Arthur H. Cash

Laurence Sterne

The Later Years

London and New York

First published in 1986 by Methuen & Co. Ltd

First published in paperback 1992
by Routledge
11 New Fetter Lane, London EC4P 4EE

Simultaneously published in the USA and Canada
by Routledge
a division of Routledge, Chapman and Hall Inc.
29 West 35th Street, New York, NY 10001

Printed in Great Britain at the
University Press, Cambridge

British Library Cataloguing in Publication Data
Cash, Arthur H.
Laurence Sterne. – Later Years. – New edn.
I. Title
823.8

Library of Congress Cataloging in Publication Data
Cash, Arthur H.
Laurence Sterne, the later years.
Bibliography: p.
Includes index
1. Sterne, Laurence, 1713–1768—Biography
2. Novelists, English—18th century—Biography.
I. Title.
PR3716.C295 1986 823′.6[B] 86-694

ISBN 0-415-08032-0

O ye POWERS! (for powers ye are, and great ones too)—which enable mortal man to tell a story worth the hearing,—that kindly shew him, where he is to begin it,—and where he is to end it,—what he is to put into it,—and what he is to leave out,—how much of it he is to cast into shade,—and whereabouts he is to throw his light!——Ye, who preside over this vast empire of biographical freebooters, and see how many scrapes and plunges your subjects hourly fall into;—will you do one thing?

(*Tristram Shandy*, III, xxiii)

for Mary

Let the torpid monk seek heaven comfortless and alone.——GOD speed him! For my own part, I fear I should never so find the way. . . . Wherever thy Providence places me, or whatever be the road I take to get to thee——give me some companion in my journey, be it only to remark to, How our shadows lengthen as the sun goes down;—to whom I may say, How fresh is the face of nature! How sweet the flowers of the field! How delicious are these fruits!

(Sterne, 'The Levite and His Concubine')

Contents

Illustrations

Plates *between* pp. 200–201

Preface

A biographical fact is nothing concrete: an event evoked in the imagination of the biographer to explain the newspaper story, the letter, the legal document before him – his primary evidence. He may carefully weigh the evidence, refine the facts, work them into what is grandiosely called a 'life', but a biographer can never know that his story is true, for biographical truth, if it exists at all, can only do so in the mind of God. A friend once asked me, 'What would you do if by a miracle Laurence Sterne should walk in through that door?' I replied, 'Ask him to forgive me.'

I have developed my story of Sterne from my own examination of the primary evidence, citing my predecessor biographers only upon those rare instances when I could not find a document which was known to them. I am in the debt of Percy Fitzgerald and Wilbur Cross for pointing the way, but I have not relied upon their judgements, their interpretations, their facts. My story of Sterne may resemble theirs in general outline, but it differs in almost every detail.

I have had the advantage of sound scholarship written by a later generation – the bibliographical studies of Kenneth Monkman and J. C. T. Oates and Oates's study of Sterneian ephemera: Harlan Hamilton's work on William Combe, the forger of Sterne letters; Gardner D. Stout Jr's annotated edition of *A Sentimental Journey*; and Alan B. Howes's collections of critical commentary. I used a computer print-out of the then unproofed explanatory notes to *Tristram Shandy* sent by the editors, Melvyn New, Richard A. Davies and W. G. Day, notes which have since been published as the third volume of the scholarly Florida *Works* of Sterne. And I have had the use of that modern research tool, the concordance – in fact, three of them, those to *Tristram Shandy* compiled by Patricia Horgan Graves, to *A Sentimental Journey* by Betty, David and John Pasta, and to the *Sermons* by Kenneth Monkman.

My greatest advantage was to have followed L. P. Curtis. Professor Curtis did not live to help me with this volume as he had helped with *The Early and Middle Years*, but I have felt his influence at every turning in the example he set of scholarly integrity and the body of work on Sterne he left. It was he who collected and edited the vast majority of Sterne letters. The reader may find at the back of this volume seven heretofore unpublished letters and locations for another eleven which have been published in recent years – all that have been found since Curtis's *Letters of Laurence Sterne* (1935). I have sometimes disagreed with Curtis's dating of letters, and given my reasons in notes, but I have nothing to object to in his renditions of the texts of Sterne's letters. His edition obviated any need on my part to seek out the manuscripts, where they exist, or the original publications. I could and have used the edition as my major primary source, and my citations of it, usually in parentheses, run into the thousands. Moreover, Curtis's notes to the *Letters* provide the most important index to Sterneian documents other than letters – more documents than were used by Fitzgerald or Cross. As Curtis once told me, he was inspired to take up the study of Sterne by his teacher, Wilbur Cross, but he learned his scholarly methods from Cross's colleague at Yale, C. B. Tinker. I hope that my book preserves something of the tradition of Professors Cross, Tinker and Curtis.

This book is not a 'critical biography', yet I have found it necessary to talk briefly about Sterne's writing in order to show how Sterne's life affected what he wrote and how his writing affected his life. I have discussed the sermons, most of them written during the early and middle years but published in the later years, primarily to show how they were received by Sterne's contemporaries. More was at stake with *Tristram Shandy*, for seven of the nine volumes were written during the years covered by this book. Discussing each instalment as I arrived at the period when Sterne wrote it, and needing to describe just which segment of the novel he was writing at a particular time, I was led to think of the novel in terms of its plots and in those terms to speculate upon Sterne's problems of how to continue or terminate it. I do not mean to imply any disagreement with those critics who think that Sterne subordinated plot and the chronological ordering of fictional events to the unfolding of an inner world. Sterne was keenly aware of the separateness of time as we sense it and time as an intellectual schema by which we parcel up the intervals between completed cycles of the heavenly bodies into calendar years and days and clock hours and minutes. He gave to his narrator a sense of self in the world which Jean-Jacques

Mayoux aptly called Tristram's 'thick present', for it contained all memory of the past. It would not be for another century and a half that William James and Henri Bergson would shape for us a notion of consciousness as a 'stream' in which impressions and thoughts are so disconnected from the outside world with its calendars and clocks as to render meaningless any attempt to describe them chronologically. Yet most students of Sterne believe, as do I, that the narrative devices which James and Bergson inspired, notably in the novels of Marcel Proust, André Gide and Virginia Woolf, can be found in *Tristram Shandy*. Nevertheless, I leave to others the task of explicating in detail Sterne's techniques and themes, having convinced myself that fully developed literary criticism would be of little use in telling the story of Sterne's life.

People gossip about a famous man and save his letters. Of Sterne's 249 surviving letters, 201 date from the period after the publication of the first two volumes of *Tristram Shandy*. The vast majority of descriptions or mentions of Sterne in the letters of his contemporaries, the newspaper accounts, the anecdotes, were written in the later period. Consequently, the story of Sterne's later years, as I tell it, is more detailed and intimate than that of his early and middle years. The first volume of this study covered forty-six years; this volume covers eight. Sterne, who so enjoyed pointing out that Tristram, having taken a year to write an account of the first day of his life, could never catch himself, would have had some amusing comment to make upon the fact that it has taken me longer to write a book about his later years than it took him to live them.

Acknowledgements

Four fellow Sterneians have been exceptionally generous with their help, having read the penultimate draft of this book and commented upon it in detail. I wish to thank Kenneth Monkman, my friend and advisor of many years, bibliographer and collector of Sterne and Honorary Curator of Shandy Hall, who supplied me with numerous pieces of information and called to my attention new evidence, including the Mortimer caricature. I am grateful to Harlan Hamilton, Professor Emeritus of Case Western Reserve University and outstanding authority on William Combe, for his long-standing support and advice, especially about Sterne's social milieu in London and Paris. My thanks too to Melvyn New, the general editor of the definitive Florida *Works* of Sterne, who taught me about Sterne's source materials and challenged many points in my comments upon the novels. I am deeply grateful to J. C. T. Oates, Fellow of Darwin College, recently retired as Librarian of the Cambridge University Library, who gave to this volume the sort of close critical reading which L. P. Curtis had given to the first, pointing out awkwardnesses in style, catching small mistakes, demanding clarity in the arguments and questioning my documentation. No doubt errors and weaknesses will be found in this book, but they will be fewer because of the devotion of these friends.

I am grateful for the advice I have been given by experts in a variety of areas. Paul-Gabriel Boucé and Frank Felsenstein helped me with my comments on Smollett, and Boucé checked my chapters on Sterne's travels in France. Gianni Azzi read the chapter on Italy and assisted me with Italian scholarship on Sterne. Georges Lamoine helped me to research the city archives at Toulouse. Ronald Paulson checked my remarks on Hogarth and Reynolds and Raleigh Trevelyan those on India. John Sutherland and John Riely gave me critical help with the appendix on the John Hamilton

Mortimer caricature group. Peter Wale translated Sterne's Latin letter. Janet Todd and Ruth Perry advised me in the matter of the status of women entertainers, and Barbara Brandon Schnorrenberg checked over my passages on Elizabeth Montagu and the Bluestockings. Dr James Swindley, the Director of the Coram Foundation, helped me through the archives of the Foundling Hospital, and D. G. C. Allen through those of the Royal Society of Arts. Rear-Admiral J. J. R. Oswald sent me information about his collateral ancestor George Oswald, and Sir Francis Dashwood, Bart., gave me material on the Hell-Fire Club. Van R. Baker sent me copies of the documents he found in southern France relating to Elizabeth and Lydia Sterne and the deaths of Lydia's children. Jan Fergus told me about Sterne's rural reading public, and Janice Thaddeus helped me in various matters, including my remarks upon David and Eva Garrick. Dr Maureen Strafford, now at the Harvard Medical School, helped me to interpret the evidence of Sterne's diseases and death. I want to thank scholars who voluntarily sent me information I would not otherwise have found: Bernhard Fabian, Richard Ribicoff, Donald D'Elia, and my friends and long-time advisors, Julia Monkman, co-curator of Shandy Hall, and C. B. L. Barr, of the York Minster Library. From time to time I have consulted members of my own department, and I am grateful for the continued encouragement and help of Jan Zlotnik Schmidt, Arthur Hack and Robert Waugh, the last of whom also helped with various translations.

It would be impossible to name all the archivists and librarians who have aided my research, but I should like to mention particularly those who kindly sent me material when I was unable to travel to their collections: E. G. W. Bill, Lambeth Palace Librarian; V. J. Kite, Bath–Wandsdyke Area Librarian; F. McKenzie and I. G. Brown of the National Library of Scotland; Robert Frost, Deputy County Archivist for West Yorkshire; C. P. C. Johnson, Lincolnshire Archivist; Edwin Green, Archivist for the Midland Bank, Ltd; S. R. Tomlinson, Bodleian Library; Rachel McClellan, Yale University Libraries; Nancy Coffin, Curator of the Robert H. Taylor Collection, Princeton University Library; Sara S. Hodson of the Huntington Library; and Edmund Berkeley Jr at the University of Virginia Library. I am grateful for the help given by the Bodleian Library staff, the staffs of the India Office Library, the National Portrait Gallery, the Courtauld Institute of Art, the Frick Art Reference Library, the Cambridge University Library, the Morgan Library, the Folger Library, the Vassar College Library, the Boston Public and New York Public Libraries, the libraries at Harvard, Yale, Princeton, Columbia, and especially the Sojourner Truth Library at the New Paltz College of the State University of New York. I have been supported by two sabbatical leaves from New Paltz College, a faculty fellowship, and several research grants from the Research Foundation of the State University of New York. I wish to thank the Master and Fellows of Darwin College for their hospitality in 1974–5 and indeed whenever I have returned to Cambridge. My thanks are due also to Sandra Gildersleave for typing and to my friend Katharine Waugh for her careful proofreading of the book.

I am grateful to the Laurence Sterne Trust for permission to publish Sterne's letter to John Blake of September 1758; the Henry E. Huntington Library for permission to publish the letter to Blake of ?5 October 1758; and the Princeton University Library for permission to publish from the Robert H. Taylor Collection yet a third letter to Blake of January 1759, and Sterne's letter to Lord Rockingham. My thanks are due to the Boston Public Library for allowing me to publish Sterne's letter to Thomas Becket of 26 September 1763, and to the Houghton Library for permission to publish Sterne's letter to Thomas Astle in the Amy Lowell Collection. I want also to thank the Dean and Chapter of York for allowing me to publish Sterne's letter to 'Reverend Sir', his note to John Clough, and Clough's reply, and the Huntington Library for allowing me to quote from the Elizabeth Montagu papers. I am grateful to Lord Brownlow, their owner, and Peter Walne of the Hertfordshire Record Office for permission to quote from the Egerton papers. My quotations from L. P. Curtis's edition of *Letters of Laurence Sterne* are by permission of the Clarendon Press, Oxford.

I am grateful for the permission I have received from the Yale Center for British Art, Paul Mellon Collection, to reproduce John Hamilton Mortimer's *A Caricature Group*; from the Laurence Sterne Trust to use Thomas Gill's print of Shandy Hall; from Westminster City Libraries Archives Department to use the print of St George's Hanover Square; and from Sir George Wombwell to use Andrea Soldi's portrait of Thomas Belasyse. Sir Joshua Reynolds's portrait of *Garrick between 'Tragedy' and 'Comedy'* is in a private collection, and Catherine Read's of Anne James with her daughter is in the collection of Sir Hector Monro; both are reproduced here with my thanks. Reynolds's portrait of the Second Marquis of Rockingham is reproduced by permission of The Lady Juliet Chair and the Trustees of Olive, Countess Fitzwilliam's Chattels Trust. I would also like to thank the copyright-holders for permission to reproduce the portrait of

John Wilkes by Robert Edge Pine (Crown Copyright) and that of Eliza Draper by John Downman (© Christie's Colour Library).

Such is the nature of biographical research that those who helped me with *Laurence Sterne: The Early and Middle Years* were also helping with *The Later Years*. I cannot very well repeat here the acknowledgements I made there, but I do want to draw attention to them and to thank once again those many friends to my work.

It is a pleasure to acknowledge my indebtedness to Mary Gordon, my wife, whose love of Sterne and whose insightful grasp of literature have profoundly affected what I have written, who read my drafts and criticized them, with a dear tact, who supported the family so that I could take leave from my teaching duties to complete the book, who gave large amounts of time which otherwise would have been devoted to her own writing so that I could write. These words seem 'tall and opake'; they do little justice to the gratitude I feel.

New Paltz, New York,
15 October 1985.

Short Titles & Abbreviations

Unless otherwise indicated, books cited in this study were published in London. When possible, Sterne's letters and major works are cited parenthetically in the editions which are named among the short titles. Other sources that are used repeatedly are cited by short titles – distinguishable in the notes because printed in roman capitals and roman small capitals. Sources that are cited once or infrequently are given, in the first citation, a full reference with standard use of italics; second and subsequent references within the chapter are simplified.

In quotations, initial and final ellipsis marks are usually omitted, an initial capital letter is sometimes assigned to the first word, and final punctuation is changed or added, so long as such changes or additions do not significantly alter the sense of what was said. Original spelling, capitalization and punctuation are preserved within the quotation.

ANECDOTES – *Literary Anecdotes of the Eighteenth Century*, ed. John Nichols, 9 vols, 1812–15.

BL – British Library, formerly called the British Museum Library.

Borthwick Institute – Borthwick Institute for Historical Research, York.

BOSWELL – James Boswell, *Life of Johnson*, ed. George Birkbeck Hill, revised L. F. Powell, 6 vols, Oxford, 1950.

CLIMENSON – *Elizabeth Montagu: The Queen of the Blue Stockings: Her Correspondence from 1720 to 1761*, ed. Emily J. Climenson, 1906.

CONNELY – Willard Connely, *Laurence Sterne as Yorick*, 1958.

CRADDOCK – Joseph Craddock, *Literary and Miscellaneous Memoirs*, 4 vols, 1828.

CROFT – John Croft, 'Anecdotes of Sterne vulgarly Tristram Shandy', in *Whitefoord Papers, Being the Correspondence and other Manuscripts of Colonel Charles Whitefoord and Caleb Whitefoord from 1739 to 1810*, ed. W. A. S. Hewins, Oxford, 1898, 223–35.

CROSS – Wilbur L. Cross, *Life and Times of Laurence Sterne*, 3rd edn, New York, 1929.

CURTIS – L. P. Curtis, notes to the LETTERS.

DEALTARY LETTERS – One letter by Sterne and five by the Reverend Dr Thomas Newton addressed to the Reverend Mr John Dealtary, at the Bodleian Library: ENG. LETT. d. 122. (Published in part by L. P. Curtis, 'New Light on Sterne', *Modern Language Notes*, LXXVI [1961], 498–501.)

DUTENS – [Louis Dutens], *Memoirs of a Traveller, Now in Retirement*, 5 vols, 1806.

EMY – Arthur H. Cash, *Laurence Sterne: The Early and Middle Years*, 1975.

EGERTON LETTERS – Letters and papers of the Reverend Dr Henry Egerton, among the family papers of Lord Brownlow, housed at the Hertfordshire County Record Office. (Published in part by Arthur H. Cash, 'Some New Sterne Letters', *TLS*, 8 April 1965, 284.)

EVANS – A. W. Evans, *Warburton and the Warburtonians: A Study in Some Eighteenth-Century Controversies*, Oxford, 1932.

GARAT – Dominique-Joseph Garat, *Mémoires Historiques sur la Vie de M. Suard*, 2 vols, Paris, 1820.

GREENWOOD – Richard Greenwood, former servant of Sterne, as interviewed by Joseph Hunter: MS in Hunter's hand at BL, Add. MSS 24446, fols 26–7. (Edited and published by James Kuist, 'New Light on Sterne: An Old Man's recollections of the Young Vicar', *PMLA*, LXXX [1965], 549–53.)

HAMILTON – Harlan Hamilton, 'William Combe and the *Original Letters of the Late Reverend Mr. Laurence Sterne* (1788)', *PMLA*, LXXXII (1967), 420–9.

HARTLEY – Lodwick Hartley, 'Sterne's Eugenius as Indiscreet Author: The Literary Career of John Hall-Stevenson', *PMLA*, LXXXVI (1971), 428–45.

HOWES – *Sterne: The Critical Heritage*, ed. Alan B. Howes, 1974.

ILLUSTRATIONS – *Illustrations of the Literary History of the Eighteenth Century*, ed. John Nichols, 8 vols, 1817–58.

JOURNAL – *Journal to Eliza*, included in LETTERS 322–400.

LETTERS – *Letters of Laurence Sterne*, ed. L. P. Curtis, Oxford, 1935.

MEDALLE – *Letters of the Late Rev. Mr. Laurence Sterne, to His Most Intimate Friends*, ed. Lydia Medalle, née Sterne, sometimes called Médalle or de Médalle, 3 vols, 1775.

Minster Library – Library of the Dean and Chapter of the Cathedral of York.

MONKMAN – Kenneth Monkman, 'Bibliography of the Early Editions of *Tristram Shandy*', *Library*, 5th series, XXV (1970), 11–39. See also Monkman's 'Bibliographical Descriptions', Appendix Five of TRISTRAM SHANDY, 907–38.

N&Q – *Notes and Queries*.

NAMIER AND BROOKE – Sir Lewis Namier and John Brooke, *House of Commons, 1754–1790*, 3 vols, 1964.

NANGLE – Benjamin Christie Nangle, *The Monthly Review, First Series, 1749–1789: Indexes of Contributors and Articles*, Oxford, 1934.

OATES – J. C. T. Oates, *Shandyism and Sentiment, 1760–1800*, Cambridge, Cambridge Bibliographical Society, 1968.

PRO – Public Record Office, London.

SENTIMENTAL JOURNEY – *A Sentimental Journey through France and Italy*, ed. Gardner D. Stout, Jr, Berkeley and Los Angeles, 1967.

SERMONS – *Sermons of Mr. Yorick* and *Sermons by the Late Rev. Mr. Sterne*, ed. Wilbur L. Cross, in *Works*, New York, 1904, Vols IX–X.

SEVEN LETTERS – *Seven Letters Written by Sterne and His Friends*, ed. W. Durrant Cooper, 1844.

STERNE'S COMEDY – Arthur H. Cash, *Sterne's Comedy of Moral Sentiments: The Ethical Dimension of the "Journey"*, Pittsburgh, 1966.

TS NOTES – Explanatory notes to *Tristram Shandy*, Florida edition of *Works of Laurence Sterne*, Vol. III, ed. Melvyn New with Richard A. Davies and W. G. Day, Gainesville, Florida, 1984.

TRISTRAM IN DUBLIN – Kenneth Monkman, '*Tristram* in Dublin', *Transactions of the Cambridge Bibliographical Society*, VII (1979), 343–68.

TRISTRAM SHANDY – *The Life and Opinions of Tristram Shandy, Gentleman*, ed. Melvyn New and Joan New, Florida edition of *Works of Laurence Sterne*, Vols I–II, paginated as one, Gainesville, Florida, 1978.

VOICES SONOROUS AND CRACKED – Arthur H. Cash, 'Voices Sonorous and Cracked: Sterne's Pulpit Oratory', in *Quick Springs of Sense: Studies in the Eighteenth Century*, ed. Larry S. Champion, Athens, Georgia, 1974, 197–209.

WALPOLE – Yale *Correspondence of Horace Walpole*, ed. W. S. Lewis *et al.*, 34 vols, New Haven, Conn., 1937–67.

WINGED SKULL – Arthur H. Cash and John M. Stedmond (eds), *The Winged Skull: Papers from the Laurence Sterne Bicentenary Conference*, Kent, Ohio, 1971, simultaneously published in London under the title *The Winged Skull: Essays on Laurence Sterne*.

WOMBWELL PAPERS – Papers and letters of Thomas Belasyse, Fourth Viscount and First Earl Fauconberg, in the possession of Captain Victor Malcolm Wombwell, formerly kept at Newburgh Priory, Coxwold, now housed at the North Yorkshire Record Office, Northallerton.

WRIGHT AND SCLATER – Arnold Wright and William Lutley Sclater, *Sterne's Eliza: Some Account of Her Life in India: with Her Letters Written between 1757 and 1774*, 1922.

London 1760

'I wrote,' said Sterne, speaking of *Tristram Shandy*, 'not to be *fed*, but to be *famous*.'[1] When he set off for London three months after the first two volumes had appeared, he little dreamed how far his ambition had been fulfilled, how many London gentlemen and noblemen and their ladies, how many lawyers, artists, politicians, ministers, well-educated people from every walk and profession were reading the book or trying to get copies, how many were impatient to meet the author or to entertain him, to savour his wit or to satisfy their curiosity about a Yorkshire parson who dared to write such naughty prose. The books were being distributed in London because Sterne had sent copies of the York printing to the famous London booksellers, Robert and James Dodsley, who were selling them on commission. Four notices had appeared in the London papers, three rather cool.[2] But the reviewer for the *London Magazine* of February had been ecstatic:

> Oh rare Tristram Shandy!—Thou very sensible—humorous—pathetick—humane—unaccountable!—what shall we call thee?—Rabelais, Cervantes, What?—Thou hast afforded us so much real pleasure in perusing thy life,—we can't call it thy life neither, since thy mother is still in labour of thee. . . . Thy uncle Toby—Thy Yorick—thy father—Dr. Slop—corporal Trim; all thy characters are excellent, and thy opinions amiable!

[1] LETTERS, 90; cf. TRISTRAM SHANDY, 237, 446.

[2] *Critical Review* for January; *Royal Female Magazine* for February; and *Monthly Review*, appended to vol. XXI (July–December 1759), 561–71, excerpted in HOWES, 46–8.

Now, at the urging of his old friend Stephen Croft, the squire of Stillington, Sterne had accepted a place in Croft's carriage to come up to London to take stock of the situation.

He had written the volumes in the throes of melancholy and illness. His twelve-year-old daughter was sickly. His wife, much given to neurotic protection of her ordinary life, had broken under the strain of watching her husband divest himself of his clerical duties and risk their fortune to write what seemed to her a mad book. She had threatened suicide, and Sterne had been forced to place her under the care of a 'lunatick doctor' at York. Sterne himself was fatally afflicted with consumption, which he had suffered since his days at Jesus College, Cambridge, when he had awakened one night having 'bled the bed full' from a haemorrhage of the lungs. When the first volumes of *Tristram Shandy* were being bound, Sterne had bundled up eight sets to send to his earliest patron, Lord Rockingham, along with a letter:

> There is an Anecdote relating to this ludicrous Satyr, which I must tell your Lord^{p}—& it is this, 'that it was every word of it wrote in affliction; & under a constant uneasiness of mind. Cervantes wrote his humorous Satyr in a Prison——& Scarron his, in pain & Anguish——such Philosophers as will account for every thing, may explain this for me.[3]

Sterne's life itself provides an explanation. Trapped in an unhappy marriage and a disintegrating body, he sought laughter as an anodyne to pain, wherever he could find it, but most especially in *Tristram Shandy.* As he would explain in the next instalment,

> If 'tis wrote against any thing,—'tis wrote, an' please your worships, against the spleen; in order, by a more frequent and a more convulsive elevation and depression of the diaphragm, and the succussations of the intercostal and abdominal muscles in laughter, to drive the *gall*

[3] Letter in Appendix I; CROFT. Sterne used the word 'anecdote' in the meaning of 'secret, private, or hitherto unpublished narratives or details of history' (*OED*). Cf. the 'Anonymous Letter': 'He told me . . . that in the Midst of these Afflictions, it was a strange Incident that his ludicrous Book should be printed off; but that there was a stranger still behind, which was, that every Sentence of it had been conceived and written under the greatest Heaviness of Heart, arising from some Hints the poor Creature had dropped of her Apprehensions; and that in her Illness he had found in her Pocket-Book [,] "*Jan. 1st, La dernier de ma vie, hélas!*"' For a discussion of the 'Anonymous Letter' as a source of information, see *EMT*, 279 and n. 2. The original publication was in the *St. James's Chronicle*, 22–4 April 1788.

> and other *bitter juices* from the gall bladder, liver and sweet-bread of his majesty's subjects, with all the inimicitious passions which belong to them, down into their duodenums. (360)

Virtually everything Sterne would do from the time when *Tristram Shandy*, I–II, appeared until his death eight years later would be calculated to strengthen his weakening frame and revive his flagging spirits.

Not the least vivifying experience was love. When Sterne had been preparing the books for the press, he had found an unexpected source of joy in a concert-hall singer, Catherine Fourmantel or Fromantel, who was completing a season at the Assembly Rooms. 'I love you to distraction Kitty—& will love you on so to Eternity' (83).

On the afternoon of 4 March Stephen Croft's carriage drew up in Golden Square before the house of Croft's daughter, Henrietta-Katherina, and her husband Nathaniel Cholmley, squire of Whitby on the North Riding coast, a couple well known to Sterne, who had married them three years before. Cholmley, erstwhile High Sheriff of Yorkshire and currently Member of Parliament for Aldborough, was convivial and generous, but his house must have seemed like a piece of the North Riding.[4] Sterne was looking for something else. He would stay only a few days. 'I have arrived here safe, & sound,' he wrote to Catherine Fourmantel on 8 March, 'except for the Hole in my heart, which you have made, like a dear enchanting Slut as you are.—I shall take Lodgings this morning in Picadilly or the Hay market, & before I seal this Letter will let you know where to direct a Letter to me; which Letter I shall wait for by the return of the post with great impatience — so write my dear Love without fail' (96).

The next morning Sterne was missing at breakfast. He had gone to the Tully's Head, the Dodsleys' famous shop in Pall Mall, to enquire about 'Tristram Shandy's works'. 'His Vanity was highly flattered,' said John Croft, Stephen's younger brother, 'when the Shopman told him, that there was not such a Book to be had in London either for Love or money.' The

[4] Cholmley, MP for Aldborough, 1758, and for Boroughbridge, 1768, is noticed in NAMIER AND BROOKE. He would soon acquire a second estate at Howsham, which he would develop as an ideal rural community complete with a retirement village for the servants. CROFT said that his London house was in Chapel Street (since renamed Aldford Street, close to Grosvenor Square), but the membership book for the Royal Society of Arts, to which Cholmley was elected on 26 March 1760, gives his address as Golden Square.

shopman, discovering who the gentleman was, took him to meet one or other of the two Dodsley brothers, who gave him a 'cordiall reception'. They were soon discussing business, not only the future of this astonishing book, but Sterne's plans to publish two volumes of sermons. Dodsley quickly learned he was talking to an entrepreneur who, if not offered favourable terms, would publish his own books. Sterne, at his own risk, had brought out the first two volumes of *Tristram Shandy* simultaneously at York and Dublin. He had deftly advertised his sermons in the second volume of *Shandy* (166–7), and before he had left York had arranged an advertisement for them in the *York Courant*, including an appeal for subscriptions.[5] 'Soon after, Mr Croft and Cholmley passing by Pall Mall in a coach, who should they see in Dodsley's Shop but Sterne who accosting them said that he was mortgaging his brains to Dodsley.' John Croft, whose account of Sterne was built upon a memory of what his brother had told him, thought that Stephen Croft and Nathaniel Cholmley immediately entered into a conference with Sterne about Dodsley's offer: 'The Gent^n advized him not to haggle, or bargain any longer about the matter, but to close the agreem^t with Dodsley.' If such advice were actually given, Sterne ignored it. He had made an appointment with James Dodsley for the following Saturday to sign a preliminary contract, and he certainly was prepared to haggle about price. Furthermore, he was waiting to see someone far more knowledgeable about bookselling – David Garrick.

The next morning Sterne called on Garrick. They had become acquainted through a brief correspondence after Sterne had been introduced – so to speak – through a letter of Catherine Fourmantel's – though Sterne himself had written it.[6] Then, a few weeks later, having heard that Garrick was saying kind things about *Tristram Shandy*, Sterne had plucked up the courage to write himself, 'to return You my Thanks, Sir, which I heartily do, for the great Service & Honour, your good Word has done me. I know not what it was (tho "I lye abominably", because I know very well) which inclined me more to wish for your Approbation, than any Other's' (86). Sterne had said in his letter that Tristram Shandy was 'a picture of myself'. Whether Garrick found it so, the record does not say, but he was impressed

[5] *York Courant*, 5 March. For the history of the publication of the York edition of *Tristram Shandy*, see MONKMAN. The hypothesis argued by Monkman and others that the first edition of the novel appeared at York is put beyond doubt by Sterne's letter to Rockingham cited above: see Appendix I. For the Dublin edition, see TRISTRAM IN DUBLIN.

[6] CROSS, 585; *EMT*, 294–5.

enough with the original to become his chief adviser in the business of publication. Though he could not be present personally at the scheduled meeting with Dodsley, he would send his friend, Richard Berenger.

But Garrick was worried about a story he had heard about the future volumes of *Tristram Shandy*: Sterne, it was rumoured, was planning to satirize Dr William Warburton, recently elevated to the bishopric of Gloucester and reputed to be the most knowledgeable bishop in England in matters of literature. Sterne, went the gossip, would send his young hero, Tristram, upon a grand tour under the guidance of Warburton as tutor. Thomas Newton, the Precentor of York, soon to become Bishop of Bristol, a friend to both Warburton and Sterne, wrote, 'I hope . . . there is no foundation of truth in the report I have heard, that Tristram is to have his education under the Tutorage of Dr Warburton. He may be as severe as he pleases upon impertinent fools & blockheads, but I do not love to see diamond cut diamond.'[7] Warburton, hardly a diamond, was a coarse-grained, ambitious man who was not above flattering the great and lying to them when it suited his purposes.[8] But he had been a collaborator with Pope, and an editor of Shakespeare. He was the author of a widely read theological work, the *Divine Legation of Moses*, a biblical scholar, and a leading polemical divine. Edward Gibbon described him as 'the Dictator and tyrant of the World of Litterature', and Samuel Johnson, in his well-known meeting with George II, had countered the king's compliment upon the breadth of his reading by saying that he had not read much, compared with Dr Warburton.[9] Unasked, this giant had recommended *Tristram Shandy*, 'warmly', as he said himself, 'to all the best company in town, except that at Arthur's', where the rakes and gamblers abode. And more: he had defended it to 'a very grave assembly' of bishops.[10] Indeed, Newton said that many people were pleased with the 'oddness and wildness' of the book, 'and no body more than the new Bp of Glocester, who says that it is wrote in the very spirit of Rabelais, and has spoke to me highly of it several times,

[7] To the Rev. Mr John Dealtary, 4 March 1760; DEALTARY LETTERS.

[8] Benjamin Boyce, *The Benevolent Man: A Life of Ralph Allen of Bath*, Cambridge, Mass., 1967, p. 123.

[9] Melvyn New, 'Sterne, Warburton, and the Burden of Exuberant Wit', *Eighteenth-Century Studies*, XV (1982), 245–74; EVANS. New argues that Warburton played a central role in Sterne's creation of *Tristram Shandy*, though a complex one since he represented in Sterne's mind both the ideal of learning to which Tristram lays claim and the sort of pedantry Tristram was satirizing.

[10] Warburton to Garrick, 7 March 1760, in *Private Correspondence of David Garrick*, 1831, I, 115–16, reproduced by CURTIS, 95.

and inquired much after the author, and last Saturday made very honorable mention of it at the Bp of Durham's before six or seven of the Bps, some of whom were rather offended with the levity of it, thinking it not in character for a clergyman.' Horace Walpole, whose wide-ranging gossip was usually as accurate as it was amusing, wrote to Sir David Dalrymple on 4 April about *Tristram Shandy*, 'Bishop Warburton . . . recommended the book to the bench of bishops and told them Mr Sterne, the author, was the English Rabelais – they had never heard of such a writer.'[11] To Garrick, Warburton's recommendation seemed like the best of fortunes for a new writer. Could it be true that Sterne actually was planning to attack this patron of his book?

Sterne flatly denied the rumour. To put the matter to rest, they agreed, Sterne would write a letter which Garrick would show to the bishop. Sterne wrote it that very evening. 'What the devill—is there no one learned blockhead throughout the many schools of misapplied science in the Christian World, to make a *tutor* of for my Tristram? . . . I should chuse a præceptor to rob him of all the immortality I intend him? O! dear Mr. G[arrick]'(93). The weight of evidence is against Sterne here. He had satirized Warburton in the first, rejected version of *Tristram Shandy* for his part in a controversy over the authorship of the Book of Job. This satire had taken the form of an allegory based on the story of Job, in which Warburton was seen as Satan, smiting poor Job from head to foot. Worse still: elsewhere in that early version Warburton had indeed appeared as the tutor of Tristram.[12] The manuscript of this early Scriblerian version of *Tristram Shandy* Sterne had shown to numerous friends. Little wonder the story about Warburton as tutor was soon bandied about. According to one unidentified anecdotist, Sterne himself admitted the truth of it later – no doubt after he had given up any hope of remaining Bishop Warburton's friend.

> On the writer of this article remonstrating with Sterne on a report at York, that he had in London denied his ever having had a thought of making Warburton the private tutor, his own words in reply were, that 'the Bishop of Gloucester had brought over a moiety of the old women to his interest.'[13]

[11] WALPOLE, XV, 66–7.
[12] 'Anonymous Letter'.
[13] Letter dated 31 August 1792 and signed 'A.B.' in *European Magazine*, XXII (October 1792), 256. Perhaps Sterne makes a covert confession in Vol. IV of TRISTRAM

But at this point, when *Tristram Shandy* was first making its way into the world, Sterne had no intention of alienating the bishop. He wrote his denial to Garrick, putting the whole rumour down to malice – malice of the very sort 'which so unfairly brought poor Yorick to his grave'. The report, he went on, might 'draw blood' from the author of *Tristram Shandy*, 'but could not harm such a man as the author of the Divine Legation—God bless him! though (by the bye, and according to the natural course of descents) the blessing should come from him to me.' Could he be introduced to his lordship? 'I have no claim to such an honour, but what arises from the honour and respect which in the progress of my work will be shewn the world I owe to so great a man' (93). Garrick sent the letter off, and Warburton replied the next day. He was pleased, he said, 'to find I have no reason to change my opinion of so agreeable and so original a writer as Mr. Sterne. . . . I shall be glad of the honour of being better known to him; and he has the additional recommendation of being your friend.'[14]

A few days later Garrick brought together these two tall, gaunt priests. 'On Sterne's first arrival in London,' said John Croft, 'Dr Warburton, then Bishop of Gloucester, sent for him and gave him a purse of money attended with severall books to improve his Stile, with proper and salutary advice for his future conduct in life and pursuits in Literature, which he totally disregarded.' The books and advice are in keeping with Warburton's character. But a purse of money? Could Croft have been mistaken about that? Probably not. Sterne himself told Catherine Fourmantel, 'I had a purse of Guineas given me Yesterday, by a Bishop' (102). Walpole in a letter of 4 April wrote, 'Bishop Warburton gave him [Sterne] a purse of gold and this compliment (which happens to be a contradiction) *that it was quite an original composition, and in the true Cervantic vain.*'[15] Warburton often patronized clergymen who wrote, and it is just possible he gave Sterne the money in

SHANDY when he has one of Tristram's readers, watching Tristram 'curvetting and frisking it away', cry, 'But your horse throws dirt; see you've splash'd a bishop' (357). CRADDOCK, VI, 204, further confirms the story, though his account is inaccurate in some details. He tells how Warburton, upon spying a copy of *Tristram Shandy* in Craddock's library, 'urged its instant removal'; but the explanation that follows is skewed: 'He was not always so violent against Sterne; Warburton corresponded with him, and nothing was urged against Tristram, till the Bishop and Sterne quarrelled, and then Sterne in print threatened to make the author of the "Divine Legation", the private tutor of his rising pupil, master Shandy.'

[14] CURTIS, 95.

[15] WALPOLE, XV, 66–7.

the hope of having the London edition of *Tristram Shandy* dedicated to him.[16] But most people must have thought what Dr John Hill finally said publicly: 'It is scarce to be credited whose liberal purse has bought off the dread of a tutor's character.' This was said in the earliest biographical account of Sterne, an article which appeared on 1 May 1760 in the *Royal Female Magazine* and was then reprinted five days later in the widely read *London Chronicle*. Sterne denied the story, of course, calling it a 'lie' (110); but the damage was done. Warburton, embarrassed, began to wonder whether he could continue to defend *Tristram Shandy* and its Rabelaisian author. He was getting ready to leave London for Prior Park, where he lived in the warm months. He would keep in touch with Garrick.

But long before this meeting with Warburton could take place, Sterne and Garrick had become fascinated with each other. On the evening of 6 March, the very day Sterne first met Garrick, he went to the Drury Lane Theatre to see his new friend perform the part of Æmilius in Home's tragedy, *The Siege of Aquilea*.[17] 'Mr. Garrick', Sterne wrote to Catherine, 'leaves nothing undone that can do me either Service or Credit.' 'Mr Garrick pays me all & more honour than I could look for, I dined with him to day.' Even more surprising, Garrick had given him 'an Order for the Liberty of his Boxes, and of every part of his house for the whole Season' (96–7) – a compliment rare enough to be remarked as far away as Paris.[18] Sterne was soon speaking of Garrick's wife, Eva Maria Veigel, erstwhile dancer at the court of Vienna,[19] as his 'kind friend'. In 1762, he wrote to Garrick from Paris, 'I see nothing like her here, and yet I have been introduced to one half

[16] The suggestion of Benjamin Boyce, *The Benevolent Man*, 256–7, who thinks the story of the purse of guineas is likely. EVANS, 227–8, however, rejects it.

[17] The performance on this day (6 March) recorded in [John Genest], *Some Account of The English Stage*, 10 vols, Bath, 1832, IV, 583, and confirmed by an uncatalogued MS, *List of plays produced at Drury Lane and Garrick's Roles in them*, in the Burney Collection, BL. An advertisement in the *Public Advertiser* of the previous day promised that the cast would also include Mrs Cibber and Thomas Davies. Yet another cast was to follow with a second performance, of *Miss in Her Teens*.

[18] In the review of *Tristram Shandy*, I–II, in *Journal Encyclopédique*, April 1760, pp. 150–1. Seats at the Drury Lane Theatre were not cheap. The cost of a box was 5*s*., the cost of Dodsley's issue of *Tristram Shandy*, I–II, if bound. The pit cost 3*s*., the first gallery 2*s*. and the upper gallery 1*s*. Ronald Hafter provides a helpful review of Sterne's and Garrick's relationship: 'Garrick and *Tristram Shandy*', *Studies in English Literature*, VII (1967), 475–89.

[19] See Janice Thaddeus, 'A Spirit Free and Female: Eva Garrick', *Eighteenth-Century Life*, in press.

of their best Goddesses' (157). 'Had she been last night upon the Tulleries, she would have annihilated a thousand French goddesses *in one single turn*' (163). Joseph Craddock said that Mrs Garrick often found fault with Sterne, 'yet both she and Mr. Garrick had a real regard for him'.[20] Indeed, they must have admired Sterne and enjoyed his company, for they opened to him their home in Southampton Street. Writing from Paris about how the Baron d'Holbach had made him welcome, Sterne said, 'his house, is now, as yours was to me, my own' (151).

But David Garrick's friendship for Sterne fell short of the ideal. True, its lasting quality is attested by his concern for Sterne's wife and daughter after Sterne's death, and by an epitaph he wrote. But he valued the friendship less than did Sterne and would soon betray him to Bishop Warburton.

On Saturday Sterne went to the Tully's Head, as appointed, to close his bargain with James Dodsley. He dealt with James because Robert Dodsley was in the process of withdrawing from the business. The firm itself remained the unchallenged leader among English booksellers. It had brought out numerous books in the previous year, among them Johnson's *Rasselas*, Goldsmith's *Enquiry into the Present State of Polite Learning*, and a second edition of Burke's *Enquiry into the Origin of our Ideas of the Sublime and Beautiful*. To this meeting came Richard Berenger, probably as Garrick's envoy.[21] This handsome, witty, popular courtier was 'a particular friend' of Garrick's. He wrote books on horsemanship, and was destined soon to be preferred as Gentleman of the Horse to George III. Berenger would sign the agreement as witness.

The paper which all parties signed that day reveals something about how they bargained. The agreement is in Sterne's hand, and one supposes he brought it to the meeting.[22] If so, he got the sum he demanded for the copyright of the first two volumes of *Tristram Shandy* – £250 in advance and £200 to be paid within six months. But he was forced to reduce his price for the yet unwritten third and fourth volumes. Originally he had written into the agreement a price of 400 guineas for III–IV. That figure is struck out and 380 guineas written in. Finally 'guineas' was lowered to 'pounds'. The

[20] CRADDOCK, I, 207.

[21] Suggested by CURTIS, 100, in his note on Berenger. John Taylor, in *Records of My Life*, 2 vols, 1832, I, 325–6, attests to Berenger's friendship with Garrick and tells a story about Garrick's raising a subscription to pay his debts.

[22] The original is bound in the Owen D. Young guardbook in the Berg Collection, New York Public Library. Published by CURTIS, 98.

agreement also stipulated that Sterne would retain the profit from the sale of the original York and Dublin editions of the first two volumes.

It was a triumph for Sterne. The sale of the first edition would easily repay the money he had borrowed to print it. How much would be left over one can only guess, but it was probably about £100. If so, he was now richer by £730.[23] Although monetary equivalents are difficult to work out, this sum might approximate £30,000 today.[24] He returned to Cholmley's, said John Croft, 'and came skipping into the room, and said that he was the richest man in Europe.'

Dodsley lost no time. Only three days later, on the 11th, a series of advertisements promising a new edition 'in a few days' commenced in the *London Chronicle* and the *Public Advertiser*.

Sterne was not yet done with his arrangements. He had brought to London a dedication which he hoped he now could use. It was to William Pitt, the 'Great Commoner', the man who as Secretary of State had guided his nation so brilliantly through the Seven Years War. Sterne, accentuating the contrast between his own two personae, the rural parson and the urbane author, slyly says that the book was written 'in a bye-corner of the kingdom, and in a retired thatch'd house'; in fact, most of it had been written in York. Ingenuously he invites the statesman's sympathy, mentioning his struggles against ill health, and more vaguely, 'other evils of life'. But evils were real enough for Sterne, and what follows is his creed for comic writing, the sincerity of which we can hardly doubt. He 'fences' against evils, says Sterne, 'by mirth; being firmly persuaded that every time a man smiles,—but much more so, when he laughs,—that it adds something to this Fragment of Life.'

> I humbly beg, Sir, that you will honour this book by taking it (not under your protection, it must protect itself, but) into the country with you; where, if I am ever told it has made you smile, or can

[23] WALPOLE, XV 66–7, was not far wrong when he reported that Sterne sold the copyright in the four volumes of the novel for £650. CROFT, however, was mistaken when he said Sterne sold the copyright for I–II plus two volumes of sermons for £600. Croft also said, 'It appears by Sterne's Accompt Book that he had received £1500 of Dodsley at different times for his Publications'; but the report is not very helpful since he did not break the figure down. I doubt whether he knew enough about Sterne's publication history to understand such a record. The attempt to locate Sterne's banking records has so far proved futile.

[24] See the discussion of monetary equivalents in Richard B. Schwartz, *Daily Life in Johnson's London*, Madison, Wisc., 1983, pp. 44–5.

> conceive it has beguiled you of one moment's pain, I shall think myself as happy as a minister of state——perhaps much happier than any one (ONE only excepted) that I have ever heard or read of.[25]

Sterne sent off a copy of the dedication to Pitt with a brief letter (103) asking for permission to print it. It appeared in the London edition.

There was yet one more thing to do for the new edition. Berenger had kindly said, 'Tell me all your wants', and Sterne wanted a frontispiece for *Tristram Shandy* by William Hogarth, with whom Berenger was acquainted. Hogarth had been an influence upon Sterne's fiction. Sterne had made three allusions in his second volume to Hogarth's celebrated *Analysis of Beauty*. In a digression on rhetoric, he had spoken of 'the *Poco piu* and the *Poco meno* of the *Italian* artists' (115), associating the concept with Hogarth's famous principle of the 'line of beauty'.[26] A few pages later he made his deft comic sketch of Dr Slop entering Shandy Hall: 'Such were the out-lines of Dr. *Slop*'s figure, which,—if you have read *Hogarth*'s analysis of beauty, and if you have not, I wish you would;—you must know, may as certainly be caricatur'd, and convey'd to the mind by three strokes as three hundred' (121). Then there was Tristram's amusing 'painting' in the words of Trim preparing to read the sermon – the very scene Sterne wanted Hogarth to draw for him. Actually, Sterne in this passage made extensive use of an English translation of Leonardo's *Treatise of Painting*;[27] but that was not easily recognized, since Hogarth used the same terms. One allusion to the line of beauty (141) was sufficient to suggest that the entire description was Hogarthian.

Using the trick which he and Garrick had used to approach Warburton, Sterne went home and wrote Berenger a letter which Berenger could carry to Hogarth. Sterne wrote it at least twice: two versions exist. 'I would give both my Ears . . . for no more than ten Strokes of *Howgarth*'s witty Chissel, to clap at the Front of my next Edition of Shandy.—The Vanity of [a]

[25] Sterne's MS copy of the dedication and the letter to Pitt were known to W. S. Taylor and J. H. Pringle, who published both in the *Correspondence of William Pitt, Earl of Chatham*, 1838, II, 12–13. CURTIS, 103–4, reproduces both, and it is from that source that I have taken my quotations. The whereabouts of the MSS is now unknown.

[26] For a discussion of how this passage reflects Hogarth, see Ronald Paulson, *Hogarth: His Life, Art, and Times*, 2 vols, New Haven, Conn., 1971, II, 302.

[27] R. F. Brissenden, 'Sterne and Painting', in *Of Books and Humankind*, ed. John Butt, 1964, pp. 93–108. Brissenden provides an entertaining anaylsis of the scene.

pretty Girl in the Hey day of her Roses & Lillies, is a fool to that of [an] Author of my Stamp. . . . The loosest Sketch in Nature, of Trim's reading the Sermon to my Father &c; w^{d} do the Business' (99). Berenger, one presumes, took the letter and a copy of *Tristram Shandy* and 'sallied out' to Hogarth's studio as Sterne had bid him. They met with success. On 25 March the advertisements running in the *London Chronicle* were changed to read, '*Next Week will be published* . . . With a Frontispiece by Mr. HOGARTH . . . The LIFE and OPINIONS of TRISTRAM SHANDY, Gent.' Hogarth had drawn the very scene which Sterne had wanted – Trim's reading of the sermon.

Did Sterne pay for the drawing, or did Hogarth, flattered by these compliments, present it to Sterne as a gift? Most scholars have assumed the latter, but the only evidence is Sterne's letter to Berenger, in which he had the temerity to suggest, in a comical vein, that a money exchange would be unthinkable: 'I would hold out my lank Purse—I would Shut my Eyes—, & You should put in your hand, & take out what you liked for it—*Ignoramus*! Blockhead! Symoniack!—This Grace is not to be bought for money—perish thee & thy Gold with thee' (99). Hogarth, who certainly did not need the money, probably laughed and sent the drawing back with his compliments.

The original drawing survives.[28] It is not one of Hogarth's best – a 'loose sketch', as Sterne had requested, but not a careful one. It was engraved by Simon-François Ravenet, and some of the copies of the second, London edition contain Ravenet's engraving in its first state. But Hogarth was unhappy with the picture. He took back his drawing and added a hat lying at Trim's feet, and a standing clock – alluding to the opening scenes of the novel. The remaining copies of the second edition contain the engraving in a second state which includes these added details.[29]

If in fact Hogarth and Sterne met face to face, the meeting came too late to grow into a friendship. Hogarth admired Sterne: he subscribed to the *Sermons*, soon to appear, and that winter made yet another illustration for *Tristram Shandy*, which would become the frontispiece to Volume III. But he had suffered some major setback to his health, perhaps a stroke, and was

[28] In the Owen D. Young guardbook, Berg Collection, New York Public Library. Technical descriptions have been made by A. P. Oppé, *Drawings of William Hogarth*, 1948, pp. 55–6; and Ronald Paulson, *Hogarth's Graphic Works*, 2 vols, New Haven, Conn., 1970, I, 281–2. Oppé expresses the opinion that the drawing is not carefully executed.

[29] MONKMAN.

producing little. Probably he lacked the energy to take on Sterne, or anyone, as a personal friend. Yet, paid for or not, the *Tristram Shandy* sketches were tokens of his esteem. Only three known prints came out of Hogarth's studio during the period 1760–1, and two of them were for Sterne.

Sterne had begun looking for his own lodgings as soon as he arrived in town. Mindful of how indiscreet it would have been for Catherine Fourmantel to write to him at Cholmley's, he deferred sending one of his letters to her for several days until he could let her know 'where to direct a Letter' (96). He looked at rooms in the theatre district and in fashionable Piccadilly. He finally settled for 'a good address'. 'My Lodgings', he wrote to Catherine, '. . . are the genteelest in Town' (102). Indeed, it would have been hard to find an address which denoted higher social status than Pall Mall, which fronted upon St James's Palace and Marlborough House. At the Friary Passage leading into St James's Park (now replaced by Marlborough Gate) stood the chairmen with their ranks of sedan chairs. Pall Mall and the park were the most fashionable promenade in London. The house in which Sterne now established himself stood toward the east end of the street, the second house from St Alban's Street (97), which at that time connected into Pall Mall at a point just east of the present Waterloo Place. All of that area was changed when John Nash's celebrated plan for Regent Street was put into effect. Nash's Royal Opera Arcade stands today on the spot where once stood the house in which Sterne lived. The parish church for the area was St James's, Piccadilly, where Sterne probably attended services and listened to the sermons of Dr Samuel Nicolls, who was a Royal Chaplain and a Prebendary of St Paul's. He had been a student at Magdalene College, Cambridge, when Sterne was at Jesus.[30] The lodgings were bespoke by Tuesday, 11 March, a week after he had arrived.[31]

[30] For the location of the house, see the map by J. Rocque, *Cities of London and Westminster* . . . , 1746, and the index to it, *Alphabetical Index of the Streets Lanes, Alleys* . . . , 1747, facsimile issued by the London Topographical Society, No. 108, 1968. Parish boundaries are shown in the map of London by Richard Horwood, 1799. Dr Samuel Nicolls is noticed in *Alumni Cantabrigienses*.

[31] Sterne's acquisition of his Pall Mall lodgings can be dated from Letter 49, to Catherine Fourmantel, in which he tells her he will not seal the letter until he has a new address. The first part was written before he had his meeting with Dodsley, therefore on the morning of Friday the 8th, the date he put on the letter. (He met Dodsley later that day.) The letter closes with the sentence 'I go to the Oratorio this night.' CURTIS, 97, argues convincingly that this

Sterne had some need of fashionable residence because he was now being courted by numerous nobles and people of wealth. In accordance with established etiquette, these high-ranking neighbours either called upon him or sent their cards. He then returned their calls. That done, invitations to dine could be extended. Since he was a clergyman of limited means, it was understood that Sterne could accept such invitations without returning them. These formalities were well under way before he was able to get away from Cholmley's house. 'I have the greatest honors paid me,' he wrote on 8 March, '& most civilities shewn me, that were ever known, from the Great; & am engaged allready to ten Noble men & men of fashion to dine' (96). The catalyst for such a stir was David Garrick: 'Mr Garrick . . . has promissed Numbers of great People to carry me to dine wth 'em' (96).

Sterne was not talking about insignificant people. 'My Lodgings is every hour full of your great People of the first Rank who strive who shall most honour me—even all the Bishops have sent their Complim$^{t[s]}$ to me, & I set out on Munday morning to pay my Visits to them all.—I am to dine w^{h} Lord Chesterfield, this week &c &c' (101). And, in a third letter to Catherine, 'I dined these 2 Days with 2 Ladies of the Bedchamber—then with, Ld Rockingham, Ld Edgecomb—Lord Wilchelsea, Lord Littleton, A Bishop—&c &c—I assure you my Kitty, that Tristram is the Fashion' (102).

So Sterne was entertained in the magnificent Chesterfield House, overlooking Hyde Park, by one of the greatest lords of England. Curious, to think of the straight-backed Chesterfield, who thought laughter not quite appropriate to a gentleman, walking through his beautiful gardens with the parson who overnight had become the most famous comic writer in England. The visit must have gone well. Sterne was emboldened to ask his lordship for a subscription to the forthcoming sermons, and Chesterfield gracious enough to give it. Not all great folk were so stiff as Chesterfield. Lord Edgecomb, as Sterne spelled it, was Richard Edgcumbe, second Baron Edgcumbe, a major-general, politician, erstwhile Lord of the Admiralty, a

refers to a performance of Handel's *Messiah* on Tuesday, 11 March. (The performance was advertised in the *London Chronicle* for 1–4 March and the *Public Advertiser*, 11 March.) So Sterne wrote this on the afternoon of the 11th, presumably at the time he added his signature and his new address in a postscript. Therefore, he had acquired his lodgings by the 11th. Although it is not material to this dating, I would point out that the middle section of the letter was written at some time between the opening paragraph and the closing sentence.

wit, and a gambler who frequented Arthur's. Very probably Sterne's hostess at his lordship's house was Ann Franks, with whom Edgcumbe had lived many years.[32] 'Wilchelsea' was Daniel Finch, eighth Earl of Winchilsea, an eccentric who, a few years later, went mad.[33] His wife, the Rt Hon. Lady Charlotte Finch, perhaps remembered Sterne kindly when she subscribed to Sterne's posthumous *Sermons*. 'Littleton' was the scholarly George, Baron Lyttelton of Frankley, author of *Dialogues of the Dead* and close friend of Sterne's cousin by marriage, Elizabeth Montagu. The Marquis of Rockingham was already his patron, and Sterne would see a lot of him in the weeks ahead. And there were dozens of others whose names we do not know. 'I have not a Moment to spare,' he wrote to Catherine Fourmantel on 1 April, 'dine to Day with a Dozen Dukes & Earls' (104). And, later that month, 'I am hurried off my Legs—by going to great People' (105–6).

'I am to be presented to the Prince' (106). Thus Sterne announced what in the eyes of many people of fashion was his greatest social coup – to be taken up by a member of the royal family. Edward Augustus, Prince of Great Britain and Ireland, Duke of Brunswick-Lüneburg, had just turned twenty-one and on 1 April 1760 had been given the title by which he is usually remembered, the Duke of York. He was second in line to the throne and among the royal children closest in affection to his brother George, the Prince of Wales. He held the rank of captain in the navy and would soon be made a rear-admiral, but he was not a good commander. The following year his naval superiors, after formally hearing complaints about his performance, would remove him from the command of the *Princess Amelia*. The 'Harlequin prince', as Elizabeth Montagu called him, rejected out of hand all the domestic virtues for which his brother as George III would be admired. He insisted upon making public appearances as an actor and musician and crudely sought the favours of women of good breeding. He had, said Walpole, 'loose and perpetually rolling eyes', white hair and white eyebrows. After he had danced with the fourteen-year-old Lady Sarah Lennox, she called him an 'ugly little white pig'. In mid-May Sterne wrote to Stephen Croft, since returned to Stillington, 'just came from a Concert

[32] CURTIS, 103; NAMIER AND BROOKE.

[33] His madness was described by Elizabeth Montagu in a MS letter to Elizabeth Vesey, 19 November 1765: Huntington Library, MO 6380.

where the D[uke] of Y[ork] perform'd—I have received great notice from him, and last week had the honour of supping with him' (110–11).[34]

The duke had a rakish retinue, and Sterne may have met through him some of his more colourful acquaintances. When he first came to London, said John Croft, 'he fell into the Company and affected a Set of Wits in London at that time, Foot, Delavall, &c.' Samuel Foote, the comedian, Garrick's most successful rival, and Foote's sidekick, Sir Francis Blake Delaval, among the most conspicuous rakes of the age, were frequent companions of the duke.[35]

What most gladdened Sterne's heart was the attention paid to him by Charles Watson Wentworth, second Marquis of Rockingham, the thirty-year-old leader of the Yorkshire Whigs and Lord Lieutenant of the North and West Ridings. This young aristocrat had known Sterne in Yorkshire, not as a political figure, for Sterne had long given up politics, but as a prebendary of the Minster. Before the first two volumes of *Tristram Shandy* were issued at York, Rockingham had ordered no fewer than eight copies. Now that the book was a success, Rockingham was not going to be outdone in celebrating the author. He first took Sterne to court (101), then to dine (102), and then a month in advance invited him to join his retinue to travel to Windsor where Rockingham would be admitted into the Order of the Garter (104). He was being rewarded with the Garter for his support of Newcastle, upon whom George II relied heavily. Although Rockingham would later form two governments, in 1765 and 1782, he never won the confidence of George III and spent most of his long political career in opposition. He is remembered for his personal integrity, for leading a party

[34] [George Edward Cokayne], *Complete Peerage*, 1910–59, XII, ii; John Charnock, *Biographia Navalis*, 6 vols, 1794–8, VI, 382–5. See also Elizabeth Montagu's comment in a letter to Leonard Smelt, 3 November [1767] at the Huntington Library, MO 4994; WALPOLE, X, 237–9 and *passim*; Walpole's *Memoirs of the Reign of King George the Third*, ed. G. F. Russell Barker, 4 vols, 1894, III, 74–5; and George Bubb Dodington, *Political Journals*, ed. John Carswell and Lewis Arnold Dralle, Oxford, 1965, pp. 178–9. For the comments of Lady Sarah Lennox (daughter of Charles, Duke of Richmond) and others, the *Correspondence of Emily, Duchess of Leinster*, ed. Brian Fitzgerald, 3 vols, Dublin, 1949–57, III, 76–7, 84, 487, 634 and *passim*. For his naval career, see William Laird Clowes, *The Royal Navy*, 1898, 193, 565 and *passim*.

[35] CROFT. CURTIS, 261, cites a story in John Croft's *Scrapeana*, 1792, to demonstrate a connection between Sterne and Foote. But I make no use of *Scrapeana* here or anywhere because it is no more than a jest-book and has no historical value. In the manner of jest writers, Croft makes free use of the names of famous comic figures, those of 'Foote', 'Tristram Shandy' and 'Yorick' among them.

as free of corruption as any of that age, and for advocating liberal causes such as greater freedom for Catholics and liberty for the American colonies.[36]

On the first of May, Sterne wrote to Stephen Croft, 'On Monday we set out with a grand retinue of Lord Rockingham's (in whose suite I move) for Windsor' (107). It was certainly a gay occasion. The company which gathered at Windsor, the papers reported, included more foreign ministers, nobles and persons of rank than had ever been assembled for such a ceremony. Three persons were to be installed – Rockingham and Earl Temple in person, and by proxy Prince Ferdinand of Brunswick, commander of the allied forces in Europe. The ceremonies, which were held on 6 May, commenced with a grand procession from the dean's house to the Royal Chapel of St George –

> The Poor Knights in their cloaks—The Prebends in their mantles—The Officers of Arms in their Tabarts—The two Knights Elect in the Under Habit of Silver Tissue, carrying their caps and feathers in their hands.—The Deputy Register of the Order, having on his Right Hand Garter bearing the King's Commission, and on his Left Black Rod with his Rod, all in their mantles.

With great pomp the knights were invested with the robes of their order, their swords belted on, their book of statutes presented. There were solemn ceremonies honouring the deceased knights of the order, including, ironically, old Lord Carlisle, who had been the chief political opponent to Rockingham's father. The knights then offered 'gold and silver' at the altar. Finally, they processed to Windsor Castle, where 'a splendid dinner was provided for the Knights and their company in the Great Guard Chamber', during which the 'styles' of the new knights were proclaimed. That evening 'there was a magnificent ball and supper.'[37]

Sterne's Yorkshire neighbours were incredulous. One wrote, 'Common-Fame says, but Common-Fame is a great Liar, that it is not only a Duke and an Earl, and a new made Bishop, who are contending for the Honour of

[36] Sterne's letter to Rockingham, dated at York, 4 December 1759, in Appendix I; George Thomas [Keppel], Earl of Albemarle, *Memoirs of the Marquis of Rockingham and His Contemporaries*, 2 vols, 1852, *passim*; NAMIER AND BROOKE; Cedrick Collyer, 'The Rockinghams and Yorkshire Politics, 1742–1761', *Publications of the Thoresby Society*, XLI (1946–53), 352–82; Ian R. Christie, *Wilkes, Wyville and Reform*, 1926, pp. 74, 202–3.

[37] *London Chronicle*, 10 May; a nearly identical account appeared in the *Public Advertiser*, 12 May.

being God-father to his dear Child Tristram, but that Men and Women too, of all Ranks and Denominations, are caressing the Father, and providing Slavering-Bibs for the Bantling.'[38] But another, as though in answer, wrote, 'He is in Vogue. He is the man of Humour, he is the toast of the British Nation.'[39] Indeed, Sterne burst upon London Society, as William Rider said, 'with an Eclat of which there have been few examples'.[40] Thomas Gray was soon writing to Thomas Wharton, 'one is invited to dinner, where he dines, a fortnight beforehand.'[41] Before long the backlog of Sterne's invitations grew to mythic proportions. 'He frequently had cards of Invitation from the Nobility and People of the first Fashion', said John Croft, 'for a month to come, that it allmost amounted to a Parliamentary Interest to have his company.' By the time Samuel Johnson spoke of Sterne's reception, the backlog had become three months – longer than Sterne's stay in London!

> It having been observed [wrote Boswell] that there was little hospitality in London; JOHNSON. 'Nay, Sir, any man who has a name, or who has the power of pleasing, will be very generally invited in London. The man, Sterne, I have been told, has had engagements for three months.' GOLDSMITH. 'And a very dull fellow.' JOHNSON. 'Why no, Sir.'[42]

Among the 'Duke of York's people' that spring was a nineteen-year-old aspiring poet from Scotland named James Boswell, who was delighted to meet the literary man of the hour. He showed Sterne a poem he had just written. Sterne, he said, responded with a caper, though they were standing in the middle of Pall Mall, patted him on the shoulder, and told him he was the child of Matthew Prior. Boswell, thrilled, went home to Scotland and wrote another poem – 'A Poetical Epistle to Doctor Sterne, Parson Yorick, and Tristram Shandy'. This piece of juvenilia, though uneven and unfinished, contains nevertheless some striking descriptions.

> By Fashon's hands compleatly drest
> He's everywhere a wellcome Guest

[38] 'Anonymous Letter'.

[39] Sir Thomas Robinson of Newby, Yorkshire, later Baron Grantham, to his son Thomas, 27 May 1760; MS in Leeds Archives Department.

[40] *Historical and Critical Account of the Living Authors of Great Britain*, 1762 (Augustan Reprint Society, No. 163, 1974).

[41] *Correspondence*, ed. Paget Toynbee and Leonard Whibley, 3 vols, Oxford, 1935, II, 670–1.

[42] BOSWELL, II, 222.

He runs about from place to place
Now with my Lord, then with his Grace
And mixing with the brilliant throng
He straight commences *Beau Garcon.*
In Ranelagh's delightfull round
Squire Tristram oft is flaunting found
A buzzing whisper flys about,
Where'er he comes they point him out;
Each Waiter with an eager eye
Observes him as he passes by
'That there is he, – do, Thomas! look
Who's wrote such a damn'd clever Book.'[43]

Boswell's poem was structured upon the idea of Sterne's remarkable transformation from slovenly rural parson to fashionably dressed, urbane social lion. Sterne's portraits bear out Boswell's point about clothing: they show Sterne in well-cut, fashionable clothes, but in clerical black and with bands. Sterne was nearly six feet tall (240), which was exceptionally tall for those days. His forehead was broad, his cheeks hollow, his nose long, thin and hooked, his lips full and hanging loosely in his gaunt face. 'My Phyz', he once said, 'is as remarkable as myself' (231). An unidentified correspondent to the *Grand Magazine* thought his very appearance incited laughter:

> there is no reading him without laughing; nay the very sight of him is reviving—for his long sharp nose, and his droll look altogether, affect our risible faculties so strongly, that there is no looking at him without laughing. . . . one cannot help laughing at his joke, even before he opens his mouth.—I only wish he was fatter—He looks as meagre as if he had pored over the metaphysical lamp.[44]

For all that, Sterne's manners were polished. He drank little, and smoked not at all.

[43] Frederick A. Pottle, 'Bozzy and Yorick', *Blackwood's Magazine*, CCXVII (1925), 297–313, summarizes the history of Boswell's meeting with Sterne and its effect upon him. Pottle quotes extensively from the poem, and quotes the best parts. The MS is housed at the Bodleian Library (Douce MS. 193). I have taken my quotation from a photographic copy of the MS kindly supplied by the Beinecke Library, Yale University.

[44] 'Animadversions on *Tristram Shandy*', by an unidentified correspondent, *Grand Magazine*, III (April 1760), 194–5. But this same writer, in defending Sterne's bawdry, which was his primary purpose, did Sterne incalculable harm. See below.

But externals cannot explain Sterne's great social success. He was, in Boswell's phrase, 'the best companion I ever knew'. On the one hand, he was celebrated for his fund of lively talk and his keen wit. On the other, he was a gregarious being who enjoyed all sorts of people and was almost never critical of them. On one rare occasion, when he had allowed himself in a letter to make a derogatory remark about another clergyman, he scolded 'my own vile passions' and crossed the passage out (248). In 1765 Elizabeth Montagu would say of Sterne:

> He has a world of good nature, he never hurt any one with his witt, he treats asses on two legs as well and gently as he does that four legged one in his book. A Man of witt (& such he certainly is with all his oddities) that never makes use of the sharp Weapon ever at his side to alarm or to wound his neighbour deserves much indulgence.[45]

It was Sterne's modesty and goodness of heart which Dr John Hill emphasized in his newspaper biography of Sterne:

> Every body is curious to see the author; and, when they see him, every body loves the man. There is a pleasantry in his conversation that always pleases; and a goodness in his heart. . . . A vain man would be exalted extremely, at the attention that is paid to him; the compliments, invitations, civilities, and applause: he sees them in another light, attributing that to novelty, which perhaps few could more justly place to the account of merit. He says he is now just like a fashionable mistress, whom every body solicits, because 'tis the fashion, but who may walk the street a fortnight, and in vain solicit corporal Stare for a dinner.

Dr Hill's account was published originally in a newspaper which he himself had recently started, the *Royal Female Magazine*, 1 May 1760, where it might have been forgotten were it not picked up and reprinted in the *London Chronicle*, 3–6 May. Sterne professed to be angry about the story, but perhaps he had to take that stand because of what Hill had said about Warburton's buying Sterne off. The account, though a piece of hack work, did Sterne's public image no harm. He might protest against its inaccuracies, but one can find twentieth-century biographical articles by

[45] MS letter to Sarah Scott, 11 April 1765: Huntington Library, MO 5820.

persons who have claims to scholarship that contain more errors than Hill's. Much of it is shammed, but it is nevertheless amusingly written. For instance, though he knew nothing much about Sterne's early career, Hill wrote, 'He seated himself quietly in the lap of the church; and if this was not yet covered with a fringed cushion, 'twas not naked.' Sterne, however, was embarrassed by Hill's sentimental story that, upon being presented to the Coxwold living, Sterne had made a gift of money and granted a pension to the widow of his predecessor. 'The story of a hundred pounds to Mrs. W[ilkinson],' Sterne wrote, 'not true, or of a *pension promised*; the merit of which I disclaim'd' (110). But the general outline of his life and career was correct, and Sterne had to admit the truth of some of the anecdotes. Hill rather ponderously told a story about how Sterne had silenced a physician who had offended the table by his pompous talk of empiric medicine. Parodying the doctor's jargon, Sterne told a story about how he had healed the adhesions in his lungs by pole vaulting and allowing himself to fall across a stone wall – a *reductio ad absurdum* of empiric medicine. Dr Hill, said Sterne, had tampered with this story so as to make readers think the doctor was an old enemy, Dr Messenger Monsey. Sterne was forced to contradict the story in London 'for the honour of my friend M[onse]y' (110), but he allowed the truth of the dialogue itself.

Even more advantageous to Sterne than Hill's little biography was the appearance in the January issue of the *Gentleman's Magazine* of the sketch of Yorick in *Tristram Shandy*, accompanied by a declaration, 'It is by some supposed to be the Character of the Author, as he himself Chuses it should be exhibited.' Both sketch and comment were repeated on 5 February in the *London Chronicle*.

But Sterne's personal charm could never account for his success without *Tristram Shandy*. Dr Hill put it well:

> A parcel of the books were sent up out of the country; they were unknown, and scarce advertised; but thus friendless they made their own way, and their author's. They have been resembled to Swift's, and equalled to Rabelais', by those who are considered as judges; and they have made their author's way to the tables of the first people in the kingdom, and to the friendship of Mr. Garrick.

Not everyone liked the book. Horace Walpole wrote:

> At present nothing is talked of, nothing admired, but what I cannot help calling a very insipid and tedious performance: it is a kind of

> novel called, *The Life and Opinions of Tristram Shandy*; the great humour of which consists in the whole narration always going backwards. I can conceive of a man saying that it would be droll to write a book in that manner, but have no notion of his persevering in executing it. It makes one smile two or three times at the beginning, but in recompense makes one yawn for two hours. . . . The best thing in it is a sermon—oddly coupled with a good deal of bawdy, and both the composition of a clergyman.[46]

But most people of sophistication found *Tristram Shandy* the most amusing book they had seen since Swift. Dr William Oliver, the Bath physician, was highly amused by the obstetrical passages and wrote to his cousin William Borlase that all sorts of people, from highly placed clergy to Beau Nash's mistress, loved and admired the book even when they did not understand it, that it had beguiled them into reading a sermon and thinking about what seldom occupied their thoughts – religion.[47]

The writer of that early enthusiastic notice of *Tristram Shandy* in the February issue of the *London Magazine* had seen clearly that it was destined to be read and admired 'by the best, if not the most numerous class of mankind'. This is not to say that Richardson, Fielding and Smollett had no readers among persons of wealth and rank. Good novels were rare, and those who had an appetite for prose fiction read most of what was printed. But *Tristram Shandy*, with its comic opening scene of Tristram's parents interrupted in the act of begetting him, its naughty puns and suggestive *aposiopeses*, had a special appeal to people who thought of themselves as freed by birth or education from the constraints of middle-class codes of conduct. Thomas Twining and his fellow students at Cambridge went about gathering signatures for their comic certificate of excellence for Tristram Shandy,[48] but the dons shook their heads. 'Mark my words,' said Richard Farmer, the classical tutor at Emmanuel, '. . . in the course of twenty years, should any one wish to refer to the book in question, he will be obliged to go to an antiquary to inquire for it.'[49]

A few prominent people were made nervous by Sterne's ability to satirize. It would have been common talk that Sterne had modelled his Dr

[46] WALPOLE, XV, 66–7.

[47] Letter of 12 July 1760, as quoted by Benjamin Boyce, *The Benevolent Man*, 256.

[48] BL, Add. MSS 39929, fol. 1.

[49] B[aptist] N[oel] Turner, 'An Account of Dr. Johnson's Visit to Cambridge, in 1765', *New Monthly Magazine*, X (1818), 385–91.

Slop upon Dr John Burton of York, and his lawyer, Didius, upon Dr Francis Topham, the prominent ecclesiastical lawyer and Master of the Faculties, and certain members of the medical profession were upset at Sterne's cutting remarks about the late Dr Richard Mead.[50] 'Fools tremble', said Hill, 'at the allusions that may be made from the present volumes, and authors dread the next.' Yet Hill insisted that Sterne was not primarily interested in personal satire and had, in fact, rewritten parts of his book so as not to offend anyone. There is an element of truth in Hill's comment. We know Sterne had toned down the satire of his original version of *Tristram Shandy*.[51] If he kept a few personal satires, he put them on the edge of the main story, that of the Shandy family. And the Shandy family was no threat to anyone: its members were readily recognizable rural types – the irascible country gentleman, the retired soldier in his garden, the shy mistress of the manor with longings to be in town, the servants. Their foibles represented universal shortcomings, and Sterne laughed at them tolerantly and lovingly. Without getting into the complicated critical problem of how Sterne's fiction reflected the moral philosophies of his age, we can say that he hit the perfect note for a public who were learning to take seriously the sentimental virtues being explained and advocated by Shaftesbury, Lord Kames and David Hume, but who had not yet lost their appetite for the boldness and stringency of the Augustans.

But if Sterne were, as Mrs Thrale put it, 'caressed by all Ranks of People with ridiculous Assiduity',[52] he established little rapport with other writers. Warburton's patronage was short-lived. Johnson never took him up at all. Smollett was standoffish and suspicious: that at least is suggested by the articles in the *Critical Review*, of which Smollett was owner. Its review of the first edition of *Tristram Shandy*, I–II, was not unfriendly, but implied that the best features of the book were imitations of Smollett: 'For instance, uncle *Toby*, Corporal *Trim*, and Dr. *Slop*, are excellent imitations of certain characters in a modern truly Cervantic performance, which we avoid naming, out of regard to the author's delicacy.'[53] Later reviews of the subsequent volumes of *Tristram Shandy* were cool. These three, Warburton, Johnson and Smollett, were the most influential figures in the world of letters.

However, as already noted, Sterne was entertained by George Lyttelton,

[50] *EMY*, 295–6. His satires of Topham and Burton: 289–91.

[51] *EMY*, 278–81.

[52] *Thraliana*, ed. Katharine C. Balderston, 2 vols, Oxford, 1942, I, 27.

[53] January 1760. Reviewer not identified.

who was the friend and patron of Fielding, the man to whom *Tom Jones* had been dedicated. In the wake of a long but undistinguished political career, including various cabinet posts, he had been elevated to the peerage with the title of Baron Lyttelton of Frankley.[54] His rather ponderous *Dialogues of the Dead* had appeared that spring and were being sold side by side with *Tristram Shandy*. One wonders what Sterne made of this pedantic, dull historian, mild-mannered, absentminded and serious. Elizabeth Montagu and Elizabeth Vesey, who would be remembered eventually as the leaders of the Bluestockings, were friends of and collaborators with Lord Lyttelton. It was an open secret that Elizabeth Montagu had written two of the *Dialogues of the Dead*, and Elizabeth Vesey would later help Lyttelton with his *History of Henry II*. This was the one literary circle which in 1760 made Sterne welcome.

Sterne had a special claim upon Mrs Montagu because she was a cousin of his wife and godmother to his daughter. To be precise, the women were half-cousins: Elizabeth Montagu's father was half-brother to Elizabeth Sterne's mother. Mrs Montagu never denied the kinship and in later years did not fail of her cousinly duty when she was needed. Nevertheless, she thought of Elizabeth Sterne as a fractious, ridiculous woman, and she carefully avoided her. As she explained in 1768 to a friend,

> Mrs Sterne is a Woman of great integrity & has many virtues, but they stand like quills upon the fretfull porcupine, ready to go forth in sharp arrows on ye least supposed offence; she w^{d} not do a wrong thing, but she does right things in a very unpleasing manner, & the only way to avoid a quarrel with her is to keep a due distance.[55]

Mrs Montagu came from the wealthy, socially prominent branch of the family. As a child she had lived for a time in the magnificent Great House in York. She also had an excellent informal education at the hands of Conyers Middleton, the great Cambridge scholar, who had married her maternal grandmother. Elizabeth herself married an intellectual, Edward Montagu of Allerthorpe, who in the course of time became one of the most distinguished mathematicians in England. He was also an astute businessman and industrialist who operated extensive coalmines in Northumberland. Although there was a difference of thirty years in their ages, Elizabeth and

[54] NAMIER AND BROOKE; *DNB*.

[55] MS letter to Leonard Smelt, [? September 1768]: Huntington Library, MO 4999.

Edward Montagu were perfect in their duties to one another. Nevertheless, there were many in the eighteenth century and even today who say that she was really in love with George Lyttelton. In 1760 Mrs Montagu was a tall, goodlooking woman of forty, childless (her one child had died early), studious, a gossip, though not a vicious one, and a prolific letter writer. Her *Essay on the Writings and Genius of Shakespeare*, which would make her reputation as a woman of letters, was ten years in the future. She was not yet that influential figure, the 'Queen of the Bluestockings', though it was about this time that she and Mrs Vesey began to assemble groups of women who called themselves 'Bluestockings'. The Montagus' house in Hill Street, Berkeley Square, had for some time been a gathering place for many of the literary figures of London, most of the bishops and highly placed clergy, and numerous nobles and wealthy gentry. For the rest of his life, Sterne would look to Elizabeth Montagu for friendship and support, which sometimes she gave, sometimes not.[56]

Probably Sterne met Elizabeth Vesey at this time. At forty-five, this interesting Anglo-Irish woman was a celebrated hostess. She spent her summers with her husband at Lucan, ten miles west of Dublin, her winters at Tunbridge Wells, Bath and London. In London the couple maintained a house in Bolton Row. In all of these places, she opened her doors to writers, scholars, intellectuals, but especially to women writers and students of letters. She had, said Montagu Pennington, 'the almost magic art of putting all her company at their ease, without the least appearance of design'. Fanny Burney, who knew her much later, talked entertainingly of her determination to break up the traditional conversational circle. 'She pushed all the smaller sofas, as well as chairs, pell-mell about the apartments . . . and her greatest delight was to place the seats back to back . . . an arrangement that could only be eluded by such a twisting of the neck as to threaten the interlocutors with a spasmodic affection.' But the amusing side of Elizabeth Vesey should not blind us to her talents. She was an excellent

[56] CLIMENSON, I, 1 ff.; NAMIER AND BROOKE; *DNB*; Frances Burney, *Memoirs of Doctor Burney*, 3 vols, 1832, II, 269–73; Katherine G. Hornbeak, 'New Light on Mrs. Montagu', *Age of Johnson*, ed. Frederick W. Hilles and Wilmarth S. Lewis, New Haven, Conn., 1949, pp. 349–61; Jane Steffenson Hagen, 'The Salon, the Queen of the Blues, and Laurence Sterne', *Susquetanna University Studies*, X, 5–15; John Taylor, *Records of My Life*, 2 vols, 1832, I, 92–3. I speculate in *EMY*, 276 and n. 2, that Sterne went to London in 1759, at which time he first met Mrs Montagu. Elizabeth Sterne, writing in 1760 and 1761, says that Sterne had seen Mrs Montagu 'these two last winters': CURTIS, 136–7.

writer – as evidenced by her letters – but without ambition to be known as a writer. Her assemblies were more like the literary salons of Paris than those of any other British woman. For many years she had been called by her women friends 'the Sylph', because, as Mrs Delany explained, she belonged to 'a race of air rather than of earth'. But her personal life was sad. Agmondesham Vesey, her second husband, who was also her cousin, was very much a creature of earth. He detested his wife's assemblies and spent his time gambling and whoring.[57]

It has often been said that Sterne became enamoured of Mrs Vesey and carried on a long sentimental flirtation with her. We are told about a tryst at Ranelagh Gardens; and sometimes we are shown a print of the couple strolling arm and arm through Ranelagh. The sentimental courtship and the walk through Ranelagh are the inventions of William Combe, the man who forged many letters that once passed for Sterne's.[58]. The print was made for an otherwise worthless jest-book, *Tristram Shandy at Ranelagh*, which appeared in June 1760.[59] Mrs Vesey might have responded to a lover who would appeal to her sympathies. Elizabeth Montagu, in making the point that Mrs Vesey would never be attracted by wealth or rank, said she would be open only to the advances of some 'weary pilgrem reposing beside a murmuring rill, or a shepherd panting beneath the spreading beach'. Sterne once addressed a letter to Elizabeth Vesey, the manuscript of which survives, but it is unlikely he ever sent it. It is perhaps the most ribald love letter he ever wrote! He puns indecently: 'intercourses of this kind are not to be dated by hours, days or months, but by the slow or rapid progress of our intimacies which can be measured only by the degrees of penetration' (137); and he audaciously interweaves sexual with religious images: 'You

[57] The best study of Mrs Vesey is probably that of Reginald Blunt, 'The Sylph', *Edinburgh Review*, CCXLII (1925), 364–79, but unfortunately he used the spurious *Original Letters of the Late Reverend Mr. Laurence Sterne* (see next note, below). See also *DNB*; John S. Crone, *A Concise Dictionary of Irish Biography*, 256; Montagu Pennington, *Memoirs of Mrs. Carter*, quoted in *Johnsonian Miscellanies*, 2 vols, 1897 [1966], II, 59; Frances Burney, *Memoirs*, II, 262–8. She is often talked about in the letters of Elizabeth Montagu, Mary Delany and Elizabeth Carter. Hannah More's poem, *Florio*, 1786, is largely about her assemblies.

[58] *Original Letters by the Late Reverend Mr. Laurence Sterne*, 1788, Letter XIX, 103–8; Letter XXXVII, 205–7. On Combe's authorship of this book, unfortunately used by CROSS and CLIMENSON, see HAMILTON and Hamilton's *Doctor Syntax: A Silhouette of William Combe, Esq.*, Kent, Ohio, 1969, pp. 142–3.

[59] Advertised in the *London Chronicle* of 21 June, and noticed in the *London Magazine* for July.

are the sweetest and best tuned of all Instruments—O Lord! I would give away my other Cassoc to touch you—but in giving this last rag of my Priesthood for this pleasure You perceive I should be left naked—if not quite dis-*Orderd*' (138). But Mrs Vesey, as Elizabeth Montagu said, was 'past the high day of the blood'. 'If her frozen virtue had ever melted before the fire of some amorous swain, it must have been one who at the foot of a Rock, shaded by a trembling willow, had languished in the moon beams.'[60] If Sterne had been foolish enough actually to send his letter, it would have instantly put an end to any budding romance or friendship. No, the probabilities are that Elizabeth Vesey meant little or nothing to Sterne except as a figure in some fantasy which he transmogrified into a piece of comic writing. A few years later he complimented her as 'interesting', a word that to Sterne meant affecting, appealing to the tender sentiments:[61] 'the interesting Mrs. Vesey, with her vocal, and fifty other accomplishments' (250); but he knew so little about her as to call her a widow when her husband was very much alive.

The Bluestocking group, if it can be called that, was not really in a position to teach Sterne or learn from him. Mrs Montagu read widely in French, Italian and English literature, but she had a dislike of novels. She and her circle shared with Warburton and many others an unspoken, perhaps only half-understood assumption that authors had the duty to spread the gospel of middle-class virtue, the good news that honesty, duty and chastity were not only possible, but immediately rewarding. The new millennium would be one of sentimental fiction. And here they made their mistake about Sterne. Moved by the sweetness in his story, they did not fully recognize that he was a subversive who delighted in being naughty and believed that people were most lovable when their imperfections showed. They would eventually withdraw from him.

The person who most fully appreciated Sterne, perhaps, was old Lord Bathurst, who had been the friend and patron of many great Augustan writers. In later years, Sterne recalled his meeting with Bathurst in 1760:

> This nobleman is an old friend of mine.—You know he was always the protector of men of wit and genius; and has had those of the last

[60] MS letter to Elizabeth Carter, 29 September [1764]: Huntington Library, MO 3130.

[61] The *OED* cites *A Sentimental Journey* as its earliest example of this word in its second meaning – appealing to or able to arouse emotions.

> century, Addison, Steele, Pope, Swift, Prior, &c. &c. always at his table.—The manner in which his notice began of me, was as singular as it was polite.—He came up to me, one day, as I was at the Princess of Wales's court. 'I want to know you, Mr. Sterne; but it is fit you should know, also, who it is that wishes this pleasure. You have heard, continued he, of an old Lord Bathurst, of whom your Popes, and Swifts, have sung and spoken so much: I have lived my life with geniuses of that cast; but have survived them; and, despairing ever to find their equals, it is some years since I have closed my accounts, and shut up my books, with thoughts of never opening them again: but you have kindled a desire in me of opening them once more before I die; which I now do; so go home and dine with me. (304–5)

Indeed, Lord Bathurst would continue to entertain Sterne for the rest of Sterne's life.

Although many people of rank and station celebrated Sterne the writer and entertaining dinner guest, there was one who did not neglect the country parson. Some two weeks after his arrival in London, Sterne received an invitation to call on his old neighbour, Lord Fauconberg, of Newburgh Priory, Coxwold. Fauconberg, a genial, fat man, seldom left his Hanover Square house; so Sterne probably thought there was nothing unusual in the summons. How astonished he must have been to hear his lordship ask if he would like to become the parson of Coxwold.[62] Sterne had not learned of the illness and death of parson Richard Wilkinson. He had known poor Wilkinson for years, and once had hired him as his assistant at Sutton and Stillington. He had never much liked him. But Sterne got on very well with Lord Fauconberg. The Sutton enclosure, enacted four years before, had greatly benefited Lord Fauconberg, and enclosures were virtually impossible to effect without the co-operation of the clergy.[63] One cannot say for sure that Fauconberg was not pleased with the prospect of having so celebrated a man as Sterne living in his village under his protection, but we know he was moved primarily by his sure sense of the

[62] That the presentment was made first orally is implied by the announcement of it in the *York Courant* of 25 March, which said that it was made 'last week', whereas Fauconberg did not sign the nomination until 28 March. See also Richard Chapman's letter about the nomination, 23 March, cited below. Other announcements were made in the *Public Advertiser* for 29 March, the *London Chronicle* for 27–9 March, and in the April issues of the *Gentleman's Magazine* and *London Magazine*.

[63] *EMY*, 260–1.

proper reciprocity between manor and village. When a friend wrote to congratulate Sterne on the preferment, he replied, 'I hope I have been of some service to his Lordship, and he has sufficiently requited me' (143).

Probably Fauconberg did not expect Sterne to do full-time duties in the parish. He seems, however, to have wanted him to live there, and may have made residence a condition of the presentation. Nothing could have suited Sterne better, for he loved Coxwold, 'a sweet retirement,' he said, 'in comparison of Sutton' (5). Coxwold was high on the edge of the Vale of York, removed from the bogs of the Great Forest. Its dry air would benefit Sterne's weak lungs, and he could move into that charming old cottage which his friends would soon dub 'Shandy Hall'. Best of all, the additional income would give him the security he needed to continue as an author. 'Tho' I have but a moment's time to spare,' he scribbled that evening to Catherine Fourmantel, 'I w^{d} not omit writing you an Acc'ount of my good Fortune; my Lord Fauconberg has this day given me a hundred & sixty pounds a year, wch I hold with all my preferment; So that all or the most part of my Sorrows and Tears are going to be wiped away' (102). It was not worth quite so much, but it would help.[64]

The formalities were concluded within a few days. Fauconberg, always precise in legal matters, wrote home to get the nomination document he had used when he preferred Mr Wilkinson. This he sent to Sterne, who copied it – as was the custom – with appropriate changes.[65] Fauconberg signed it on 28 March. The next day Sterne was at the Grosvenor Square house of Archbishop John Gilbert of York, who with the help of his scrivener soon finished the business. They presented Sterne with a parchment 'collation' – his legal proof of the preferment – and entered the appointment in the archbishop's *Act Book*.[66] Nothing remained but to be inducted to the Church of St Michael when he got to Coxwold. He planned, he said, to go there in May (104), but he did not actually arrive until June.

[64] Discussed in Chapter 2, below.

[65] Lord Fauconberg's steward, Richard Chapman, wrote on 23 March: 'I am extremely glad your Lordship hath thought proper to Nominate Mr Sterne to Coxwold living, of which I have acquainted Mrs Wilkinson this Day, and got Mr. Wilkinsons Nomination which I have Sent Inclosed' (WOMBWELL PAPERS). CURTIS thought it odd that the document should be in Sterne's hand, and reproduced it in LETTERS, facing p. 102. But it seems to have been the custom: at the Borthwick Institute there are numerous nominations in the hands of the nominees.

[66] *Act Book (Institutions) 1755–1768*, fol. 113, at the Borthwick Institute. The collation, signed at 'Our House in Grosvenor Square' 29 March, is now at the BL: Add. Chart. 16166.

On 20 March 1760 Sterne sat down in the studio of Joshua Reynolds, rested his right arm on a small table, as the painter directed, inclined his head lightly on his right hand, and peered amusedly but searchingly at Reynolds as he went to work. This was the first of eight sittings which would result in the splendid 'Lansdowne portrait' now prominently displayed at the National Portrait Gallery. The large, ungainly, half-deaf artist, who talked so intelligently and worked so rapidly with his brushes and paints, must have enchanted Sterne. Reynolds, now aged thirty-seven, had been a fashionable portrait painter for six or seven years, but was still living with his spinster sister in the studio he had set up in as a young man in Great Newport, a cobblestoned street crowded with vendors and small shops. He would move later this very year to a spacious and elegant studio in Leicester Fields opposite Hogarth's. He worked at great speed, turning out three or four portraits a week, often after only three or four sittings. Both Stephen Croft and Nathaniel Cholmley were sitting for him during this same period. Reynolds completed Cholmley's picture in three sittings, Croft's in four. But Sterne sat eight times.[67] Was Reynolds spurred on by conversations with Sterne about Hogarth? The London edition of *Tristram Shandy* with Hogarth's frontispiece appeared midway in the course of Sterne's sittings. Could they have failed to talk about it? In any event, Reynolds was determined to paint very well the celebrated Mr Sterne. The result was one of his greatest portraits.

The painting was not commissioned in the way that Stephen Croft would have commissioned his own portrait. It was, rather, a joint business venture of Sterne and Reynolds. Sterne would have the right to have it engraved and used as a frontispiece for his sermons. He promptly called in the man who had engraved the Hogarth sketch for *Tristram Shandy*, Simon-François Ravenet, who made a line engraving for the book. Reynolds or

[67] Reynolds's appointment book, now at Burlington House, records Sterne's sittings on 20, 25 and 29 March; 3, 6, 19, 20 and 21 April. I presume that the 'Mr Chumley' who sat for Reynolds on 14 April and 9 and 10 May was Nathaniel Cholmley. Stephen Croft sat on 17, 19, 21 and 25 March, the last on a day when Sterne also had a sitting. Opposite Reynolds's note about Sterne's sitting on 6 April is a note, 'Stephen Croft Esqr at York to send a letter at Mr Smelt's', suggesting that Croft was present at Sterne's sitting. For details about Reynolds's studio, life and appearance, see Derek Hudson, *Sir Joshua Reynolds: a Personal Study*, 1958, *passim*. In 1974 the painting was put up for sale, and various buyers from abroad expressed an interest. The National Portrait Gallery mounted a massive and ultimately successful campaign to raise the funds with which to purchase it.

Sterne or both of them also called in Edward Fisher, who executed a skilful mezzotint. It is unclear who had the rights to the framable prints produced by Fisher. Reynolds sold at least some of them; Fisher probably sold others; and it is just possible that Sterne may have sold some, perhaps through Dodsley's shop. It is difficult to know whether he was talking about Ravenet's frontispiece or Fisher's mezzotint when he wrote to Catherine Fourmantel, 'There is a fine print going to be done of me—so I shall make the most of myself, & sell both inside and out' (105). The word *fine* suggests the mezzotint, the higher form of the art. But Reynolds himself kept the painting, which he exhibited at the Society of Artists in 1761 and 1768. After Sterne's death he sold it to Sterne's admirer, John Fitzpatrick, second Earl of Upper Ossory.[68]

It seems likely that Sterne and Reynolds became personal friends, and even more likely that Reynolds supplanted Hogarth as an influence upon Sterne's aesthetic theory. Reynolds subscribed to Sterne's sermons in both 1760 and 1766. Sterne in turn complimented him quite gratuitously early in the third volume of *Tristram Shandy* (188), and he made use of one of Reynolds's *Idler* essays in a satire upon 'connoisseurs', by which Sterne meant people who assess the arts according to mechanical rules. Reynolds's essay had appeared as *Idler* No. 76, one of a sequence of three by Reynolds. It had not yet been republished and was available only in the original publication in the *Universal Chronicle*, for 27 September 1759.[69] It is unlikely Sterne would have found it unless Reynolds had told him about it or given him a copy. Sterne's little satire, in the twelfth chapter of his third volume,

[68] For a history of the painting, engravings and other copies, see 'Portraits of Sterne', appended to *EMY*. Reynolds's involvement in the sale of prints is evidenced in his account book, now at the Fitzwilliam Museum, in which, under the date 26 March 1766, he wrote, 'Mr Smart for Mr Sternes Print 0/5/0/'. The price is noteworthy. It is sometimes said that Reynolds presented the portrait to Sterne as a gift. Though that remains a remote possibility, it is unlikely. The source of the story is a letter forged by William Combe, Letter No. XXII in *Original Letters of the Late Reverend Mr. Laurence Sterne*, 1788, pp. 121–5. At his death, Sterne was in possession of an unidentified portrait of himself which was sold in the autumn of 1768 with other of his effects in London by his wife's brother-in-law, the Rev. John Botham (LETTERS, 441). It is only remotely possible that this was the Reynolds portrait and that Botham sold it to Ossory. If so, Botham would have had to lend it to Reynolds for exhibition at the Society of Artists exhibition of 1768, and that seems unlikely, given Botham's mean disposition and the chaotic condition of Sterne's estate.

[69] At that date the newspaper bore the title *Payne's Universal Chronicle*: Stanley Morison, *The English Newspaper*, Cambridge, 1932, pp. 136–9.

attacks critics of several arts – acting, prose fiction, epic poetry and, finally, painting. One brief passage, in the satire on connoisseurs of painting, makes use of Reynolds's essay. Interestingly, the chief target of Reynolds was Hogarth. Today, students of Sterne are in some disagreement about whether Sterne's passage is also aimed at Hogarth. Sterne made fun of critics who insist that a painting contain pyramidal forms: 'Not one principle of the *pyramid* in any one group!' exclaims Sterne's connoisseur (214). Some readers may have taken this to be an allusion to Hogarth's *Analysis*, in which the pyramid is discussed as one of the shapes of universal interest. On the other hand, he might have been alluding to the aesthetics of Giles Hussey, whose entire system was based upon the figure of the triangle. Though Hogarth and his friends may not have thought twice about the passage, Sterne never again complimented Hogarth in *Tristram Shandy*. But in the seventh volume he called Reynolds the 'son of Apollo' (590). It looks as though Reynolds had convinced Sterne that Hogarth's aesthetic or aesthetic systems of that general type were too constricting. They would hardly suit an author who said that his way of writing was 'religious' because 'I begin with writing the first sentence——and trusting to Almighty God for the second' (656).[70]

Reynolds's portrait was soon common gossip. 'Tristram Shandy is still a greater object of admiration,' wrote Thomas Gray to Thomas Wharton on 22 April, 'the Man as well as the Book. . . . his portrait is done by Reynolds, and now engraving.'[71]

The London edition of *Tristram Shandy*, I–II made its appearance on 2 April and rapidly sold out. The Dodsleys brought out another, and possibly a third edition that spring and yet another toward the end of the year.[72]

[70] Sterne's use of Reynolds's *Idler* essay and his shift of loyalty to Reynolds was first remarked by Willian Holtz, 'Sterne, Reynolds, and Hogarth: Biographical Inferences from a Borrowing', *Art Bulletin*, XLVIII (1966), 82–4; see also Holtz's expanded discussion in *Image and Immortality: A Study of 'Tristram Shandy'*, Providence, Rhode Island, Brown University Press, 1970, especially pp. 21–38. Ronald Paulson, in his review of Holtz's book for *Philological Quarterly*, L (1971), 484–5, argued that Sterne's passage was not aimed specifically at Hogarth, and might have referred to Giles Hussey. For further discussion of the relationship of *Tristram Shandy* to Reynolds, see R. F. Brissenden, 'Sterne and Painting'; for expanded commentary on Sterne and Hogarth, see Paulson's *Hogarth*, II, 304–6.

[71] *Correspondence*, II, 670. If Gray was referring to the Fisher mezzotint, which seems likely, Reynolds or Sterne and Reynolds together lost no time in getting started with the production and sale of prints.

[72] For a definitive statement about what editions of *Tristram Shandy* appeared during

With one exception, no new formal reviews appeared. The exception was by Edmund Burke, not yet the famous politician, but editor and chief writer for the *Annual Register*. In the third volume of the *Register*, which appeared in late May or early June, Burke bravely grappled with the problem how to evaluate such an unusual book as *Tristram Shandy*, but the result is not impressive. The satires, he said, were 'spirited, poignant, and often extremely just', but the digressive method a 'blemish'. The characters were lively but 'somewhat overcharged'.[73]

Unfortunately for Sterne, a great many things appeared in print that made no claim to the status of a review. A controversy, if it can be called that, broke out in the newspapers over the so-called indecencies of the book. It began with an unsigned letter to the *Universal Magazine of Knowledge and Pleasure* for April. The writer took a moderate enough position, but he argued that, however justified in some circumstances, immodest words and *double entendres* could not be condoned in a book by a clergyman.[74] Another attitude was expressed by an unidentified writer whose letter appeared in the *Grand Magazine* for April under the title 'Animadversions on *Tristram Shandy*'. Here was a friend Sterne might well have done without. He praised the book for its lasciviousness and, preposterous as it sounds, for the enjoyable titillations raised by obstetrical discussions, which no one could read 'without feeling a violent itching and propensity, to make work for the sons and daughters of *Pilumnus* and *Lucina*' – i.e. the deities of childbearing. Some Grub Street printer saw fit to run off this fatuous argument as a pamphlet under the title *Letter from a Son of Comus to the Author of Tristram Shandy*.

Such a defence could only encourage Sterne's attackers to see indecency

Sterne's lifetime, see MONKMAN and TRISTRAM IN DUBLIN. Kenneth Monkman, having demonstrated that Sterne published a Dublin edition as well as one at York, raises the question whether or not we can continue to call Dodsley's edition the 'second'. Does not the term now belong to the Dublin edition, which appeared a day or two after the York?

In Appendix V of TRISTRAM SHANDY, Monkman lists three editions of I–II published by Dodsley in 1760 (as well as one in 1763 and another in 1767). The second of these, which Monkman calls the third edition, appeared slightly earlier than he thought. It was advertised in the *Public Advertiser*, 27 May, p. 4, in an appendix to the announcement of the publication of *Sermons*, I–II. Monkman cites as the earliest advertisement that in the *Public Advertiser* for 5 June.

[73] HOWES, 106–7. The identification of Burke was made by Thomas W. Copeland, 'Edmund Burke and the Book Reviews in Dodsley's *Annual Register*', *PMLA*, LVII (1942), 446–68.

[74] HOWES, 62–3.

where others saw no more than playful wit. 'Obscenity', 'bawdry', 'pruriency' are words used by Oliver Goldsmith to describe *Tristram Shandy*. Goldsmith was engaged in writing a series of 'Chinese Letters' in the *Public Ledger*, subsequently published as *The Citizen of the World*. He devoted the letter of 30 June to *Tristram Shandy* without naming either the book or the author. 'Pruriency', said Goldsmith,

> has always been found to give most pleasure to a few very old gentlemen, who being in some measure dead to other sensations, feel the force of the jest with double violence on the organs of risibility.
>
> An author who writes in this manner is generally sure therefore of having the very old and the impotent among his admirers; for these he may properly be said to write, and from these he ought to expect his reward, his works being often a very proper succedaneum to cantharides, or an assa fœtida pill. His pen should be considered in the same useful light as the squirt of an apothecary, both being directed to the same generous ends.[75]

Not a single clever or thoughtful defence of *Tristram Shandy* appeared in print, but the attacks appeared in ranks, especially during the month of May. In the *Public Ledger* there was a letter from 'Ebenezer Plain-cloth', purporting to be a Quaker,[76] and in the *Grand Magazine* for May 'An Admonitory Lyrick Epistle to the Rev. Tristram Shandy', which was at once a criticism of Sterne and a travesty upon the recently published *Two Lyrick Epistles* by Sterne's friend Hall-Stevenson:

> Your humour
> Is like an ulcer or a tumour,
> Always gathering and running
> Corrupted matter;
> Religion is but lint and plaister
> That by confining, make it run the nastier;
> I wish you were both modester and fatter.

[75] Quoted from *Collected Works*, ed. Arthur Friedman, 5 vols, Oxford, 1966, II, 222, but amended according to Friedman's notes to represent the version which appeared in the *Public Ledger*. CROSS, 227–8, 233–4, seems to say that Goldsmith also wrote a series of letters in the *Public Ledger* 'from Mr. Tristram Shandy to his friend Bob Busby', but I have been unable to confirm this.

[76] CROSS, 228.

Less unpleasant was a verse satire in the May issue of the *Gentleman's Magazine*:

> Ye ladies so fair,
> And beaus debonair,
> Do all in your power that can be,
> The author to shame,
> And publisher blame,
> That gave him six hundred for *Shandy*.

When the *Grand Magazine* of June appeared, it contained a dreadful engraved copy of the Reynolds painting and an elaborate critique in the form of a dialogue – 'An Account of the Rev. Mr. St**** and his Writing'. This author, says one of the speakers, 'has discovered a new method of talking bawdy *astronomically*; and has made *four stars* (which, perhaps, may stand for the four Satellites of *Jupiter*) convey ideas which have set all the maidens a madding, have tickled the whole bench of bishops, and put all his readers in good humour.' But, answers another, the book's being patronized by the bishops, 'has encouraged every scribbler to mimic the reverend writer's manner. . . . if this taste prevails, we need not wonder to see in some future novel, the words which are chalked out on church walls, boldly printed in *Italics*.'

A Genuine Letter from a Methodist Preacher in the Country to Laurence Sterne, M.A. Prebendary of York, a widely read pamphlet, may indeed have been written by a nonconformist preacher; but, when a pirated version of it appeared in the autumn under the title *A Letter from the Rev. George Whitfield, B.A. to the Rev. Laurence Sterne, M.A.*, it was promptly and correctly labelled 'spurious' by the *Gentleman's Magazine*.[77] If one scabby sheep spoils a flock, asks the preacher, what will a scabby shepherd do?

> Oh Sterne! thou art scabby, and such is the leprosy of thy mind that it is not to be cured like the leprosy of the body, by dipping nine times in the river Jordan. . . . *Tristram Shandy* is as it were an anti-gospel, and seems to have been penned by the hand of Antichrist himself.[78]

[77] Issue for October, p. 491. The text under the two titles is identical, but the preliminary matter of the first is omitted from the second, of which there is another edition dated 1761. Both were printed by the Garland Press in the series 'The Life and Times of Seven Major British Writers', *Sterneiana*, V, New York, 1976.

[78] First edition, p. 2. Extracted in HOWES, 100–1.

It may have been to this book Sterne was alluding when he wrote to Stephen Croft, 'There is a shilling pamphlet wrote against Tristram.—I wish they would write a hundred such' (107). He would soon change his mind.

Criticism which had the grace, at least, of sincerity was followed by a flood of imitations, jest-books and less easily catagorized ephemera. *Explanatory Remarks upon the Life and Opinions of Tristram Shandy . . . by Jeremiah Kunastrokius, M.D.* offered annotations upon certain details in what the author conceived to be a Shandean manner.[79] *The Clockmaker's Outcry against the Author of the Life and Opinions of Tristram Shandy*, purporting to be an attack upon Sterne's 'indecencies', opened with a shocking pseudo-dedication to 'the Most Humble of Christian Prelates' which satirized Bishop Warburton. In an explanation of the title, which alludes, of course, to the clock that popped into Mrs Shandy's head while her husband was doing his marital duty, the author says, 'No modest lady now dares to mention a word about *winding-up a clock*, without exposing herself to the sly leers and jokes of the family, to her frequent confusion. Nay; the common expression of street-walkers is, "Sir, will you have your clock wound-up?" '[80] The spawn of *Tristram Shandy* was soon producing another generation. In July appeared *The Clockmaker's Political Humbug*.[81] According to the *British Magazine*, *Yorick's Meditations upon Various Interesting and Important Subjects* was the 'best imitation of the Shandean Humour that has yet appeared'. It was excerpted in the *Critical Review* for July and the *Nottingham Courant* of 20 September, and pirated in Dublin. It too had offspring – *A Supplement to the Life and Opinions of Tristram Shandy, by the Author of Yorick's Meditations*.[82]

Certain pamphlets and sheets, capitalizing on the names Tristram or Yorick, were really nothing more than the common and perennial jest-book – *Yorick's Jests; The Cream of the Jest . . . Dedicated to Poor Yorick*; *Tristram Shandy's Bon Mots*; *Tristram Shandy's Jests . . . Taken from Actual Conversation*;

[79] Said by OATES to be the earliest pamphlet on *Tristram Shandy*. Announced in the *Public Advertiser* of 23 April and the *Gentleman's Magazine* for May. Some copies were sold by Dodsley. Reviewed in the *Critical Review* of April. Extracted in HOWES, 62, and printed in the Garland Press series, *Sterneiana*, III, New York, 1976.

[80] Reviewed unfavourably in the *Critical Review* for May, p. 413. Advertisements appeared as far away as York: *York Courant*, 10 June. Reissued in the Garland Press series, *Sterneiana*, III, New York, 1976.

[81] Advertised in the *York Courant* for 8 July.

[82] OATES; *NCBEL*. Both are printed in the Garland Press series, *Sterneiana*, IV, New York, 1975.

and *Tristram Shandy at Ranelagh*. About this last a writer for the *London Magazine* said, 'If Tristram Shandy has done any mischief, 'tis in raising such a swarm of filthy pamphleteers, to din the ears and poison the eyes of the public.'[83]

Some things were harmless enough. 'A Receipt for a Soup for Tristram Shandy', a poem in the *Gentleman's Magazine* for June, seemed innocent; few realized it was cribbed from a poem by John Gay.[84] There was also *Tristram Shandy: A New Game at Cards*, which gave rules for a game played with 'a pack from which all the cards below the sevens had been thrown out except the four of Clubs and the deuce of Hearts.'[85] And there appeared a slip ballad called *Tristram Shandy*, which began: 'Early on a summer morning, it was down by Portsmouth Ferry O!'[86] Others were downright bawdy. *The Life and Opinions of Miss Sukey Shandy of Bow-Street* was a pale reflection of *Fanny Hill*. The *London Magazine* called it 'a wretchedly-dull catch penny performance'.[87] *The Life and Opinions of Jeremiah Kunastrokius*, a mock biography, and *A Shandean Essay on Human Passions, by Caleb McWhim*, were not much better.[88]

There was a pamphlet mocking George Lyttelton's *Dialogues of the Dead* called *Dialogues of the Living: Particulars between the following celebrated Personages, 1. Parson Tristram and the Revd. Mr. Sterne, on the Danger, Sin, and Folly of being Righteous Over-much*.[89] Finally, a so-called imitation entitled *Tristram Shandy in a Reverie* was noticed by the *Critical Review* as 'the most stupid, unmeaning, silly attempt to humour, that ever insulted the public curiosity after every thing that bears the name of Shandy'.[90] 'God forgive me', wrote Sterne that summer, 'for the Volumes of Ribaldry I've been the cause of' (118).

[83] *London Magazine*, quoted in OATES. Advertised in the *Public Advertiser*, 20 June, and the *London Chronicle*, 19–21 June. On *Bon Mots*, reissued by Garland Press, *Sterneiana*, III, New York, 1976, see OATES and CURTIS, 111. Others advertised in the *York Courant*, 12 June 1760, 17 June 1760, and *Public Advertiser*, 12 May 1760.

[84] George L. Barnett, *N&Q*, CLXXXV (1943), 346–7.

[85] Published in the *Grand Magazine* for May and later as a pamphlet (so advertised in the same periodical for June and in the *York Courant* for 15 July).

[86] *NCBEL*.

[87] OATES. Advertised in the *London Chronicle* for 19–21 June. Printed in the Garland Press series, *Sterneiana*, II, New York, 1975.

[88] *NCBEL*.

[89] OATES.

[90] OATES, who quotes from the *Critical Review* of December 1760, p. 493. Published 30 May; advertised *Public Advertiser*, 2 June, and *York Courant*, 1 July.

In the meanwhile Sterne, in the quiet eye of this storm, was preparing for the press the *Sermons of Mr. Yorick*, I–II – making sure that the engraving of the Reynolds portrait was ready, writing a preface, doing some editing. Whether by design or chance, on 18 May, the Sunday before they were to be released, Sterne preached before the lawyers, judges and 'a numerous and polite audience' at the chapel of Serjeants' Inn, which stood at the corner of Fleet Street and Chancery Lane. At this venerable institution lawyers took advanced degrees to qualify themselves as judges. Serjeants' Inn has since been disbanded, in 1910, and its buildings pulled down.[91] An invitation to preach before such a distinguished audience would have been considered an honour in any circumstances, but especially gratifying at this time. Did Sterne, one wonders, write the playful news release which was printed in the *Public Ledger* of Tuesday, 20 May?

> On Sunday morning last the rev. Mr. Laurence Sterne, editor of Mr. Yorick's sermons, preached at Serjeants-Inn Chapel, Chancery-Lane, to a numerous and polite audience.

One cannot but wonder whether there was any connection between the invitation to Serjeants' Inn and Sterne's friendship with the lawyer, Samuel Salt, remembered today as Charles Lamb's 'Lovel'. John Thomas Smith in his memoirs recalled meeting Salt as an older man, who told him that 'he was one of the few who buried Sterne'.[92] Upon this slim evidence one might guess that Salt was Sterne's legal counsel in London. Samuel Salt, some ten years younger than Sterne, was serving in 1760 as Under-Treasurer of the Inner Temple. He later had a distinguished career as Bencher and Treasurer, and he was parliamentary member for Liskeard and later Aldeburgh. He was depicted by Charles Lamb as the absentminded 'Lovel' in *Essays of Elia* – a thin disguise for the master to Lamb's father, a scrivener.

[91] Sterne wrote to Stephen Croft: 'I preach before the Judges on Sunday—my sermons come out on Thursday after—' (110). A plaque may be seen on the corner commemorating the site as that of 'Old Serjeants' Inn 1415–1910'. A search of the few remaining records revealed nothing about the sermon: *Records and Documents Concerning Serjeants' Inn*, collected by H. C. King, 1922, and housed at the Lincoln's Inn Library.

[92] John Thomas Smith, *A Book for a Rainy Day*, ed. Wilfred Whitten, 1905, p. 100. On Salt, see *DNB*; NAMIER AND BROOKE; obituary in *Gentleman's Magazine*, July 1792, 678; John Hutchinson, *Notable Middle Templars*, 1902; F. V. Morley, *Lamb before 'Elia'*, 1932, *passim*; *A Calendar of the Inner Temple Records*, ed. R. A. Roberts, 1936, V, *passim*; and Charles Lamb, *Essays of Elia*, in *Works*, ed. Alfred Ainger, 12 vols, 1899–1900, I.

Salt's sister Anne Fenton, the widow of a certain Thomas Fenton who had died in 1744, may have been 'My Witty Widow Mrs. F' to whom Sterne addressed a letter the following August.[93]

On Monday, the day after Sterne preached at Serjeants' Inn, he met with Dodsley to cement their agreements. The documents they signed have vanished, but we have an imperfect set of notes by someone who saw them.[94] A second contract was drawn up for the sale of the copyright in *Tristram Shandy*, III–IV, with no change in the price they had already agreed upon – £380. Did Samuel Salt insist upon a more binding contract? And there was some sort of receipt for money Sterne received for both sermons and novel, though the note about this does not specify the price of the sermons. Sterne himself later told his banker he had sold the copyright in the first two volumes of sermons for 400 guineas (190) – an astonishing price.

Moreover, Sterne had already taken in a great deal of money in subscriptions. The list of subscribers which he was preparing to turn over to the printer was one of the most impressive of the mid-eighteenth century, not necessarily for its length, though it was quite long, containing 661 names (and a postscript apologizing for incompleteness), but for the quality of the subscribers. There were the names of five bishops, including Warburton, and any number of nobles – Lord Chesterfield, Lord Rockingham, Lord Temple, Lord Edgcumbe, Lord Lyttelton, Lord Rochford. There were prominent politicians: Charles Townshend, John Wilkes and Sir George Saville. One finds the names of Elizabeth Montagu, Garrick, Hogarth, Reynolds, and the Poet Laureate William Whitehead. It is touching to read the name of Lynford Caryl, Sterne's old tutor from Jesus College, and that of Jeremiah Rawson, the husband of Sterne's cousin, Frances, one of his playmates from his childhood days in Halifax; and amusing to see the name of the forger-to-be of Sterne letters, William Combe. There are any number of old Yorkshire friends and allies – John Fountayne, Dean of York; Richard Osbaldeston, formerly Dean, now Bishop of Carlisle; Lord Fauconberg; Nathaniel Cholmley; Stephen Croft; John Hall(-Stevenson); William Phillips Lee, who financed the first publication of *Tristram Shandy*; and such old drinking companions as

[93] Genealogy of the Salt family in *N&Q*, 7th series, VI (1888), 85.

[94] 'Literary Remuneration', *Willis's Current Notes*, November 1854, pp. 90–2.

Nathaniel Garland and Marmaduke Fothergill. It is hard to imagine a higher compliment than this list of subscribers.

The two volumes appeared on Thursday, 22 May,[95] under the title, *The Sermons of Mr. Yorick.* A second title-page acknowledged them to be 'Sermons by Laurence Sterne, A.M. Prebendary of York, and Vicar of Sutton-on-the-Forest, and Stillington near York' (he had forgotten to tell the printer that now he also had the title, Curate of Coxwold). In a brief preface Sterne apologized for using the name of Yorick: the sermon, he said, 'which gave rise to the publication of these' was Yorick's sermon, and Yorick was a name better known than Sterne. He had added the second title-page, to 'ease the minds of those who see a jest, and the danger which lurks under it, where no jest was meant'.

Sterne made excuses for borrowing from other sermonists. Although he had tried to give due credit when he was aware of the borrowing, he suspected he had missed some – 'but 'tis only a suspicion, for I do not remember it is so'. This apology served for a century. Not until Percy Fitzgerald's *Life* of 1864 did anyone raise a serious question about Sterne's borrowings in the sermons. Actually, about 11 per cent of the sentences are plagiarized.[96] In this regard Sterne's sermons are not much different from those of most Anglican divines, who in fact were encouraged to borrow. But plagiarism in a homespun homily delivered to a rural congregation was one thing, in a published sermon another. Sterne excused himself in saying that not one of his sermons was composed 'with any thoughts of being printed'. For all that, he was not entirely scrupulous in publishing them – though his was a venial sin.

If Sterne's readers in 1760 were aware of his borrowings, they cared little. They were far more interested in the unusual tone and style. These were

[95] *Public Advertiser*, 22 May; *London Chronicle*, 20–2 May. Advertisements had begun in the *Public Advertiser* for 2 May and *London Chronicle*, 6–8 May. Announced also in the *Gentleman's Magazine* for May, p. 251.

[96] This figure may have to be revised when the Florida *Works of Laurence Sterne* volume of sermons appears. The figure given here is calculated from the number of words in passages which Lansing Van der Heyden Hammond thought were plagiarized – in *Laurence Sterne's 'Sermons of Mr. Yorick'*, New Haven, Conn., 1948. Hammond's total number of words has been discounted by a third to allow for his double entries and for the many 'borrowings' he lists which are so different in wording from the 'sources' that one hesitates to accept his judgement. The numerous weaknesses of Hammond's study are explored by James Downey in 'The Sermons of Mr. Yorick: A Reassessment of Hammond', *English Studies in Canada*, IV, 1978, pp. 193–211.

the shortest sermons most of them had ever seen or heard.[97] They were without the usual homiletic devices of headings and subdivisions.[98] Instead of the typical perorations and recapitulations, they found the most abrupt endings they had ever seen. The style little resembled the cool, reasoning prose of the Latitudinarians or the passionate calls to repentance of the Methodists. Sterne's devices were taken from secular literature and drama: arresting, often paradoxical opening statements, digressions, character sketches, dialogues, tableaux – devices which lend themselves well to a preacher who regards the pulpit as a stage. Thomas Gray saw at once how Sterne's sermons verged upon drama: 'Have you read his Sermons?' he asked Thomas Wharton; 'they are in the style I think most proper for the Pulpit, & show a very strong imagination & sensible heart: but you see him often tottering on the verge of laughter, & ready to throw his perriwig in the face of his audience.'[99] Indeed, Sterne referred to characters in his sermons as the '*dramatis personæ*' (I, 295), and he had Walter Shandy speak of the sermon in *Tristram Shandy* as 'dramatic' (165). In that advertisement in the *York Courant* which he had arranged shortly before coming to London, he had proposed to publish 'THE DRAMATIC SERMONS of MR. YORICK'. Years later, Caleb Whitefoord recalled this discarded title and said that only with the greatest difficulty was Sterne persuaded to drop this 'allusion to the church and the playhouse'.[100] In Corporal Trim, Sterne painted an ideal preacher of dramatic sermons, not only in his posture, gestures and intonations, but in his feelings:

> I should have read it ten times better, Sir, answered *Trim*, but that my heart was so full.—That was the very reason, *Trim*, replied my father, which made thee read the sermon as well as thou hast done. (164–5)

Sermons, said Sterne in the preface, should come 'more from the heart than the head' – the very point which he later had Yorick make in the scene of the visitation dinner in *Tristram Shandy* (376–7). The heart of the preacher

[97] William Seward was told by a Bath bookseller's boy that Bishop John Hinchcliffe of Peterborough once sent a servant to Leake's shop on the Parade, to get Smallridge's Sermons. The man asked instead for '*small religious* Sermons and the Bookseller after examining his Catalogue for the *smallest* sent him Sterne's': *Thraliana*, Vol. I, fol. 57.

[98] In this discussion of the sermons, I draw upon James Downey's essay on Sterne in the *Eighteenth-Century Pulpit*, Oxford, 1969.

[99] *Correspondence*, II, 681.

[100] Reported by Isaac D'Israeli, *Miscellanies of Literature*, 1884, p. 31.

must touch the heart of the reader or listener, and mediating this meeting are the language and rhetoric of the passions.

> I know not whether the remark is to our honour or otherwise, that the lessons of wisdom have never such a power over us, as when they are wrought into the heart, through the ground-work of a story which engages the passions: Is it that we are like iron, and must first be heated before we can be wrought upon? or, Is the heart so in love with deceit, that where a true report will not reach it, we must cheat it with a fable, in order to come at truth? (I, 319)

Indeed, Sterne's major theological message is the divinity of love. True, he was not a formal, academic theologian. He accepted without question the teachings of the church, and he presumed the tenets of the Latitudinarianism typical of Anglican leaders during the first half of the eighteenth century, especially in the doctrine of the perfect correspondence between 'natural' (i.e. rational) religion and revealed religion,[101] but he had little or no interest in justifying these points philosophically. Not until the sermon on 'Humility' in Volume IV, 1766, did Sterne pose a question in Christology, and the Holy Ghost he mentioned but rarely. What interested him was man – his psychology, his morality, his happiness, his capacity for self-judgement, wisdom and love. One of his goals was to teach us to respect ourselves, and he wrote a sermon on the 'Vindication of Human Nature'. Another was to show that pleasure is not sinful. What he said years later about *A Sentimental Journey* might have been said about the sermons he presented to the world in 1760: 'my design in it was to teach us to love the world and our fellow creatures better than we do—so it runs most upon those gentler passions and affections, which aid so much to it' (401). Of these goals, love of our fellow creatures was the principal. Sterne wanted to show us how to attain for ourselves the 'settled principle of humanity and goodness' (I, 45) which motivated the Good Samaritan.

> 'Tis observable in many places of Scripture, that our blessed Saviour, in describing the day of judgment, does it in such a manner, as if the great inquiry then, was to relate principally to this one virtue of compassion. . . . to intimate to us, that a charitable and benevolent

[101] Arthur H. Cash. 'The Sermon in *Tristram Shandy*', *ELH*, XXXI (1964), 395–417.

> disposition is so principal and ruling a part of a man's character, as to be a considerable test by itself of the whole frame and temper of his mind, with which all other virtues and vices respectively rise and fall, and will almost necessarily be connected. (I, 50–1)

On the whole, the public was delighted with Sterne's performance as a sermonist. 'I like them extremely,' said Georgina, Countess Cowper, 'and I think he must be a good man.'[102] Boswell thought Sterne 'the most taking composer of sermons that I ever read',[103] and described how the sermons were received in the fashionable world:

> On Sterne's discourses we grew mad;
> Sermons, where are they to be had?
> A strange enthusiastic rage
> for sacred text now seis'd the age.
> Around St. James' every table
> was partly gay and partly sable.
>
> . . .
>
> My Lady Betty, hob or nob!
> Great was the patience of old Job.
> Sir Smart breaks out, and one and all
> Adore St. Peter and St. Paul.[104]

'It is with pleasure', said the *Critical Review* of May, 'that we behold this son of Comus descending from the chair of mirth and frolick, to inspire sentiments of piety, and read lectures in morality, to that very audience whose hearts he has captivated with good-natured wit, and facetious humour.' But the reviewer for the *Royal Female Magazine*, while praising the sermons themselves, expressed a suspicion about the character of the author. Owen Ruffhead, writing for the *Monthly Review* of May, praised the sermons too, but then attacked Sterne for calling them Yorick's sermons – 'the greatest outrage against Sense and Decency, that has been offered since the first establishment of Christianity'. 'We have read of a Yorick', he went on, ' . . . in an obscene Romance. . . . Must obscenity then be the handmaid

[102] *Autobiography and Correspondence of Mary Granville, Mrs. Delany*, ed. Augusta Waddington Hall, Lady Llandover, 6 vols, 1861–2, III, 602.

[103] Pottle, 'Bozzy and Yorick'.

[104] Boswell's MS, cited above.

to Religion – and must the exordium to a sermon, be a smutty tale?'[105] Thus Ruffhead signalled a hostility toward Sterne among reviewers which would continue with little relief for the rest of Sterne's career. Nevertheless, the public bought the *Sermons of Mr. Yorick*. The Dodsleys published a second edition in July,[106] and by 1769 the number of editions had reached eleven.

Behind the public figure of 'Mr Yorick' or 'Tristram Shandy' was the private man, Lorry Sterne, as his friends often called him, about whose thoughts and activities we know less. He was in constant touch with his family in York, though his letters to them have not survived. Elizabeth had been released from the house of the 'lunatick doctor' in late March or early April. By May she was running short of funds, and Sterne wrote to Stephen Croft, asking that he advance her 10 guineas out of the money which would fall due to him in the summer.[107] One would like to know whether he called upon his sister Catherine, who was living in London as the wife of a publican. Sterne had been estranged from her for many years, and would continue so, though he was saddened by the separation.[108]

Much of the time he spent with his dearest friend, John Hall-Stevenson, who was living that winter in the house he maintained in John Street, Berkeley Square.[109] Boswell, who had a slight acquaintance with Hall (as he

[105] HOWES, 76–8.

[106] *Public Advertiser*, 21 July. For the later editions, see *NCBEL*, and CROSS, 600–1. Joyce Hemlow was mistaken in saying that Lady Sarah Pennington recommended Sterne's sermons in *An Unfortunate Mother's Advice to Her Absent Daughter*, 1761: see Hemlow's *History of Fanny Burney*, Oxford, 1958, pp. 18–19; cf. Pennington, p. 39. Two of Sterne's sermons were included in the four-volume anthology compiled by W. W. Rose, *The Practical Preacher*, published by Becket and Dehondt, 1762.

[107] LETTERS, 107. Sterne paid Croft back in October when he requested payment of what was due to him as Vicar of Stillington, but deducted the 10 guineas: LETTERS, 123.

[108] Sterne mentioned his sister in the 1761 'Memorandums' which he left his wife when he went abroad; in the event Elizabeth should be left a widow and their daughter should predecease her, 'Leave my Sister, something worthy of Y^r^self': LETTERS, 147. The sister is also mentioned in a passage in Sterne's 'Memoir' written in September 1758: 'Catherine, still living, but most unhappily estranged from me by my uncle's wickedness, and her own folly': LETTERS, 3. For Sterne's quarrels with his sister, see *EMY*, 145–6, 237 and *passim*. The evidence for dating the greater part of the 'Memoir' in 1758 will be published by Kenneth Monkman in his facsimile reproduction of the recently discovered MS, now in press.

[109] The location of Hall's house was indicated by Sterne in the 'Memorandums' of 1761. 'My friend Mr Halls St John Street'; (LETTERS, 146), which CURTIS, 148, correctly identified as John Street near Berkeley Square. Jean-Baptiste Tollot addressed a letter to Hall, 8 January 1764, to 'John Street, near Charles Street, Berkley

was usually called), spoke of the two men as though they were inseparable. Boswell could manage to show Sterne his poem, he said, only by holding him back from Hall in the street.

Sterne's persistence in this oldest and most cherished of his friendships inevitably damaged his public image. Hall moved in a circle of rakes, including John Wilkes and Sir Francis Dashwood, and was probably a member of the famous Hell-Fire Club, which met on Dashwood's estate at West Wycombe, Buckinghamshire.[110] Hall cared nothing for appearances. He was a man filled with rage. He hated his wife and her family, and adamantly refused to use her family name, Stevenson, which he had taken when he married. His estate on the North Riding coast, Skelton Castle, was still the gathering place for a circle of friends who shared his love of sports and literature, especially French literature. He was fluent in French and Latin. This gathering of pleasure-loving sportsmen with literary pretensions Sterne named the 'Demoniacs' (140), alluding to their delight in the language and trappings of gothic diabolism. In this they were probably influenced by the Hell-Fire Club, sometimes called 'the Rabelaisian Monks of Medmenham Abbey'.

There was in Hall's personality an odd streak of idealism. He was acquainted with many of the French *philosophes*, who are usually said to have laid the intellectual foundations of the French Revolution. He tried himself to become a revolutionary of sorts: in 1761 he offered his services as propagandist to John Wilkes. Wilkes liked Hall, and never quarrelled with him, as he did with many of his friends. But he declined to make him his aide-de-camp, probably because the more talented Charles Churchill appeared on the scene.[111] Even Hall's dreadful verse had a theory behind it which Hall said he derived from La Fontaine. No doubt he thought of its pornographic or near-pornographic images as a just defiance of prudes.

Square' (SEVEN LETTERS). According to Horace B[enjamin] Wheatley, *London Past and Present*, 3 vols, 1891, II, 310, John Street, now gone, once led from Hill Street to Charles Street, perhaps where the present Hays Mews makes this connection. A study of the rate books reveals no name of Hall or Hall-Stevenson; he must have rented the house. In later years he changed his London residence to No. 3 Berkeley Street, on the other, north-east side of the square (John Hope's letter to Hall of 1783, in SEVEN LETTERS).

[110] Donald McCormick, in *The Hell-Fire Club*, 1958, lists him among the 'probable' members. John Wilkes was one of the known regular members. See Hall-Stevenson's letters to Wilkes at the BL, Add. MSS 30,867, fols 181, 188, 199. On the Demoniacs, see *EMT*, 185–95.

[111] HARTLEY.

For all that, Hall was a weak man of limited talents. Nowhere did his weakness show more obviously than in his capitalizing upon the success of his friend Sterne to launch his own literary career. On 17 April, two weeks after the London edition of *Tristram Shandy*, the Dodsleys issued Hall's first book, a thin volume entitled *Two Lyrick Epistles: One to My Cousin Shandy on His Coming to Town; and the Other to the Grown Gentlewomen, the Misses of *****.[112] The first is addressed to 'Dear Shandy', and passes itself off as a welcome to Sterne upon his arrival at London. Sterne is compared at length to Jonah swallowed by the whale. The second is an indecent piece which purports to warn two young women of York about the dangers of seduction in the big town. Both verge upon the absurd. Although the author was not named on the title-page, Hall's authorship was an open secret. Thomas Gray wrote to Thomas Wharton, 'Your Friend Mr. Hall has printed two Lyrick Epistles. . . . They seem to me to be absolute madness.'[113] The book got a scathing review in the *Critical Review*, prompting Hall to write an angry answer, which he could not induce Dodsley to publish. It was issued that summer by Mary Cooper under the title *A Nosegay and a Simile for Reviewers, a Lyric Epistle* – an attack which the *Monthly Review* (July 1760) found an amusing performance, knowing it did not refer to them.

Though Sterne denied any involvement in Hall's *Two Lyrick Epistles*, he probably had seen the poems in manuscript. There was even a rumour in London that he had written them. He was informed of this by Bishop Warburton, in a gingerly worded letter of that summer:

> There are two Odes, as they are call'd, printed by Dodsley. Whoever was the author, he appears to be a monster of impiety and lewdness—yet such is the malignity of the scribblers, some have given them to your friend Hall; and others, which is still more impossible, to yourself. . . . But this might arise from a tale equally groundless and malignant, that you had shewn them to your acquaintances in *M.S.* before they were given to the public.[114]

Sterne replied, pleading innocence, but in so weak a manner as to suggest that he was not being candid.

> the first ode, which places me and the author in a ridiculous light, was sent to me in a cover without a name, which, after striking out some

[112] Announced in the *Public Advertiser*, 17 April, and the *London Chronicle*, 15–17 April.

[113] *Correspondence*, II, 671.

[114] LETTERS, 113.

> parts, as a whimsical performance, I showed to some acquaintance; and as Mr. Garrick had told me, some time before, he would write me an ode, for a day or two I supposed it came from him. I found afterwards it was sent me from Mr. Hall; for from a nineteen years' total interruption of all correspondence with him, I had forgot his hand, which at last when I recollected, I sent it back. (115)

The detail about not corresponding with Hall for nineteen years is untrue: we know they were exchanging letters in 1758,[115] and probably they wrote to each other often. From Warburton's standpoint, it was shocking that Sterne actually could have seen the poems and yet stood quietly by while they were published. From another, it may seem touching that Sterne was willing to put his public image in jeopardy so as not to interfere with his friend's attempt to start his own writing career. In any event, it was obvious to most people how much Sterne and Hall loved one another. They soon identified Hall with Sterne's character, Eugenius, the faithful friend of *Tristram Shandy* and eventually of *A Sentimental Journey*.[116]

Catherine Fourmantel arrived in London about the third week in April, and thereafter Sterne saw less of Hall and other friends. Catherine settled into rooms in Meard's Court, Soho.[117] We have three letters written to her there. In all three Sterne makes excuses for not seeing her when she expected him. As a result, other biographers have said Sterne was growing tired of Catherine. But this interpretation will hardly hold, since in each letter he names a specific day and hour when he will come to his 'dear Kitty'. The letters show a man pressed by invitations to appear in the fashionable world where Catherine cannot accompany him. He can be with her in the afternoon, he writes, but not in the evening as they had planned; so he is sending a ticket to the play in the hope she will be entertained. 'You are a most engaging Creature; and I never spend an Evening with you, but I leave a fresh part of my heart behind me—You will get me all, piece by piece, I find, before all is over' (107). In the next (if it is the next, for the

[115] Sterne to the Rev. John Blake, [? 5 October 1758]: Appendix I.

[116] Sterne's daughter, Lydia, in 1770, begging Hall to join with Wilkes in writing a life of Sterne, told him, ''twill prove that Eugenius was the friend of Yorick' (LETTERS, 453). In *EMT*, 53, I argued that it was unlikely Sterne had Hall in mind when he developed the character. Lydia's comment weakens my argument. I now think that Sterne intended the identification.

[117] One of Sterne's letters was addressed to her at 'Merds Court St Anne, Soho': LETTERS, 109.

dates of the letters are uncertain[118]), he writes to remind her that he cannot drink tea with her, as was their expectation; 'I will however contrive to give my dear friend a Call at four o'Clock—tho' by the by, I think it not quite prudent—but what has prudence, my dear Girl, to do with Love? In this I have no Gover[n]ment, at least not half so much as I ought' (109). In the third he apologizes for his inability to come to her during the week: 'I am as much a Prisoner as if I was in Jayl.—I beg dear Girl, You will believe I d[o] not spend an hour where I wish—for I wish to be with You always' (109). He will, however, see her on Friday at two o'clock. These letters reveal no lack of interest or lack of love, but rather a concern for appearances.

In a carefree mood Sterne might call prudence an 'understrapping Virtue' (76), but there was nothing carefree about his calls at Meard's Court. Sterne's uncle, Dr Jaques Sterne, Precentor of York and Archdeacon of Cleveland, may have openly kept a mistress, but that freedom for clergymen had passed with his generation. Sterne, as a parson, a prebendary, and a dignitary of the spiritual courts, was expected to keep up at least an appearance of respectability. Catherine, as a singer, had to live with a social status little higher than that of a prostitute.[119] Her mother, who had accompanied her to York and was living with her in London, if she behaved like most women in her position, would have encouraged her daughter to use her charms to their advantage. Women in the performing arts had rarely made their way into polite society, and then only when protected by powerful men, usually relatives. Catherine, whose birth and death were of so little consequence that no one has found a record of either, had no such advantage. Sterne may have been wishing for the death of his troublesome wife when he wrote to Catherine, 'God will open a Dore, when we shall sometime be much more together, & enjoy Our Desires without fear or Interruption' (104), but Catherine would have been wise enough to know that he was not thinking about marriage.

Still, there is no reason to conclude that Sterne and Catherine were not in love. They were very companionable. He shared with her the joys of his success: most of what we know about his being lionized is through his letters to her. One of his gestures toward her has seemed ridiculous or

[118] Although these letters, numbered 56, 58 and 59 in LETTERS, cannot be demonstrably assigned to the spring of 1760, Sterne's excitement about numerous pressing invitations suggests that period.

[119] See Mary Nash, *The Provoked Wife: The Life and Times of Susannah Cibber*, Boston, Mass., and Toronto, 1977, pp. 267–83 and *passim*.

shocking to some writers: while they were still in York, Sterne had sent her a copy of his published sermon, *The Case of Elijah and the Widow of Zerephath, Consider'd*, telling her, 'I see something of the same kind & gentle disposition in your heart, which I have painted in the Prophet's' (83). There is no reason why a man of Sterne's sophistication should not have looked for and responded to moral virtues in a mistress. Shaftesbury, Hutcheson and other of the 'sentimental' moralists had argued that it was just these virtues which explained why a man would go to all the trouble of developing and maintaining a liaison with a mistress. One could never explain such long-lasting relationships as the product of raw sexual desire, for that could be satisfied at little trouble or expense by a common prostitute. But a mistress offered more than sex: she offered generosity, sympathy, tenderness, loyalty – qualities, the philosophers argued, that could only be called moral virtues.[120] Sterne's relationship with Catherine seems to exemplify the point. He assures her of his fidelity, telling her she shall ever find him 'the same Man of Honour & Truth' (105). He, in turn, is touched by her loyalty: when she writes from York about another man who is courting her, he responds, 'It would have stabb'd my Soul, to have thought such a fellow could have the Liberty of coming near you—I therefore take this proof of y^r^ Love and good principles, most kindly—& have as much faith & dependence upon You in it, as if I was at y^r^ Elbow.—would to God, I was at this moment,—for I am sitting solitary & alone in my bed Chamber' (97). For Catherine Fourmantel, Sterne had 'the truest friendship . . . that ever Man bore towards a Woman—where ever I am, my heart is warm towards you & ever shall be, till it is cold for ever' (97).

We do not know when this affair came to an end, but probably it did not survive Sterne's absence in France from 1762 until 1764. Since the record of Catherine's singing career ceases during that same period, it is possible that she married and gave up her career, or that she died then.[121] Be that as it

[120] Shaftesbury's *Characteristics of Men, Manners, Opinions, Times*, ed. John M. Robertson, 1900, I, 310–11; Francis Hutcheson, *Inquiry into the Original of Our Ideas of Beauty and Virtue*, 1738, 250, 258; and Hume, *Enquiry Concerning the Principles of Morals*, in *Enquiries*, ed. L. A. Selby-Bigge, Oxford, 1902, p. 300.

[121] The last record of Catherine is a benefit concert for 'Miss Formantel' at the Great Room, Dean Street (Mrs Theresa Cornelys's concerts), on 4 February 1763: [John Genest], *London Stage*, Part IV, ed. George Winchester Stone, Jr, 1962, p. 977. The difficulty of tracing the life of Catherine Fourmantel is compounded by the variant spellings of her name. At Colchester there were a great many Dutch Huguenots with the names of Fromantel, Fromanteel, Fromanteil, Fromantle,

may, Sterne was to fall in love with other women in the period following his sojourn in the south of France, but never again with the joy he felt in his love for Catherine Fourmantel.

Sterne could not keep the affair a secret. Inevitably friends began to notice his absences, and the story got around.[122] Garrick knew everything that was going on in the theatrical world, and he had an acquaintance with Catherine. Moreover, when Catherine failed to get an engagement at Ranelagh upon her return to London, Sterne asked Garrick's help. She had been a regular singer at Ranelagh in 1758 and 1759,[123] but could not arrange another engagement by correspondence from York. When she wrote to Sterne about it, he replied, 'never, my dear Girl, be dejected. . . . Thou

---

Formantel, Formanteel, Furmantel, Furmantil, etc.: *Register of Baptisms in the Dutch Church at Colchester from 1645 to 1728* (Publications of the Huguenot Society of London, Vol. 12), 1905. In fact there is no certainty that Catherine herself spelled her name in the manner traditional among Sterneians – *Fourmantel*. Genest called her 'Formantel'. John Baker in his *Diary*, 1931, 109, called her 'Miss Fromantel'. The two published collections of songs sung by her also give her name as 'Fromantel'. Sterne spelled her name 'Formantel' (97) and 'Formantelle' (109). The tradition of spelling it 'Fourmantel' seems to have been launched by the shadowy Mrs Henry Watson, who once possessed Sterne's letters and left a highly fanciful account of Catherine now preserved with the letters at the Morgan Library. Much of it was repeated by Isaac D'Israeli in *Miscellanies of Literature*, edition of 1884, pp. 29–33. But Mrs Watson's notion that Catherine came from a French Huguenot family named Berenger de Fourmantel cannot be disproved. In the publications of the Huguenot Society of London there exists one but only one record of a person of similar name: in the French chapel in Leicester Fields, a Jean Beranger de Formentel appeared as a witness to the marriage of Emanuel de Seret and Emée Reid on 7 February 1733: *Registre des Eglises de Glasshouse Street et de Leicester Fields*, XXIX, 148 (cited by CURTIS, 465).

[122] In Sterne's letter to Mrs Fenton of 3 August he responds in sequence to two things she had said in such a way as to suggest that she has asked him about Catherine Fourmantel and the song written for her and then teased him about all the time he spent with her and not his other friends. Sterne, after saying that the song was written at Garrick's (see below), writes: 'I deny it I was not lost two days before I left town—I was lost all the time I was there, and never found till I got to this Shandy-castle of mine.—Next winter I intend to sojourn amongst you with more decorum, and will neither be lost nor found any where' (120). I take this as evidence that Sterne's absences were noted and were connected to Catherine Fourmantel.

[123] She is known to have sung at Ranelagh in the spring of 1758: *Diary of John Baker*, ed. P. C. Yorke, 1931, p. 109, cited by CURTIS, 465. In July of that year appeared *Ten Favourite Songs Sung by Miss Fromantel at Ranelagh, Music by Mr Oswald*, cited in the coverage of Catherine Fourmantel in *A Biographical Dictionary of Actors, Actresses, Musicians, Dancers . . . 1660–1800*, ed. Philips H. Highfill, Jr, Kalman A. Burnim and Edward A. Langaus, Carbondale and Edwardsville, Ill. 1973–, V, 1978, pp. 376–7.

mayst be assured nothing in this world shall be a wanting—that I can do with Discretion' (105). By that summer she had the engagement. We know this through a thin volume published on 30 August, *A Collection of New Songs Sung by Mr. Beard, Miss Stevenson, and Miss Fromantel at Ranelagh.* What sold this songbook, which went into at least two editions,[124] was the name of John Beard, the most famous singer in England. One song bears the title 'Dialogue, Sung by Mr Beard & Miss Fromentel'. The 'Swain' opens a pastoral conversation about British liberty:

How imperfect the Joys of the Soul
How insipid Life's Journey must be,
How unsocial the Seasons must roll,
To the Wretches who dare not be free.

The 'Nymph' replies:

Ev'ry Youth loyal Courage can fire,
To the Fair kind and constant must prove:
British Maids shall their Merit admire,
And reward them with Beauty and Love.

Then there is a 'Duetto':

Blooming Plenty shall smile on our Fields,
Sweet Contentment shall prompt us to sing;
And our own be what Industry yields,
Long as George, gracious George, is our King.

This light treatment of the themes of love and patriotism is comic as verse, but its full ironic tone is to be found only in performance. In the final refrain, complimenting 'George, gracious George', one hears woven into the melody distinct strains from 'Rule Brittania', a song that had become so popular during the Seven Years War that theatre audiences demanded to sing it night after night, sometimes several times in one evening.[125] The composer named on the title-page is Joseph Baildon, a well-known writer of songs performed in the pleasure gardens and concert halls.[126] It is remotely

[124] Advertised in the *Public Advertiser*, 30 August 1760. The copy in the Rowe Music Library at King's College Library, Cambridge, is a later edition, 1765.

[125] R. Grundy Heape, *Georgian York*, 1937, p. 14.

[126] Joseph Baildon (?1727–74) was a singer and lay-vicar of Westminster Abbey. In 1762 he became organist of St Luke's, Old

possible that Laurence Sterne, an amateur musician, collaborated with Baildon. It is virtually certain he composed the words. 'Who told you', he asked Mrs Fenton, 'Garrick wrote the medley for Baird?—'Twas wrote in his house, however, and before I left town' (120). So it seems Sterne not only talked to Garrick about getting Catherine an engagement, but wrote a song for her that Garrick could use for that purpose.[127]

Garrick, who once had an affair with an actress he loved, Peg Woffington, may have felt some sympathy for Sterne and Catherine, but in the end decided not to put his own reputation in jeopardy for their sakes. Bold enough to recommend a naughty book by a parson, he was not bold enough to continue his support when the parson himself began to get a reputation for naughtiness. He decided to speak to Bishop Warburton, and for that purpose employed Richard Berenger. In mid-June Warburton wrote to him from Prior Park:

> I must not forget to thank you for the hints I received from you by Mr. Berenger, concerning our heteroclite Parson. I heard enough of his conduct in town since I left it, to make me think he would soon lose the fruits of all the advantage he had gained by a successful effort, and would disable me from appearing as his friend or well-wisher.[128]

Sterne, who continued to treat Garrick as a friend, may never have discovered what lay behind the severe letters that Warburton would write that summer and may not have been aware that he had acquired a reputation for misbehaviour.

He was fully aware, however, that the bishops – most of them – were withholding their judgement of him until they saw the next two volumes of *Tristram Shandy*. Archbishop Gilbert himself had warned him and extracted from him a promise to reform.[129]

Street, and All Saints, Fulham. He won the Catch Club first prize for a catch in 1763 and for a glee in 1766 (*Grove's Dictionary of Music and Musicians*, 1954).

[127] Garrick would not have been stopped by his well-known quarrel with Beard, which did not begin until a year later when Beard took over the management of the Covent Garden Theatre.

[128] CURTIS, 114. Warburton's adjective for Sterne, 'heteroclite', he borrowed from Sterne's description of Yorick: TRISTRAM SHANDY, 27.

[129] Dr Thomas Newton wrote to the Rev. John Dealtary on 26 February 1761, soon after Volumes III–IV appeared: 'Our Archp is very angry with him for having broke his promise': DEALTARY LETTERS.

Undaunted, he purchased a chaise, the first he had ever owned, and toward the end of May set out for York in what John Croft called 'a superior style'.

2

Writer & Parson 1760–1761

Sterne returned to York in late May 1760. John Courtney, a young lawyer of Beverley, was in York on 31 May when he wrote in his diary, 'Saw Mr. Sterne Author of Tristram Shandy this Even: as I was reading his Sermons in Booksellers Shop.'[1] No doubt Sterne had stopped at the Sign of the Bible in Stonegate, whence had been issued the first edition of *Tristram Shandy*, I–II, to visit the new owner, John Hinxman. By then he would have rejoined his family in the house he leased for them in the Minster Yard. Elizabeth was much recovered from her mental breakdown, and Lydia was flourishing once more. Elizabeth and Sterne must have come to an agreement about how they would pattern their lives in the future: they would live as a family in Coxwold during the warm months, when Sterne would superintend the parish and do his writing. In the autumn he would go to London to publish what he had written, while Elizabeth and Lydia would return to York where they could be among friends and enjoy the theatre and other amenities of a 'town life'.[2]

By the first of June he had made the sixteen-mile trip to Coxwold.[3] Soon thereafter he underwent, for the third time, the ancient ritual of initiation into parochial office. The churchwardens gathered at the church door. One of them laid Sterne's hand upon the old iron key standing in the lock. As

[1] Humberside Record Office, Beverley: DDX/60.

[2] Courtney wrote in his diary under 14 February 1761, 'This night was at the Play [in York] & saw for the first time the New Entertainment of Harlequin Salamander, the Statue Scene, very well done by Fitzmaurice. I had a great deal of Conversation wth Mrs. Sterne, Tristram Shandys Wife.'

[3] Datable from Richard Chapman's letter to Lord Fauconberg of 1 June. Unless otherwise mentioned, Chapman's letters are found among the WOMBWELL PAPERS.

Sterne stood thus, another read off the archbishop's collation. Sterne then unlocked the door, walked into the tower, and tolled the bell. Thus he became Curate of Coxwold.

But it was no time for celebration, for the village was in mourning for Lady Catherine Fauconberg, the wife of Sterne's patron, who had died in London a day or two after Sterne left.[4] Lady Catherine had been a Catholic, and no doubt there had been a quiet funeral mass in London. There would be no funeral in Coxwold, though Sterne's first sad duty would be to bury the lady. Her body arrived on 12 June and was interred in the church forthwith. Richard Chapman, Lord Fauconberg's chief steward, wrote to his master, 'Every thing was ready and done according to your Lordship's order, and her Ladyship's Body was put into the Vault Just as 12 oClock Struck.'[5] Sterne must have said one or two of the prayers appointed in his own *Book of Common Prayer*.

The village he saw as he stepped out of the church was small. About half of the 158 families of Coxwold parish lived in outlying hamlets. The churchyard sloped toward a stream that flowed down from Old Byland; on the opposite side rose a lovely long hill belonging to Newburgh Priory, Lord Fauconberg's seat, upon which were seen cultivated strips of open-field farms, enclosed pastures and woodlands. To the north the Hambleton Hills rose abruptly, the beginning of high moors that rolled toward the North Sea thirty miles away. The air was dry and healthful. Across the fields one caught sight of Byland Abbey, a beautiful gothic ruin. The mile-and-a-half walk over Brink Hill to the abbey became Sterne's favourite. The village was dominated by St Michael's, a graceful fifteenth-century church with an unusual octagonal tower and small flying buttresses. Close by stood a Jacobean house in which was conducted a grammar school for the sons of squires and prosperous yeomen – five boarders in 1760 – and a village school where the children of the poor learned their letters. The master, the Rev. Mr Robert Midgley, who lived in the house, served both schools with the help of an usher. To the west of the church stood Colville Hall, a handsome seventeenth-century farm, now occupied by tenant farmers. All of these buildings may still be seen, as well as a hospital for ten old men established by Lord Fauconberg's father. Another for old women has vanished. Many of

[4] Died 29 May: Cokayne's *Peerage*, 1910, V, 266. Chapman, in his letter of 1 June, spoke of ordering mourning dress for the old men and women of the two Coxwold hospitals.

[5] Chapman to Fauconberg, 13 June 1760.

the small houses one sees today were there in Sterne's time, but virtually all were repaired and refaced in the nineteenth century. The village probably was as charming in 1760 as it is today.[6]

Sterne's new title was that of 'curate', later called 'perpetual curate' to distinguish the office from that of a hired assistant curate. In the eighteenth century the parson of a parish was called 'rector' if all of the tithes were paid directly to him, 'vicar' if the rights to the great tithes had been sold off and replaced with a stipend, and 'curate' if rights to both the great and small tithes had been sold and the income was entirely from a stipend. Things were seldom so neat. Coxwold had undergone many changes and had been combined with several other parishes. In the course of this complex history, its land holdings had been sold and its tithes bargained away, except for those of the township of Raskelf which had been brought into Coxwold parish. The tithes of Raskelf provided the largest part of Sterne's income. The impropriator of the other tithes and the patron of the living was Trinity College, Cambridge; but, in the way so typical of that age, tithes and patronage were leased repeatedly to the Belasyse family, of which Lord Fauconberg was now head. His lordship's obligation to the curate was a stipend of £30. There were also fees for weddings, funerals, and the like, though they did not amount to much. The total value of the living was about £140 per annum.[7]

This was not the first gift Sterne had received from Lord Fauconberg. In 1750 Fauconberg had presented him to the commissaryship of the Peculiar Court of Alne and Tollerton, a judgeship in the spiritual courts which brought him £5 or £6 a year. Sterne might well have concluded that he

[6] William Page (ed.), *Victoria History of the County of York: North Riding*, 2 vols, 1923, II, 8–24; Thomas Gill, *Vallis Eboracensis*, 1852, pp. 185–99.

[7] Because the value of livings depended so largely upon the income from farmland, they were difficult to estimate. Archbishop Drummond in 1762 valued Coxwold living at £120 (CURTIS, 165), but Sterne's neighbour, the Rev. Mr Robert Midgley, who was in a better position to know, thought it worth £140: Midgley to James Erskine of Alva, 29 September 1760, National Library of Scotland, MS 5081, fol. 73. The *York Courant* announcement of the preferment on 25 March 1760 also set the value at £140. In one letter Sterne said it was worth £160 (102), in another £100 (143); in both cases he was seeking rhetorical effects. Details on the curacy from George Lawton, *Collectio Rerum Ecclesiasticarum de Deoecesi Eboracensi*, 2 vols paginated as one, 1840, pp. 428–31; *Archbishop Drummond's Visitation Returns*, 1764, MS at Borthwick Institute; MS terrier dated 13 October 1760 and signed by Sterne and two churchwardens, also at the Borthwick Institute; MS terrier presented at the Drummond primary visitation at Thirsk, 27 June 1764, signed by Sterne's curate, James Kilner, and two churchwardens, bound with parish registers.

would be next in line for Coxwold, but when the living fell vacant in 1753 Fauconberg passed him over to prefer Sterne's former assistant at Sutton, Richard Wilkinson. It must have rankled, waiting another seven years in the damp air of Sutton.

For the first two years Sterne personally supervised the parish, though he had a curate – R. H. Atkinson, as he signed himself in the parish registers, an unlicensed assistant who had been called in while Mr Wilkinson was still alive. Sterne distributed the annual dole, completed a terrier, or inventory, for the parish, and no doubt performed numerous other, unrecorded tasks. But he seems to have been remiss in keeping up the parish registers, for no baptisms or burials were recorded during the periods when he was in residence. He was a little better about recording the marriages he performed, the first on 10 June 1760.[8] In 1761 he directed extensive repairs of the church fabric. Unhappy with the architect's plan for pews which would leave half the congregation with their backs to the pulpit and set off, as Sterne said, an unchristian dispute for the better seats, he offered a plan of his own in which 'all face the Parson alike'.[9] Sterne's arrangement of pews and the unusual alter rail he designed may still be seen at the church, though the backs and sides of the pews were lowered in 1906 by cutting 18 inches off the bottom. Likewise the pulpit from which Sterne preached was reduced from three decks to two.

And Sterne officiated at church services and preached: 'Eloquent in the pulpit & not at all mute out of it,' said Mr Midgley, the schoolmaster.[10] 'I gave Your Lordship's Service to M[r] Sterne,' wrote Richard Chapman to his master on 20 July, 'whose Doctrine, (tho Chiefly Extempory) takes so well amongs the Congregation that the Church can Scarce Contain the Number of People that appear every Sunday.' Sterne's reputation as an author meant little to the parishioners, most of whom could not even read. Nevertheless, to the labourers and farmers of Coxwold, Sterne was famous, not as an author, but as a preacher. They would have heard how 'he never preached

[8] Parish registers at Borthwick Institute. The MS with them entitled *Parish Charities, 1693–1766* reveals Sterne distributing the annual dole to the poor on 19 October 1760 and 18 October 1761.

[9] Chapman to Fauconberg, 25 September 1761, in CURTIS, 145. This letter was published originally in the Royal Historical MSS Commission report, *Various Collections*, II, 1903, p. 188. Curtis appears to have made use of the original, then among the WOMBWELL PAPERS, but the letter is no longer with the collection.

[10] Robert Midgley to James Erskine of Alva, Coxwold, 29 September 1760: National Library of Scotland, MS 5081, fol. 73.

at Sutton but half the congregation were in tears – the Minster was crowded whenever it was known that he was to preach.'[11] Sterne did not disappoint them. 'His parishioners are much taken with his preaching,' reported Midgley in December 1760,[12] and in 1761, when the church was torn up for repairs, Chapman, who had temporarily lost his pew, was forced to write to Lord Fauconberg to ask permission to sit in his lordship's pew because he could find no other seat in the crowded church.[13] But 1760 and 1761 would be the last years Sterne would preach regularly. In France in 1762 he was repeatedly struck down by illnesses which left him weak in body and almost voiceless, putting a virtual stop to his long preaching career.[14]

In June or July 1760, Sterne brought his wife and daughter to that charming house standing at the west end of the village which his friends would soon 'christen' Shandy Hall (380). Originally a fifteenth-century timber house of a type built by prosperous yeomen, it had probably been the house of the reeve to the abbots of Newburgh. It had undergone extensive changes in the seventeenth century: a floor had been inserted, dividing the open hall horizontally into a ground and upper storey, each partitioned into rooms and passageways. Chambers had been finished, gables cut in the roof, and a brick veneer laid over the timber walls. Sterne, with the help of Lord Fauconberg, would eventually make other changes – adding the boxlike extension to the west, refurbishing bedrooms, building a stable, coachhouse and garden summerhouse. The end product of these alterations was a charming but odd house, its formal west end contrasting with the east end, dominated by a huge medieval chimney, which served a

[11] GREENWOOD.

[12] Robert Midgley to James Erskine of Alva, Coxwold, 12 December 1760: National Library of Scotland, MS 5081, fols 92–3.

[13] Chapman to Fauconberg, 6 September 1761. Only two of Sterne's sermons can be shown to have been preached at Coxwold, both written in connection with the accession of George III. Sermon XXI, 'National Mercies Considered', SERMONS, I, 335–49, Sterne indicated in a footnote was read 'On the Inauguration of his present Majesty'. Since Sermon XL, 'Asa: – A Thanksgiving Sermon', SERMONS, II, 299–312, was preached at the time of the coronation (see below), one presumes that 'National Mercies' was preached at the time of the accession. George II died on Saturday, 25 October 1760; allowing for the time it took for the news to reach Coxwold, one concludes that Sterne preached the sermon on 2 November 1760. For reasons that are hard to understand, Sterne included this dull piece in his third volume of sermons, 1766, but passed over the charming 'Asa', which is preserved for us only because his daughter published it among the posthumous sermons, 1769.

[14] VOICES SONOROUS AND CRACKED.

kitchen fireplace large enough to sit in. 'A delicious retreat' Sterne called it (366). The house was not legally a parsonage and did not belong to the church, but it had long been the traditional residence of the curates of Coxwold, who rented it from Lord Fauconberg. Sterne paid £12 a year for his 'Philosophical Hut' (228), and here he wrote seven more volumes of *Tristram Shandy* and all of *A Sentimental Journey*.

Sterne's social life was limited, of course, as it would be in any village. He made a friendly gesture the first summer toward his neighbour Midgley, the schoolmaster: he read him a satire of church lawyers that he had just written – a piece which would appear in the twenty-ninth chapter of Volume IV – in which Kysarcius demonstrates to the clergy and lawyers at the visitation dinner that a mother is not of kin to her child. But Midgley found it, he said, 'far above my Comprehension, & so I was no further Inquisitive about it.' Poor Midgley was terrified of Sterne, 'whose superior Talents I readily Subscribe to', of his wife, 'almost as Ingenious as Himself', and even of Lydia, albeit she was only thirteen years old – a 'very quick Girl'. Once, in an unguarded moment, he called Sterne 'our Romantick Hero', but, frightened at what he had said, begged his correspondent not to repeat it: 'I woud *by no means* depretiate Him who is far my Superiror in Every thing. I shall always make it my End[eavou]r to be well wth him . . . as Neighbors Should, Especially Clergymen.' One may imagine Sterne's reaction to such a man, especially when he learned that Midgley had written a book called *The Compendious School-Master*. Sterne had more success with the usher, Thomas Newton, who read the third and fourth volumes of *Shandy* in manuscript and pronounced them better than the first two. Richard Chapman did not think Newton was 'cut out for this World', but he had attained priest's orders in 1758 and was destined to follow Midgley in 1761 as master of the school and Curate of Husthwaite and Carleton Chapel, and to follow Sterne as Curate of Coxwold in 1768.[15]

Sterne often saw Lord Fauconberg, who lived during the warm months at Newburgh Priory, a mile to the east. The house had originally been a twelfth-century Augustinian priory. At the dissolution, Henry VIII granted

[15] The two letters of Midgley to Erskine cited above; Midgley obituary in *York Courant*, 2 June 1761; *DNB* article on Midgley's uncle, Robert Midgley, MD; S. L. Ollard and P. C. Walker (eds), *Archbishop Herring's Visitation Returns, 1743*, 5 vols, 1927–31; Archbishop Drummond's *Visitation Returns, 1764*; *Chapter Acts*, 22 August 1761, at the Minster Library; Chapman to Fauconberg, 1 November 1761.

it to a lawyer in holy orders, Anthony Bellasis, a man notorious for his assistance in the destruction of the monasteries of Yorkshire. He was also one of the clergy who declared invalid Henry's marriage to Anne of Cleves. The Rev. Dr Bellasis did not take possession of the priory himself, but signed it over to his nephew and heir, William, who established the Belasyse family there. William pulled down most of the buildings and converted others to a Tudor style. Sterne's patron, who had inherited in 1718, tried hard to reshape these Tudor structures into something Georgian, but, not being a bold architect, he ended with a graceless set of buildings, as odd as Shandy Hall.[16]

Thomas Belasyse, fourth Viscount Fauconberg, fourth Baron Fauconberg, and first Earl Fauconberg by the second creation, had inherited Newburgh in a state of near-bankruptcy. His father had died in Brussels, where he had fled from his creditors. The son turned out to be a vigorous manager who brought the estate into order and eventually enlarged his fortunes by a prudent marriage. By the time Sterne came to Coxwold, Fauconberg had lands at Coxwold, Husthwaite, Oulston, Thornton, Old Byland, Hapwich, Lund, Yearsley, Alne, Tollerton, Easingwold and Sutton-on-the-Forest. Sterne once estimated his income at £6000 per annum.[17] He had the patronage of the churches at Coxwold, Alne, Brafferton, Wigginton and Birdforth Chapel.

Fauconberg had a keen sense of hierarchical order, and in more than one record we find him standing firmly behind his dependants when they were in need.[18] But his insistence upon his own rights in every tittle could be oppressive. In 1757 Sterne had been drawn into an unpleasant affair at Huby, a hamlet which lay within the parish of Sutton-on-the-Forest. A servant boy of Huby had been kicked to death by a mare belonging to his master, George Wilson. Lord Fauconberg, in accordance with an ancient law, had demanded the horse as a 'deodand'. By this law, an animal which

[16] John Cornforth, 'Newburgh Priory, Yorkshire', *Country Life*, CLV, 28 February, 7 March and 14 March 1974.

[17] Sterne reported this income in his 'Papist Report' of 1767: see below.

[18] Two letters of Fauconberg to the Earl of Loudoun, dated 3 May and 8 May 1756, at the Huntington Library (MSS 1099, 1129), reveal him using his influence to help a tenant, Mary Walker of Easingwold, in her attempt to obtain the release of her husband, who had been irregularly charged with a crime, so that he could be impressed into the navy as a man of bad character. At the Minster Library (BB 25) is a letter of Fauconberg's dated 15 December 1779 challenging the entire Dean and Chapter because they illegally had granted a marriage licence which should have been issued by his lordship's commisary of the Peculiar Court of Alne and Tollerton; the fee in question was £4.

had occasioned a human death would be sacrificed to God as an expiation, but in a form which local people often found less than satisfactory: the animal had to be given to the lord of the manor, who would see that its worth was distributed in alms or put to whatever charitable uses he saw fit. The owner of the horse refused, and Sterne tried to bury the whole matter by burying the boy. Lord Fauconberg insisted upon his rights. Ten days after the death, the body was exhumed, an inquest held, the death by kicking declared, and the deodand claimed.[19]

Curiously, in the Elizabethan era the Belasyse family had reverted to the Roman religion, though more often than not the heads of the family had conformed. One of them had married the daughter of no less a Protestant than Oliver Cromwell, and a crude stone crypt in the attic of the priory is thought to contain part of Cromwell's desecrated body. But Lord Fauconberg's father had openly declared his popery and kept two Roman Catholic priests in residence. Lord Fauconberg himself, for twenty years after he inherited, had followed his father's tradition, and during this period had become the unchallenged leader of the North Riding Roman Catholics. But his wife's papist family gave him constant trouble over her inheritance in Staffordshire, and his own mother-in-law took him to court. Roman Catholic lawyers were involved on both sides, and the quarrels often looked like Staffordshire versus Yorkshire papists. Fauconberg finally lost patience and in 1743 apostatized. He took the oaths of allegiance and abjuration, subscribed to the declaration, and took his seat in the House of Lords. George II was pleased to present him with a King James Bible and to make him Lord of the Bedchamber and member of the Privy Council. Already a Whig, Fauconberg became a staunch supporter of Walpole and Newcastle. In 1756 he was elevated to an earldom. Catholic leadership in the North Riding passed to his friend and neighbour, Lord Fairfax of Gilling Castle. Although Fauconberg saw to it that his son and heir, Henry, was reared a Protestant, his wife and two daughters continued in the Catholic faith.[20]

In the summer of 1767, Sterne, along with the incumbents of parishes all

[19] William Chapman (brother to Richard) to Lord Fauconberg, 24 May and 29 May 1757; Thomas Mitchell (a York lawyer) to Lord Fauconberg, 24 May and 28 May 1757, in WOMBWELL PAPERS.

[20] For details of Lord Fauconberg's history, his marriage, his quarrels with the Catholic community, see Hugh Aveling, *The Northern Catholics: The Catholic Recusants of the North Riding of Yorkshire, 1558–1790*, 1966, esp. pp. 372–3, 396–8. A history of the house and the family is being written by Geoffrey Ridsdill Smith. Aveling thinks it likely that Lord Fauconberg reverted to Catholicism on his deathbed.

over England, supplied information on local Catholics for a parliamentary survey. The questionnaire which Sterne completed and sent to the archbishop does not survive, but we have a digest made by one of the archbishop's scribes, who set the information side by side with that gleaned in earlier, similar reports. According to this document, thirty-eight Catholics had been living in Coxwold in 1706, ninety-six in 1735, forty in 1748. Sterne, in 1767, reported the number up again, to ninety-seven, perhaps 15 per cent of the population. Another document entitled 'Resident Persons of Estate, Papists or Reputed Papists' lists Lord Fauconberg, 'now a Protest^{t}', and his two daughters.[21]

Lord Fauconberg may have been making a statement about his commitment to Protestantism when he appointed Sterne, whose dislike of Catholics was well known. Sterne's most famous sermon, the 'Abuses of Conscience, Considered', which he had included in *Tristram Shandy*, contains a strong attack upon Roman Catholicism. Eleven of his forty-five known sermons specifically attack papism, and seven of these Sterne published in 1760 and 1766 after his preferment to Coxwold. Numerous other sermons make sharp jabs and sarcastic allusions.[22] But Sterne's attitude underwent a gradual change, as we see from his novels. The first seven volumes of *Tristram Shandy* contain many satirical thrusts against Catholics, especially in the treatment of Dr Slop, but these are virtually absent in the last two. The incident with the monk in *A Sentimental Journey*, ending with the famous exchange of snuffboxes as tokens of the friendship between the mendicant monk and the English parson, is often taken as a plea for religious tolerance. It may be that Sterne's views of Roman Catholicism softened late in his life, in part because of his exposure to the religion abroad, and in part

[21] Borthwick Institute: *Parishes wth ye greater Number of Papists* and *Resident Persons of Estate, Papists or Reputed Papists* (shelved together under the number R. Bp. H 2. 9 [70–87]). For the letter Sterne wrote pertaining to the report, see Appendix I.

[22] The brief allusions to Roman Catholicism in the sermons are too numerous to list. The seven extended attacks which Sterne himself published are found in SERMONS V, VI, IX, X, XIV, XIX, XXVII. Others, in the posthumously published SERMONS, are in XXXI, XXXVII and XXXVIII. Sterne's political essays during the period of 1741 to 1747 often contain barbed comments about papism. In one, written during the rebellion of 1745–6, he attacks 'those very People, whose Principles, whose Religion and Riches, have been the Means of forming this unnatural Rebellion', but he makes exception of 'our own neighbouring Gentry (from whom is our natural Support)', meaning, no doubt, Lord Fauconberg and Lord Fairfax: *York Journal; or, Protestant Courant* (renamed, in 1749, the *Protestant York Courant*), 1 July 1746.

because he had discovered at Coxwold that it need not be feared. It is noteworthy that in the 1767 papist report Sterne did not tell everything he knew. He reported the chapel at the hamlet of Angram, but not that at Oulston, and he did not list any resident priests. It was well known that first Lord Fauconberg and then Lady Catherine had kept a priest at Newburgh, and one record from 1795 indicates a priest in residence at Oulston.[23] It seems likely that priests were present in the parish in 1767, but Sterne just did not report them. He had probably cultivated a habit of turning aside whenever he glimpsed a strange gentleman dressed in sober brown and ignoring parishioners who stayed away from St Michael's but gathered on a Sunday morning at Oulston or Angram.

Clerical preferments in eighteenth-century England were seldom without a political dimension. In 1738 Sterne had been preferred to the Tory parish of Sutton-on-the-Forest in the expectation that he would do his best to bring the village into the Whig camp. No such arduous task faced him in Coxwold. Since English Catholics had, by and large, remained loyal during the rebellion, they were now tolerated by Parliament and Crown. Politically, the parish was well under the control of the Whig Fauconberg, whose chief agents were his steward, Richard Chapman, and his steward's brother, William, an independent farmer, and usually president of the vestry. Between them, they ran the parish as Lord Fauconberg wished it to be run.

Sterne's political responsibility to his patron had to do, not with Coxwold, but with Sutton-on-the-Forest, and he had already discharged much of it. Fauconberg, a major landholder and legally lord of the manor at Sutton, had needed Sterne's support for the land enclosure there, of which he and the squire, Philip Harland, were to be the major recipients. Mr

[23] S. L. Ollard and P. C. Walker, in *Archbishop Herring's Visitation Returns*, IV, 190, 196, 202, discussed the priests at Coxwold in 1743. A note of Archbishop Herring, dated 11 December 1747, attached to a papist list of 1743, names one of the priests of Coxwold as 'Moor' (Borthwick Institute, R. Bp. H 2. 9 [64–9]). No doubt this was Thomas Moore (or More) who lived at Angram, a brother of Zachariah Steward Moore, and uncle of Sterne's friend from the Demoniac group, Zachary Harmage Moore of North and South Loftus: 'Registration of Papists Estates', *Quarter Session Records: North Riding Record Society*, VIII, 1890, p. 44. On the family, see Aveling, *The Northern Catholics*, 398–9. On Zachary Harmage Moore, see *EMT*, 186. On Lady Mary Fauconberg's rebuilding Oulston chapel in 1795, see Page (ed.), *Victoria History: North Riding*. For the state of Catholic recusancy in England at this time, see Aveling, *The Northern Catholics*, and T. J. Holt, 'A Further Note on some Eighteenth-Century Statistics', *Recusant History*, XI (1971), 160–1.

Wilkinson's timely death had put it into Fauconberg's power to repay Sterne amply. This is not to imply that the enclosure at Sutton-on-the-Forest was a conspiracy to defraud the poor. On the contrary, the history of Sutton had amply demonstrated the inadequacy of open-field farming under the authority of the vestry, for acre upon acre of common land now stood barren as a result of centuries of abuse. The purpose of the enclosure was to put this useless land into the hands of entrepreneurs with capital ample to reclaim it and return it to production. No doubt the labourers who lived as squatters on the common were dispossessed of their homes – how many we do not know. But Lord Fauconberg could congratulate himself because in his own mind his reclaiming of this land was at once a service to England and a profit to himself and his heirs.

The Sutton Enclosure Bill had been brought in in 1756, but the legalities had begun to drag. Throughout the spring of 1760, when Sterne moved to Coxwold, the commissioners appointed by Parliament were meeting and making their investigations and striking their bargains with the persons involved. But the entire procedure had reached an impasse over the question of taxes for which each awardee would be responsible. Richard Chapman's letters to Lord Fauconberg are full of descriptions of meetings and arguments, and especially the obstreperousness of Philip Harland, the Tory squire of Sutton and Sterne's old opponent. But Sterne, it seems, finally succeeded in negotiating this critical agreement. 'Last Tuesday,' wrote Chapman on 6 July 1760, 'Mr Sterne went along with me to Sutton in order to give his Assistance in Settleing the Rentals and Assessm^ts^, which was not agreed to till that Day.' From that point on the Sutton enclosure was no longer in doubt.[24]

Sterne always deferred to Lord Fauconberg, but it was the sort of deference which any rural parson would give to a local nobleman. He wrote dutifully from abroad, but in an open, easy manner. Once, in France, he went to considerable trouble to ship Fauconberg a hogshead of Bordeaux wine (200). He was a frequent guest at Newburgh, but complained that its master demanded his presence too often and too much: 'from morning to night every mom^t^ of this day held in Bondage at my friend L^d^ ffauconberg's' (358). He could not always be himself, he told Hall, 'being so much, which I cannot avoid, at Lord F[auconberg]'s who oppresses me to death with

[24] Richard Chapman to Lord Fauconberg, 30 March, 27 April, 11 May and 6 July 1760. For a full account of the Sutton enclosure, *EMY*, 259–61.

civility' (290). But his lordship seemed unaware. He franked Sterne's letters and gave him support as a writer. He subscribed to the *Sermons* of 1760 and 1766 and to *A Sentimental Journey*, agreed to Sterne's plan to divide his time between Coxwold and London, and never complained when Sterne stopped preaching.

Sterne's clerical obligations outside Coxwold more often than not had become troublesome. Sutton and Stillington were being looked after by William Raper, a young man who had grown up in Coxwold. He was without licence or holy orders and he had a bad reputation.[25] In the spring of 1761, Sterne replaced Raper with another local man, but one who had attained holy orders, Marmaduke Callis, thirty years old and a native of Pocklington. Callis typified that large group of exploited clergy, without university degrees or political influence, who eked out a bare living in the hire of pluralists, often taking complete charge of parishes from which the parsons were absent. For four years Callis had worked for the Rev. Mr Cornelius Rickaby at Bridlington, helping him to look after three parishes and one chapelry for £20 a year, the lowest pay curates of that time were ever given. His salary had not been increased in 1760 when he was ordained a priest. Sterne's offer of £32 and the use of Sutton vicarage and garden must have looked good at the time. In the next few years Callis performed his duties, but he disliked the job and tried several times to break his contact. Eventually he brought Sterne serious troubles.[26]

Sterne's preferments in the spiritual courts, of which he had once been proud, had grown onerous. He divested himself of the task of presiding at the tiny prebendal court of North Newbald, associated with his stall at the Minster, by the simple and not uncommon expedient of asking the Curate of North Newbald, Anthony Almond, to serve in his place. He was also

[25] Chapman wrote to Lord Fauconberg about him on 16 March 1760, 'he hath a bad Character and has behaved very Ill for which Mr. Hugill Discharged him from Smeaton'; see also *EMY*, 282–3.

[26] Callis's history can be pieced together from various sources. His service with Mr Rickaby, at Bridlington, Bempton, Flamborough and Grindale Chapel, is recorded in the Archbishop's *Act Book (Institutions)*, *1755–1768*, Borthwick Institute, R. I. AB. 14, p. 63. His service to Sterne's parishes is recorded in the registers of Sutton and Stillington, now kept at the Borthwick Institute. Sterne's promise to pay Callis £16 per annum for each of the parishes is written out in two holograph notes to the Dean and Chapter, dated and signed by Sterne 6 September 1761 (Minster Library BB 25). The licence is recorded in *Chapter Acts*, at the Minster Library, under date of 26 September, and the Chapter's deliberations are described in a note by the recorder, John Clough, written on one of Sterne's notes.

commissary, that is, judge, of the Peculiar Court of Alne and Tollerton, which was ordinary to three parishes. It usually met in the spring. In 1760 Sterne did not get around to convening it until November, and then he did not come himself, but asked Joseph Slack, Vicar of Alne, to preside. He did put in an appearance in July of 1761 and yet again in 1765; but thereafter he was represented by substitutes. His third and largest spiritual court was the Deanery Court, commonly called the Peculiar Court of Pickering and Pocklington, which served nineteen parishes and chapelries. Traditionally it met in two annual visitations, one at Pickering and one at Pocklington. In 1759, when Sterne was engrossed in writing the first two volumes of *Tristram Shandy*, he completely neglected to call the court into session. In 1760 he combined the meetings and then sent his old friend the Rev. Joseph Bridges to preside. He held another combined session at Pickering on 8 June 1761 over which he personally presided, but that would be his last appearance there.[27]

Another obligation was to represent his own parishes, Sutton, Stillington and Coxwold, at still other spiritual courts that had jurisdiction over them. He could easily get out of representing Stillington, for that parish was visited separately by the prebendaries of Stillington; protocol allowed an absentee parson to send his curate in his place, and Sterne did that throughout his years of fame. There was more pressure to appear personally as the representative of Sutton and Coxwold at the visitations of the Cleveland Archdeaconry Court held at Thirsk. Sterne did not show up in 1760, though he put in an appearance the next year. More surprising is his failure to come to Archbishop Gilbert's primary visitation at Thirsk in September of 1760. He later sent the documents he was to have exhibited to the archepiscopal recorder at York, who duly noted them down.[28]

[27] For detailed discussions of Sterne's experiences in the spiritual courts, see *EMY*, Ch. 12, and Arthur H. Cash, 'Sterne as a Judge in the Spiritual Courts: The Groundwork of *A Political Romance*', in *English Writers of the Eighteenth Century*, ed. John H. Middendorf, New York, 1971, pp. 17–36.

[28] The Cleveland Archdeaconry Court records are at the Borthwick Institute, R. VI. F. 1–4; those for Stillington Prebendal Court at the Minster Library. Although Archbishop Gilbert had come to the See of York in 1757, he did not get around to making the customary primary visitation until 1759–60. He came to Thirsk to hold one section of the visitation on 11 September 1760. Sterne did not appear. At the back of the *Exhibit Book* (Borthwick Institute, R. V. C. 21) is an appendix marked 'Exhibits sent to York Since the Visitation'. Sterne's name is included. Sterne's collation to Coxwold, the paper signed in London by Archbishop Gilbert, should have been exhibited by him at the Archdeaconry Court of 1760, but it is

Sterne found the quiet of Coxwold good for his writing, but restless by nature he needed to get away now and again. Almost every autumn he made the journey over the moors to Skelton Castle, Hall's seat near Saltburn-by-the-Sea. He often went to Harrogate, the spa which lay fifteen miles west of Coxwold. But his chief recreation was the celebrated York Race Week, held every August. One can still see the handsome grandstand at Knavesmire from which Sterne cheered on his favourite horses. In the evening there were rounds of entertainments and dinners. He became a member of the Assembly Rooms, and every year (when he was not out of the country) the *York Courant* listed his name among those attending the Race Week balls. There he would see many of his old friends, not only from Yorkshire but from London, for people came from all over the country to take part in the festivities. Lord Rockingham inevitably opened the ceremonies. Stephen Croft and Nathaniel Cholmley and their families were always at the balls. Hall usually came. So did Sterne's old enemies, Dr John Burton and Dr Francis Topham. In 1761 the Duke of York put in an appearance, saluted by cannon from the ships riding at anchor in the river and by the ringing of all the church bells. He reviewed the militia, met the dignitaries at the Minster, and attended a ball at the Assembly Rooms. No doubt Sterne met him on many of these occasions, and probably he was among the guests when the duke was entertained by Nathaniel Cholmley.[29]

But Coxwold was the centre of his new life. His house, he wrote to a friend, was 'within a mile of his Lordship's seat, and park. 'Tis a very agreeable ride out in the chaise, I purchased for my wife.—Lyd has a poney which she delights in.—Whilst they take these diversions, I am scribbling away at my Tristram' (143). Sterne took to gardening. 'Your letter', he wrote to another correspondent, 'will find me either pruneing, or digging or trenching, or weeding, or hacking up old roots, or wheeling away Rubbish' (122). In 1767 he would write:

> I am as happy as a prince, at Coxwould—and I wish you could see in how princely a manner I live—'tis a land of plenty. I sit down . . . to venison, fish and wild fowl, or a couple of fowls or ducks, with curds,

marked 'Exhibited at Thirsk 1761', and signed by Robert Jubb, the recorder (BL, Add. Charters 16166).

[29] *York Courant*, 18 August 1761; Thomas Beckwith's MS *History of York* at the Minster Library. Assembly Room lists appeared in the *York Courant*, 26 August 1760 and 1 September 1761. Sterne's visits to Skelton Castle and Harrogate in 1761: LETTERS, 142.

> and strawberries, and cream, and all the simple plenty which a rich valley . . . can produce—with a clean cloth on my table—and a bottle of wine on my right hand to drink your health. I have a hundred hens and chickens about my yard—and not a parishioner catches a hare, or a rabbet, or a trout, but he brings it as an offering to me. (353)

In early June, Sterne set to work on Volumes III–IV of *Shandy*. He must have worked in the little study to the right of the entrance door to Shandy Hall, sitting and pacing, nervously pulling his wig over one eye and then pushing it from side to side.[30] He worked rapidly, substantially finishing Volume III within two months.[31] 'Now I wish to God, I was at your elbow,' he wrote to Mrs Fenton on 3 August; 'I have just finished one volume of Shandy, and I want to read it to some one who I know can taste and relish humour' (120). Obviously, he did not think Elizabeth was a fit judge of his work. Volume IV took no more than another four months, and perhaps less. He had a good draft by mid-November.[32] These are the longest volumes of the entire novel, a fifth longer than the first two. Sterne seems to have known just where he was going. And he was pleased with the result. He wrote to Mrs Fenton, 'I think there is more laughable humour,—with equal degree of Cervantik Satyr—if not more than in the last—but we are bad Judges of the merit of our Children' (120–1).

He did nothing to clean up *Tristram Shandy*, despite his promise to Archbishop Gilbert. When the Rev. Robert Brown of the Presbyterian church at Utrecht wrote expressing his incredulity that Sterne should be in holy orders, Sterne replied, 'Be assured I am an unworthy Labourer in the Vineyeard—and I verily believe some of the Lords of it, wish me out' (122). Bishop Warburton had put him on notice: 'You have it in your power', Warburton wrote that summer, 'to make that, which is an amusement to yourself and others, useful to both: at least, you should above all things,

[30] The gesture was described by GREENWOOD, though he was recalling Sterne in the study at Sutton twenty years earlier.

[31] In his letter to Warburton of 9 June he says 'I am just sitting down to go on with Tristram' (112). He wrote this letter from York. It is possible that he began working on the book in the house in the Minster Yard, but more likely that he was speaking loosely.

[32] Roughly halfway through the fourth volume, in Chapter 13, Sterne made an allusion to the accession of George III: 'Heaven prosper the manufacturers of paper under this propitious reign, which is now open'd to us' (342). George II died on 25 October. Since it had taken him two months to get this far, one presumes that he would have completed the volume in about four.

beware of its becomeing hurtful to either, by any violations of decency and good manners.'[33] Sterne replied:

> Be assured, my lord, that willingly and knowingly I will give no offence to any mortal by anything which I think can look like the least violation either of decency or good manners; and yet, with all the caution of a heart void of offence or intention of giving it, I may find it very hard, in writing such a book as 'Tristram Shandy', to mutilate everything in it down to the prudish humour of every particular. I will, however, do my best; though laugh, my lord, I will, and as loud as I can too. (115)

Warburton, not in the least satisfied, shot back, 'You say you will continue to laugh aloud. In good time. But one who was no more that even a man of spirit would wish to laugh in good company, where priests and virgins may be present.'[34] So pleased was Warburton with this retort that he made a copy of the letter and showed it to friends. The following winter, after *Tristram Shandy*, III–IV, had appeared, Richard Hurd, the future Bishop of Worcester, wrote to William Mason about Sterne, 'he does not seem capable of following the advice which one gave him – *of laughing in such a manner, as that Virgins and Priests might laugh with him.*'[35] The parting shot, however, was Sterne's. He hoarded Warburton's words for a year and then made use of them in his fifth volume: Trim, trying to tell Walter and Toby that young master Tristram has been circumcised by a falling window sash, but at a loss for words, 'by the help of his forefinger, laid flat upon the table,

[33] Warburton's letter, dated from Prior Park, 15 June 1760, in LETTERS, 112–14. In this same letter Warburton asked about the authorship of the *Two Lyrick Epistles*, in reply to which Sterne denied any correspondence with Hall: see above, Chapter 1.

[34] Warburton's letter, dated from Prior Park, 26 June, in LETTERS, 118–19. Sterne wrote to a friend, Mary Macartney, about this time, complaining about the 'volumes of Ribaldry' that his book had provoked; 'the Bishop of Glocester . . . has wrote me a congratulatory Letter therupon—the Summ total of all w[ch] is—That we bear the Sufferings of other people with great Philosophy—I only wish one could bear the excellencies of some people with the same Indifference' (118). The letter to Mary Macartney is numbered 64 in LETTERS; but Sterne's comment about Warburton's congratulating him seems to refer to Warburton's letter of 26 June, in which the bishop said to Sterne, 'Do not expect your friends to pity you for the trash and ribaldy scribbled against you; they will be apter to congratulate you upon it' (119) – a letter to which Curtis in LETTERS assigned the number of 65. He might have been better advised to reverse the two letters.

[35] *Correspondence of Richard Hurd and William Mason*, ed. Ernest Harold Pearce and Leonard Whibley, Cambridge, 1932, p. 53.

and the edge of his hand striking a-cross it at right angles, made a shift to tell his story so, that priests and virgins might have listened to it.'[36] In the third and fourth volumes the *double entendres* and sexual innuendoes abound. In the fourth Sterne sends Tristram 'curvetting and frisking it away' on a lively hobby horse, his story, but a bystander cries to him, 'your horse throws dirt; see you've splash'd a bishop' (357). And in the last chapter he all but flings Warburton's advice in his face: Tristram promises to tell soon the story of Uncle Toby's amours with the Widow Wadman and, when he does, he says,' I shall not be at all nice in the choice of my words . . . and the thing I *hope* is, that your worships and reverences are not offended—if you are, depend upon't I'll give you something, my good gentry, next year, to be offended at' (401).

Sterne knew that the charge of indecency was unjust, that his fiction offered not the least threat to morals. He would not be deterred from expressing his comic vision of man's inner life, which included the absurd intrusion of sexual awareness or desire into the thoughts and feelings of people who would rather be free of these disturbances. A fundamental joke was to demonstrate to the reader himself, or more especially *her*self, how she could not keep her thoughts pure. Tristram could taint them with the greatest ease – by refusing to define the word *crevice*, in one instance (258), and insisting upon a definition of the word *nose*, in another (262); in either case madam or sir would inevitably take what Tristram calls the 'dirty road'. But this is playful only, not the least arousing. Sterne's attitude is summed up in an anecdote. He once asked a Yorkshire lady if she had read *Tristram Shandy*;

> 'I have not , Mr. Sterne,' was the answer; 'and, to be plain with you, I am informed it is not proper for female perusal.' —'My dear good lady,' replied the author, 'do not be gulled by such stories; the book is like your young heir there, (pointing to a child of three years old, who was rolling on the carpet in his white tunics) he shews at times a good deal that is usually concealed, but it is all in perfect innocence!'[37]

[36] TRISTRAM SHANDY, 453. The parody was pointed out by Michael O. Houlahan, 'William Warburton and *Tristram Shandy*: An Ironic Source', *N & Q*, 217 (1972), 378–9. In Volume IX, Sterne named Warburton's book the *Divine Legation of Moses*: 'for what has this book done more than the Legation of Moses, or the Tale of a Tub, that it may not swim down the gutter of Time along with them?' (754)

[37] *Ballantyne's Novelist's Library*, 1823, V, xvi.

Sterne was committed to the two stories, or plots, with which he had launched the first two volumes. One of these was the story of Uncle Toby's recovery from his wound, a prolonged quest for physical and mental health which begins in London, moves to the bowling green, and terminates in his amour with Mrs Wadman. Sterne had virtually outlined Toby's story in Volumes I–II,[38] but he was in no hurry to tell it. He set it aside completely in III–IV, taking up instead the other story: that of Walter Shandy's comic attempt to create a perfect child by begetting, rearing and educating it upon principles of 'reason' and 'science' – a prideful scheme which is ironically frustrated by a series of disasters for poor Tristram, the subject of these experiments. Volume I had opened with the first of these disasters – as Walter sees them – the bungled conception that dooms Tristram to a frail constitution. Within a few pages Tristram had promised the stories of the birth and baptism, and by the close of Volume II Sterne had brought upon the scene both the midwife and the man-midwife.

Volumes III–IV are devoted entirely to the continuation of this satirical story, and in that sense they are the simplest volumes of the entire novel. Sterne keeps on violating in his playful way the rules of fiction, offering an 'Author's Preface' in the twentieth chapter of the third volume and 'removing' a ten-page chapter; but these devices are not disorienting. Apart from one or two flashbacks, there is no jumping about in time. Everything is anchored to three major events told in chronological order – the birth, including the discovery that the child's nose has been broken by the forceps; the hasty baptism in which he receives what his father thinks is the worst of all Christian names; and the visitation dinner where the Shandy brothers try in vain to find a way of changing the name.

The digressions, too, Sterne justified in terms of this story, or the telling of it. Musing upon the difficulties he faces in making us understand his world, Tristram notes that he has been writing for a year but has got no further than the first day of his life. Demonstrably, he is living 365 times faster than he is writing: 'I shall never overtake myself' (341–2).[39] We can

[38] TRISTRAM SHANDY, 75–6, 86–9, 117. The notion that Toby's hobby is a quest for health was suggested by Jean-Jacques Mayoux, 'Variations on the Time-sense in *Tristram Shandy*', in WINGED SKULL.

[39] Bertrand Russell in *Principles of Mathematics*, ch. 43, in a discussion of infinity, explicates the 'Tristram Shandy paradox' side by side with Zeno's paradox of Achilles, maintaining on formal mathematical grounds that Tristram, 'if he had lived for ever, and not wearied of his task, then, even if his life had continued as

hardly doubt that Sterne intended some of the digressions as delights in and of themselves. 'Slawkenbergius's Tale' can certainly stand alone. Nevertheless, Tristram insists that he offered it to us only because it said so much about his father's obsession with noble noses – 'an institute of all that was necessary to be known of noses' (285). At another point Sterne uses a digression to defend David Garrick against a group of theatrical malcontents who had attacked Garrick's acting in the press (212–13),[40] but he has Tristram insist that his remarks are no more than a commentary upon 'connoisseurs', which in turn comments upon Bishop Ernulf's curse. So the schematic simplicity of Volumes III-IV was no barrier to Sterne's contemporary satires or the development of his major themes on the complexities and ambiguities of human communication.

Tristram had said in the first volume he would offer us both his life *and* opinions,

> hoping and expecting that your knowledge of my character, and of what kind of a mortal I am, by the one, would give you a better relish for the other: As you proceed further with me, the slight acquaintance which is now beginning betwixt us, will grow into familiarity; and that, unless one of us is in fault, will terminate in friendship.——*O diem præclarum*!——nothing which has touched me will be thought trifling in its nature, or tedious in it's telling. (9)

As this suggests, the rickety construct of story, digressions and symposia is actually self-containing: the life and opinions are used to familiarize us with the narrator, who, becoming real to us through those means, speaks in a manner in keeping with his character. As a scheme, this is not very different from that of other first-person novels. In Defoe's *Moll Flanders*, for instance, Moll's story and Moll's commentary serve to develop her character as storyteller and moralist. We then judge the story, to a large degree, upon the consistency or inconsistency we find between Moll the character, as child or woman, being moulded by these events, and Moll the narrator and mature moralist who comments upon them. But the proportions in Defoe's narrative differ from those in Sterne's. Moll has a great many events to tell of and is given little room for talk about them or herself or the other people

eventfully as it began, no part of his biography would have remained unwritten.'

[40] George Winchester Stone, Jr, and George M. Kahrl, *David Garrick*, Carbondale and Edwardsville, Ill., 1979, pp. 149–50.

involved. Tristram, however, with but a handful of events to tell of, allows himself seemingly unlimited freedom to talk about his family, himself, or the world at large, so long as he can find some tenuous link between his remarks and the story.

This mass of opinion emanates from the ample mind of Tristram, a narrator whom Sterne created in the Renaissance tradition of 'learned wit'.[41] Not only is Tristram unstinting in his own opinions, but he tries to give us a sense of the vast hobby-horsical learning of his father and uncle. Sterne himself did not possess such a fund of knowledge, but he developed characters who had it. He did so by drawing upon source books. To be sure, Sterne was a man of learning. He could quote from memory, for example, his favourite Shakespearian plays. And so steeped was he in the Bible that its phrases came often to mind, probably without his being aware of it.[42] But Shakespeare and the Bible are not what give the dense texture of recondite allusion that marks every page of *Tristram Shandy*. To build up this larger-than-life erudition, Sterne had to be deliberate, even systematic.

As a sermonist, Sterne seems to have followed the common practice of compiling collections of sayings on specific topics.[43] Although no commonplace books belonging to him have been found, it seems highly likely that he had such books and drew upon them from time to time as he worked on *Tristram Shandy*. Otherwise, he could hardly have written, say, the chapter on sleep (345–7), which strings together passages or images from Cervantes, Montaigne, Shakespeare, the Bible and perhaps Sir Philip Sidney.[44]

[41] D. W. Jefferson, '*Tristram Shandy* and the Tradition of Learned Wit', *Essays in Criticism*, I (1951), 225–48; Howard Anderson, 'Associationism and Wit in *Tristram Shandy*', *Philological Quarterly*, XLVIII (1969), 27–41; Jonathan Lamb, 'Sterne's System of Imitation', *Modern Language Review*, LXXVI (1981), 794–810; Lamb, '"Uniting and Reconciling Every Thing": Book-Wit in *Tristram Shandy*', *Southern Review*, VII (1974), 236–45.

[42] On some of Sterne's uses of the Bible and Shakespeare, see Arthur Sherbo, 'Some Not-so-hidden Allusions in *Tristram Shandy*', in Sherbo's *Studies in the Eighteenth-Century Novel*, East Lansing, Mich., 1969, pp. 128–35.

[43] Graham Petrie, 'A Rhetorical Topic in *Tristram Shandy*', *Modern Language Review*, LXV (1970), 261–2.

[44] TS NOTES enables me to make statements about Sterne's sources or allusions with no documentation other than the page numbers in TRISTRAM SHANDY. Readers who want further information should consult the notes for those pages, where they will find the source identified and sometimes quoted. Often they will find further references to the scholarship which led to the attribution or to the outstanding critical discussions of the relationship between the source and the novel.

Books in his possession Sterne consulted directly. He was a lover of books and an avaricious collector. In the summer of 1761, when the library of the late Rev. Mr Clarke, schoolmaster of Wakefield, was put up for sale, Sterne bought the entire collection – 700 volumes, 'dog cheap – and many good' – and spent a week setting them up at Shandy Hall (142).[45] Those particular books, of course, did not affect Volumes III–IV, written in 1760; for them Sterne relied upon an older, smaller library which he seems to have moved from the house in the Minster Yard to Coxwold.

No doubt Sterne had some curious, out-of-the-way books, but one must not suppose that he had consulted all the rare books mentioned in the novel. Tristram the fictional narrator knew Bruscambille's prologue upon long noses, but Sterne the author had never laid eyes on Bruscambille's *Prologues*: he took the entire description from Rabelais (266). 'The nine volumes of *Tristram Shandy*', says the general editor of the Florida *Works* of Sterne, 'are liberally sprinkled with names of authors he never read, books he knew little or nothing about.'[46] What is more typical of Sterne is his discovery of the ridiculous in books widely read by his contemporaries. The legal argument so hilariously presented in the scene of the visitation dinner in Volume IV demonstrating that a mother is of no kin to her child (389–91) Sterne took from a frequently consulted law book which he probably ran into in his capacity as a judge in the spiritual courts, Henry Swinburne's *Briefe Treatise of Testaments and Last Wills* (1590), reissued numerous times.

[45] W. G. Day, 'Sterne's Books', *Library*, 5th series, XXXI (1976), 245–8, speculates that this collection had belonged to Clarke, master of the Free School at Wakefield. Day makes the point in connection with his discussion of the book-sale catalogue issued in 1768 by Todd and Sotheran of York. The catalogue has been much used by scholars because it includes the books put up for sale by Sterne's family after his death. The difficulty is that it also included other collections. It was reissued in 1930 under the misleading title, *A Facsimile Reproduction of a Unique Catalogue of Laurence Sterne's Library*, with a preface by Charles Whibley which does nothing to warn against its misuse. Actually, one cannot distinguish Sterne's books from others. Kenneth Monkman has showed that the file of the *York Courant: or Weekly Advertiser*, which one might have guessed had belonged to Sterne, belonged to another clergyman: 'Sterne, Hamlet, and Yorick: Some New Material', WINGED SKULL, 112–23. Stephen Park's subsequent facsimile edition of the catalogue has an introduction which states the facts more carefully: *Sale Catalogues of Libraries of Eminant Persons*, No. 5, 1972, pp. 257–356. The most thoroughgoing assessment is that of Day, who concludes pessimistically, 'At the moment all one can say is that the more than 2,500 lots offered by Todd and Sotheran from 25 August 1768 included an unknown number of books owned by Sterne but did not include all of the books he owned.'

[46] TS NOTES, 24.

The twelfth-century anathema of Bishop Ernulf of Rochester, which Sterne presented in both Latin and English (202–11), he took from two sources: Thomas Hearne's edition, *Textus Roffensis* (Oxford, 1720), provided the Latin, and the *Gentleman's Magazine* (September 1745) the English. Sterne, not completely happy with either, made numerous small changes in both.[47] He probably had kept them since the days of the rebellion, when he might have intended a more serious use, to discredit the papism of the rebels.

But what gives *Tristram Shandy* its particular stamp are the few works Sterne turned to again and again – his 'reference works', so to speak. For political and military history, he used Nicholas Tindal's two-volume *Continuation of Mr. Rapin de Thoyras' History of England, from the Revolution to the Accession of King George II*, though in Volumes III–IV he had less use for it than in others. For technical or scientific information, especially about fortifications and military machines, he used Ephraim Chambers's *Cyclopaedia: or, an Universal Dictionary of Arts and Sciences*. From Robert Burton's *Anatomy of Melancholy* he took many things, but especially classical lore. For instance, when he needed a vow which would contrast with the medieval curse of Bishop Ernulf, he had Tristram swear 'by the golden beard of Jupiter', and incorporated into the oath a description of the classical deities taken directly out of Burton (211). He repeatedly plundered Rabelais, which he knew in the celebrated translation of Thomas Urquhart and Peter Motteux with notes by John Ozell, and he often helped himself to information or passages in Ozell's notes. Which editions he used is uncertain.[48] Tindal, Burton, Chambers and Ozell's notes he treated as so

[47] TRISTRAM SHANDY, Appendix 8, pp. 952–7.

[48] It is unlikely that we shall ever establish with certainty which editions Sterne used. The only external evidence, such as it is, is contained in the Todd and Sotheran catalogue discussed in the above notes. Internal evidence is more helpful, but not conclusive. In some cases, a study of Sterne's borrowings narrows the field but still does not pinpoint a particular edition. If he borrowed material not included in a book until a late edition, we know he used that or a subsequent edition, but not exactly which edition from this narrowed group. The editors of TS NOTES use editions within these narrowed groups; but, not believing that the priority of the Todd and Sotheran catalogue has been demonstrated, they have used the editions within these groups which were most readily available to them.

Tindal's *History*, Vols III–IV (which are the continuation of Rapin de Thoyras's initial two volumes), is listed twice in the catalogue – an undated listing, and the edition of 1732. The editors of the *Works* use the edition of 1743–7.

Burton's *Anatomy* is listed in the catalogue in the edition of 1652, but does not specify which of the two sixth editions published that year. The edition of 1638, used by the editors of the *Works*, is the last which Burton himself corrected and

much public property and felt no obligation to give them credit even when he took whole sentences or paragraphs.

Other great writers he usually named or alluded to in some obvious way, probably because he wanted his reader to associate *Tristram Shandy* with them – Cervantes, Montaigne, Locke and usually Rabelais. He specifically cited Montaigne,[49] for instance, to justify his 'tearing out' of the twenty-fourth chapter of Volume IV. To explain 'true Shandeism' he borrowed an image obviously from Cervantes – 'Was I left like *Sancho Pança*, to chuse my kingdom . . .' (402).

The case of Locke is less clear. Sterne may have paraphrased the *Essay Concerning Human Understanding*,[50] but these passages do not demonstrate any intimate knowledge of Locke because he might have found these very quotations in Chambers's *Cyclopaedia* under such headings as 'Time', 'Duration' or 'Idea'.[51] True, Sterne once told Jean-Baptiste Suard that he had taken up the study of Locke in his youth and continued it for the rest of his life,[52] but he did not always agree with Locke. In the 'Author's Preface' in Volume III, perhaps Sterne's most important justification of his fiction, he specifically takes issue with Locke's notion that the talent for wit and the talent for judgement are not to be found coexisting in one person – a notion which seemed to Sterne to deny the very possibility of constructive laughter.

Although Sterne often borrowed information and plagiarized passages, he copied almost nothing verbatim. If he took a list of names from Chambers, for instance, he would add another to it, often a fictional name. If

contains new materials that Sterne dipped into; so we know Sterne used it or a subsequent edition. (See G. W. Day, 'Some Source Passages for *Tristram Shandy*', *N & Q*, CCXVI (1971), 58–60.)

Chambers's *Cyclopaedia* appears in the catalogue in the 1738 edition. The editors use that of 1741–3, which they think differs little.

The translation of Rabelais by Urquhart and Motteux is listed in the catalogue twice: editions of 1708 and 1737. But the 1737 edition is the first which contained the notes by Ozell which Sterne frequently made use of. So Sterne necessarily used the edition of 1737 or a later one. The editors make use of the 1750 edition, which they believe differs little from 1737.

[49] The Todd and Sotheran catalogue lists the editions of 1711 and 1738. The editors of TS NOTES use that of 1738.

[50] TRISTRAM SHANDY, 222–5, 280–1. In all probability, Sterne used the fourth or a subsequent edition. The fourth, the last corrected and amended by Locke, appeared in 1699 but is dated 1700.

[51] TS NOTES, 17. The discussion of Sterne's use of his major sources in TS NOTES, 12–24, is invaluable.

[52] GARAT, II, 148–9. Garat seems to quote from or summarize some memoir left by Suard, but the original has vanished.

he borrowed a passage from Burton, he would add a piece of information taken from another source. He went to a great deal of trouble to check his political and military history against Tindal, but he worried not the least about obstetrical history: the obstetrical forceps were not known in England in 1718, the year of Tristram's birth. Accuracy was never his intent; the illusion of accuracy was.

In November 1760, Sterne finished his draft of Volumes III–IV. He was in a bad mood and angry with his wife. Elizabeth was unhappy in Coxwold, as perhaps she would be anywhere. In a state of self-pity she had written to Elizabeth Montagu:

> Cou'd Mrs Montagu think this the way to make a bad Husband better, she might indeed have found a better, which I have often Urged, though to little purpose, namely, shewing some little mark of kindness or regard to me as a Kindswoman, I meant not such as would have cost her money but indeed this neither she or any one of the Robinsons [Mrs Montagu's family] vouchsafed to do . . . so that surely never poor Girl who had done no one thing to merit such neglect—was ever so cast off by her Relations as I have been.[53]

From this letter we learn that Elizabeth had embroiled herself and Elizabeth Montagu in an old quarrel between Sterne and Dr William Herring, the Diocesan Chancellor. Dr Herring, a seventy-year-old lawyer-priest who had been brought into the church of York by his late cousin, Archbishop Thomas Herring, was not only a residentiary canon of the Minster, but, in his capacities as Diocesan Chancellor and Official Principal of the Consistory Court, the chief judiciary of the archbishops of York. He and Sterne had been allies in various church quarrels for a decade, but they had fallen out in the spring of 1759 over the question of who should have the next residentiaryship at the Minster. Sterne wanted it for himself and took the step of moving into the Minster Yard so that he would be in a position to obtain it. Herring wanted it for his son, also named William, the Prebendary of Apesthorpe at York as well as Dean of St Asaph and Precentor of Salisbury.[54]

Early in 1760, soon after Sterne had brought out the first volumes of

[53] Huntington Library, MS 5088; reproduced by CURTIS, 137.

[54] For the careers of Dr William Herring (1691–1762) and his son William (1718–74), see *EMT*, 227 and n. 2, where the errors of several authorities are corrected. On Sterne's attempt to obtain a residentiaryship, *EMT*, 268 and n. 2.

Tristram Shandy at York, Herring had brought up the matter again. 'Letters & Conversations', Elizabeth told her cousin, Elizabeth Montagu, 'pass'd betwixt them . . . on this subject.' Now, in the autumn of the year, Herring began again to stir up trouble.[55] Sterne, hearing that the older man had been blackening his reputation to Dean Fountayne, sat down and wrote a 'long pathetic Letter' to Fountayne about 'the hard measure I have re[ceive]d' (147) and demonstrating to his own satisfaction 'that I was as much a protection of the Dean of York – as he to me' (135). Fountayne replied at once, and his letter, said Sterne, 'has made me easy with regard to my Views in the Church of York; & . . . has cemented the Dean & myself beyond the power of any future breach' (136).

But Dr Herring would not desist, and somehow during the autumn of 1760 he drew Sterne and Elizabeth Montagu into the quarrel. Elizabeth Sterne wrote to her cousin protesting that she had known nothing about Sterne's and Herring's quarrel until 'the Chancellor wrote his 1st Letter, w[ch]

[55] I have reconstructed this quarrel and its aftermath from three documents: (1) Elizabeth Sterne's letter to Elizabeth Montagu, cited above; (2) Sterne's letter to Mrs Montagu, also undated, No. 75 in LETTERS; and (3) the 'Memorandums' Sterne left his wife when he went abroad – No. 81 in LETTERS. Sterne dated the 'Memorandums' 28 December 1761. I would argue that the other two were written in the autumn of 1760 and thus place the story of Sterne's anger with his wife and with Mrs Montagu in that period.

Elizabeth Sterne's letter to Mrs Montagu was written at a time when the Sternes as a family had been living in the country but had established a house in York to which the wife and daughter would go when Sterne left for London. Thus it was written after the spring of 1759, when the family first established a house in York, and before 1762, when they went abroad, never to return to England as a family. During that period Sterne is known to have travelled to London in the spring of 1760, the autumn of 1760 and the autumn of 1761. It is also likely that Sterne went to London early in 1759 (*EMT*, 276), but I rule out that year because Elizabeth would not have been apt to return during the warm months to the only country house they had then – in Sutton-on-the-Forest. The journey to London in Stephen Croft's carriage in the spring of 1760 is not a possible time because Elizabeth remained in York thoughout that period. Sterne's trip to London in the autumn of 1761 is ruled out by the fact that he was not quarrelling with Elizabeth: they had arrived at a truce and were upon good terms – for them (LETTERS, 140, 143). Thus, by a process of elimination, I place Elizabeth's letter in the autumn of 1760.

Sterne's letter to Mrs Montagu (No. 75 of LETTERS) obviously postdates Elizabeth Sterne's letter. It also antedates the 'Memorandums', as CURTIS pointed out. But Curtis places it too late – the spring of 1761. I doubt that Sterne would have allowed a quarrel with Mrs Montagu to drag on all winter: she was too important as a patron. More probably he forced the issue without delay and quickly obtained the peace with Mrs Montagu indicated in his letter. So I place Letter No. 75 in the month he arrived in town – December 1760.

Mr Sterne communicated to me'. Whatever was in that letter, it made Sterne accuse his wife of betraying him. Since Elizabeth wrote to Mrs Montagu begging her to 'do all that was in her power to undo the mischeif', one guessed that Elizabeth had said something hurtful of Sterne in a letter to her cousin which Mrs Montagu began to repeat in London. In any event, Sterne learned through Herring's letter that Mrs Montagu was saying derogatory things about him; and his wife, as she herself said, 'must expect to the last hour of my Life to be reproach'd by Mr Sterne as the blaster of his fortunes'. Nothing loath to stand up for himself, Sterne wrote an angry letter to Elizabeth Montagu telling her in plain terms that she was mistaken about him.

Having finished his work on the third and fourth volumes of *Tristram Shandy*, he employed someone to make a copy, left it in the hands of Stephen Croft at Stillington, and departed for London.[56]

Soon after his arrival, Samuel Torriano, secretary to Archbishop Gilbert and a close friend of Mrs Montagu, knocked at the door of Sterne's Pall Mall lodgings.[57] He had brought a letter of apology from Mrs Montagu and an invitation to dine. In replying, Sterne declared he was 'ten times more oppress'd with the excesse of your candour & goodness than I was before with the subject of my complaint.'

> Dr Herring, was I suppose the person, who interested himself in the honour of the Dean of York, & requested that act of friendship to be done the Dean, by bringing about a Separation betwixt the Dean & myself—the poor Gentleman has been labouring this point many Years—but not out of Zeal for the Dean's Character, but to secure the next Residentiaryship to the Dean of St Asaph his Son; he has outwitted himself at last, & has now all the foul play to settle with his

[56] After Sterne got to London late in this year, Stephen Croft wrote to him about his reaction and that of other 'friends at Stillington' to the chapter on noses. He must have been looking at a manuscript after Sterne left Yorkshire. See LETTERS, 126. Sterne was in Coxwold until at least 16 November, on which day he performed a wedding there. He arrived in London on 6 December: Newton's letter of 9 December, below.

[57] Lacking any evidence where Sterne lodged during his London visits of winter 1760–1 and autumn 1761, one must presume he returned to the Pall Mall lodgings he had taken in March 1760. Country people who regularly wintered in London but owned no house there usually took the same quarters year after year.

Conscience, without gaining, or being ever likely to gain his purpose. (135)

He enclosed for her perusal a copy of the letter he had written the month before to Dean Fountayne, the answer to which had been for him so gratifying. And he assured her that he was past his anger toward his wife: 'there is not an honest Man, who will not do me the Justice to say, I have ever given her the Character of as moral & virtuous a woman as ever God made—What Occasion'd Discontent ever betwixt us, is now no more—We have settled Acc^{ts} to each others Satisfaction & honour—& I am persuaded shall end our days with out one word of reproach or even Incivility' (136). During the next two years, Sterne would try to live up to this ideal of domestic peace.

But Mrs Montagu, if indeed she had gossiped about Sterne, did him little harm. His social life among the rich and powerful picked up where it had left off the previous spring. 'I have been in such a continual hurry since the moment I arrived here—what with my books, and what with visiters, and visiting' (126), he wrote to Croft on Christmas Day. Archbishop Gilbert, though waiting to see the new volumes of *Shandy*, had entertained him the day after he arrived in London.[58] And he had gone to one of the lavish balls given by the Countess of Northumberland (130). 'I never dined at home once since I arrived,' he told Croft in January, 'am fourteen dinners deep engaged just now' (128).[59] Little wonder that the compiler of *Ways to Kill Care: A Collection of Original Songs* should say in his dedication to 'Tristram Shandy':

> Who is more thought of, heard of, or talked of, by dukes, dutchesses, lords, ladies, earls, marquisses, countesses, and common whores, than Tristram Shandy? My Lord Groom's favourite running nag is no more called by that worn-out hackney'd name of Othello, Black and all black, Jenny Diver, or Little Davy, but Tristram Shandy: nor my Lady Lovepuppy's lap-dog, that filthy odious one of Veny, but by that more dear name of all names, Tristram Shandy.

[58] Dr Thomas Newton to the Rev. John Dealtary, 9 December 1760, speaking of the previous Sunday (7 December): 'Laury Sterne was there [at the Archbishop's house], who it seems arrived in town the night before': DEALTARY LETTERS.

[59] One such engagement was a dinner given by a Mr Upton, where Thomas Hollis was introduced to him on 20 February 1761: see Hollis's MS diary, 6 vols, I, fol. 142, at the Houghton Library.

Nothing better demonstrates the point than the painting which George Stubbs exhibited at the Society of Artists 1762, of a racehorse named 'Tristram Shandy'.[60]

Early in 1761, Sterne struck up a friendship with John Spencer and his wife, and in February went off with them to their estate at Wimbledon for a few days' visit (130). Spencer, a great-grandson of the Duke of Marlborough, master of Althorp in Northamptonshire, of Wimbledon Park, and of Spencer House, St James's Place, one of the finest houses in London, was among the most magnificent aristocrats of England. The prudent alliances of the great duke and his sons had resulted in a family fortune so vast that a decision had been made to divide it between the main line, which retained the title, and the cadet line, of which Sterne's friend was the head. In the British system as it then existed, it would have been almost impossible to deny such a man a peerage. And on 3 April 1761 he was created Baron Spencer of Althorp and Viscount Spencer of Althorp; in 1765 he was created Earl Spencer. When Sterne met him, he was twenty-six years old and of a fragile constitution.[61]

Sterne was full of devotion for Spencer's wife, Margaret Georgiana. Although well connected on the side of her mother, who was daughter and co-heiress of General Lewis Mordaunt, on her father's side she was the grandchild of an upholsterer. However, her father, Stephen Poyntz, had become a courtier and diplomat and favourite of George II. Margaret Georgiana had married John Spencer the day after his twenty-first birthday in a secret ceremony held in his mother's dressing room at Althorp, though there were 500 people in the house at the time. The couple then proceeded up to London accompanied by a cavalcade of horsemen so enormous it alarmed the villagers, who thought it was another Jacobite rebellion. They presented themselves to George II, who was godfather to the bride, wearing diamonds given them by the old Duchess of Marlborough worth, it was said, £100,000, including Spencer's diamond shoebuckles, alone worth £30,000. Lady Spencer, as she soon would be, was reputed to be beautiful

[60] OATES, from whom I have also taken the quotation from *Ways to Kill Care*.

[61] G. E. C[okayne], *Complete Peerage*, 1953, XII, 153; Burke's *Peerage*, 1963; NAMIER AND BROOKE. On Spencer's estates and houses, Ian Nairn and Nikolaus Pevsner, *Surrey* (Buildings of England series, Penguin), Harmondsworth, 1971, p. 521; John Summerson, *Georgian London*, 1970, p. 249 and plate 12b; E[dwin] Beresford Chancellor, *The Eighteenth Century in London*, [1920], 153–4. Since the couple subscribed to Sermons III–IV, 1766, but not to Sermons I–II, 1760, I presume Sterne did not make their acquaintance until the winter of 1761.

and intelligent. At a later date she became a special friend to David Garrick, who in a long correspondence with her commented repeatedly on her naturalness in whatever she said or wrote. Little wonder that Sterne should fall under her spell: the next year he would dedicate to her the 'Story of Le Fever' in Volume VI of *Tristram Shandy*.[62]

During his absence in Yorkshire, Sterne had been elected to the burgeoning Society for the Encouragement of Arts, Manufactures and Commerce, usually called at that time the Society of Arts, but known since 1909 as the Royal Society of Arts. This interesting organization, established only six years before, had already had a remarkable effect upon the applied sciences and polite arts, largely through the prizes it gave for outstanding accomplishment in agriculture, husbandry, chemistry, methods and machines of manufacture, drawing, sculpture, engraving, and the like. The handsome house next to the Adelphi designed by Robert and James Adams which became their permanent headquarters had not yet been built; they were meeting at this period in rooms in Castle Court, Strand (the present Agar Street), which they rented from Sir John Fielding. The society was in a period of expansion, and had grown to well over a thousand members, including a great many people known to Sterne. Among them were Yorkshire Whigs, Sir George Saville, Lord Rockingham and Nathaniel Cholmley; many fine gentlemen, such as John Spencer, Francis Dashwood and Lord Chesterfield; literary people, Johnson, Gibbon and Lord Lyttelton; and numerous artists. Hall was a member, as was Garrick. So was Elizabeth Montagu, the first woman to be elected, and the most active of all women members of that century. Sterne, however, was nominated by none

[62] Additional information on Mrs Spencer from *Autobiography and Correspondence of Mary Granville, Mrs. Delany*, ed. Augusta Waddington Hall, Lady Llanover, 6 vols; 1861–2, III, 305, 340, 399–402 and *passim*; *Georgiana: Extracts from the Correspondence of Georgiana, Duchess of Devonshire*, ed. Earl of Bessborough, 1955: Fanny Burney, *Diary and Letters*, ed. Charlotte Barrett, 6 vols, 1904–5, II, 233–4; CLIMENSON, II, 148; *Letters of David Garrick and Georgiana Countess Spencer, 1759–1779*, ed. Earl Spencer and Christopher Dobson, Cambridge, 1960.

The couple had two children and were expecting a third. The eldest daughter became Georgiana Cavendish, Duchess of Devonshire (1757–1806), the queen of London society, who, after being scandalously treated by her husband, became something of a scandal herself. The son, George John (1758–1834), who became the second earl, had a long political career and served as First Lord of the Admiralty from 1794 to 1801, when he supported Nelson; he collected the great library at Althorp which became in time the foundation collection of the Rylands Library. A second daughter, Henrietta Frances, was born on 16 June 1761. She eventually married Frederick, Earl of Bessborough, and became the mother of the celebrated Lady Caroline Lamb.

of these, but by a certain Thomas Ryder, who gave his address as Lincoln's Inn. Sterne paid his annual assessment of two guineas on 3 March 1761, but whether he participated in any of the meetings is not known. Attendance records for large meetings were not kept. He had the privilege of sitting on any committee he wished, but so far as anyone has discovered he did not avail himself of these opportunities. He soon lost whatever interest he had, for he did not again pay his assessments. The society, however, did not lose interest in Sterne. The walls of the great room of the Adams building, in which the society still meets, are covered with six vast murals by James Barry – completed in 1798. In the sixth, *Elysium, or the State of Final Retribution*, Barry, as he said, brought together 'those great and good men of all ages and nations, who were cultivators and benefactors of mankind', placed them in the light of God which emanates from the top left corner, and turned them away from the abyss in the lower right. There, peering over the head of Alexander Pope, is the smiling face of Laurence Sterne, finger on his temple as in the Reynolds portrait; he seems to be turning his back to those next to him – Gray, Mason and Goldsmith.[63]

During the winter of 1760–1, London was buzzing with rumours about the new king, the government he was apt to form, the possibility of withdrawal from the German war. Everyone knew that the Earl of Bute's interest with the king was so great as to make him a central figure in any new government. 'I wish you was here to see what changes of looks and political reasoning, have taken place in every company, and coffee-house since last year,' Sterne wrote to Stephen Croft on Christmas Day; 'we shall be soon Prussians and Anti-Prussians, B[ute]'s and Anti-B[ute]'s, and those distinctions will just do as well as Whig and Tory—and for aught I know serve the same ends' (126). He gave Croft a description of the new king's style of conduct: 'He rises every morning at six to do business—rides out at eight to a minute, returns at nine to give himself up to his people.—By persisting, 'tis thought he will oblige his M[inister]s and dependants, to dispatch affairs with him many hours sooner than of late' (126). Sterne went to the Commons and sat in the balcony of St Stephen's Chapel – since replaced by the Houses of Parliament – to hear Pitt debate the matter of the German campaign; but he was disappointed: 'There never was so full a

[63] James Barry, *Account of a Series of Pictures in the Great Room . . .*, 1783, as quoted in the society's pamphlet, *The Paintings by James Barry*; two MSS in the Society Library, *Subscription Book*, Vol. I, and *Committee Minutes*, 1758 ff.; Derek Hudson and Kenneth W. Luckhurst, *Royal Society of Arts, 1754–1954*, 1954.

house—the gallery full to the top—I was there all the day—when, lo! a political fit of the gout seized the great combattant—he entered not the lists' (129). The new government took charge on 19 March. 'The court is turning topsy-turvy,' wrote Sterne, '. . . a peace inevitable—Stocks rise—the peers this moment kissing hands, &c. &c. (this week may be christened the kiss-hands week) for a hundred changes will happen in consequence of these' (132–3). Pitt and Newcastle proved strong enough to remain in office, but were forced to share it in a triumvirate with Bute, who would indeed succeed in ending the war as the king wished, but at the sacrifice of his own political career.

Sterne knew several of the politicians involved in these changes. Charles Townshend, the new Secretary of War, was 'my friend' (130); Sir Francis Dashwood, the new Treasurer of the Chamber, was an intimate of Hall's; and there is one anecdote which links Sterne to the Duke of Newcastle.[64] In December he dined with George Bubb Doddington, whose Pall Mall lodgings were in the house opposite Sterne's. Doddington had been a central figure in the Leicester House faction of the late Frederick, Prince of Wales, and his guests on this occasion were mostly men who had served the king when he was himself Prince of Wales; they would soon be preferred in the new court – Lord Masham, William Breton and David Mallet.[65]

Although Sterne himself was no longer very active in politics, his acquaintance with politicians was now so wide that the normal order of things was reversed and he found himself petitioned by the Squire of Stillington to intercede on behalf of his son. In February of 1760, Stephen Croft, the son, had been commissioned at the lowest officer rank in the cavalry, that of cornet, in the Second or Royal North Britain Regiment of Dragoons. His father, anxious to get him promoted, pressed Sterne to use his influence. At first Sterne was enthusiastic: 'I have enquired every where about Stephen's affair, and can hear nothing—My friend, Mr. Charles T[ownshend], will be now secretary of war—he bid me wish him joy of it, though not in possession.—I will ask him' (130). Young Stephen's

[64] *Monthly Visitor*, I (February 1798, pp. 124–5), published the following anecdote: 'The duke of Newcastle being one day engaged in conversation with the late witty author of Tristram Shandy, and observing that men of genius were unfit to be employed, being generally incapable of business; the wit sarcastically replied – "They are not incapable, my lord duke, but above it; a sprightly, generous horse is able to carry a pack-saddle as well as an ass; but he is too good to be put to the drudgery." '

[65] *Political Journals of George Bubb Doddington*, ed. John Carswell and Lewis Arnold Dralle, Oxford, 1965, p. 407.

regiment had been sent to Germany, where the war was going badly for the allies. 'I was told yesterday by a Colonel, from Germany,' Sterne had written earlier, 'that out of two battalions of nine hundred men, to which he belong'd, but seventy-one left!' (127). Stephen, however, was in England. So, when Sterne managed to meet Townshend's assistant for breakfast, he was advised not to press the case.

> You must know that the numbers of officers who have left their regiments in Germany, for the pleasures of the town, have been a long topic for merriment; as you see them in St. James's Coffee-house, and the park, every hour, enquiring, open mouth, how things go on in Germany, and what news?—when they should have been there to have furnished news themselves—but the worst part has been, that many of them have left their brother officers on their duty, and in the fatigues of it, and have come with no end but to make friends, to be put unfairly over the *heads of those* who were left risking *their lives*.—In this attempt there have been some but too successful, which has justly raised ill-blood and complaints from the officers who staid behind—the upshot has been, that they have every soul been ordered off, and woe be to him ('tis said) who shall be found listening. Now just to mention our friend's case whilst this cry is on foot, I think would be doing more hurt than good, but if you think otherwise, I will go with all my heart and mention it to Mr. T[ownshend], for to do more I am too inconsiderable a person to pretend to. (132)

Young Croft was recommissioned at the rank of captain in the Second or Queen's Regiment of Dragoon Guards on 20 October 1761, but whether Sterne's influence helped we do not know. He joined his new regiment on 18 November; but by then the war in Germany was over.[66]

Meanwhile, Sterne was editing *Tristram Shandy*, III–IV. Most authors in that age did their own editing. Sterne would have been the person to make arrangements with Hogarth for the frontispiece and with Ravenet to engrave it.[67] One can imagine how resistant the printers must have been to

[66] Printed army list for 1765 at PRO: IND 5455, p. 23.

[67] The first edition of Vol. III had the Simon-François Ravenet engraving. For the second and subsequent editions it was re-engraved by J. Ryland. The original drawing, in the Berg Collection of the New York Public Library, is described by Ronald Paulson, *Hogarth's Graphic Works*, 2 vols, New Haven, Conn., 1965, I, 282; and A. P. Oppé, *The Drawings of William Hogarth*, New York, 1948, pp.56–7.

the idea of omitting the page numbers of the pages which Tristram says he has 'torn out'. (Nine page numbers representing the missing Chapter 24 of Volume IV are omitted in all good editions of the novel.) One detail of Volume III is especially noteworthy – the marbled leaf. The leaf for each copy of the book was prepared individually, marbled on both sides, but with margins kept clean, hand-stamped with the page numbers, and tipped in when the sheets were gathered and bound. This lengthy and costly process demonstrates the care Sterne gave to the physical production of his books.[68]

He also continued to tinker with the text. He could at times be stubborn when others suggested changes in his wording. The year before, when a friend had objected to the syntax of a sentence in *A Political Romance*, Sterne had taken the trouble to write a defence of his complicated and not entirely logical sentence, but would change nothing.[69] By contrast, on his own initiative he made many changes. When the first two volumes were printed at York, Sterne had corrected the proofs himself so that 'it shall go perfect into the world' (81). In transposing his sermon *The Abuses of Conscience, Considered* from the original published version (1750) into the second volume of *Tristram Shandy*, he made almost ninety small changes.[70] A comparison of the manuscripts of *A Sentimental Journey* with the printed text reveals the same meticulous care.[71] Though the manuscripts of *Tristram Shandy* do not survive, we can still find evidence of last-minute changes or additions. Sterne had said that he finished Volume III in August; but one finds in the novel a sentence which he must have written during the winter because it alludes to the new ministry: 'Had the parlour-door open'd and turn'd upon its hinges, as a door should do—— —Or for example, as cleverly as our government has been turning upon its hinges' (240). The entire fourth chapter of Volume III is another late interpolation, for he there complains about the nine months' annoyance he has suffered since May when the *Monthly Review*-ers attacked him.[72]

[68] W. G. Day, '*Tristram Shandy*: The Marbled Leaf', *Library*, 5th series, XXVII (1972), 143–5.

[69] Sterne to the Rev. John Blake, [21–30 January 1759], in Appendix I.

[70] Melvyn New, 'Sterne as Editor: The "Abuses of Conscience" Sermon', *Studies in Eighteenth-Century Culture*, VIII, ed. Roseann Runte, Madison, Wisc., 1979, pp. 243–51.

[71] Discussed by Stout in notes to SENTIMENTAL JOURNEY, 49–57, 295–307.

[72] Both these suggestions were made by the editors of TS NOTES in their notes to TRISTRAM SHANDY, 190 and 240. In complaining about the *Monthly Review*-ers' treatment of him in the previous May, Tristram says he has been disturbed 'these

Meanwhile, Stephen Croft and some other Yorkshire friends had finished reading the manuscript of the new volumes which Sterne had left behind. Worried, Croft wrote to Sterne in London, and Sterne replied:

> I am not much in pain upon what gives my kind friends at Stillington so much on the chapter of *Noses*—because, as the principal satire throughout that part is levelled at those learned blockheads, who, in all ages, have wasted their time and much learning upon points as foolish—it shifts off the idea of what you fear, to another point—and 'tis thought here very good—'twill pass muster—I mean not with all—no—no! I shall be attacked and pelted, either from cellars or garrets, write what I will—and besides, must expect to have a party against me of many hundreds—who either do not—or will not laugh.—'Tis enough if I divide the world;—at least I will rest contented with it. (126)

In mid-January he wrote to Croft again: 'Tristram will be out the twentieth—there is a great rout made about him before he enters the stage—whether this will be of use or not, I can't say—some wits of the first magnitude here, both as to wit and station, engage me success—time will show' (126).

Sterne was anxious about a spurious third volume which had appeared in the late summer of 1760 and taken in a good many people.[73] One busy Grub Street hack, thinking the volume genuine, rushed into print with *A Supplement to the Life and Opinions of Tristram Shandy . . . Volume III.*[74] The matter became serious when the *Critical Review*, already displeased with Sterne, accepted this third volume as genuine and gave it a bad review in their September issue: 'To speak without a figure, we never perused a more

last nine months together'. If this were written in the summer of 1760, it would necessarily refer to the late months of 1759, which would be inexplicable. But if Sterne added the comment shortly before going to press in late January 1761, nine months previous would have been late April or early May 1760. Tristram says, in fact, that the critics were storming at him 'last May'. Thus, Sterne would be referring to the review of the *Sermons* by Owen Ruffhead in the May issue of the *Monthly Review* – the review which criticized Sterne for publishing them as the sermons 'of Mr Yorick'.

[73] CROSS, 231, and other writers on Sterne attribute this work to John Carr. Reissued in the Garland Press series, *Sterneiana*, I, New York, 1975.

[74] The title-page to the *Supplement* announces it to be 'by the author of *Yorick's Meditations*'. Published 17 December: OATES.

stupid, unmeaning, and senseless performance than the third volume of Tristram Shandy.' Alarmed, Sterne took out an advertisement in the *York Courant*, which appeared on 7 October:

> TRISTRAM SHANDY. Whereas several Advertisements have lately appeared in the London and other Papers, intimating that the third Volume of Tristram Shandy was published . . . such [a] Volume is entirely unknown, in every Respect, to the Author of the two first; . . . the third and fourth Volumes, will come out about Christmas next, printed only for R. and J. Dodsley, in Pall-mall, London, and J. Hinxmann, in Stonegate, York.

One would suppose Sterne made a similar announcement in London, but as yet none has been found.

Advertisements of the genuine volumes commenced in the *Public Advertiser* on 19 December 1760. Since the new instalment would stimulate a demand for Volumes I–II, the Dodleys brought out a new edition of them, the fourth, on 21 December.[75]

Volumes III–IV of *Tristram Shandy* were published on 29 January 1761.[76] The advertisement announcing their appearance was placed in the *London Chronicle* dated 27–29 January, and it included offers of the new edition of I–II and the *Sermons*. In the customary manner, the advertisement was repeated six times unchanged.

A Dublin edition appeared simultaneously, presumably with Sterne's authority, but it had hardly been sold when an unscrupulous Dublin bookseller, Henry Saunders, brought out a cheap, pirated edition of Volumes I–IV. Sterne could not have made much on his Dublin venture this time.[77]

In London, sales were brisk at first, but then slackened off. Dodsley told his printers that no more copies would be needed, and they began to dismantle the plates. Then came an unexpected surge of demand in mid-February, and Dodsley found himself running out of copies. 'We are going on with a second edition, as fast as possible,' Sterne wrote to Stephen Croft

[75] Ralph Straus, *Robert Dodsley*, New York, 1910, pp. 370 ff. Described in TRISTRAM SHANDY, Appendix Five, II, 913, 920–1, where publication is given as possibly 29 January 1761 on the grounds of an advertisement in the *London Chronicle* of that date.

[76] Straus, *Robert Dodsley*, gives the date of publication as 30 January, but does not cite his evidence. Descriptions of the first edition may be found in MONKMAN and in TRISTRAM SHANDY, Appendix Five, 923–7.

[77] TRISTRAM IN DUBLIN.

on the eighteenth (130). Dodsley now had his printers reset the already distributed plates, which they combined with those that had remained set, and early in March brought out a second edition – of sorts.[78]

Brief announcements of Volumes III–IV appeared in the *Gentleman's Magazine* for January and the February issues of the *British Magazine* and the *London Magazine*. The first genuine review was written for the February *Monthly Review* by Owen Ruffhead, the stiff-necked critic who had been so hard on Sterne for attaching the name of Yorick to his sermons.[79] Sterne had incautiously complained of him in Volume III (190–1). Ruffhead was now outraged again.

> What would be venial in the farcical Author of the *Minor* [Samuel Foote], would be highly reprehensible from the pen of a Divine. In short, there is a certain faculty called *Discretion*, which reasonable men will ever esteem; tho' you, the arch *Prebend* Mr. *Yorick*, Alias *Tristram Shandy*, have done all in your power to laugh it out of fashion.

Then, evoking an old and quite illogical euphemism for matters sexual, he pronounced the volumes 'dull'. 'Yes, indeed, Mr. Tristram, you are dull, *very dull*. . . . We are sick of your uncle Toby's wound in his groin; we have had enough of his revelines and breastworks.'

'One half of town abuse my book as bitterly, as the other half cry it up to the skies,' said Sterne in his letter to Croft (129). No doubt Sterne's wealthy, well-placed clientele enjoyed the volumes and told him so, but little was said in favour of the books in print. The unidentified writer for the *Critical Review* made a thoughtful, scholarly comment upon the origins of Sterne's comedy, the 'patern and prototype' of which he found to be Rabelais, not Cervantes. He complimented the books for their 'pertinent observations on life and characters, humourous incidents, poignant ridicule, and marks of taste and erudition'. On the other hand, 'Most of the apostrophes and digressions are mere tittle-tattle', and the performance is 'blameable for some gross expressions, impure ideas, and a general want of

[78] The second edition of Vol. III is announced on the title-page, but the second edition of Vol. IV, which was put on sale with it, is undeclared. Neither is completely new: some sheets are identical with the first edition, some corrected, some entirely new. As MONKMAN suggests, Dodsley seems to have changed his mind in response to an unexpected demand. The frontispiece was re-engraved for the second edition by 'J. Ryland', i.e. Joseph Ryeland or Ryland; but why this was deemed necessary is a mystery. See also Melvyn New's introduction for TRISTRAM SHANDY, 824–5.

[79] Identified by NANGLE.

decorum.'[80] The entire essay was reprinted in the *London Chronicle* for 30 April–2 May.

Some few disliked the volumes on aesthetic grounds. Horace Walpole found them 'the dregs of nonsense',[81] and Richard Hurd thought that 'this broad Humour, even at its best, can never be endured in a work of length.'[82] But most of the objection was moral. Archbishop Gilbert and virtually all of the clergy and bishops were angry, said Dr Thomas Newton:

> The last two vol[s] of Tristram Shandy have had quite contrary success to the two former. It is almost as much the fashion to run these down, as it was to cry up the others. Not that I think there is that great difference between them, but certainly these are inferior in wit & humor, and in other respects are more gross & offensive. Our Archp is very angry with him for having broke his promise, and the last time he called there which is a month ago, he would not see him. All the Bps & Clergy cry out shame upon him. All the graver part of the world are highly offended . . . and the Bp of Gloucester & I & all his friends are sorry for him. He has not come near us, and I believe is almost ashamed to see us.[83]

One may doubt it was shame which kept Sterne away from his erstwhile patrons among the clergy, but there can be little doubt that Newton correctly assessed the reaction of 'the graver part of the world'. Dean Delany, in Dublin, 'is not a little offended with Mr. Sterne,' said his wife; but then she added, 'his book is read here as in London, and seems to divert more than it offends.'[84] Samuel Richardson had read the first two volumes, but would not touch the next two. To his friend Mark Hildesley, Bishop of Sodor and Man, he wrote, 'execrable I cannot but call them; for I am told that the third and fourth volumes are worse, if possible, than the two first; which, only, I have had the patience to run through. One extenuating circumstance attends his works, that they are too gross to be inflaming.' He

[80] HOWES, 125–7. Smollett was no longer reviewing, though he still had control of the *Critical Review*. Four reviewers from this period have been identified, but it cannot be determined who wrote this one. See Derek Roper, 'Smollett's "Four Gentlemen": The First Contributors to the *Critical Review*', *Review of English Studies*, X (1959), 38–44.

[81] WALPOLE, XVI, 44.

[82] *Correspondence* of Hurd and Mason, 53.

[83] DEALTARY LETTERS, 26 February 1761.

[84] *Autobiography and Correspondence of Mary Granville, Mrs. Delany*, III, 593; see also p. 588.

sent along to Hildesley an imaginary dialogue which, he said, had been written by his daughter and a lady friend of hers: 'his own character as a clergyman', says one lady to the other, 'seems much impeached by printing such gross and vulgar tales, as no decent mind can endure without extreme disgust!' Hildesley replied on 1 April:

> Your strictures, good Sir, upon the indelicately witty Yorick, from that little I accidentally read of shameless-Shandy (for that little was enough to forbid me to read more) I believe to be very just. . . .
>
> That corrupt nature should be pleased with what ministers plentifully to the foul imagination of the polluted heart, is not strange; but, that spiritual men, and ecclesiastical dignitaries should countenanc[e] and encourage such a production, is hardly capable of any sort of defence. However, I hear from several, and those very good hands, that now the laugh is pretty well subsided, many begin to be heartily ashamed at that which had raised it.[85]

Dr William Dodd wrote a poetic epistle 'To the Author of Tristram Shandy, on the Publication of His Third and Fourth Volumes'.

> . . . the time will come, when you shall feel
> Stabs in your heart more sharp than stabs of steel,
> When conscience loud shall thunder in your ear,
> And all your wide spread ill in horrid form appear!
>   Prevent the hour, for pity's sake I ask,
> And oh perform your own advised task;
> Search your own heart, you'll find the debt is large,
> And haste! perform the duties of your charge;
> Leave the vile town, nor wish it in your power
> To shine the giddy meteor of an hour,
> Ah! you have talents,—do not misapply;
> Ah! you have time,—seize, seize, it, ere it fly;
> Strait seize it, for too short you needs must own,
> Whate'er of life remaineth to atone
> For all the filth diffus'd and evil you have done.[86]

[85] *Correspondence of Samuel Richardson*, ed. Anna Laetitia Barbauld, 6 vols, 1804, V, 144–54. Richardson's letter was erroneously dated 24 September 1761 by Mrs Barbauld, but it was obviously written between the publication of *Tristram Shandy*, III–IV, and Hildesley's answer, dated 1 April 1761. The MS of Hildesley's letter of 1 April is now in the Morgan Library.

[86] ILLUSTRATIONS, V, 780. I do not know where the original was published.

This was the same Dr Dodd who in 1777 was hanged for forging the name of his old pupil, Lord Chesterfield, to a bond for £4200. Most of Sterne's critics were men of good character, to be sure, but the situation did seem to invite hypocrisy. The most successful pornographer of his age, John Cleland, the author of *Fanny Hill*, adjudged Sterne guilty. Boswell recorded the story:

> *CLELAND*. Sterne's bawdy *was* too plain. I reproved him, saying, 'It gives no sensations.' Said he: You have furnished me with a vindication. It can do no harm.' 'But,' *I said*, 'If you had a pupil who wrote C—on a wall, would not you flogg him?' He never forgave me. *FRASER*: That was a hard knock to Sterne. *BOSWELL*: 'A knock against the WALL.'[87]

Even Grub Street was cool to Volumes III–IV. Only one imitation appeared – *The Life and Opinions of Bertram Montfichet, Esq.*[88] There was an addition to that series of parasitical *Explanatory Remarks . . . by the Author of the First*.[89] But obviously the name Tristram Shandy had lost its magic.

Sales began to fall off. Two months after the second edition appeared, Dodsley re-ran in the *London Chronicle* for 19–21 May the exact advertisement he had used in January to announce the first edition: 'This Day was published, / Price Four Shillings sewd, / With a Frontispiece by Mr. Hogarth . . .' – a not very scrupulous device to boost the flagging sales.[90]

Warburton, of course, was galled that Sterne had ignored his advice – 'that egregious Puppy who has received of me the most friendly services and has repaid them as all such men do. Not but that I deserved as much, for tho' Nature sowed in him the seeds of *Puppybility*, yet I cultivated them

[87] *Private Papers of James Boswell*, ed. Geoffrey Scott and Frederick Pottle, 18 vols, Mount Vernon, NY, 1928–34, XIII, 220. The conversation took place in 1779; Cleland's meeting with Sterne cannot be dated precisely, but it postdates *Tristram Shandy*, I–II, for Cleland was probably alluding to the sixth chapter of the second volume: 'My sister, mayhap, quoth my uncle *Toby*, does not choose to let a man come so near her ****' (116).

[88] Kenneth Monkman and J. C. T. Oates, 'Towards a Sterne Bibliography', WINGED SKULL, 279–310; reissued in Garland Press series, *Sterneiana*, VI–VII, New York, 1975.

[89] Copy at the Beinecke Library, Yale University.

[90] That the advertisement was no more than a sales device and not an announcement of a new edition is a moot point. Melvyn New, however, in his introduction to TRISTRAM SHANDY, 824–5, argues that it was a sales device, and Kenneth Monkman, as he said in a recent conversation, has come to the same view.

when I brought him out into the world.'[91] Nevertheless, he had cause to write to Mason, '"*Tristram Shandy*" is fallen apace from this height of glory.'[92] And Garrick, reported Dr Newton, was emboldened to give Sterne some advice: 'Mr. Sterne,' he said, 'you are in a very bad state of health; I would advise you to go into the country, to keep quiet upon your living, to take care of your health, and if you write any more of these things, be sure to mend your hand.'[93]

In March a rumour began to circulate at York that Sterne had been denied the court. When Stephen Croft wrote to ask about it, Sterne replied, 'You made me and my friends here very merry with the accounts current at York, of my being forbid the court—but they do not consider what a considerable person they make of me, when they suppose either my going, or my not going there, is a point that ever enters the K[ing]'s head' (132). He was not damaged by the criticism, Sterne insisted, but one seems to hear him whistling in the dark:

> where I had one friend last year, who did me honour, I have three now.—If my enemies knew that by this rage of abuse, and ill will, they were effectually serving the interests both of myself, and works, they would be more quiet—but it has been the fate of my betters, who have found, that the way to fame, is like the way to heaven—through much tribulation—and till I shall have the honour to be as much mal-treated as Rabelais, and Swift were, I must continue humble; for I have not filled up the measure of half their *persecutions*. (132)

While Sterne was protesting his good fortune, Charles Churchill stole centre stage. Churchill, also in holy orders, published on 14 March 1761 his biting satire of the theatre, the *Rosciad*, which attacked virtually every actor, manager and playwright except Garrick. Its popularity was enormous. In 1764 Sterne would tell David Hume, then the rage of Paris, that his own vogue in London had lasted only one winter.[94]

But if Sterne's popularity fell off slightly or underwent a change, it

[91] BL, Add. MSS 32563, fol. 17, as quoted by EVANS, 231.

[92] BL, Add. MSS 32563, fol. 11, as quoted by CURTIS, 96.

[93] The words are Newton's in his letter to John Dealtary of 26 February 1761: DEALTARY LETTERS.

[94] *Letters of David Hume*, ed. J. Y. T. Greig, 2 vols, Oxford, 1932, I, 6 and n.

mattered little to his writing career. With the exception of Volume IX, first editions of the volumes of *Tristram Shandy* would consist of 4000 copies, and all of them would be sold, though not always quickly. Sterne could manage to keep a clientele of 4000 readers without being the favourite of the entire reading public. Moreover, he had probably been introduced personally to about half of the people who bought his books, and many had become his friends. He would continue for the rest of his life a pet of the fashionable world.

He was liked too by an odd variety of people, and indeed liked them in turn. Thomas Hollis, scion of a wealthy Baptist family in London, benefactors of Harvard College, was a paranoiac, reclusive book-collector, scholar and private publisher. He wrote in his diary under the date of 21 March 1761, 'Mr Hewett, & the Rev. Mr Sterne (Tristram Shandy) with me in the morning.' Hewett was that garrulous world traveller and former colonel of the Leicestershire Volunteers, whose rhetorical antics fascinated Hollis and Smollett, both of whom left brief memoirs of him. He had long been a member of the Demoniacs.[95]

Sterne seems to have spent a good deal of time with Hall and those of the Demoniacs who were in town, and at least once went with them to Ranelagh (139–40). This may be the period in which he wrote the *Impromptu*, published by his daughter with the letters of 1775. According to 'S.P.', who sent Lydia the manuscript, 'This was quite an *Impromptu* of Yorick's after he had been thoroughly *soused.*—He drew it up in a few moments without stopping his pen.' It is an amusing little *jeu d'esprit* about the insubstantiality of a coat:

> This a coat for a rainy day? do pray madam hold it up to that window—did you ever see such an *illustrious* coat since the day you could distinguish between a coat and a pair of breeches?——My lady did not understand derivatives, and so she could not see quite through my splendid pun. Pope Sixtus would have blinded her with the same 'darkness of excessive light'. What a flood of it breaks in thro' this rent? what an irradiation beams through that? what twinklings—

[95] For Hollis, see *DNB*. His paranoia about the Catholics, whose spies he thought he saw everywhere, is apparent in his *Diary*, at the Houghton Library. The entry about Sterne and Hewett, Vol. I, fol. 149. His memoir of Hewett appears in Hollis's *Memoirs*, 2 vols, 1780, I, 324–5. Smollett's memoir of him: *Humphry Clinker*, II, Matthew Bramble's letter of 4 July. For Hewett: *EMY*, 190, CURTIS, 202–3.

what sparklings as you wave it before your eyes in the broad face of the sun?[96]

Two of the most conspicuous events in Sterne's public life that spring happened only a few days apart. On Sunday, 3 May, he preached a charity sermon at the Foundling Hospital, and on the following Saturday the Society of Artists opened an exhibition in which Sterne's face was prominently displayed. The two events are curiously interrelated.

The Foundling Hospital, historically one of the most important service institutions in English history, had always been associated with musicians and artists. Handel, for instance, had given the organ in the chapel and from it had often conducted the children in performances of the *Messiah*. Hogarth had been one of its earliest and most faithful patrons, donating various of his great paintings. These and other paintings the hospital displayed on the walls of the room in which the governors met, and the display gave rise to a notion that exhibitions of art need not be confined to the houses of the rich. In 1759 the governors called a meeting of artists to discuss the possibility of mounting a special exhibition. Curiously, the meeting was chaired by John Wilkes, representing the governors of the Foundling Hospital. Out of that meeting grew the first exclusively professional organization of painters, sculptors and engravers – the Society of Artists. Reynolds was a chief organizer. Hogarth, in poor health, did not come in until late, but then became very active. Early in 1760 the artists, with the assistance of Samuel Johnson,[97] petitioned the Society of Arts for permission to hold an exhibition in the society's rooms. The exhibition opened on 21 April 1760 and was in many ways a resounding success. But the professional artists were unhappy that the society had permitted the exhibition of paintings by amateurs and had announced prizes among these that the professionals had not competed for. A large group of professional artists broke away to form the Society of Artists (later called the Incorporated Society of Artists); others that continued to hold exhibition under the patronage of the Society of Arts came to be called the Free Society of Artists.[98]

[96] *Works*, ed. Wilbur Cross, 12 vols, 1904, VII, 263–7. There is no way of dating this piece.

[97] James L. Clifford, 'Johnson and the Society of Artists', in *The Augustan Milieu*, ed. Henry Knight Miller *et al.*, Oxford, 1970, pp. 333–48.

[98] William T. Whitley, *Artists and their Friends in England, 1700–1799*, 2 vols, 1928, I, 173–6; Ronald Paulson, *Hogarth: His Life, Art, and Times*, 2 vols, New Haven, Conn., and London, 1971, II, 318–23; D. G. C. Allan, 'Artists and the Society in the Eighteenth Century', *Journal of the Royal*

A year later, on 9 May 1761, the Society of Artists opened their own exhibition in Spring Gardens, Charing Cross, in rooms rented from an auctioneer – the first exhibition in history organized exclusively by professional artists for their own benefit. Among the five paintings Reynolds displayed was No. 82, 'Half length of Dr. Sterne' – the great Lansdowne portrait of the year before. An unidentified young officer, in a letter to his family, expressed his admiration of the portrait in which, he said, Sterne appeared 'in as facitious a humour as if he would tell you a story of Tristram Shandy'.[99] Simon-François Ravenet exhibited a 'Head of Doctor Sterne', No. 210, presumably the drawing after Reynolds from which he did the line engraving for the frontispiece to the *Sermons of Mr. Yorick*. Edward Fisher displayed his 'Mezzotint of Dr. Sterne', No. 189, the excellent print of the Reynolds which Sterne or Reynolds or both had commissioned.[100] In the age before the camera, few had such public exposure.

Hogarth did not show his drawings for *Tristram Shandy*. He seems not to have thought any of his recent work worth displaying; so he put up only earlier paintings. But the atmosphere of co-operation among artists may have worked in Sterne's favour another way. As was pointed out in the previous chapter, Sterne, in Volume III of *Tristram Shandy*, had paraphrased an *Idler* essay in which Reynolds had attacked Hogarth; yet Hogarth, far from taking offence, had drawn another sketch to serve as frontispiece for the very volume. To be sure, he may not have read the book. On the other hand, he may have thought himself slighted but declined to make a protest which might have embroiled him in a quarrel with Reynolds.[101]

Society of Arts, CXXXII (1984), 204–7, 271–6.

[99] Quoted by Whitley from an unidentified document.

[100] Algernon Graves, *The Society of Artists of Great Britain, 1760–1791, The Free Society of Artists, 1761–1783, a Complete Dictionary of Contributors and their Works*, 1907; *EMY*, 301–2.

[101] Reynolds's three *Idler* essays in which Hogarth was attacked are Numbers 76 (the one Sterne made use of), 79 and 82. A week after the Society of Artists exhibition opened, the *London Chronicle*, 14 May, published the three essays, slightly cut. The *St. James's Chronicle*, which had been recently established by Garrick, Bonnell Thornton and George Colman the Elder, largely to support the arts, had been very supportive of Reynolds, but the editors did not take up the challenge. Instead they found numerous occasions to praise both Hogarth and Reynolds. See Paulson, *Hogarth*, II, 329–34. The essays were offprinted from the collected edition of October 1761 and sold under the title *Three Letters to the Idler*: see the *Idler* and the *Adventurer*, ed. W. J. Bate, John M. Bullitt and L. F. Powell, Vol. II of the Yale edition of the *Works of Samuel Johnson*, New Haven, Conn., and London, 1963, p. 235, n. 1.

Sterne's invitation to preach at the Foundling Hospital may also indicate that he was in the good graces of Hogarth, who was still a governor, though not so active at this point as formerly. The governors were a curious mixture of artists and clergymen and of puritan types and rakes. George Whatley, the man who sent Sterne an invitation, was a strait-laced person, though an indefatigable worker for the charity.[102] By contrast, Sir Francis Dashwood and John Wilkes, notorious rakes, were also governors. A major task of this body was fund-raising, for in 1761 the hospital was so short of money it could no longer afford to take in new children. In this situation, the two or three charity sermons given every year became an important source of income. Wealthy people came from all over the town to these services, and the collection plates were large.

On 25 March Sterne responded to Mr Whatley's invitation and promised that on 5 April he would deliver a short sermon, 'and *flap* you in my turn:—preaching (you must know) is a theologic flap upon the heart, as the dunning for a promise is a political flap upon the memory:—both the one and the other is useless where men have *wit enough* to be honest' (134).

Sterne did not deliver his sermon on 5 April, as originally planned, but on 3 May, the Sunday before the Society of Artists exhibition. On Saturday, the governors ran an announcement in the *Public Advertiser*, naming Sterne and explaining, 'As the sums of Money granted by Parliament are applied towards the Maintenance of the Children only, the great and useful Purposes of this Charity cannot be executed without the Assistance of Charitable and Well-disposed Persons.'

The Hospital for the Maintenance and Education of Exposed and Deserted Young Children is still in operation, though it is usually referred to as the Coram Foundation. It was Captain Thomas Coram whose heroic efforts had originally established the hospital. The buildings in Holborn, then a rural area north of the town, were begun in 1742. Today on the site of the old hospital is a children's park, Coram Fields. The buildings are gone, for now children are placed in foster homes. All that remain are the gate and

[102] CROSS and CURTIS were mistaken in thinking that in 1761 George Whatley was the treasurer of the Foundling Hospital. At that time he was only a governor, though a member of the subcommittee which exercised the most authority. The treasurer was Taylor White. Whatley, a merchant and minor diplomat, become the author of *Reflections on the Principles of Trade in General*, 1769. In 1772 he was elected vice-president of the Board of Governors and in 1779 treasurer: *European Magazine*, XIX (1791), 240; *Monthly Reposity of Theology and General Literature*, I (1806), 136–8; Nichols and Wray (see below), *passim*.

the colonnades which then framed the courtyard.[103] 'I will take care', Sterne had written to Whatley, 'to be walking under some colonnade, in or about the Hospital; about a quarter before eleven' (134).

The sermon Sterne preached eventually appeared among the *Sermons of Mr. Yorick*, Volume IV (1766) – 'The Parable of the Rich Man and Lazarus Considered'.[104] It is a carefully written comment upon the doctrine of retribution and the virtue of charity, calculated for a wealthy audience, and building finally into a passionate appeal on behalf of poor children. The *Lloyd's Evening Post* of the next day described a 'numerous audience, several of whom were persons of distinction', who had contributed 'a handsome Collection'. To be precise, as the treasurer reported to the governors, the collection came to £55. 9*s*. 2*d*.[105] The only eyewitness account was left by Charles Brietzcke, a Polish servant to the Duke of Grafton. Under 3 May he wrote in his diary, 'At the Foundling to Dr. Sterne, the Author of Tristram Shandy, whose preaching, to me was as indifferent as his Writings are. Saw Miss Stanley in the Green Park but She took no Notice of poor me.'[106]

In mid-May Sterne returned to his family in York and shortly thereafter took them to Coxwold. 'I should have walked about the streets of York ten days,' wrote Sterne to Hall, 'as a proper medium to have passed thro', before I entered upon my rest' (139). After London, Coxwold seemed no more than a 'cuckoldly retreat' – punning on the name of the village – and country life seemed a misery.

> I have not managed my miseries like a wise man—and if God, for my consolation under them, had not poured forth the spirit of Shandeism

[103] The more recently built offices of the Coram Foundation stand in Brunswick Square, adjacent to Coram Fields. Two excellent histories of the Foundling Hospital have been written: Reginald H. Nichols and Francis Aslett Wray, *History of the Foundling Hospital*, Oxford and London 1935; and Ruth K. McClure, *Coram's Children: The London Foundling Hospital in the Eighteenth Century*, New Haven, Conn., and London, 1981. The MS minutes at the Foundation offices entitled *General Commmittee*, No. 7, contain minutes of the board meeting for 29 April 1761, in which it was ordered 'That a Paragraph be inserted in the Daily Papers that a charity Sermon will be Preached in the Chapel of this Hospital on Sunday next by the Rev[d] M[r] Sterne.'

[104] No. VIII in the fourth volume, 1766; No. XXIII in SERMONS, ii, 21-39. Sterne's note says only 'Charity Sermon at St. Andrew's, Holborn'. The only St Andrew's Church in Holborn was the hospital chapel.

[105] Minutes of the meeting of 6 May recorded in *General Committee*, No. 7. Announcements of Sterne's sermon were made also in the *Gentleman's Magazine* for May, p. 233, and the *Annual Register* for 1761, p. 105.

[106] Emma Hailey in *N&Q*, new series, II (January–December 1955), 443.

into me, which will not suffer me to think two moments upon any grave subject, I would else, just now lay down and die—die——and yet, in a half an hour's time, I'll lay a guinea, I shall be as merry as a monkey—and as mischevious too, and forget it all. . . . Oh, Lord! now you are going to Ranelagh to-night, and I am sitting, sorrowful as the prophet was when the voice cried out to him and said, 'what do'st thou here, Elijah?'—'Tis well the spirit does not make the same at Coxwold—for unless for the few sheep left me to take care of, in this wilderness, I might as well, nay better, be at Mecca. (139–40)

Sterne took up parochial duties again, assisted by his unlicensed curate. All the summer and autumn of 1761 he preached regularly. He made the required appearances in the spiritual courts. And he wrote. 'To-morrow morning, (if Heaven permit),' he said to Hall in June, 'I begin the fifth volume of Shandy—I care not a curse for the critics—I'll load my vehicle with what goods *he* sends me, and they may take 'em off my hands, or let them alone' (140). Then, lest he take himself too seriously, he added, 'I am very valourous—and 'tis in proportion as we retire from the world and see it in its true dimensions, that we despise it—no bad rant!' He was having second thoughts about country life.

In August he took a holiday. He went to York for Race Week, where he saw Lord Rockingham, the Duke of York, and numerous friends and acquaintances.[107] Soon thereafter Hall, back from London, took him off to Skelton Castle for a few days among the Demoniacs.[108]

Elizabeth did not accompany him on these jaunts, but neither did she resist his going. With surprising equanimity, Elizabeth had decided to accept even his friendship with Hall. 'She swears you are a fellow of wit, though humourous; a funny jolly soul, though somewhat splenetic; and (bating the love of women) as honest as *gold*—how do you like the simile?' (140). From Sterne's condescending tone we gather that her opinion was not to be trusted. But they were still honouring the truce they had declared

[107] *York Courant*, 18 August, 1 September 1761.

[108] LETTERS, 142. While there, he was annoyed by another guest, unidentified, whom he thought pompous. 'Panty' is their old friend, the Rev. Mr Robert Lascelles: 'Panty is mistaken, I quarrel with no one.—There was that coxcomb of ———in the house, who lost temper with me for no reason upon earth but that I could not fall down and worship a brazen image of learning and eloquence, which he set up to the persecution of all true believers—I sat down upon *his altar*, and whistled in the time of his divine service—and broke down his carved work, and kicked his incense pot to the D[evil], so he retreated.'

after their quarrel of 1760, and Shandy Hall was free of domestic squabbles for the time. 'As to matrimony,' Sterne said to Hall, 'I should be a beast to rail at it, for my wife is easy—but the world is not.' Elizabeth had said she would welcome a life in which they were often separated,[109] 'but not in anger is this declaration made—but in pure sober good-sense, built on sound experience' (140). She had even gone so far as to urge Sterne to tutor some nobleman's son whom he could take on the grand tour. As subsequent events show, Elizabeth was quite serious in her opinion that separation was good for them. And Sterne was not going to discourage a notion which so suited his own desires.

The affairs of York Minster meant nothing to him now, and he attended no meetings of the Dean and Chapter. Besides, he had fallen out with Dean Fountayne once more and arrived at an opinion of him which he would not again change – 'a very corrupt man'. He began to question his wisdom in having written the Latin sermon, or *concio ad clerum*, with which Fountayne had obtained the Doctor of Divinity degree at Cambridge. 'He got Honour by it,' grumbled Sterne, 'What Got I?' (147). The DD degree taken *per saltum* entailed a large fee and required a *clerum*, to be preached at Great St Mary's before the undergraduates. Sterne, who in London was often called 'Doctor Sterne', began now to think of taking the degree himself. 'I have wrote a clerum,' he told Hall, 'whether I shall take my doctor's degree or no—I am much in doubt, but I trow not' (142). He never did.

On 22 September 1761 the coronation of His Majesty George III was celebrated throughout his realms. The celebration at Coxwold was a remarkable affair designed by Sterne and the churchwardens for the entertainment and instruction, not only of the villagers, but of people from all over the North Riding. In the end a mob of 3000 crowded into the village. Sterne and the churchwardens purchased a 'Scotch ox' from Lord Fauconberg's herd which was to be roasted whole on a spit. Moreover, as Richard Chapman wrote on 20 September, 'Mr. Sterne hath prevailed with me to give 'im a Bushil of Wheat for Bread so that all the Poor in the Parish may be Satisfied——there will also be a collection for a Drink for 'em.' The entire village was engaged in baking the bread and preparing the drink and

[109] I take this to be Sterne's meaning, though the text of the letter is probably imperfect at this point: 'had I staid from her a second longer it would have been a burning shame – else she declares herself happier without me' (140). The text in LETTERS is based upon MEDALLE, who bowdlerized many of the letters, especially in points concerning her mother.

the bullock. In the manner of the ancient Greeks, the horns of the animal were to be gilded. 'My parishioners will, I suppose, be very merry upon the occasion' (143). They were. A letter of Chapman's describes the day:

> Here a fine ox with his horns gilt was roasted whole in the middle of the town, after which the Bells put in for Church, where an Excelent Sermon was Preached Extempory on the Occation by Mr Sterne, and gave great Content to every hearer, the Church was quite full, both quire and Isle to the very Door.

Sterne may have memorized his sermon, but it was not extemporized. It appeared among his posthumous sermons – 'Asa: A Thanksgiving Sermon', that delightful homily upon a youthful king who brings to a conclusion the war begun by his predecessor – an unmistakable allusion to the new monarch's policy of peace.[110] 'About 3 o'Clock,' Chapman continued,

> the Ox was cut up and Distributed Amongst at least 3000 People, after which two Barrils of Ale was Distributed amongst those that could get nearest to 'em, Ringing of Bells Squibs and Crackers Tarr Barrills and Bonefires, &c and a Ball in the Evening Concluded the Joyful Day.[111]

Since it was not at Newburgh Priory, one supposes the ball was held in the hall of the Tudor school building.

Meanwhile, 'I go on with Tristram' (142). In the seventeenth chapter of the fifth volume, Sterne named the date upon which he – or Tristram – was writing: 10 August 1761. A month later he was well into the sixth volume. To Lady Dacre he said in September, 'I am scribbling away at my Tristram. These two volumes are, I think, the best.—I shall write as long as I live, 'tis, in fact, my hobby-horse' (143). He must have written through the noise of saws and hammers that autumn as Lord Fauconberg's workmen built a stable behind Shandy Hall.[112] He had a good draft of both volumes early in November.

[110] The sermon, which appears in SERMONS as No. XL, can be identified as the one preached upon this occasion because the *York Courant*, 29 September 1761, ran an account of the festivities at Coxwold (given in CURTIS, 146) in which they named the text of Sterne's sermon. Sterne may have given them the story.

[111] CURTIS, 145–6, published originally in the report by the Royal Historical Manuscripts Commission, *Various Collections*, II (1903), 188–9. Curtis appears to have made use of the original, then among WOMBWELL PAPERS, but the letter is no longer with the collection.

[112] Richard Chapman wrote to Lord Fauconberg, 6 August 1761, 'Mr Sterne is

Sterne's manner in V–VI was much the same as in the previous volumes. He twitted his critics as asses (491–2) or Dutch commentators (517). He poked fun at Warburton for his role in the controversy over the historicity of Job (441–2), and probably Warburton is the principal target in Parson Yorick's laughable description of polemic divines as the battling Gymnast and Tripet – a passage Yorick reads or pretends to read from Rabelais: in fact, Sterne had considerably altered it (463–4). He continued to rely heavily upon Burton, Chambers, Locke and Rabelais, and his satire of educational theory made extensive use of Obadiah Walker's *Of Education, Especially of Young Gentlemen* (1673).[113] But this time, turning his laughter inward, he made fun of himself as plagiarist. Tristram vows to lock up the study where his source books are and to throw the key down his 90-foot well (407, 551). Then he scolds himself and all plagiarists in a passage which Sterne had stolen from Robert Burton's complaint against plagiarists!

> Shall we for ever make new books, as apothecaries make new mixtures, by pouring only out of one vessel into another?
>
> Are we for ever to be twisting, and untwisting the same rope? for ever in the same track—for ever at the same pace? (408)

In Volume V and the first half of VI, Sterne completed the story of Walter Shandy's attempt to beget and rear the perfect child. He had Tristram explain that his father 'had lost, by his own computation, full three fourths of me—that is, he had been unfortunate in his three first great casts for me—my geniture, nose, and name' (445). The last fourth is the primary topic of Volumes V–VI, Tristram's education. Walter, ever more circumspect than is called for, carefully sets down his educational theory in a book, the *Tristra-pædia*, but at such a slow rate that the boy, growing faster than the book, is 'neglected' and 'abandoned' to the care and influence of his mother (448). The narrative is not so neatly structured as in the previous two volumes. The two episodes which are fully developed and rendered in vivid detail – the news of Bobby's death, and the Story of Le Fever – do not serve as nuclei for the narrative. They are not part of one chronological sequence, and the digressions, flashbacks and symposia are not necessarily

very much put about for want of a Stable, he has been at me sev[l] times to mention it to your Lordship, if you please to let one be Built for four or five Stands he will pay your Lordship Twelvepence p. pound for what it Costs Building, which may be added to the Rent—': WOMBWELL PAPERS. The stables may be seen today.

[113] Here again, my discussion of Sterne's sources depends heavily upon TS NOTES.

tied to them. Such unity as one finds is imparted through the theme of education – in the broadest sense of the word. We find a hilarious satire of over-refined educationalism in Walter's theory: the North-West Passage to the intellectual world, explains Walter, is the auxiliary verb, in demonstration of which point Walter takes the company upon that comic dance of the white bear through half a dozen pages of the *Tristra-pædia* (484–7). There is a rich, diverse commentary upon related matters – the evolution of language in the digression on the word *whiskers* (409–15); rote learning in Trim's recitation of his catechism (468–70); the ideal tutor in Le Fever's son (498, 520); rhetoric failed in Walter Shandy's funeral oration (418–26); and rhetoric successful in Trim's dropping his hat (432–3). In ironic contrast to Walter's vaunted rationalism, the events in Tristram's life begin to look less and less like the Platonic heaven and more and more like primitive rites of passage. Tristram is circumcised, albeit by accident (449–50). Unconsciously on Walter's part, he has Tristram undergo the puberty rite of 'breeching' (520–33). Finally, in two contrasting funeral scenes, the death of Bobby and the death of Le Fever, we are exposed to the perfectly blundered and perfectly celebrated rites of death.

In the twentieth chapter of the sixth volume, Sterne abruptly drops this story and without apology takes up his other plot – the story of Toby, Trim and the Widow Wadman. He first brings us up to date on the progress of the war upon the bowling green and the old soldiers' miniature town, a perfect Proteus, which served in succession as Landen, Trerebach, Santvliet, Drussen, Hagenau, Ostend, Menin, Aeth and Dendermond (540) – and Liele, on that great day in which Corporal Trim contrived to make the miniature cannon puff tobacco smoke (542–9). This poignant comedy is brought to a close when Fate 'basely patched up the peace of *Utrecht*' (551), ending the campaign and giving Mrs Wadman her chance to seduce Uncle Toby. With the promise of that story, Sterne concluded Volume VI.

Sterne completed his work by putting before the new volumes two mottoes chosen with an eye to those who had criticized him as an indecent priest. He attributed them to Horace and Erasmus, though in fact he took both from Burton's *Anatomy*. 'If I speak too lightly or freely,' goes Burton's version of Horace, 'you will indulge this liberty.' The so-called Erasmus quotation he lifted from Burton's apologetic preface: 'If any quarrelsome persons should censure my jesting as either too light for a divine or too satirical for a decent Christian—not I, but Democritus said it.' Sterne initially intended to include a third, more audacious motto, but decided at the last minute to withdraw it. He had, in fact, quoted a canon law from the fourth-century Second Council of Carthage: 'If any priest or monk engages in jesting words, raising laughter, let him be damned.' Before Sterne actually struck the motto from the manuscript, someone at the printer's shop – or so it seems – had stolen the volumes and sold them to the Dublin printer, Henry Saunders, who in 1762 published a pirated edition including all three mottoes.[114] Since it was exposed, Sterne included the third motto in the second edition when it appeared in 1767.

Sterne had over-exerted himself. In the late autumn he fell ill again. It may be that he came down with a dread disease which spread through the North Riding. 'Almost every body hereabouts are bad in Colds, ague's, and Fevers,' Chapman wrote on 1 November to Lord Fauconberg; and he added ominously, 'a great Many Dies.' On 1 January Sterne wrote to Lady Dacre,

> Indeed I am very ill, having broke a vessel in my lungs—hard writing in the summer, together with preaching, which I have not strength for, is ever fatal to me—but I cannot avoid the latter yet, and the former is too pleasurable to be given up. (150)

Sterne had decided to go to France in search of a more healthful climate. 'I shall set off with great hopes of its efficacy, and shall write to my wife and daughter to come and join me at Paris, else my stay could not be so long' (150). Biographers have supposed that the illness which drove Sterne to France had attacked him in London. Their evidence appears to have been that striking passage in *Tristram Shandy*, VII, when Tristram is interrupted in the midst of telling Eugenius a tawdry story:

> . . . DEATH himself knocked at my door—ye bad him come again; and in so gay a tone of careless indifference, did ye do it, that he doubted of his commission——
>
> '——There must certainly be some mistake in this matter,' quoth he.
>
> . . .Thou has had a narrow escape, Tristram, said Eugenius, taking hold of my hand as I finish'd my story——
>
> But there is no *living*, Eugenius, replied I, at this rate: for as this *son of a whore* has found out my lodgings . . . had I not better, Eugenius, fly for my life? (576–7)

[114] TRISTRAM IN DUBLIN.

The passage exemplifies, not the way an author records events in his life, but the way he idealizes and transforms his experiences. Sterne's decision to go abroad was made in Yorkshire, and it was not a hasty one.[115] He gave a power of attorney to Stephen Croft, who had promised to look after his affairs at Sutton and Stillington, though he wrote the document so carelessly that he had to replace it later (171–2, 176). He arranged for Richard Chapman to manage things for him at Coxwold (201). He already had a well-qualified curate at Sutton and Stillington. Now he was hiring one for Coxwold.

In November he sent his family to their winter house in the Minster Yard, but he lingered on in Coxwold waiting for James Kilner, the new curate. Kilner had taken deacon's orders and was a candidate for the priesthood. He came at a salary of £30, plus the fees, which brought another £3. He had a second position worth an additional £11 assisting Mr Newton, who had taken charge of the grammar and village schools on the death of Mr Midgley. It was a good income for a hired curate. But Kilner was another of those poor clerics without a university degree who would spend his life assisting one parson after another. He was painfully timid, and probably quite holy. He served Coxwold faithfully until Sterne died.[116]

Kilner finally arrived, and Sterne set off for London, stopping briefly at York. He arranged an advertisement for the new volumes, which would be run in the *York Courant* on 1 December.[117] He visited his wife and daughter. A letter arrived from Hall at Skelton Castle, and he sat down in a coffee house to answer it – a revealing letter written entirely in Latin.

> I do not know what is the matter with me, but I am sick and tired of my wife more than ever—and I am possessed by a Devil who drives me to town—and you are possessed by this selfsame evil spirit who

[115] I have changed my position in this matter. In two previous essays I presumed that Sterne fell ill in London: 'Some New Sterne Letters', *TLS*, 8 April 1965, 284; and VOICES SONOROUS AND CRACKED. A noteworthy comment upon Sterne's health and its effect upon his fiction is that of W. B. C. Watkins, 'Yorick Revisited', in his *Perilous Balance*, Princeton, NJ, 1939, pp. 99–156.

[116] CURTIS, 165; correspondence between Kilner and Archbishop Drummond at the Borthwick Institute, R. Bp. 5; Sterne's nomination for a licence, Borthwick Institute: R.IV. A. 1764, p. 11; *Act Book (Institutions), 1755–1768*, fol. 285 (Borthwick Institute: R.I. AB. 14).

[117] The first appearance of Kilner's name in the Coxwold registers was also on 1 December. This correspondence suggests that Sterne left Coxwold late in November and stopped in York. It is possible he was in London as early as 26 November, when an advertisement similar to that in the *Courant* appeared in the *London Chronicle*; or he may have made that arrangement by post.

holds you here in the desert to be tempted by your serving maids[118] and troubled to distraction by your wife—believe me, Antony, this is not the way to salvation in this world or the next. . . . you are not saying in your heart often enough, 'I Antony of the crazy castle am already forty odd years old and have completed my fourth decade and it is time to cure myself, to make myself, Antony, a happy man, a free man, and to do some good to myself, as Soloman exhorts us, that nothing is better in this life than that a man live merrily, and eat and drink and enjoy good things, because this is his portion and dowery in this world.'

And now I intend to write you to say that I ought not to be reprimanded for rushing off to London, because God is my witness I am not hurrying there out of pride or to show myself off; that devil who entered me is not a powerless devil like his cousin Lucifer—but he is a lascivious devil who will not leave me alone; for what with not sleeping with my wife, I am unbearably horny—and I am done to death by desire—and I am made foolish; so you will excuse me, my dear Antony, because you too have been done to death by desire and have travelled over land and sea and have rushed around like a devil with that same devil driving you. I have a lot to write to you—but I am writing this letter in a coffee house full of loud-mouthed companions who do not let me think a single thought.

Greet my friend Panty, whose letter I will reply to—greet my friends in the house of Guisborough, and I beg you to believe me most firmly held in the chains of cousinness and love to you, my Antony.

L. STERNE[119]

[118] An allusion to St Anthony the Abbot, the father of Christian monasticism, who is traditionally believed to have been tempted in the desert by, among other things, naked ladies.

[119] Translation based upon the text in LETTERS, 124–5. Although I must bear responsibility for the translation, I was assisted by Peter Wale of Titirangi, Auckland.

CURTIS, following Wilbur Cross, dated the letter December 1760 (No. 69 in LETTERS). I believe it should be dated November 1761. Sterne wrote the letter from a York coffee house upon the eve, more or less, of his departure for London. The only possible occasions were (1) his journey to London in early December 1760 or (2) his journey of late November 1761. I rule out an earlier visit because Sterne speaks of the possibility of going to town to seek to promote himself or to seek glory – something he would not have said before the appearance of *Tristram Shandy*, I–II. No later date will do because he speaks of living with his wife. The couple never lived together in England after 1761. Of these two possible dates, Curtis assigned the

If he actually had any liaisons with women when he got to London, they have remained a secret.

earlier, but I believe the later more probable. As we have seen, in the autumn of 1760, Sterne and his wife were quarrelling, and he departed from her in anger; but in the autumn of 1761 they had worked out a *modus vivendi*: they would maintain a peaceful home but would welcome periods of separation (140). So Sterne when he went to London in 1761 felt free to have affairs. That he did so is suggested by the 'Memorandums' he prepared for Elizabeth when he was getting ready to go abroad: he would not set down the name of the woman who had a portrait of him (? Catherine Fourmantel), but he would write it in a sealed billet in Mrs Montagu's hand (148). So the Latin letter reflects Sterne's situation in the autumn of 1761: he makes no complaint about his wife, but indicates he has little or no sexual commerce with her; his sexual interests are all in London.

It is puzzling that Lydia Sterne should have included this letter in her edition, *Letters of the Late Rev. Mr. Laurence Sterne, to His Most Intimate Friends*, 1775, since she went to such extremes in that edition to protect her mother. Lydia either forged Letter 1, as CURTIS believed, or, as I believe, redated and readdressed a letter Sterne had written to Eliza Draper so as to make it seem to be addressed to her mother at the time Sterne was courting her (*EMT*, 81–2, n. 3). She would surely not have published the Latin letter had she been able to read it. So the question becomes: who advised her to publish it? No doubt Hall-Stevenson was primarily responsible, since he gave her the original. He had never had much love for Elizabeth Sterne, and he probably had become annoyed with Lydia, who had her mother's knack for alienating her friends. Moreover, being such an enemy to the church, Hall probably delighted in exposing Sterne's indiscretions. But, since Lydia's chief adviser for the edition, and the person to whom she dedicated it, was David Garrick, suspicion also falls upon him.

Paris
1761–1762

Sterne arrived at London in late November 1761. Soon thereafter he met Dr Samuel Johnson – a meeting so displeasing to Johnson that he made certain it did not happen again. The story begins with Sterne's calling upon Lord and Lady Spencer to show them a dedication he had written and to ask permission to print it before the new volumes. The books themselves he hoped to dedicate to his lordship:

> they are the best my talents, with such bad health as I have, could produce:—had providence granted me a larger stock of either, they had been a much more proper present to your Lordship.

The 'Story of Le Fever', that sweet, sad story of how Uncle Toby and Trim take under their care a dying officer and his boy, Sterne wanted to dedicate to Lady Spencer:[1]

> I beg your Lordship will forgive me, if, at the same time I dedicate this work to you, I join Lady SPENCER, in the liberty I take of inscribing the story of *Le Fever* in the sixth volume to her name; for which I have no other motive, which my heart has informed me of, but that the story is a humane one. (405)

The loose syntax of this had repercussions. Lord and Lady Spencer granted the permission, and Sterne went off to Sir Joshua Reynolds's. There among

[1] A MS of the 'Story of Le Fever' used to be preserved at Spencer House. It was endorsed in Lord Spencer's hand, 'The Story of Le Fever, sent to me by Sterne before it was published': *Second Report of the Royal Commission on Historical Manuscripts*, 1871, p. 20.

the assembled guests was Dr Johnson. 'In a company where I lately was,' Johnson later reported,

> Tristram Shandy introduced himself; and Tristram Shandy had scarcely sat down, when he informed us that he had been writing a Dedication to Lord Spencer; and sponte suâ he pulled it out of his pocket; and sponte suâ, for nobody desired him, he began to read it; and before he had read half a dozen lines, sponte meâ, sir, I told him it was not English, sir.[2]

What happened next is recorded in a second anecdote:

> I was but once, said Johnson, in Sterne's company, and then his only attempt at merriment consisted in his display of a drawing too indecently gross to have delighted even in a brothel.[3]

The third scene of this comedy was told by Phillipina Lady Knight:

> Doctor Johnson was so much hurt by the Indelicate Conversation of Laurence Sterne that he quited his Company one Evening at Sir J Reynolds', and soon after told Miss Reynolds y[t] he would rather give up the pleasure of her brother's society then meet such a Contemptible Priest as Sterne.[4]

[2] 'Account of Dr. Johnson's Visit to Cambridge, in 1765', a letter signed by B[aptist] N[oel] Turner, 17 October 1818, and published in the *New Monthly Magazine*, X (1 December 1818), 385–91; reprinted in ILLUSTRATIONS, VI, 156. Since the remark was made in 1765, Melvyn New in TS NOTES, 338, suggests that Johnson might have been talking about another, later dedication to Spencer written for Volumes VII–VIII (published January 1765) but suppressed for some reason. The hypothesis rests upon Johnson's saying that he met Sterne 'lately'. Since the anecdote represents only Turner's memory of Johnson's words, I do not think one ought to give so much weight to the word. The alternative explanation, which New also lays out, is the simpler: that Johnson in 1765 was talking about his meeting with Sterne in 1761.

[3] George Steevens, 'Johnsoniana', *European Magazine*, VII (January 1785), 51–5. These are miscellaneous anecdotes and sayings of Johnson collected from public papers because, said Steevens, 'we have every reason to rely on their authenticity'. But we do not know where Steevens found this particular story and why he thought it authentic. 'Johnsoniana' was included by Sir John Hawkins in his edition of Johnson's *Works*, 1787, XI, 195–216. On the basis of that source, George Birkbeck Hill repeated the anecdote in BOSWELL, II, 222, n. 2, and L. F. Powell left it undisturbed.

[4] Marginal note in Phillipina Lady Knight's copy of Boswell's *Life*, 1st edn, 1791, II, 503, opposite Johnson's remarks to Boswell in 1784 on obscenity and impiety being repressed in good company. Lady Knight (1727–99), widow of Admiral Sir Joseph Knight, frequented Johnson's house

The scene is only as reliable as its three sources, but all three have been used by reputable Johnsonian scholars. That the three things happened together is implied in Johnson's saying that he met Sterne only once. Sterne, then, caught off guard by Johnson's attack upon his prose style, struck back with the first weapon that came to hand, a pornographic picture which he had in his other pocket. Johnson quitted the field, threatening to stay away if Reynolds continued to entertain Sterne. There is nothing unlikely about the story. Reynolds did not stop seeing Sterne, but no doubt he stopped inviting him when Johnson was to be present.[5]

Sterne had a great deal to do, for he had become his own publisher once more. If Dodsley was the one who backed out of the arrangement, it may have been because of the bad press, which was continuing. In October 1761 there had appeared a scurrilous pamphlet entitled *A Funeral Discourse, Occasioned by the Much Lamented Death of Mr. Yorick, Prebendary of Y—k and Author*, a mock funeral sermon for Yorick's dead wit, peppered with scandalous, inaccurate gossip. On the other hand, Sterne, who had proved his abilities as a publisher with the first edition of Tristram Shandy, I–II,

---

as a friend of Anna Williams, Johnson's hostess. Other of her anecdotes have been accepted without question. See BOSWELL, VI. Her copy of the *Life* is now at the Princeton University Library.

[5] Johnson's dislike of Sterne never abated. The following anecdotes are told of him. 'Mr. Sterne, it may be supposed, was no great favourite with Dr. Johnson, and a lady once ventured to ask the grave doctor, how he liked Yorick's Sermons.—"I know nothing about them, Madam," was his reply. But sometime afterwards, forgetting himself, he severely censured them; and the lady very aptly retorted: "I understood you to say, Sir, that you had never read them."—"No, Madam, I did read them, but it was in a stage-coach; I should not have even deigned to have looked at them, had I been at large."' (CRADDOCK, I, 208.)

'I [Mr. Wiggins, the Lichfield draper] then showed him Sterne's *Sermons*. "Sir," said he, "do you ever read any others?" "Yes, Doctor; I read Sherlock, Tillotson, Beveridge, and others." "Ay, Sir, *there* you drink the cup of salvation to the bottom; here you have merely the froth from the surface."' (*Johnsonian Miscellanies*, ed. George Birkbeck Hill, 2 vols, 1897, II, 429.)

'Her vivacity [Miss Monckton's] enchanted the Sage, and they used to talk together with all imaginable ease. A singular instance happened one evening, when she insisted that some of Sterne's writings were very pathetic. Johnson bluntly denied it. "I am sure (said she) they have affected *me*."—"why (said Johnson, smiling, and rolling himself about,) "that is, because, dearest, you're a dunce."' (BOSWELL, IV, 109.)

'I censured some ludicrous fantastick dialogues between two coach-horses, and other such stuff, which Baretti had lately published. He joined with me, and said, "Nothing odd will do long. *Tristram Shandy* did not last."' (BOSWELL, II, 449.)

See also BOSWELL, II, 222, cited above, Chapter 1.

may have been the one who made the break. In any event, he had known Dodsley was out before he left Yorkshire, though he had not completed his new arrangements. The advance advertisements he had placed in the *London Chronicle* for 24–6 November and the *York Courant* of 1 December had named no bookseller. But the advertisements for the new volumes which commenced on 17 December in the *London Chronicle* and other newspapers named the booksellers T. Becket and P. A. Dehondt at the Tully's Head in the Strand, and added the information. 'sold by all Booksellers in Town and Country'.[6]

Sterne had little or nothing to do with the Dutch partner, Peter Dehondt, but Thomas Becket became his most important business associate and in time one of his closest friends. As a bookseller, Becket's star was rising, largely because of the patronage of David Garrick. 'A plain, stirring, honest, agreeable fellow,' Garrick said of him; 'He is not over genteel in his address. I call him the *worm*, from an agreeable vermicular motion he has with his arms and legs.'[7] Becket undertook to be Sterne's principal bookseller and the agent who would distribute his books to other booksellers and collect the money from them. Sterne would take the financial risk, perhaps with borrowed money, and make the principal business agreements. He purchased the paper from William Edmonds, a stationer in the Poultry.[8] He arranged for the printing at the shop of William Strahan, remembered today as the publisher and friend of Johnson and Hume.[9]

Sterne may also have intended a Dublin edition, but he was pushed out by the piratical bookseller, Henry Saunders. Saunders, who had already pirated Volumes I–IV, now brought out V–VI at a cost so low no one could

[6] *London Chronicle* for 15–17 and 17–19 December; the *Public Advertiser* for 16, 17, 18 and 19 December; the *St. James's Chronicle* for 17–19 December.

[7] Garrick to Berenger, 3 March 1771, in Historical Manuscripts Commission Report, *Fortescue*, I, 160. CURTIS, 167–8, has an excellent summary of the known information about Becket.

[8] CURTIS's identification of him as a William Edmonds, stationer in the Poultry (169), is confirmed by a letter of Lydia Sterne which has recently come to light in the collection of the Houghton Library, undated but clearly addressed to Becket in December 1768.

[9] MONKMAN, 25–6, explains: 'Sterne had not simply changed publishers. He had gone into the game again himself, as he had done with the York edition. We know this because, fortunately, he chose William Strahan as printer, and the record remains in one of his ledgers in the British Museum: "Decr Revd Mr Sterne Tristram Shandy, Vol. 5 & 6th 20 sheets N° 4000 @ £2:10:0", followed by the happy touch: "Drink-money to the Men, by Order £1:1:0." The bill came to £51.1*s*.'

compete – 120 pages for $6\frac{1}{2}d$. Sterne never regained control of his books in Ireland.[10]

Hall must have got to London shortly after Sterne, and no doubt they talked much about publishing. Hall's second book, *Fables for Grown Gentlemen; or, a Fable for Every Day in the Week*, was published by Dodsley on 11 December 1761, only a few days before Sterne's volumes appeared.[11] This book was less offensive than Hall's productions of the year before, but also less entertaining. Here he used the animal fable for purposes of social or political satire. Hall was a sportsman, and his pictures of animals, especially dogs, can be winning. But the satire is enervated, and the jerky verse, which Hall thought resembled a Fontaine's, annoying. The best piece is probably 'The Dog and the Cat', a satire of self-serving politicians which likens William Pitt, who had stepped down from the cabinet, and Henry Legge, who had been dismissed as Chancellor of the Exchequer, to a dog and cat who had co-operated in order to get the spoils from the master's table. 'The Wild Ducks and the Water Spaniel' was timely: it made fun of Spain for her threat to enter the war in support of France – something which indeed happened a few days later.

On 21 December, the day before the new volumes were to appear, Sterne went to court, where the new king attended. By an unfortunate circumstance, he was introduced to His Majesty along with the biblical scholar, Alexander Cruden. Cruden, a brilliant, saintly, mad and lovable Scotsman, had just brought out the second edition of his great *Concordance to the Holy Scriptures*, which would be put up for sale side by side with *Tristram Shandy*, V–VI. The king paid the closest attention to Cruden, 'taking him by the hand, and thanking him for the service he had done to the cause of religion'. But to Sterne

> the King made so slight a bow, that the disappointed Author told the noble Lord by whom he was presented that he was confident that the King could not have distinctly heard his name, and begged to be presented a second time. On his name being again announced, the King replied to the Nobleman, 'My Lord, you have told me so already.'[12]

[10] TRISTRAM IN DUBLIN.

[11] Date given by Ralph Straus, *Robert Dodsley, Poet, Publisher, and Playwright*, 1910, p. 375.

[12] Told by the Rev. Mr Jonas Dennis, *A Key to the Regalia; or, The Emblematic Design of the Various Forms Observed in the Ceremonial of a Coronation*, 1820, pp. 102–3, n.

Tristram Shandy, V–VI, was published on 22 December 1761. Advertisements announcing its appearance on 'this day' were run in the *Public Advertiser* and the *St. James's Chronicle*.[13] The similar advertisement in the *London Chronicle* for 19–22 December carried an unusual additional announcement: 'Every book is signed by the author.' Sterne was probably worried about a pamphlet which had appeared just three days before, the *Life and Amours of Hafen Slawkenbergius, Author of the Institute of Noses*, which, said the advertisement in the *London Chronicle*, was printed 'in the Size and Manner of Tristram Shandy, in order that so valuable a Supplement may be preserved by being bound at the End of the Sixth Volume.'[14] So Sterne took unusual precautions against forgery: he sat at the bindery and signed every copy of Volume V. He may not have predicted that his signature would become a sort of trademark which his public would expect in subsequent instalments.

The books were received with no great éclat. '*Tristram Shandy* may perhaps go on a little longer,' wrote Boswell in his journal; 'but we will not follow him. With all his drollery there is a sameness of extravagance which tires us. We have just a succession of Surprise, surprise, surprise.'[15] What little commendation they received was limited to the sentimental scenes. The January *Gentleman's Magazine* ran an excerpt from the 'Story of Le Fever', praising it as a '*master-piece of its kind*', which '*does the Writer great credit*'. The announcement in the *British Magazine* for January complimented the 'many pathetick touches of nature'. There were two genuine reviews. That in the *Critical Review* for January deplored Sterne's attempt to imitate Rabelais; but, 'if our author has sometimes lost sight of Rabelais, he has directed his eye to a still greater original, even nature herself. The episode of Le Fever is beautifully pathetic, and exhibits the character of Toby and his corporal in such a point of view, as must endear them to every reader of sensibility.'[16] John Langhorne, a minor poet and hack, covered the volumes for the January issue of the *Monthly Review*. He once again decried Sterne's behaviour as a priest and insisted that his excellence lay 'not so much in the humorous as in the pathetic; and in this

[13] A second edition of the volumes appeared in 1767: MONKMAN.

[14] Also advertised in the *St. James's Chronicle* for 24–6 December and included, along with *Tristram Shandy*, V–VI, in the *Gentleman's Magazine* book list in the December issue.

[15] *Private Papers*, ed. Geoffrey Scott, 19 vols, 1928–34, I, 127.

[16] HOWES, 138–40.

opinion we have been confirmed by the . . . story of Le Fever.'[17] Sterne did not much resist this line of comment. As he wrote to Lady Dacre,[18] '"Le Fever's story has beguiled your ladyship of your tears," and the thought of the accusing spirit flying up heaven's chancery with the oath, you are kind enough to say is sublime—my friend, Mr. Garrick, thinks so too, and I am most vain of his approbation' (150).

Relatively little ephemera appeared. There was another in the series of admonitory letters: *An Admonitory Letter to the Rev Mr S—— upon the Publication of his Fifth and Sixth Volumes . . . by a Layman.*[19] There was also some bogus scholarship in *The Life, Travels, and Adventures of Christopher Wagstaff, Gentleman, Grandfather to Tristram Shandy* (1762).[20] This thin volume opens with a preface that attempts to demonstrate that Sterne had copied John Dunton's *Voyage Round the World* (1691), but the narrative which follows is a mish-mash of Sternean imitations and passages from Dunton. It was printed by Sterne's erstwhile bookseller in York, John Hinxman, who had recently moved his business to London.

The clergy, on the whole, were silent about Volumes V–VI. Some of them may have found the books acceptable because of the sentimental parts. But there is a more likely explanation. In the spring and summer of 1761 there had been a great mortality among the bishops. Hoadley of Winchester died in April, Sherlock of London in July, and Archbishop Gilbert of York in August. The shift of prelates which followed was advantageous to Sterne. Dr Thomas Newton, Precentor of York, whose letters we have often cited, was elevated to the See of Bristol. Although Newton was never known to gainsay his friend Warburton, he liked Sterne personally. To London came Thomas Hayter, once Subdean of the Minster and Archdeacon of York, a man with whom Sterne had been allied in Yorkshire politics years before. Hayter lived but one year more and at his death was followed at London by a much closer friend of Sterne's, Richard Osbaldeston, the former Dean of York. But most important was the elevation to the See of York of Robert Hay Drummond. Drummond was a Yorkshireman who seems to have known Sterne previously. Born Robert Hay, second son of George Hay, Earl of Kinnoul, he had taken the name of

[17] HOWES, 140–1.

[18] Tentatively identified by CURTIS, 143–4, as Anne Pratt (1719–1806), wife of Thomas Barrett-Lennard (1717–86), afterwards seventeenth Baron Dacre of the South. Curtis thought that Letters 79, 82 and 96 were addressed to her.

[19] *NCBEL*.

[20] Reissued in the Garland Press series, *Sterneiana*, VIII, New York, 1975.

Drummond to become principal heir of his great-grandfather, William Drummond, Viscount Strathallan. As a royal chaplain, he had accompanied George II on his German campaigns and preached before him the victory sermon after Dettingen. He became Bishop of St Asaph at a young age, was translated to Salisbury in 1761, and four months later to York. He would soon become Lord High Almoner and member of the Privy Council of George III. But wealth and power did not corrupt Drummond. Unlike most aristocratic bishops, he was a hard worker who reorganized and reformed the administration of the northern church. He was devoted to his wife and numerous children and spent all the time he could afford with his family at Broadsworth, his estate close to Doncaster. His conviviality and hospitality were well known, and his hospitality extended to Sterne. 'In his Grace's *Concio ad clerum*,' Sterne would write, 'I do not find myself a very principal figure, but in his private hours, he is always most cordial to me.'[21] And in the *Journal to Eliza* he would describe him as 'this good Prelate, who is one of our most refined Wits—& the most of a gentleman of our order' (380). Drummond became Sterne's protector, not legally, and perhaps not out of any intention, but simply by paying no attention to any criticism levelled against his celebrated subordinate. Sterne would never again feel such weight of moral pressure as had been brought to bear upon him the year before.

Bishop Warburton, however, did not change his mind: 'Sterne has published his fifth and sixth Volumes of Tristram,' he wrote to Hurd on 27 December. 'They are wrote pretty much like the first and second; but whether they will restore his reputation . . . with the publick, is another question.—The fellow himself is an irrecoverable scoundrel.'[22]

By contrast, Sterne at this juncture was high in the estimation of Elizabeth Montagu. He came to her for sympathy in his troubles with his wife and showed her Elizabeth's letters. 'I have seen many letters of hers from York to him,' she later wrote to her sister, '& she was always taking frump at somebody & for ever in quarrels & frabbles.'[23] Mrs Montagu included him in her dinner parties, where he sat at table with her favourite

[21] This sentence, taken from William Combe's largely forged *Original Letters*, 1788 (Letter V, 26–7), is one of the few which HAMILTON believes can be accepted as genuine. Information on Archbishop Drummond from *DNB*.

[22] *Letters from a Late Eminent Prelate to One of His Friends*, 1809, p. 335.

[23] Letter to Sarah Scott, 11 April 1765: Huntington Library, MO 5820. Since Elizabeth was abroad from 1762, Mrs Montagu was recalling letters Sterne had showed her in 1760 and 1761.

friends. One of these was the elder statesman, William Pulteney, Earl of Bath, then in his seventy-seventh year. She had commissioned Reynolds to paint the old man, but was unhappy with the likeness. To entice him back to Reynolds's studio and to put him in a good mood for the sitting, she promised him the company of Sterne. He wrote in answer,

> On Wednesday about one of the clock, I will most certainly be, at Mr. Reynolds's, to mend my sickly looks, and to sitt down in my Chair, as I should do; instead of being half standing, which criticism of Mr. Sternes, I think perfectly right. As for my looks I fear, they will not be much mended, by any Physick of Mr. Reynolds. He has made an old man, look as if he was in pain, which an old man generally is, and so far he is right.[24]

Elizabeth Montagu, delighted with herself for having managed a confluence of three such 'great and extraordinary subjects' as Bath, Reynolds and Sterne, sent a note to Elizabeth Vesey inviting her to join the fun.

> Will my dear Mrs. Vesey go with me tomorrow at half an hour after one to Mr. Reynolds, where my Lord Bath is to sit for his picture? Where y[e] facetious author of Tristram Shandy is to make him smile? and where you may see the historical picture in which the Muses of Tragedy and Comedy are disputing for Mr. Garrick? If all these temptations cannot allure you, what more can I offer?[25]

The meeting of the great ones took place on the afternoon of 30 December, three days before Sterne left for Paris.

The problem of how Sterne was to get into France while she was at war with England must have occupied much of Sterne's attention in the last weeks of 1761. By now it seemed inevitable that the peace policy of Bute would eventually carry the day, but the imminent war with Spain would delay the peace. The frontiers of France remained officially closed. Nevertheless, Sterne with the help of friends found a way: he would travel

[24] Reginald Blunt (ed.), *Mrs. Montagu: 'Queen of the Blues': Her Letters and Friendships from 1762 to 1800*, 2 vols, [1923], I, 14. See also Lord Bath's letter to Mrs Montagu in CLIMENSON, II, 269. Algernon Graves and William Vine Cronin in *History and Works of Sir Joshua Reynolds*, 4 vols, 1899, I, 63–4, describe the painting. They say Lord Bath presented it to Mrs Montagu, but I think it more likely that she commissioned it.

[25] Blunt, *Mrs. Montagu*, I, 14. Graves and Cronin also describe the picture of 'Garrick between Tragedy and Comedy' in *History and Works*, I, 350–1.

in the diplomatic party of George Pitt, later to be created Earl Rivers of Stratfieldsaye, who had just been made Envoy Extraordinary and Minister Plenipotentiary to the Court of Turin.[26]

In all probability the arrangement had been made through the Rev. Dr Henry Egerton, squire and Rector of Settrington, near Malton, Chancellor of Hereford Cathedral and Treasurer of Bangor, a clergyman so wealthy that, as William Mason told him, '£1,000 will hardly fill one of your hollow teeth.'[27] When he was in London, 'Henry the Great', as Sterne called him, lived in the house of his mother, Lady Betty Egerton, widow of the Bishop of Hereford and mother to the Bishop of Bangor – Henry's eldest brother, John. Lady Betty kept about her in her house in Albemarle Street a tribe of sons and daughters and their families, most of whom Sterne had met at York races.[28] 'Let me tell You how much I am debtor to You all,' Sterne

[26] EGERTON LETTERS. George Pitt (1721–1803) was the eldest son of George Pitt of Stratfieldsaye, Hampshire. He attended Winchester School and Magdalen College, Oxford. He was a handsome, polished man, and in his youth had been a favourite of Lady Mary Wortley Montague. He married Penelope, daughter of Sir Hervey Atkins of Surrey, by whom he had several children. She was considered a beauty and was celebrated by Walpole in his poem, 'The Beauties'. But he could not be faithful, and the couple finally separated. He represented Shaftesbury in the Commons, 1742–7, and Dorset, 1747–77. He had been a member of the opposition during the reign of George II, and so was rewarded by George III by being made a Groom of the Bedchamber in 1760, Envoy Extraordinary and Minister Plenipotentiary to Turin, 1762–4, and to Spain, 1770. Created Baron Rivers of Stratfieldsaye, 1776, and Baron Rivers of Sudeley Castle, 1802. See *DNB*; NAMIER AND BROOKE; DUTENS, II, 56–60 and *passim*; John Heneage Jesse, *George Selwyn and His Contemporaries*, 4 vols, 1843–4, I, 322; D. B. Horn, *British Diplomatic Representatives, 1689–1789*, 1932.

[27] Quoted by Kenneth Monkman, letter to the editor, *TLS*, 6 May 1965.

[28] Dr Henry Egerton, the father (1688–1746), had been Rector of Whitchurch, Shropshire, Prebendary of Christ Church, Oxford, and from 1723/4 Bishop of Hereford. He was the son of John Egerton, third Earl of Bridgewater (1646–1700/1). Dr Egerton married Lady Elizabeth Anna Bentinck (d. 1765), daughter of William, Earl of Portland. Their eldest son was John (1721–87), Rector of Ross, Hertfordshire, Prebend of Hertford Cathedral; Chaplain in Ordinary to George II; Dean of Hereford, 1750; Bishop of Bangor, 1756; Bishop of Coventry and Lichfield, 1768; Bishop of Durham, 1771. His wife was Lady Anne Sophia, daughter and co-heiress of Henry de Grey, Duke of Kent. The second son was Lt-Col. William Egerton, who had various ranks in the second troop of Horse Guards and represented Brackley in the Commons, 1768–80. He served as a yeoman clerk of the Jewel Office, and from 1779 until his death in 1783 as Lt-Governor of the Scilly Islands. The youngest son, Charles, had various ranks in the 94th Foot, but spent twenty-five years as a half-pay officer. He died 1793. Henry Egerton and his brothers were first cousins to Francis Egerton, third Duke of Bridgewater (1736–1803), the famous 'Canal Duke', who had completed

would write from Dover, '& That I love & reverance you, from the *highest* to the lowest. . . . I hate the word when I am talking of the Egertons.'[29] And a month later he wrote to Henry, 'I verily believe I owe to your good Offices my Life—& I tell the story of y[r] kindness to me every day.'[30] It may be that the family had performed some extraordinary service such as taking Sterne into their house or nursing him. But more probably Sterne was thanking them for making the arrangements for him to travel in Pitt's party. The Egerton family had a particular friend in Richard Phelps, a scholarly, entertaining man who wrote Latin verses and sang tenor at the Catch Club.[31] Phelps in turn was a friend of Pitt, with whom he served in the Dorset Militia, and was going to Turin with him as his secretary. No doubt Phelps, at the Egertons' request, had interceded on Sterne's behalf.

In all probability Pitt was taking several other people besides Sterne. It was customary for a travelling diplomat to bring along ten or twelve gentlemen or even ladies who would otherwise not have been able to cross the border.[32] Mrs Pitt was to accompany her husband.[33] The way would be made easy for this party, since Pitt, as Minister to Turin, was expected to play a role in the peace negotiations. It was well known that the Kingdom of

in 1761 the first of his canals, that between Worsley and Salford. See Robert Clutterbuck, *History and Antiquities of the County of Hertford*, 3 vols, 1815, I, 390–2; Le Neve and Hardy, *Fasti Ecclesiæ Anglicanæ*, 3 vols, 1854; army lists; *Registrum Orielense*, ed. Charles Lancelot Shadwell, 2 vols, 1902, II, 118–19; NAMIER AND BROOKE; *DNB* article on John Egerton (1721–87); *Journal of the Commissioners for Trade and Plantations, 1768–1775*, 1937, *passim*; and the 'Ashridge II Collection' of papers at the Hertfordshire Record Office, AH 2161, 2162, and others.

[29] EGERTON LETTERS.

[30] Sterne to Henry Egerton, Paris, 8 March: EGERTON LETTERS.

[31] Richard Phelps (d. 1771) was born at Eye, Hereford, son of Rev. Mr George Phelps, Custos of the College of Hereford and Rector of All Saints, Hereford. He attended Winchester School, where he became a friend of George Pitt, and New College, Oxford. He travelled as tutor to the Duke of Beaufort and others, served in the Dorsetshire Regiment of Militia, and was a member of the Catch Club and the Society of Dilettanti. Secretary to the legation at Turin 1761–3; Under-Secretary of State to the fourth Earl of Sandwich; Provost Marshal of the Leeward Islands, 1768. See Horn, *British Diplomatic Representatives*; ILLUSTRATIONS, I, 713–21; ANECDOTES, III, 135, 144, 613; *Journal of the Commissioners for Trade and Plantations 1764–1767*, 1936, pp. viii, 2, 109, 314; Frank Spencer, *The Fourth Earl of Sandwich*, 1961, p. 72; Leslie Lewis, *Connoisseurs and Secret Agents*, 1961, pp. 25–6.

[32] Pitt's predecessor at Turin, Stuart Mackenzie, when he set out for Turin in 1758, took along a dozen gentlemen and noblemen who needed the help of a diplomat to cross the border: reported by DUTENS, I, 166–8.

[33] WALPOLE, XXI, 548.

Sardinia, of which Turin was the capital, had begun quiet, unofficial negotiations.

'Dear Garrick,' Sterne wrote on 24 December, two days after the new volumes appeared, 'upon reviewing my finances, this morning, wth some unforeseen expences—I find I should set out with 20 p^{ds} less—than a prudent man ought—will You lend me twenty pounds [?]' (146). Garrick did. Garrick and Becket had agreed to look after Sterne's finances, Becket to collect the money from the sale of the volumes and Garrick to invest it in stocks (147). Sterne settled with his landlord, for he was giving up his Pall Mall lodgings. He was sending his trunks to Hall's house in John Street, including one full of sermons (146). He called upon Archbishop Drummond and asked permission to leave, which His Grace 'most humanely' gave (150). The request and the permission were polite formalities; neither was required in canon law.

He put in Mrs Montagu's hands a will, leaving everything to Elizabeth and Lydia. It eventually vanished, probably because Sterne destroyed it. But the document he left with it survives in manuscript, dated 28 December 1761 and headed 'Memorandums Left with Mrs Montague, In Case I should die abroad'. If he should die, he told Elizabeth, she should publish the sermons in the trunk at Hall's – '2 Vols, to be picked out of them—NB. There are enough for 3 Vol^{s}' (146).

> My Letters, in my Bureau at Coxwould & a Bundle in the Trunk with my Sermons–
>
> Note. The large pile of Letters in the Garrets at York, to be sifted over, in search for some either of Wit, or Humor—or what is better than both—of Humanity & good nature—these will make a couple of Vol^{s} more.—and as not one of 'em was ever wrote, like Popes or Voitures to be printed, they are more likely to be read. (146)

If she needed them, Elizabeth had his permission to publish *A Political Romance*, which three years before Sterne had published, and then withdrawn from circulation, and the *Concio ad clerum* he had written for Dean Fountayne to get his doctor's degree. Elizabeth was to collect the money due from Sterne's livings, sell the farms, the library, and the copyright to Volumes V–VI; this money she was to lay out in government securities. He plucked up the courage to say something which revealed an interest in another woman; he told her he would leave a sealed billet in which was the name of a woman who had the painting of himself and his friend dressed as mountebank and macaroni. Recollecting those painful times when he had kept Elizabeth's small fortune from the hands of his grasping mother, he commanded her not to impoverish herself to Lydia's husband if Lydia were to marry. 'I charge you,—I charge you over again, (that you may remember it ye more and ballance it more)—That upon no Delusive prospect, or promise from any one, You leave Y^{r}self DEPENDENT; reserve enough for y^{r} comfort—or let her wait y^{r} Death' (147). The thought brought to mind his sister Catherine. 'If Lydia sh^{d} dye before You: Leave my Sister, something worthy of Y^{r}self—in Case You do not think it meet to purchase an annuity for your greater Comfort: if You chuse that—do it in God's name' (147). Having said that, he was ready to depart.

On 2 January 1762 the *Public Advertiser* announced:

> This Morning the Hon. George Pitt, Member in the present Parliament for Dorsetshire, will set out from his House in Bolton-Row for Dover, in order to embark for the Court of Turin on his Embassy.[34]

At the moment there was much excitement over Spain's belated entry into the war. The public knew that England had broken off diplomatic relations with Spain two days before and that the Spanish ambassador had left London. Actually, as Pitt would have known, the king had declared war on Spain on 2 January, the day the party left London, though the declaration would not be published until the fourth. It was not until 6 January that the *Public Advertiser* noticed Sterne's departure:

> The Rev. Mr. Sterne, Author of Tristram Shandy, is gone to Paris for the Recovery of his Health, which has been in a declining Way for some Time Past.

Pitt and Phelps travelled in their militia uniforms, the better to assert their authority. By 4 January they were in Chatham, then the chief clearing house for travellers going abroad and the chief arsenal of the navy. 'Here am I intent upon Regimental matters,' Phelps wrote to Henry Egerton, 'as we are detain'd a day or two, upon account of some Barrack disputes. . . . waiting for answers from Commissioners, Quarter Masters, &c is almost as bad as attending a wind.'[35] Sterne walked along the waterfront where a

[34] The same notice was carried in the *London Chronicle* for 31 December–2 January.

[35] Phelps to Henry Egerton, Chatham, 4 January: EGERTON LETTERS.

multitude of boats rode at anchor and looked at the warehouses and repair yards and factories for making ropes and chains and nautical gear.[36] The sea air blowing up the mouth of the Medway delighted him and convinced him his lungs were mending. He scribbled a hasty note to enclose in Phelps's letter:

Chatham, Tuesday

My dear friend—

Chatham! Yes-Yes, here I am—no matter why or wherefore—but what is more material, I am much mended even at Chatham!—Goodness! What shall . . . the balsamic air of Languedoc do for me—when this Puddle Dock has set me up. God bless you all.

Y^rs in Domino
LS[37]

Their difficulties at Chatham took up most of the week.

At Dover, the party lodged at the Cross Keys[38] while awaiting a wind. Phelps wrote to Egerton again saying that Sterne did not look well, but made the mistake of letting Sterne know what he had written. Sterne was furious:

> Phelps is a son of a Bitch for saying I was worse than when I left You for I am ten, nay 15 per Cent better, only he took his Idea of me, from a pale sour face I set one morning upon a fit of the Gripes, the pains of wch I kept to myself tho I could not the mortified Looks, which he took to be the forerunners of my Exit not into France, but into the Vale of Jehosophat.[39]

The party crossed in a packet belonging to the Huguenot family of Minet, and if the breeze was strong could easily have made the crossing in three hours.[40] Most passengers got sick – as did Tristram Shandy:

[36] Described engagingly by Daniel Defoe in his *Tour thro' the Whole Island of Great Britain*, 2nd edn, 1738, I, 151–5. One need not take seriously Tristram's comment in Volume VII of TRISTRAM SHANDY, 'I never ... took notice of the dock of Chatham' (577).

[37] EGERTON LETTERS.

[38] Presumed from the fact that Sterne in June instructed his wife to lodge there (177).

[39] Sterne to Henry Egerton, Dover, [11 January 1762]: EGERTON LETTERS.

[40] CURTIS, 168, 465, discusses the packet boats owned by William Minet and Co. and the nephew, Hughes Minet, who was acquainted with Sterne and his family. The Rev. William Cole, Rector of Bletchley,

Pray captain, quoth I, as I was going down into the cabin, is a man never overtaken by *Death* in this passage?

Why, there is not time for a man to be sick in it, replied he——What a cursed lyar! for I am sick as a horse, quoth I, already——what a brain!——upside down!——hey dey! the cells are broke loose one into another. . . .

Sick! sick! sick! sick!——(578)

At Calais there would have been French customs officers and military officers to get past. They put in at the Lyon d'Argent, 'the master a Turk in grain' (177), said Sterne in his first reference to Pierre Quillacq, called Dessin, whom Sterne was to immortalize in the opening pages of *A Sentimental Journey*. Dessin, who had recently leased the inn, was not yet well known to English travellers, but the inn itself was famous in England as the best and most comfortable in Calais.[41]

From Calais through the rest of the journey, Pitt and his group would have been spied upon constantly. It had been so throughout the war. Louis Dutens, chargé d'affaires at Turin, who was awaiting Pitt's arrival, had often spoken in his dispatches to Whitehall of the spies about him when he travelled through France, at one time complaining that they were so numerous as to prevent him from carrying on his own intelligence activities.[42]

It is tempting to look into Sterne's fiction for evidence of his experience as a traveller, but caution is needed. Sterne wrote the travel narrative in

described his crossing on 17 October 1765: 'Very fine day. At 10 o'Clock in the Morning I went aboard the Pacquet Boat, & arrived at Calais in 3 Hours & 4 or 5 Minutes, during which Time every Passenger was sick except myself, it being a rough Sea, tho' an exceeding fine Day': *A Journal of My Journey to Paris in the Year 1765*, ed. Francis Griffin Stokes, 1931, p. 6.

[41] CURTIS, 175, 177–8, 261. The friar, Father Felix, whom Mrs Piozzi met at Calais, is sometimes said to have been Sterne's model for the Monk of *A Sentimental Journey*. But Mrs Piozzi had not intended the identification: she made no mention of Sterne in her account, *Observations and Reflections Made in the Course of a Journey through France, Italy, and Germany*, ed. Herbert Barrows, Ann Arbor, n.d., 4. The anonymous author of *The American Wanderer through Various Parts of Europe*, 1783, enquired of Dessin about Sterne's Monk and was assured 'that no monk any way answering that description, ever in his time, lived at Calais' (216–17).

[42] DUTENS, I, 220–2, described his spying activities while serving as chargé d'affaires. His description of the spies who hampered him in Paris is contained in his decoded dispatch dated 10 March [?1761] among the numerous dispatches of Dutens and Pitt at the PRO: SP 92, Vol. 69.

Tristram Shandy, VII, and *A Sentimental Journey* while sitting at his ease in his study in Coxwold. When he wanted facts, he took them from post books and travel books. He was perfectly open about this in *Tristram Shandy*, which is in part a satire upon travellers and travel books. Tristram says in Chapter 4 that he knows nothing about Calais, and then goes on slyly to suggest that by 'drawing this from that' and 'putting this and that together' he could easily write a chapter on Calais anyway (580). He then proceeds to do just that, lifting all his material straight out of Jean Aimar Piganiol de la Force, *Nouveau Voyage de France*.[43] We do not know how much Sterne actually saw of Calais on this journey, but we know he would pass through the town three more times before he wrote the Calais scenes of *A Sentimental Journey*.

The party left Calais on the Paris stage, one or more 'great lumbering coaches' each holding as many as ten persons, including the servants who sat on the top. Two postillions rode, shouting and cursing, upon two of the eight small horses that dragged each of these ungainly machines. Yet they went at 'a tolerably good rate', thanks to a well-paved road.[44]

Inevitably they would have changed horses at Montreuil, where Sterne set two amusing scenes. What interested Tristram was Janatone, the daughter of the innkeeper, and his meditation upon 'the principles of change' in the frame of a beautiful woman becomes a commentary upon the mutability of all that he values in the physical world. In *A Sentimental Journey* Sterne has Yorick stay the night at Montreuil. (The posting inn, then called the Hôtel de la Cour de France, is still standing). There Yorick hires his servant, La Fleur; and there he experiences his first public act of charity in France, fumbling all of his moral principles by trying to distribute eight coins to sixteen beggars. Neither narrative gives any sense of the village of Montreuil with its beautiful medieval buildings and walls. Sterne's Montreuil passages might as well have been placed in any village in France so long as it had a posting inn.[45]

[43] Van R. Baker, 'Sterne and Piganiol de la Force: The Making of Volume VII of *Tristram Shandy*', *Comparative Literature Studies*, XIII (1976), 5–14.

[44] Cole, *Journal*, described the Dover–Paris stagecoach. I surmise that the party took the stage because Pitt did not purchase a carriage for himself and Phelps until he got to Paris. In TRISTRAM SHANDY, Tristram remarks the smallness of French post-horses (605).

[45] The inn at Montreuil is named and described by Cole, *Journal*, 347. An unidentified German admirer of Sterne wrote an amusing essay about his visits to Calais and Montreuil in 1770. At Calais he was shown 'Sterne's room', only to discover that the building had just been built. At

Beyond Montreuil a traveller bound for Paris had to choose one of three routes, all described by Tristram: via Lille, via Amiens or via Beauvais (579). No doubt Sterne was consulting his copy of Jaillot's *Liste générale des postes de France*.[46] Tristram finally decides upon the Amiens route, though oddly by way of Chantilly, which did not lie on it or any of the routes (598). Since the details about Chantilly which appear in the novel were available to Sterne in his source books, one suspects that he never set foot in that town. His purpose was not historical, but aesthetic. In all probability, George Pitt and his party took the most direct route, that through Beauvais, the route travelled by neither Tristram nor Yorick.

The party arrived in Paris on or about 17 January. Sterne took lodgings in the Faubourg Saint-Germain, where most Englishmen stayed. He liked his rooms, though he complained of the expense of heating them; and he liked the wood fire: ''tis most pleasant and most healthy firing . . . if I can get wood at Coxwold, I will always have a little' (155). There were new boulevards in Saint-Germain, built after Louis XIV demolished the old right-bank fortifications, but most of Paris was made up of ancient timber houses rearing high above narrow, smelly streets through which carriages rattled at dangerous speeds. 'The streets', says Tristram Shandy as he enters Paris, '. . . are nasty . . . no one gives the wall!' (599). Tristram is amazed, as we suppose Sterne was, at the number of cooks' shops and barbers' shops, and the sight of barbers wearing swords like gentlemen.

Among the fifteen or sixteen British men 'of distinction' and their servants who were in Paris at this time (152) was a thirteen-year-old boy and his tutor, who may have come in Pitt's party. Young Charles James Fox was destined to become the brilliant leader of the opposition in the

Montreuil he met the family of Varennes, who operated the Hôtel de la Cour de France, and decided that Janatone's surname must have been Varennes: *Repository of Arts, Literature, Fashions, Manufactures, &c* (sometimes called *Ackerman's Repository* because published by R. Ackerman in the Strand), 3rd series, V (July–December 1825), 188–94: Cole said that the family who operated the inn was named Varein or Warren. As to La Fleur, the *European Magazine*, vol. 18 (July–December, 1790), 173–4, 268, 346–7, has an article on the 'real' La Fleur, his service with Sterne, and his life thereafter. CROSS, 408, n., thought it 'untrustworthy as a whole; but it has behind it a real La Fleur and vague traditions.' CURTIS, 268, called it 'questionable'. Gardner Stout, Jr, in his notes to SENTIMENTAL JOURNEY, 342, rejected it as 'entirely fictitious'. I agree with Stout and presume that La Fleur is the creature of Sterne's imagination.

[46] This was an annual publication by the Jaillot family. Sterne's use of it was demonstrated by Van Baker.

Commons during the ministry of the younger Pitt, and was the chief spokesman of his age for such liberal causes as freedom for slaves, self-government for Ireland, and independence for the American colonies.[47] His tutor, a young Anglo-Irish gentleman, George Macartney, would become England's first ambassador to China. Macartney was the protégé of the boy's father, the famous parliamentarian and minister, Henry Fox, soon to be created Baron Holland, who would launch Macartney upon his long diplomatic career. Macartney had every qualification for a diplomat. He was handsome, affable, charming to ladies, with a ready wit and excellent memory, and never known to have had an original idea.[48] Fox had taken Charles James, his second son, out of Eton to make his grand tour. He supplied the boy with daily gambling money and hoped he would lose no time learning the manly arts of drinking and whoring.[49] The lad was not ready, and after four months asked to be sent back to school. For his first three months in Paris, Sterne shared rooms with these new, young friends, and his first explorations of taverns and churches and street theatres and legitimate theatres were made in their company.[50] They went together to see the great actress Clairon (152) and to Versailles, where Sterne had a commission of some sort to carry out for Garrick (151). At one point, Sterne gave Macartney a holiday and took charge of the boy himself for a week in the country.[51]

Late in February, Sterne had a falling-out with Pitt and Phelps. Sterne

[47] Since Charles James Fox is said to have stayed abroad only four months and left in mid-April, he must have arrived about the time Sterne did.

[48] For the career of George Macartney (1737–1806), afterwards Baron Macartney of Parkhurst, see Helen H. Robbins, *Our First Ambassador to China*, 1908; the obituary in the *Gentleman's Magazine* for April 1806, p. 387; *DNB*; NAMIER AND BROOKE; CURTIS, 405–6. His career was launched by Henry Fox, who obtained for him his first diplomatic post, that of Envoy Extraordinary and Minister Plenipotentiary to Russia: see Fox's letter to him, 22 May 1764, BL, Add. MSS 51399, fol. 8.

[49] Henry Fox's ideas about how to rear his sons are described by Robbins, *Our First Ambassador*, 11, and Jesse, *George Selwyn*, II, 216–33.

[50] Sterne speaks of making excursions with Fox and/or Macartney on 31 January (151, 152), 11 February (159) and 8 March (EGERTON LETTERS). When M. de la Borde went looking for Sterne and Macartney, he found them in a common lodging. On 19 April Sterne wrote, 'Mr. Fox, and Mr. Macartny, having left Paris, I live altogether in French families' (163). From these hints I conclude that from mid-January to mid-April Sterne shared a lodging with Fox and Macartney.

[51] Sterne writing to Lord Fauconberg on 10 April says he wrote last 'from St. Germains where I retired for a week w^h^ young Mr Fox' (159). CROSS, 293, assumes, correctly I believe, that this was Saint-Germain-en-Laye, west of Paris, and not the Fauborg Saint-Germain.

kept up appearances, writing to Garrick that Pitt had behaved to him 'like a man of good breeding, and good nature' (152). Nevertheless, as we learn from a letter written by Phelps from Turin, Sterne was angry with them both:

> We have not heard a word from Tristram Shandy ever since we left him at Paris five or six weeks ago: I am afraid that Mr Pitt and particularly myself are out of his good graces. Tristram is an Author, and as such, tenacious of the privilege which all great Authors claim of being the best Judges of their own Merit. We ventur'd to give him some little Advice during our stay at Paris, which I believe would do him no harm if practis'd in other Meridians as well as those of France: Tristram receiv'd it as an Author; you need not therefore enquire how he approv'd of the Physick or those who ventur'd to administer it.[52]

Sterne was in no mood to accept gratuitous criticism of his writing or his behaviour. He might have forgiven Phelps, who had an unstained reputation, but he must have thought it impertinent of Pitt, a womanizer who, by his ill-treatment, would soon drive away his wife. Though handsome and polished in his externals, Pitt was, said Walpole, 'brutal and half-mad'.[53]

The departure of these diplomats on the first or second day of March[54] did not put an end to the spying. When some letters Sterne had addressed to Lord Fauconberg vanished in the mails, Sterne suspected they had been intercepted: 'thank God there was no Treason in any one of them', he commented ironically (159).

Two weeks after he reached Paris, a report spread about London that Sterne had died abroad. 'Private letters from Paris', said the *British Chronicle* for 1–3 February, 'bring an account of the death of the Rev. Mr. Sterne, Author of Tristram Shandy'.[55] The news reached Coxwold by the 7th,[56] and Sterne's congregation went into mourning.[57] Then on the 12th the *Public Advertiser* printed a correction: 'The Report of the Death of the Rev. Mr. Sterne, Author of Tristram Shandy is not true; Letters from Paris of the

[52] Phelps to Henry Egerton, Turin, 24 March 1762: EGERTON LETTERS.

[53] NAMIER AND BROOKE; DUTENS, II, 56–60.

[54] They arrived at Turin on 6 March: Horn, *British Diplomatic Representatives*.

[55] Identical accounts were carried in the *London Chronicle*, 2–4 February, and the *Public Advertiser*, 4 February.

[56] Richard Chapman to Lord Fauconberg, 7 February: WOMBWELL PAPERS.

[57] Chapman to Fauconberg, 14 February.

20th of last Month, mention that Gentleman to be in good Health.' Elizabeth and Lydia in York had learned that Sterne was alive, and Lydia wrote at once to Sterne's parishes to tell them.

But Sterne dead was more newsworthy that Sterne alive. Despite the 12 February announcement of his good health, the *British Chronicle* of the 15th ran an epitaph –

> STERNE! Rest for ever, and no longer fear
> The Critic's malice, and the Wittling's sneer;
> The gate of Envy now is clos'd on thee,
> And Fame her hundred doors shall open free.

Three days later the *St. James's Chronicle* printed a letter from a soldier without a regiment reacting to the news of the death of one who had created in Uncle Toby 'the greatest Character that human Nature can attain to'. But the *St. James's Chronicle* for 6–9 March made amends with a poem celebrating the good news – a comic piece by no less a lover of literature than John Nichols:[58]

> How! *Shandy* dead! (a well-bred Lady cries)
> . . .
> No more dear Satire through the Nation reign
> With *Shandy* fled to *Pluto*'s drear Domain!

Then 'Sir *John Fopling*' brings the news that 'Illustrious *Yorick's* still alive and well': so the lady sends her cards about to invite her friends 'to share a gen'ral Rout'.

Sterne, who followed the news of his own death and resurrection as the English papers arrived in Paris, laughingly told Egerton that he now had the perfect excuse for not writing, being 'above all Epistolary Correspondence, after my death'. But then, 'I find by the last english papers here, I am once more alive. . . . Strange! that a man should be so inconsistent!'[59]

In fact, Sterne had recovered his health remarkably. 'Well! here I am, my friend,' he had written to Garrick on 31 January, 'as much improved in my health for the time, as ever your friendship could wish, or at least your faith give credit to' (151). To Elizabeth he wrote, 'I have got a colour into my

[58] Identified by Professor Richard Rabicoff.

[59] Sterne to Henry Egerton, 8 March: EGERTON LETTERS. Hereinafter, throughout this chapter, Sterne's comments to Henry Egerton are taken from this long letter.

face now, though I came with no more than there is in a dishclout' (155). He had consulted the 'doctors of the Sorbonne' soon after his arrival (151), and they, learning he intended to go to Toulouse after Paris, had advised him to stay on in Paris, at least for a time. By 19 March, he had decided not to go south at all (158). To Egerton he wrote, 'The Physicians here tell me, I shall find myself in the spring—& that tho Toulouse w^{d} have done me service in the winter—the seasons are against it in the heat of Summer—I therefore think I shall stay here til May . . . and return thro Holland to London ab^{t} ye end of June.' So, with the pleasant prospect before him of a convalescence in Paris, he sought a passport.

Passports for Englishmen were issued only upon the approval of the Duc de Choiseul, Secretary of State for Foreign Affairs, Minister of War and Minister of the Navy, effectively the prime minister, though never designated such. This great man could seldom be approached personally – as Yorick discovered in *A Sentimental Journey* (208). So an Englishman had to find people who had access to him, as well as French citizens known to him who would vouch for the person's behaviour and countersign his passport.[60] Sterne wrote to Garrick on 31 January – mistaking the duke's rank – 'My application to the Count de Choisuiel goes on swimmingly, for not only Mr. Pelletiere . . . has undertaken my affair, but the Count de Limbourgh – the Baron d'Holbach, has offered any security for the inoffensiveness of my behavior in France' (151). One or more of these well-known men[61] may have signed the passport, but the person who actually got it for him in all probability was the anglophile general, Claude de Thiard, Comte de Bissy. De Bissy had been elected to the Academy as the translator of Bolingbroke, though it was said he paid another to do much of the work.[62]

[60] French passports from this era have two places for sponsors to sign. Pitt, in a dispatch from Turin on 10 March, told how he had attempted to wait upon Choiseul at Versailles to thank him for his passport, was not admitted, but was sent 'a Civil Message' through the Sardinian ambassador: PRO: SP. 92. vol. 69, 10 March 1762.

[61] For 'Pelletiere' and d'Holbach, see below. 'Limbourgh' was identified by CURTIS, 152, as Damian August Philipp Karl (1721–97), Graf von Limburgh-Styrum, Dean of the secularized bishopric of Speyer, and later Prince-Bishop. There was a count by the name of Choiseul – César-Gabriel de Choiseul (1712–85), Comte de Choiseul, Minister for Foreign Affairs, created 2 November 1762 Duc de Choiseul-Praslin, a cousin to Etienne-François de Choiseul-Stainville (1719–85), Duc de Choiseul and First Minister of France. The contexts clearly indicate that all Sterne's references are to the First Minister.

[62] Charles Collé, *Journal et mémoires*, ed. Honoré Bonhomme, 3 vols, Paris, 1868, I, 250–6. A biographical sketch of Bissy may be found in the *Biographie universelle*.

’Twas an odd incident when I was introduced to the Count de Bissie, which I was at his desire—I found him reading Tristram—this grandee does me great honours, and gives me leave to go a private way through his apartments into the palais royal, to view the Duke of Orleans’ collections, every day I have time. (151)

Thus Sterne made it easy for us to identify the ‘Count de B****’ of *A Sentimental Journey*, whom Yorick found reading Shakespeare (215). Sterne would hardly have represented this man as the person who obtained Yorick’s passport and introduced him into French society unless the Comte de Bissy had actually performed these services for him.

De Bissy found occasion to introduce Sterne to the Duc d’Orléans. The duke’s late father, Philippe, Duc d’Orléans, a cousin to the king, much his senior in years, had served as regent during the king’s minority. The son, who continued to reside in the Palais-Royal, had inherited the wealth, but not the power and ambition of his father. After an honourable military career, in which he had attained the rank of lieutenant-general, he had settled into a life of pleasure. He was fat. His mistress, Mlle le Marquis, was an actress, and he was enamoured of the drama. He had theatres built at the Palais-Royal and some of his country houses, and he kept as permanent members of his household the dramatists Charles Collé and Bernard-Joseph Saurin. The collection of paintings at the Palais-Royal, which Sterne went so often to see, was the finest in France.[63]

Another member of his table at the Palais-Royal was a playwright, actor and painter, Louis Carogis, remembered today by his stage-name, Carmontelle. This former soldier, who probably met the duke during their army service, kept his patron amused by doing watercolour portraits of his guests. ‘The Duke of Orleans’, said Sterne, ‘has suffered my portrait to be added to the number of some odd men in his collection; and a gentleman who lives with him has taken it most expressively, at full length’ (157–8). Carmontelle’s portraits, all watercolours, are charming, though the artist was curiously limited: he could paint his subjects only in profile. Unfortunately, his original picture of Sterne has been lost. Two copies survive, however; and in these we see Sterne leaning on the back of a chair,

[63] Collé also left numerous stories about his master. For a summary of Orléans’s career, *Biographie universelle*.

dressed in clerical black, but in a suit of elegant cut with lace ruffles and bands – no mean figure for a Parisian salon.[64]

'I have found little difficulties [*sic*] in getting into some of the best Circles,' Sterne told Henry Egerton on 8 March, '& am moving on with ten times the rapidity I ever moved before; for Lo! I am going this night to the Prince of Contis.' The handsome, powerful Louis-François de Bourbon, Prince de Conti, brother-in-law to the Duc d'Orléans, was commander-in-chief of the French armies and Grand Prieur de France. After years of opposition to a court dominated by the king's mistress, Mme de Pompadour, he had recently swung round to its support and was now throwing his enormous political influence behind Choiseul's peace overtures.[65] Conti was pleased enough by Sterne to ask him back to his entertainments at least one more time (155).

At first Sterne was delighted with these attentions from the great and powerful. 'Be it known,' he told Garrick,

> I Shandy it away fifty times more than I was ever wont, talk more nonsense than ever you heard me talk in your days—and to all sorts of people. *Qui de diable est ce homme là*—said Choiseul, t'other day—ce Chevalier Shandy—You'll think me as vain as a devil, was I to tell you the rest of the dialogue. (157)

His calendar began to fill up. 'Except Ash Wensday,' he told Egerton, 'I have not once eat at my own expence, & believe I shall not do it again, during my stay. The french Love such a nonsensical fellow as I am.'

Phelps, who before his departure had shared some of this social life, had a more jaundiced view of Sterne at the dinner table:

> Tristram is so well recover'd as to talk more bad French in one day, than would serve a reasonable man a whole Month. He talks à tort et à travers to whoever sits next to him wherever he happens to be.[66]

One cannot but wonder how Sterne got on so well when his French was so

[64] For a description of the painting and its provenance, *EMY*, 307–8; information on his life and work in *Biographie universelle* and the introduction to François-Anatole Gruyer, *Les Portraits de Carmontelle*, Paris, 1902.

[65] George Thomas [Keppel], Earl of Albermarle, *Memoirs of the Marquis of Rockingham and His Contemporaries*, 2 vols, 1852; WALPOLE, *passim*; DUTENS, III, 74–5.

[66] Phelps to Egerton, 12 February: EGERTON LETTERS.

bad. 'I speak it fast and fluent,' he told Elizabeth, 'but incorrect both in accent and phrase.' Then he added, with more confidence than he had cause for, 'but the French tell me I speak it most surprisingly well for the time. In six weeks I shall get over all difficulties, having got over one of the worst, which is to understand whatever is said by others, which I own I found much trouble in at first' (155). In June he said more modestly, 'I speak French tolerably – but I only wish to be understood' (177). In July he told a good story of himself in a letter to Lady Dacre:

> I splutter French so as to be understood—but I have had a droll adventure here in which my Latin was of some service to me—I hired a chaise and a horse to go about seven miles into the country, but *Shandean like*, did not take notice that the horse was almost dead when I took him—Before I got half way the poor animal dropp'd down dead—so I was forced to appear before the police, and began to tell my story in French, which was, that the poor beast had to do with a worse beast than himself, namely *his master*, who had driven him all the day before (Jehu like) and that he had neither had corn, or hay, therefore I was not to pay for the horse—but I might as well have whistled, as have spoke French, and I believe my Latin was equal to my uncle Toby's Lilabulero—being not understood because of it's purity, but by dint of words I forced my judge to do me justice—no common thing by the way in France. (178–9)

The very artificiality of the conventions for spoken Latin among educated people everywhere in Europe may have saved the day for Sterne. But French he never mastered in its spoken form, though his written French may have been respectable.[67]

Great princes like Orléans and Conti, who were largely independent of the monarch, might choose to winter in Paris, but most of the nobility were forced to spend the cold months at Versailles, where the king lived and the court was held. Sterne met few of them, though there was an unidentified nobleman who asked him to spend a month at his country estate – an

[67] In Volume VII of TRISTRAM SHANDY, Tristram's joyful cry, 'VIVA LA JOIA! FIDON LA TRISTESSA!' (650), is a fairly accurate rendition of the southern pronunciation of the standard French of that day for 'Vive la joie! Fi donc la tristesse!' Other oddities to modern ears of his French phrasing in letters and novels may represent conventions of the time or typical English French. For a contrary view, see Henry H. Breen, 'The Drummer's Letter', *N&Q*, 1st series, VIII (1853), 153–4.

invitation which Sterne eventually declined.[68] Sterne was entertained primarily in Paris, where with few exceptions social life was in the hands of the bourgeoisie – not the industrial or mercantile class of Marxian theory, but the rich 'bourgeoisie d'Ancien Régime' who did not work, but lived off rents and sinecures.

Among these were the immensely wealthy *fermiers généraux*, who collected taxes for the Crown, retaining a percentage. One such was Jean-Benjamin de la Borde. 'I must make You smile,' Sterne said to Egerton,

> tho' I am known by the Title thro Paris, of Monsr Le *Chanoin*—I am oftener spoke of by that of Chevalier de Shandy—twas oweing to a piece of pleasantry wch happened upon going wth Mr Macartney to see Mon^{r} De Bord's House wch they say is the finest in Paris—The Porter refused us admittance, alledging orders had been given that the house sh^{d} not be shewn—but desired our Names. Le Chevalier de Shandy & Mon^{r} Macartney were given in—& the next morning M^{r} De Bord the Farmer Genl came to wait upon us, & invited us to dinner when we were treated not like Knights of the Post but Princes of the blood.

De la Borde was an *amateur* and composer of music. No doubt Sterne and Macartney were required after dinner to listen to a concert in which his company of musicians played his uninspired pieces.[69]

Another of that sort was Alexandre-Jean-Joseph Le Riche de La Popelinière, the wealthiest of the *fermiers*, a man whom Sterne described as living 'like a sovereign prince'. 'He did me the honour last night to send me an invitation to his house, while I stayed here – that is, to his music and table' (155). He was, however, not so much an eminent *amateur* as a notorious cuckold. A few years before, his wife had been found to have a secret passage leading from the back of her fireplace into the fireplace of the house next door, where lived her lover, the Duc de Richelieu.[70] Sterne satirized La Popelinière in *A Sentimental Journey* as 'Mons. P**** the farmer general' who asked Yorick about English taxes: 'They were very considerable, he heard—If we knew but how to collect them, said I, making him a low bow. I could never have been invited to Mons. P****'s concerts upon any other terms' (262).

[68] Sterne to Egerton, 8 March.

[69] Collé, *Journal et mémoires*, III, 46.

[70] Marmontel, *Mémoires*, ed. Brigit Patmore, 1930, 115–24. See also *Mémoires inédits de Madame la Comtesse de Genlis*, 8 vols, Paris, 1825, I, 67–82; *Mémoires de Madame d'Epinay*, ed. Paul Boiteau, Paris, 1865, I, 384–7; II, 472–3; CURTIS, 156.

Yet another host who engaged in domestic theatre and concerts was Charles-Ernest, Baron de Bagge, Chamberlain to the King of Prussia. Although Sterne reported his entertainment 'very fine, both music and company' (155), some doubts intrude. Bagge, though himself a shockingly bad violinist, used to pay his musicians to take violin lessons from him.[71]

It would have been the natural order of things for Sterne to have been introduced into the salon of Madame du Deffand, the brilliant hostess who, though of modest means, entertained the outstanding politicians, artists and intellectuals of the day. Choiseul often came there. D'Alembert, the greatest mathematician in France (as well as physicist, polemicist and the most brilliant talker in Paris), was her star guest. He was the secret lover of Madame du Deffand's niece, Julie de Lespinasse, if in fact the younger woman was her niece. The lurid accounts of her origin are not conclusive. In time Mlle de Lespinasse became a special champion of Sterne. 'It was she who made in Paris the reputation of the "Sentimental Journey," ' said the Chevalier de Guibert in his memoir of her; she read and reread Sterne and became his translator. Though no translations survive, there are several 'morceaux' written in what she conceived to be the manner of the *Journey*.[72] Moreover, she had, said de Guibert, the incredble patience to 'decipher' *Tristram Shandy*. Sterne may also have attended the salon of Madame Geoffrin, the greatest patroness of arts of the time, a woman who was admired by and admired Mlle de Lespinasse, though she was the arch-rival of her aunt.[73]

Initially, Sterne was caught up in 'the delights of this place, which in the *scavoir vivre*, exceed all the places, I believe, in this section of the globe' (151). As in London in 1760, 'I have just now a fortnight's dinners and

[71] CURTIS, 156; CROSS, 306.

[72] Listed by Francis Brown Barton, *Etude sur l'influence de Laurence Sterne en France au dix-huitième siècle*, Paris, 1911, 41, n. 1; 154–7.

[73] Jesse, *George Selwyn*, II, 342–9; Marmontel, *Mémoires*, 270–3; S. G. Tallentyre, *Women of the Salons*, 1901; WALPOLE, III, xxvi–xxx; *Unpublished Correspondence of Madame du Deffand with D'Alembert, Montesquieu, et al.*, trans. Mrs Meeke, 2 vols, 1810; *Letters to and from Madame du Deffand and Julie de Lespinasse*, ed. Warren Hunting Smith, New Haven, Conn., 1938; *Correspondance complète de Mme du Deffand avec la Duchesse de Choiseul, et al.*, ed. M. and Marquis de Sainte-Aulaire, 3 vols, Paris, 1877; Marquise du Deffand, *Lettres à Horace Walpole*, ed. Mrs Paget Toynbee, 3 vols, 1912; *Letters of Mlle de Lespinasse*, trans. Katharine Prescott Wormeley, 1902; *Lettres inédities de Mlle de Lespinasse à Condorcet, et al.*, ed. Charles Henry, Paris, 1887; Janine Bouissounouse, *Julie: The Life of Mademoiselle de Lespinasse, Her Salon, Her Friends, Her Loves*, trans. Pierre de Fontnouvelle, New York, 1962.

suppers upon my hands' (151). If he was puzzling to his French hosts, that only amused him. 'As in London,' he told Garrick, 'I have the honour of having done and said a thousand things I never did or dream'd of—and yet I dream abundantly' (157). He was even willing to attribute the recovery of his health to this life.

> I laugh 'till I cry, and in the same tender moments *cry 'til I laugh*. I Shandy it more than ever, and verily do believe, that by mere Shandeism sublimated by a laughter-loving people, I fence as much against infirmities, as I do by the benefit of air and climate. (163)

But his ardour began to cool. 'I have been introduced to one half of their best Goddesses, and in a month more shall be admitted to the shrines of the other half—but I neither worship—or fall (much) upon my knees before them: but on the contrary, have converted many unto Shandeism' (157). By April, the style of the salons was losing its charm:

> Here every thing is hyperbolized—and if a woman is but simply pleased—'tis *Je suis charmée*—and if she is charmed 'tis nothing less, than that she is *ravi*-sh'd—and when ravi-sh'd, (which may happen) there is nothing left for her but to fly to the other world for a metaphor, and swear, qu'elle etoit toute *extasiée* . . . and there is scarce a woman who understands the *bon ton*, but is seven times in a day in downright extasy—that is, the devil's in her—by a small mistake of one world for the other. (161–2)

In August, after he had moved on to Toulouse, he wrote to Hall, 'The humour is over for France, and Frenchmen' (181); and on 19 October, again to Hall,

> the ground work of my *ennui* is more to the eternal platitude of the French characters—little variety, no originality in it at all—than to any other cause—for they are very civil—but civility itself, in that uniform, wearies and bodders one to death—If I do not mind, I shall grow most stupid and sententious. (186)

This gradual disillusionment probably underlies the scene which concludes the Paris section of *A Sentimental Journey*. But Sterne's satire of vain ladies and foppish gentlemen is kept at a general level. Of the six persons whose names he rendered in initial letters, only half have been satisfactorily identified. 'Mons. P**** the farmer general' (262) is surely

Sterne's erstwhile host, La Popelinière, but the man had been dead five years by the time Sterne wrote. 'Mons. D***' and 'the Abbe M***', who talk against revealed religion in their encyclopedia (265), must be Diderot and Morellet; but, as we shall see, these were friends whom Sterne was teasing amicably. When he does give a full name for one figure, it turns out to be an idle conceit: 'Count de Faineant' (266) may be translated 'Lord Lounger' or 'Count Sloth'. Sterne made fun of the salons of Paris, but he protected his individual hosts. Primarily, let it be noted, the satire is directed against Yorick himself. Having learned from a beggar the utility of flattery, Yorick flatters his way through Paris. But he grows ashamed of such a 'dishonest *reckoning* . . . the gain of a slave', and so departs Paris and the 'children of Art' in search of children of nature. If Sterne made such a self-discovery, he did not talk about it in the letters we have.

But Sterne never tired of one group of friends he made in Paris – the intellectuals. Soon after his arrival he was introduced to two men who played host to outstanding writers and thinkers, the Baron d'Holbach and 'Pelletier', and through them met many of the celebrated *philosophes*. 'Pelletier', as everyone called him, was Michel-Etienne Lepeletier, Comte de Saint-Fargeau, the youthful Advocate-General and President of the Parlement of Paris. He was a bright and amusing little man, though said to have only a 'weak and flighty head'.[74] D'Holbach was a far more important figure for Sterne, and indeed for French history.

Born Paul-Henri Thiry, he acquired the name of d'Holbach when he was adopted by a wealthy uncle. His family was a *nouveau riche* Flemish family, and he was called 'Baron' only by courtesy – because he was Master of Hees in Holland. His French citizenship was by naturalization. From his days at the University of Leyden, where he made friends with John Wilkes and numerous other English, he became a passionate student of English fiction and philosophy. In 1754 he succeeded his father-in-law, by purchase, as a syndic of the Compagnie de Conseillers-Secrétaires du Roi, a sinecure as a sort of banker for the king. He then purchased a large house – which still stands at No. 8, rue de Moulins – and settled down to a life of pleasure and study. His house soon became the centre of Parisian intellectual life. To his dinners on Sunday and Thursday afternoons came the *philosophes*, poets, playwrights and numerous foreign visitors. The attention he gave to Sterne

[74] Marmontel, *Mémoires*, 218–20.

was an honour Sterne shared with David Hume, David Garrick, Benjamin Franklin, Joseph Priestley, Lord Shelburne, and others.[75]

D'Holbach has usually been treated by historians as the host to those thinkers who laid the intellectual foundations of the French Revolution. Only recently has he been recognized as a philosopher in his own right and a major influence among those who gathered at his table. He produced eleven books – only one under his own name – and wrote some four hundred articles for the *Encyclopédie*. The *Encyclopédie* itself would never have been completed without his secret support. It had been started by Diderot and d'Alembert in 1750, but the government withdrew the imprimatur in 1758 and d'Alembert resigned. Diderot, d'Holbach and the Chevalier de Jaucourt went underground with the project and before 1772 illegally published twenty-seven more volumes.

At the tables of Pelletier and d'Holbach, Sterne met most of the outstanding intellectuals and writers in France. Not Voltaire, however, or Rousseau, both of whom were living away from Paris at this time. But it is certain he knew Diderot; d'Alembert; the Comte de Buffon, who was in the midst of his forty-four-volume *Histoire naturelle*; the abbé Morellet, theologian and economist; Crébillon *fils*, the novelist; and Suard, the journalist and student of English letters. Although he does not mention them by name, Sterne probably knew all the members of d'Holbach's coterie from this period – Le Roy, the sportsman and naturalist; Marmontel, the playwright and novelist; the abbé Raynal, historian; Dr Roux, the chemist; and Saint-Lambert, poet and philosopher. On this or some later visit, he made the acquaintance of the Neapolitan economist, that handsome little 'Harlequin', the abbé Ferdinando Galiani.

Wit, so treasured in the eighteenth century, was not the most admired virtue in this circle. D'Holbach, according to Sterne, was 'the great protector of wits, and the Scavans who are no wits' (151). It was intellect that counted here, and the search for a true description of the world. But it was an atmosphere into which an Englishman such as Sterne could fit easily because the *philosophes* were very much under the influence of recent English thought and current English writers – Locke, Shaftesbury, Hartley,

[75] Alan Charles Kors, *D'Holbach's Coterie: An Enlightenment in Paris*, Princeton, NJ, 1976; W. H. Wickwar, *Baron D'Holbach: A Prelude to the French Revolution*, 1935; Pierre Naville, *Paul Thiry d'Holbach et la philosophie scientifique au xviiie siècle*, Paris, 1943; René Hubert, *D'Holbach et ses amis*, Paris, 1928; Andre Morellet, *Mémoires inédits*, 2 vols, Paris, 2nd edn, 1822, I, 131–41; GARAT, I, 207–25; Marmontel, *Mémoires*, 276–9.

Berkeley, Hume, Priestley, and others. They made up a true intellectual community, as Sterne's description of the scene to Henry Egerton reveals:

> There is nothing in this place wch has given me more pleasure than the Connections I have made wth Y^e^ Crebillions, D'Allemberg, Bufon, Diderot & the rest of a large Circle of men of wit & learning whom I meet twice a week at Baron de Holbach's, & Pelletiers Tables—what makes these men truly entertaining & desirable, is, that they have the art, notwithstanding their Wits, of living together without biting or scratching—an infinitude of gaity & civility reigns among them—& w^t^ is no small art, Every man leaves the Room wth a better Opinion of his own Talents than when he entered.

Sterne's plural, 'the Crebillions', suggests that he made the acquaintance of both Prosper-Jolyot de Crébillon, the father, and Claude-Prosper-Jolyot de Crébillon, the son. That is distinctly possible, since the two had recently been reconciled after years of estrangement. Crébillon *père*, under the urging of Madame de Pompadour, had come out of retirement to complete and produce with great success his tragedy, *Catilina*. He died in June of this very year, 1762. Crébillon *fils* was the favourite guest of Pelletier, said to have kept the table in an uproar. He was a novelist, whose most famous book Sterne knew and admired and would one day speak about in *A Sentimental Journey* (188) – *Les Égarements du cœur et de l'esprit* (1736). 'Crebillion has made a convention with me,' Sterne told Garrick,

> which, if he is not too lazy, will be no bad *persiflage*—as soon as I get to Thoulouse he has agreed to write me an expostulat[o]ry letter upon the indecorums of T. Shandy—which is to be answered by recrimination upon the liberties in his own works—these are to be printed together—Crebillion against Sterne—Sterne against Crebillion—the copy to be sold, and the money equally divided. (162)

But nothing came of the plan.[76]

Sterne's name is often linked with that of a younger member of the d'Holbach circle, Jean-Baptiste-Antoine Suard, the journalist reviewer who

[76] *Biographie universelle*; the introductions to the Bonamy Dobrée translation of the *Sofa*, 1927, and the Barbara Bray translation of the *Wayward Head and Heart*, 1963; and the *Correspondance littéraire . . . par Grimm, Diderot, Raynal, et al.*, ed. Maurice Tourneaux, 16 vols, Paris, 1877–82, V, 199 and *passim*.

introduced the French public to a great deal of English literature. One supposes they met in 1762, since three years later Suard wrote, 'We have seen Mr. Sterne in Paris several times.' We know about the friendship primarily through Suard's biographer, Dominique-Joseph Garat. Suard was initially amused by Sterne: 'his person perfectly resembles his book,' he wrote. 'He came to France for his health, which, though deplorable, did not affect his gaiety.'[77] With the passage of time, he became less enthusiastic.

Possibly the most important friendship which Sterne made in France – at least for the history of literature – was that with Denis Diderot, the chief editor of the *Encyclopédie*, mathematician, playwright, novelist and philosopher – one of the most exciting intellects of his age. Diderot, a large, rough-hewn man, who looked like a porter and talked like a Socrates, was fascinated by the tall, spare English parson. He put into Sterne's hands a tragedy, translated from his original French, in the hope Sterne would recommend it – 'The Natural Son, or, the Triumph of Virtue, in five acts'. Sterne was in doubt. He wrote to Garrick, 'It has too much sentiment in it, (at least for me) the speeches too long, and savour too much of *preaching*—this may be a second reason, it is not to my taste—'Tis all love, love, love, throughout . . .' (162). But he thought it might be printed and sent it to Thomas Becket: 'I . . . think it will not do for *our stage* – tis y[r] business to consider whether it will do for printing' (166). Eventually it was printed in London, not by Becket, but by Dodsley, and under another title – *Dorval, or the Test of Virtue*, 1767. In May Sterne instructed Becket to send some books for Diderot – a curious assortment: the works of Chaucer, Locke, Pope, Colley Cibber,[78] Tillotson's sermons, the six volumes of *Tristram Shandy*

[77] *Gazette littéraire de l'Europe*, V, (20 March 1765), 41–3. GARAT was distrusted by Suard's widow; but I see no reason to doubt the authenticity of the few things he says about Sterne and Suard. He passed on Suard's best critique of Sterne – an essay on *Tristram Shandy*, GARAT, II, 137–41; another on *A Sentimental Journey*, II, 141–6, is not so good. Sterne did not meet Suard's wife in 1762, as has been said, for Suard married only in 1766. During the time Sterne knew him, Suard was liberal in his political and social views. He was very close to John Wilkes, whose election for Middlesex he supported in the press; and he later supported American independence. But he grew more and more conservative. In 1794 during the revolution, he refused refuge to Condorcet, the mathematician and philosopher, whom Suard had known in the d'Holbach circle; Condorcet was taken by the police the next day and the day after that committed suicide in prison. Information on Suard from GARAT; Kors, *D'Holbach's Coterie*; *Biographie universelle*; Frank A. Hedgcock, *A Cosmopolitan Actor: David Garrick and his French Friends*, 1912, pp. 217–18, n. 3 and *passim*.

[78] See Melvyn New, 'The Dunce Revisited: Colley Cibber and *Tristram Shandy*', *South Atlantic Quarterly*, LXXII (1973), 547–59.

('NB. These place to my Acc^{t} for they are for a present to him—'), and others: 'I am forced to inclose the Card itself wch We have rec^{d} from Mr Diderot—because I have not been able to make it all out' (167). The books arrived in August (183–4), and in October Diderot wrote to Sophie Volland that he was gluttonously devouring 'the craziest, wisest, and gayest of books. . . . the English Rabelais.'[79] Much later Diderot was to write, in imitation of *Tristram Shandy*, *Jacques le fataliste*, a work of significance in the history of the French novel.[80]

Diderot, d'Holbach, Roux and Saint-Lambert were radical atheists, and most of the others were in one degree or another liberal deists. Only the year before, d'Holbach had published his highly successful critique, *Le Christianisme dévoilé*, though not under his own name. But far more important to the *philosophes* than atheism was the principle of religious tolerance, which Marmontel and the abbé Morellet had championed. So men of the cloth were made welcome so long as they could justify their position intelligently while maintaining the *bon ton* of the table. Sterne, who upon a later occasion defended one of his sermons with no loss of cheer to no less a sceptic than David Hume (218), seems to have won acceptance. He never hid his orthodoxy, and he was delighted when a 'Lady of Quality' – unidentified – translated into French his sermon, the 'House of Feasting and the House of Mourning Described'. The lady proposed to publish it for Lent, 'to give ye people here a specimen of my Sermons—so You see,' he said to Egerton, 'I shall be Lent Preacher at Paris, tho' I shall never have the hon^{r} at London.' No copy of the sermon has been found, so probably the lady's scheme was never carried through. In *A Sentimental Journey* Sterne playfully teased his philosophical friends about their atheism. Yorick, making his way upward in the salons of Paris, meets a great lady whom he flatters into a comic religious conversion. 'She affirmed to Mons. D[iderot] and the Abbe M[orellet], that in one half hour I had said more for revealed religion, than all their Encyclopedia had said against it' (265). This was less than fair to the *Encyclopédistes*. Morellet was a conservative in his theology. He wrote most of the theological articles in the *Encyclopédie*, such as those on 'God' and 'Soul', maintaining an orthodox, though liberal position, whereas the atheism of the principal editors was distinctly played down.

[79] *Lettres à Sophie Volland*, ed. André Babelon, Paris, 1930, II, 194–5.

[80] Arthur M. Wilson, *Diderot*, New York, 1972, p. 668. For another analysis of the relationship of the two novels, see J. Robert Loy, *Diderot's Determined Fatalist: A Critical Appreciation of 'Jacques le Fataliste'*, New York, 1950, pp. 32–50.

Did they know Sterne's work in 1762? Richard Phelps said they did not:

> He meets with great Civilities from the people to whom he has been recommended, and luckily for him (I mean as an Author) he ascribes it entirely to the life and Opinions of Mr Shandy – but alass! there are not five people in Paris possess'd of a Tristram Shandy, nor one of those who are, who pretends to understand it. They know however that Tristram is a great Genius in his own Country, and he would very probably be so in this, if he would but learn to speak before he attempts talking.[81]

Phelps was certainly right about salons such as those of de la Borde and de Bagge. In the d'Holbach circle a few who had mastered English may have read *Tristram Shandy*. D'Holbach had English books sent regularly from London, and his friends borrowed them freely. Probably none of them understood the novel. Even Voltaire was puzzled: he wrote to his friend Algarotti in the autumn of 1760, 'Have you read Tristram Shandi? 'Tis a very unaccountable book; an original one. They run mad about it in England.'[82] Others knew about the book through the reviews in the *Journal Encyclopédique* – which were uniformly damning. 'Parler à tort et à travers,' said the reviewer of Volumes III–IV, 'entasser bouffonneries sur bouffonneries, saletés sur saletés, répandre sur le tour un tour original & singulier: voilà tout le mérite de cette production.' There seems to be no way to explain why Sterne 'was received abroad with great distinction', as Mrs Montagu said, except the reputation which had followed him from England.[83] And this was Phelps's explanation: 'They know however that Tristram is a great Genius in his own Country.'

[81] Phelps to Egerton, 12 February: Hertfordshire Record Office, AH 2238.

[82] *Œuvres complètes*, ed. T. Rasherman, W. H. Barber, *et al.*, Geneva, 1968–, *Correspondance*, Vol. XXII (1972), 119. The editors in their notes to this letter, which is numbered D9227, and to Letter D20565 in Vol. XLIV (1976), 175, say that Pierre Frénais translated the first two volumes of *Tristram Shandy* in 1760, the remaining in 1777. I have been unable to confirm this. All other sources and experts I have consulted say that Frénais did indeed make the first translation of the novel, but his first two volumes appeared in 1776, expanded to four in 1777; two rival translations of the remaining volumes, neither by Frénais, appeared in 1785: OATES; Francis Brown Barton, *Etude*, 149–57 and *passim*. Other of Voltaire's comments on Sterne in HOWES, *passim*.

[83] Huntington Library: MO 5820; reviews of Sterne in the *Journal Encyclopédique* are for *Tristram Shandy*, I–II, April 1760, pp. 150–1; *Sermons*, I–II, June 1760, pp. 141–3; *Tristram Shandy*, III–IV, May 1761, pp. 131–2; V–VI, March 1762, pp. 143–4; IX, March 1767, p. 145. I have found no review of *Tristram*

During the winter and spring of 1762, Sterne dined at d'Holbach's, he said, twice a week, and he treated the baron's house, he told Garrick, as his own (151). It is an interesting spectacle – Sterne in such close and protracted contact with the very men who worked out and made popular the concepts used by the French revolutionaries to justify their actions. Not every person at d'Holbach's table wrote for the *Encyclopédie*. Suard maintained he did not. But most of them had written and would continue to write secretly for it. They were not themselves revolutionaries; they were subversives. They made free use of the existing social structure to lead a comfortable life while carrying out their subversive activity. D'Holbach had his sinecure; Diderot had spent time in prison, but he was now enjoying the protection of the Crown as a member of the Academy; d'Alembert was perpetual secretary to the Academy; Le Roy was the lieutenant of the royal hunt; Buffon the keeper of the king's gardens; and Galiani was secretary to the Neapolitan embassy to Paris. Their main revolutionary action was the writing and publishing of the *Encyclopédie* itself, where they opposed Crown and judiciary, attacked the church establishment, and advocated political freedom, economic dignity, and other ideals of the Enlightenment. They could hardly have done such work without the connivance of the police. Crébillon *fils* inherited the post of royal censor from his father and later became police censor as well. Suard received secret mail from John Wilkes in care of Monsieur Le Noir, 'Lieutenant Général de Police à Paris'.[84] Little wonder that Diderot, when he discovered a spy on the staff of the *Encyclopédie*, a copyist, did not even think of going further underground, but fired the man and then went to the police and complained.[85] The *Encyclopédistes* were not going to challenge Sterne's comfortable bargain with the political and social establishment. For all that, they were still idealists, and Sterne may have caught some of their idealism. The most striking of his scenes which express Enlightenment ideals were written after the spring of 1762 – the episodes in *Tristram Shandy* of the mad peasant girl, Maria (780–4), and the black girl who will not kill the flies (747–8); the stories in

Shandy, VII–VIII, or of *Sermons*, III–IV. None of these was written by J.-B.-A. Suard, who reviewed Sterne in the *Gazette littéraire de l'Europe*, when he began to publish it in 1764: see Alfred C. Hunter, *J.-B.-A. Suard*, Paris, 1925, pp. 77–8.

[84] John Wilkes's address book: BL, Add. MSS 30892.

[85] Wilson, *Diderot*. But some policemen considered Diderot dangerous: see the description of police files on writers in Paris by Robert Darnton, *The Great Cat Massacre and Other Episodes in French Cultural History*, New York, 1984, pp. 145–89.

A Sentimental Journey of Yorick's friendship with the papist monk (99–103), his admiration for the peasant family that dance their prayers of thanksgiving (280–4), and the passage on slavery and the Bastille (201–3).

Sterne's delight in the company of d'Holbach and his friends never palled, even when he grew weary of other French society. His daughter said, 'I remember my Father complain'd at Toulouse that by conversing much with the French his understanding diminish'd every day.'[86] It did not diminish among the *philosophes*. Later, when writing to Paris, he seldom failed to send greetings to d'Holbach and his circle. When he was again setting out for Paris in 1765, he happily looked forward to a reunion with them: 'I shall enjoy myself a week or ten days at Paris with my friends, particularly the Baron d'Holbach, and the rest of the joyous sett' (258). The group, in turn, never lost interest in Sterne. In 1766, when Volumes III–IV of the *Sermons* appeared, among the subscribers were the deist, Crébillon, and the atheists, Diderot and d'Holbach.

In April Sterne changed his plans once again and decided to send for his family and to pass the winter with them in Toulouse. He had two reasons. First, the doctors of the Sorbonne had changed their opinion and told him that a winter in the south, 'free from coughs & colds', was the very thing needed to strengthen his lungs; after that, they said, 'they shall look upon my Cure as compleat' (160). A winter in Toulouse, he was now convinced, would 'fortify' his constitution 'beyond all danger' (162). But what finally determined him was the state of his daughter's health. He had heard she was failing in March (155). The asthma she suffered from was growing worse, and by April he was convinced that 'unless something more than bare Medecines can be done for her, she will be lost' (160). Toulouse, then, offered promise for his own recovery, and for his daughter 'the last remedy of a warmer and softer air' (163). He went to Versailles once more to seek passports for his wife and child (163). He took sight-unseen a house in Toulouse (160). In May he began a series of letters to Elizabeth about their journey, touching in their concern for her and Lydia's comfort and safety. They were to 'rise early and gallop away in the cool', to bring tea to last for the trip as far as Paris, to bring a Scotch mill to make snuff, and the like (170).

On 16 March, Sterne and his friends were up all night watching the terrifying fire at the Saint-Germain fair, which turned night into day and

86 LETTERS, 456.

threatened the entire town. An enormous area of temporary wooden shops, opened during each Lent by merchants and artisans who came from all over the country, was completely destroyed.[87] 'Hundreds of unhappy people are now going crying along the streets, ruined totally by it,' Sterne wrote in a letter to Elizabeth,

> and many fled out in their shirts, and have not only lost their goods and merchandize, but all the money they have been taking these six weeks. *Oh! ces moments de malheur sont terribles*, said my barber to me as he was shaving me this morning; and the good-natured fellow uttered it with so moving an accent, that I could have found it in my heart to have cried over the perishable and uncertain tenure of every good in this life. (154).

In April, Charles James Fox and George Macartney returned to England and Sterne moved in with a French family, probably to improve his French (163). He needed that, for, as the warm weather approached and the salons began to close, he found himself more and more in the company of Englishmen. He struck up a friendship with two Yorkshiremen, Thomas Thornhill, squire of Fixby, and his younger brother, George, who had a house in Diddington. These two jolly, if somewhat infantile, bachelors in their late twenties, were inseparable from their erstwhile tutor, now their guide, the sixty-three-year-old Genevan apothecary, intellectual and poet, Jean-Baptiste Tollot, a man well known to the d'Holbach circle, to John Wilkes and to John Hall-Stevenson. The Thornhill party would be Sterne's companions upon several future occasions. Sterne, excited as he was by the company of the *philosophes*, was also perfectly happy in the company of these lighthearted men. Tollot wrote to Hall on 4 April:

> I sometimes envy the happy disposition of your friend Mr. Sterne; everything is rose colored to this happy mortal, and whatever appears to other eyes in a sad or melancholy aspect presents to his an appearance of gaiety or laughter. He pursues only pleasure, and he is not like others who, when they are tearful, no longer can enjoy life, for he drinks the *bowl* to the last drop even though it provides not enough to quench a thirst like his.

Certain envious folk, Sterne told Tollot, had tried to convince him he had

[87] Numerous eyewitness accounts of the fire were collected by Guillaume Baston, *Mémoires*, Paris, 1897–9, I, 140–9.

not long to live, even though he had no alarming symptoms and was in better health than they. In any case, said Sterne, his health was not going to stop him from drinking champagne when the occasion called for it.[88]

One member of this little English coterie was Lawson Trotter, Hall's uncle (181). Trotter, the brother of Hall's mother, had inherited Skelton Castle, which had been in his family for two centuries; but in 1732 he sold it to Hall's father. Later he joined the rebel cause, and when the rebellion failed he followed Prince Charles Edward into exile.[89] Four years later, when Thomas Thornhill was made High Sheriff for Yorkshire, Sterne must have mused upon the irony of their all sitting down to whist in the capital of the foreign power that had sponsored Charles Edward's rebellion and with whom England was still at war.

Sterne also knew an Irishwoman in Paris, a former actress, now a struggling playwright. Elizabeth Griffiths was the 'lady of talents' (162) who had translated Diderot's *Fils naturel*. When Sterne sent the play to Becket, he referred to her as 'a friend' (166). Mrs Griffiths, now in her mid-thirties, had been born into a Dublin theatrical family and had experienced some success as an actress in Dublin and London. She married, retired from stage, and devoted herself to writing. Her husband, Richard Griffiths, also Irish and also a writer, Sterne would meet at Scarborough in 1767. The Griffithses were living apart in 1762. He had a post in the customs. She lived in Paris, where she had made herself useful as a translator to Marmontel, Beaumarchais, Diderot, and other writers who hoped for an English audience.[90]

Having ample time on his hands, Sterne felt free to indulge his love of

[88] Cooper in SEVEN LETTERS did not give the full letter; I base my translation and summary upon the MS, at the Beinecke Library. For a sketch of Tollot, CURTIS, 187–8. His connection with Wilkes is revealed in Wilkes's correspondence: BL, Add. MSS 30868, fol. 198; 30869, fol. 76. He is not to be confused with the Englishman of similar name, Charles Tollet of Betley Hall, Staffordshire, a man of intellectual bent (see CURTIS, 169), who did Sterne the favour of carrying packages from Paris to London. For the Thornhill brothers, see CURTIS, 173.

[89] *EMY*, 54; CURTIS, 182; J. W. Ord, *History and Antiquities of Cleveland*, 1846, pp. 252–8; Robert Surtees, *History and Antiquities of Durham*, 4 vols, 1816–40, II, 291–2.

[90] *DNB*; obituary in *Gentleman's Magazine*, 5 January 1793; *Biographical Dictionary of Actors, Actresses, Musicians, Dancers . . . 1660–1800*, ed. Philips H. Highfill, Jr, Kalman A. Burnim and Edward A. Langhaus, Carbondale, Ill., 1973–. The identification of Mrs Griffiths as the translator of Diderot's drama was first made by Hedgcock, *A Cosmopolitan Actor*, 152, n. 1. The article on her in *European Magazine*, March 1782, is not to be trusted.

theatre. He went often to the Comédie-Française. With Fox and Macartney, he saw the great actress Clairon in La Touche's *Iphigénie en Tauride* – 'She is extremely great' (152). The entire English colony took boxes and went together to see Préville – 'Mercury himself' – in de Boissy's *Le Français à Londres* (152). He also went to the second licensed theatre, the Opéra Comique, which had recently merged with the Comédie Italienne and was offering opera (162). One can hardly doubt that he also enjoyed the highly developed, unlicensed street theatres set up on platforms on bridges and in squares, and the private theatre of the Prince de Conti and other of his hosts; but about these he left no comment in his letters.

The commentary about theatre is written for Garrick, and Sterne seems to have thought of himself as Garrick's advance agent. Garrick was planning to come to Paris as soon as he could safely bring his wife. So we find Sterne running errands for him, sending him some 'comic operas' (157), pronouncing upon Diderot's drama, buying and sending a pamphlet Garrick had requested on 'tragical declamation' as well as another in verse that Sterne thought 'worth reading' (151), and reporting on performances. He did not always like what he saw. He grew tired of the Comédie-Française because 'they act scarce any thing but tragedies . . . I cannot bear preaching—I fancy I got a surfeit of it in my younger days' (157). And he grew tired of the incessant talk about theatre:

> the whole City of Paris is *bewitch'd* with the comic opera, and if it was not for the affairs of the Jesuits, which takes up one half of our talk, the comic opera would have it all—It is a tragical nuisance in all companies as it is, and was it not for some sudden starts and dashes—of Shandeism, which now and then either breaks the thread, or entangles it so, that the devil himself would be puzzled in winding it off—I should die a martyr—this by the way I never will—(157)

But how much praise could be given to French acting when he was writing to the greatest English actor? 'They have nothing here, which gives the nerves so smart a blow as those great characters in the hands of G[arrick]! but I forgot I am writing to the man himself' (157).

> Here the comic actors [i.e. from the Opéra Comique] were never so low—the tragedians hold up their heads—in all senses. I have known *one little man* support the theatrical world, like a David Atlas, upon his shoulders, but Preville can't do half as much here, though Mad.

> Clairon stands by him, and sets her back to his—she is very great, however, and highly improved since you saw her—she also supports her dignity at table, and has her public day every Thursday, when she *gives to eat*, (as they say here) to all that are hungry and dry. (162)

Garrick, Sterne learned, was much talked of in Paris: 'these last two days you have happened to engross the whole conversation at two great houses where I was at dinner' (162). The French found it a problem 'that one and the same man should possess such tragic and comic powers, and in such an equilibrio' (162). But it is not likely that Sterne – or Garrick, for that matter – could have predicted the sensation Garrick's entrance into Paris the next year would cause. In 1762 Sterne was admired in the salons of Paris. In 1763 and 1764, Garrick was adored.

Joseph Craddock told a story about meeting Sterne at the Drury Lane and saying to him, '"As you are so intimate with Garrick, I wonder that you have never undertaken to write a Comedy." He seemed quite struck, and after a pause, with tears in his eyes, replied, "I fear I do not possess the proper talent for it, and I am utterly unaquainted with the business of the stage."'[91] It may be that Sterne did not feel competent to write for the theatre, but the tears in his eyes speak worlds about his talent for acting. At this sort of spontaneous, informal acting, he was expert. One day in Paris he was walking toward the Pont Neuf through an area crowded with people watching mountebanks, some of whom were on horseback, jugglers and actors. Stopping on the bridge to admire the pedestalled statue of Henri IV, he noticed that the crowd was watching him. 'Why are you all looking at me?' he cried; 'do as I do, all of you!' Thereupon he threw himself down on his knees before the statue, and the entire crowd followed suit. No slave, said Garat, who told this story, ever rendered to Henri IV such homage as this Englishman.[92]

Sterne's delight in exercising this ability could get him into trouble. On 4 June 1762, Lord Tavistock invited the handful of English left in Paris to a dinner to celebrate the king's birthday. Tavistock, heir to the great Duke of Bedford, had come to Paris with his father, who was now in charge of peace negotiations. Among Tavistock's guests were Sterne and Louis Dutens, who had handed over the embassy at Turin to Pitt and Phelps and was on his way back to England. Dutens told the story of what happened between him and 'the famous Sterne . . . the Rabelais of England':

[91] CRADDOCK, I, 207–8.

[92] GARAT, II, 148.

> We were very jovial during dinner; and drank, in the English manner, the toasts of the day. The conversation turned upon Turin, which several of the company were on the point of visiting: upon which Mr. Sterne, addressing himself to me, asked me if I knew Mr. D[utens], naming me. I replied, 'Yes, very intimately.' The whole company began to laugh; and Sterne, who did not suppose me so near him, imagined that this Mr. D[utens] must be a very singular character, since the mention of the name alone excited merriment. 'Is not he rather a strange fellow?' added he, immediately. 'Yes,' replied I, 'an original.'—'I thought so,' continued he; 'I have heard him spoken of:' and then he began to draw a picture of me, the truth of which I pretended to acknowledge; while Sterne, seeing that the subject amused the company, invented from his fertile imagination many stories, which he related in his way, to the great diversion of us all. I was the first who withdrew; and I had scarcely left the house, when they told him who I was: they persuaded him that I had restrained myself at the time from respect to Lord Tavistock; but that I was not to be offended with impunity, and that he might expect to see me on the next day, to demand satisfaction for the improper language which he had used concerning me. Indeed he thought he had carried his raillery too far, for he was a little merry: he therefore came the following morning to see me, and to beg pardon for any thing that he might have said to offend me; excusing himself by that circumstance, and by the great desire he had to amuse the company, who had appeared so merrily disposed from the moment he first mentioned my name. I stopped him short at once, by assuring him that I was as much amused at his mistake as any of the party; that he had said nothing which could offend me; and that, if he had known the man he had spoken to as well as I did, he might have said much worse things of him. He was delighted with my answer, requested my friendship, and went away highly pleased with me.[93]

It is not surprising that a natural actor who was also a preacher should have interested himself in the most famous pulpit orator in France. Sterne had no hesitations about attending a Roman mass so that he could hear this man, the abbé Denis-Xavier Clément:

[93] DUTENS, II, 5–8.

> Most excellent indeed! his matter solid, and to the purpose; his manner, more than theatrical, and greater, both in his action and delivery, than Madame Clairon. . . . he has infinite variety, and keeps up the attention by it wonderfully; his pulpit, oblong, with three seats in it, into which he occasionally casts himself; goes on, then rises, by a graduation of four steps, each of which he profits by, as his discourse inclines him: in short, 'tis a stage, and the variety of his tones would make you imagine there were no less than five or six actors on it together. (154–5)

Ironically, two months later Sterne suffered the first of two attacks which virtually robbed him of his voice and left him unable to preach. The first of these, possibly a case of pneumonia, happened at Versailles, to which he had returned to seek passports for his family. 'I was unhappily . . . attack'd with a fever,' he told Archbishop Drummond,

> which has ended the worst way it could for me, in a *defluxion Poitrine* as the french Physicians call it—it is generally fatal to weak Lungs, so that I have lost in ten days all I have gain'd since I came here—& from a relaxation of my lungs have lost my voice entirely, that twill be much if I ever quite recover it—This evil, sends me directly to Toulouse, for wch I set out from the Place the moment my Family arrives. (164)

This was followed six or seven weeks later by a haemorrhage of the lungs which nearly killed him. 'I had the same accident I had at Cambridge,' he told Hall, recalling the fright he had had during their college years, 'of breaking a vessel in my lungs.'

> It happen'd in the night, and I bled the bed full, and finding in the morning I was likely to bleed to death, I sent immediately for a surgeon to bleed me at both arms—this saved me, and with lying speechless three days I recovered upon my back in bed. (180)

The first of these attacks filled his lungs with fluid; the second with blood. Both affected his voice. In the spring of the following year, Sterne wrote to Drummond again, telling him about the second attack and explaining that he had been left unfit for preaching.

> I have preached too much, my Lord, already; and was my age to be computed either by the number of sermons I have preached, or the

> infirmities they have brought upon me, I might be truly said to have the claim of a *Miles emeritus*, and was there a Hotel des Invalides for a reception of such established upon any salutary plain betwixt here and Arabia Felix, I w^{d} beg your Grace's interest to help me into it. (196)

Sterne also alluded to his voicelessness in *Tristram Shandy*, VII, which he wrote in the autumn of 1764: Tristram, contemplating a flight from Death into France, speaks to Eugenius about that '*son of a whore*', Death: 'I have forty volumes to write, and forty thousand things to say and do, which no body in the world will say and do for me, except thyself; and as thou seest he has got me by the throat (for Eugenius could scarce hear me speak across the table)' (576). Sterne never again recovered the full use of his voice.[94]

Between these two attacks, Sterne went back to work on *Tristram Shandy*. He told Becket on 12 May that he would have something ready for the press early the next year (167), and a few days later wrote again, 'I am very hard at Work and when I am got down to my house at Toulouse in the South of France you will soon see ab^{t} What' (169).

He was beginning to worry about money. 'When we are got to Toulouse,' he wrote to Elizabeth, 'we must begin to turn the penny' (172). Of the 4000 copies printed of Volumes V–VI of *Tristram*, about 1000 remained unsold. He tried to get Becket to buy them, but Becket declined. So he was forced to rely upon Elizabeth to try to sell them when she passed through London.

Sterne's fussy, worried letters to Elizabeth continued. She must bring £300 in her pocket, some of it for buying clothes. Lydia must have two 'slight negligees', Elizabeth 'a gown or two'. They could buy painted linens, silk and lace cheaply in Paris. 'In this country nothing must be spared for the back—and if you dine on an onion, and lay in a garret seven stories high, you must not betray it in your cloaths, according to which you are well or ill look'd on' (172). 'I long to see you both, you may be assured, my dear wife and child, after so long a separation' (171). He was sorry for all the business matters she had to take care of, but 'Do all for the best, as He who guides all things, will I hope do for us—so heav'n preserve you both' (172).

So Elizabeth made the final arrangements with Stephen Croft, who would find substitutes to take over Sterne's duties in the spiritual courts

94 For a discussion of the evidence that Sterne's voice was damaged during this period and how that damage led to his reputation as a poor preacher, see VOICES SONOROUS AND CRACKED.

and collect the income from Sutton and Stillington parishes. She sought and presumably found a tenant for the farms at Raskelf associated with Sterne's Coxwold livings (171–2), and she represented her husband in the last stages of the Sutton enclosure (176). She vacated their rented house in the Minster Yard, and on 19 June their household furniture, including an eight-day clock, was sold at auction. The chaise and horses Sterne had bought in London in 1760 were put up for sale, along with a saddle horse and all their tack and gear.[95]

Elizabeth and Lydia reached London about 22 June. Elizabeth Montagu, who was leaving or had left for the country, was not in a position to take them in. They stayed instead with a couple, Mr and Mrs E——(Lydia Sterne's habit of deleting names from the letters is maddening), probably the stationer from whom Sterne purchased the paper for his volume, William Edmonds, and his wife.[96] They put Elizabeth and Lydia up in their London house or possibly, as Sterne suggested, in rooms close by (174). Presumably Edmonds accompanied Elizabeth, as Sterne asked him, on her important business transaction – an attempt to sell the remaining copies of *Tristram Shandy*, V–VI, and the sale of the copyright in those volumes. 'Mark', Sterne scolded, 'to keep these things distinct in your head—but Becket I have ever found to be a man of probity, and I dare say you will have very litle trouble in finishing matters with him—and I would rather wish you to treat with him than with another man—but whoever buys the fifth and sixth volumes of Shandy's, must have the nay-say of the seventh and eighth' (174). Elizabeth did not succeed in either sale, and Sterne would continue to be plagued with the unsold copies for another three years.

Sterne had heard about 'a good natured kind of a trader' who had escorted an Englishwoman from London to Paris, and had a notion to get him to help Elizabeth and Lydia (176), but we do not know whether the man actually accompanied them. 'I wish I was with you . . .', Sterne wrote in his last letter to Elizabeth before her departure, 'to strew roses on your

[95] Advertisement in the *York Courant*, 8 June 1762.

[96] The identification was made by CURTIS, 169, 175, n. 2. After Sterne's death, Edmonds supported Lydia and her mother in their project to publish more of Sterne's sermons and collected subscriptions for them: LETTERS, 441; Lydia's holograph letter to Becket, December 1768, at the Houghton Library, cited above. Edmonds should not be confused with a man of similar name who worked as an employee or business associate of Becket. Sterne may not have known this man well: he called him at various times *Edmands* (199), *Edmundson* (211) and *Edmunds* (Sterne to Becket, 26 September 1763: Appendix I).

way—but I shall have time and occasion to shew you I am not wanting—Now, my dears, once more pluck up your spirits—trust in God—in me—and in yourselves' (176–7).

They got to Calais without mishap, and there they picked up a chaise which Thomas Thornhill had left for them when he passed through on his way home. Carriages had become very dear because the government had confiscated most of them to send to the army in Germany. It was generous of Thornhill to sell his to Sterne, and so cheaply that 'tis like making a present of it' (173). 'Send for your chaise into the courtyard,' Sterne wrote, 'and see all is tight—Buy a chain at Calais strong enough not to be cut off, and let your portmanteau be tied on the forepart of your chaise for fear of a dog's trick—so God bless you both' (174–5).

They arrived in Paris on 8 July. How worried Elizabeth must have been to find her husband so pale and drawn. Lydia did not notice. 'My wife and daughter are arrived,' Sterne wrote to Lady Dacre, 'the latter does nothing but look out of the window, and complain of the torment of being frizzled.—I wish she may ever remain a child of nature—I hate children of art' (179).

The Sterne Family Abroad 1762–1764

In the middle of the hottest July anyone could remember, 'as hot as *Nebuchadnezzar's oven*', (180), the family set out on a three-week journey to Toulouse. They might have gone the direct route and reached their destination in four days, but they chose the longer, scenic route through Dijon, Mâcon, Lyons and Nîmes, then westward across Languedoc to Toulouse.[1]

> In our journey we suffered so much from the heats, it gives me pain to remember it—I never saw a cloud from Paris to Nismes half as broad as a twenty-four sols piece.—Good God! we were toasted, roasted, grill'd, stew'd and carbonaded on one side or other all the way—and being all done enough (*assez cuits*) in the day, we were eat up at night by bugs, and other unswept out vermin, the legal inhabitants (if length of possession gives the right) of every inn we lay at. (182–3)

They travelled in the chaise Sterne had bought from Thornhill, a curious vehicle that looked as though it seated only two, but a third passenger could sit at the floor level with his or her feet in a lower 'cave' toward the front of the vehicle. Sterne and his daughter took turns putting their feet in the cave. But Sterne had overloaded the vehicle, and between Beaucaire and

[1] LETTERS, 181–3. In TRISTRAM SHANDY, VII, Tristram follows the route taken by the Sterne family, with one exception: he goes from Lyons to Avignon by the Rhône ferry. Although his description of this water trip (622–3) is accurate geographically, it is unlikely Sterne and his family took it. In the novel, Tristram can choose to go by water because his carriage had broken down and he had sold it. The Sterne family retained their carriage beyond that point: it broke down between Beaucaire and Nîmes. So they had either gone by land or, which seems unlikely, had taken the carriage on board the boat.

Nîmes a wheel broke 'into ten thousand pieces'. The postillions turned out to be

> two dough-hearted fools, and fell a crying—Nothing was to be done! By heaven, quoth I, pulling off my coat and waistcoat, something shall be done, for I'll thrash you both within an inch of your lives—and then make you take each of you a horse, and ride like two devils to the next post for a cart to carry my baggage, and a wheel to carry ourselves. (183)

They sat waiting on a dusty, unpaved road for five hours. All sorts of people were going to and coming from the fair at Beaucaire. 'We were ask'd by every soul who pass'd by us, if we were going to the fair. . . . No wonder, quoth I, we have goods enough! *vous avez raison mes amis*—.'

Toulouse, lying on the flatlands through which wound the River Garonne, was surrounded by mountains. Its houses were the Mediterranean type – stucco exteriors with much ornamental ironwork and inner courtyards. Indeed, it had once been the centre of Mediterranean civilization, the capital of ancient Aquitaine. Although it had fallen to the kings of France in the thirteenth century, it still had much autonomy and its own *parlement*. Now a town of some 50,000, it had long spilled over its medieval walls. There was an ancient university and the Académie des Jeux Floraux. But Sterne was not very impressed. He thought of Toulouse as a backwater town, 'out of the road of all intelligence' (186). And there were the *vents d'autan*, the winds out of the southern mountains that blew for days at a time and drove people mad.

It was a restless time in France. The Seven Years War had upset the economy, and France was torn by internecine struggles. The Jansenists and Jesuits were at each other's throats. During the past year, the Jesuits had lost one legal battle after another in the Jansenist-dominated *parlements*. The charges against the society had arisen originally from a bankruptcy suit, but became charges of treason when subpoenaed documents revealed a policy of political conspiracy, insurgency and even regicide. In August 1762 the society was officially suppressed in France. The Parlement of Toulouse, during Sterne's stay in that city, promulgated a series of orders to seize their property. The rules of the society were countermanded, and members were prohibited from wearing the Jesuit habit. Only the interference of the king prevented their being bodily banished from the nation.[2]

[2] For a summary of the Jesuit affair, see John Lough, *An Introduction to Eighteenth-*

Worse still, a threat of violence hung over Toulouse because of recent widespread conflict between Catholics and Protestants. The war had evoked old fears on the part of the majority Catholics, many of whom believed that Protestants were controlled by foreign governments and were designing the overthrow of the king – a mirror image of English fears of Catholics. In February of this year, 1762, a Huguenot minister and three of his congregation were hanged at Toulouse for having conducted an illegal religious service. Only days later a young man from a Huguenot family committed suicide, and a story spread about that he had recently converted to Catholicism. It was widely believed that all Protestants were fanatics who would rather see one of their number dead than converted. The young man's family was arrested and accused of murder. In court they were unable to demonstrate that the death was by suicide, though all evidence points to that, and the prosecution was unable to demonstrate that the young man had converted. Nevertheless, the father, Jean Calas, a respectable citizen of sixty-four, was condemned. On 9 March, in the centre of the Place Saint-Georges, he was broken on the wheel for two hours, the authorities trying all the while to get him to implicate the others. He was heroically silent. Finally he was strangled to death by the hangman. Public sentiment turned, and the family was released. Later they were arrested again, their property was seized, and they were banished from Toulouse. Still later they were allowed to return and were compensated for the loss of their property.[3]

Sterne never spoke of the Calas affair in the letters we have, but he had been in Paris when it was going on, in daily contact with the *philosophes*, who were much exercised about it. A flood of pamphlets had appeared in support of the Calas family which considerably influenced the courts. Morellet published a *Manuel des inquisiteurs*, his edition of a fourteenth-century work which set out in cold detail what tortures might be used to elicit confessions and evidence. It was Morellet's shocking point that they were still legal.[4]

Century France, 1960, pp. 180–1. The measures taken by the Parlement of Toulouse are described in J.-B.-Auguste d'Aldéguier, *Histoire de la ville de Toulouse*, 4 vols, Toulouse, 1833–5, IV, 319; and Pierre Barthès, *Toulouse au XVIIIe siècle*, ed. E. Lamouzèle, Toulouse, 1914, pp. 219–23. Sterne referred to the affair in LETTERS, 157, 160–1, and alluded to it in TRISTRAM SHANDY, VII: when Tristram in Lyons goes to see a Chinese dictionary in the library of the Jesuit college, he finds that the Jesuits '*had got the cholic*' (642).

[3] David D. Bien, *The Calas Affair: Persecution, Toleration, and Heresy in Eighteenth-Century Toulouse*, Princeton, NJ, 1960.

[4] Alan Charles Kors, *D'Holbach's Coterie: An Enlightenment in Paris*, Princeton, NJ, 1976, p. 123.

But it was Voltaire, said Diderot, who should be given primary credit for having rehabilitated the Calas family – a deed, said Diderot, 'which I would give all I possess to have done'.[5] The pity of the case certainly stirred Voltaire, but there was more to it than that: a gross injustice, apparent to all, had been perpetrated without a single infraction of the law.

Not all the Catholic clergy were unfriendly to Protestants. The Sternes could hardly have settled there without the 'good natured offices' of a certain abbé MacCarthy. This man, who was a friend of Hall's, had obtained their house for them and now looked after many details, taking in their mail, showing them how to apportion their expenses, and performing other services. There have been attempts to identify abbé MacCarthy, none very convincing, except the suggestion that he was a member of the Irish-French family of MacCarthy-Reagh.[6]

Sterne and his family were delighted with their house, 'elegant beyond any thing I look'd for' (183) and standing on 'the prettiest situation in Toulouse' (181).

> 'Tis built in the form of a hotel, with a pretty court towards the town—and behind, the best gardens in Toulouse, laid out in serpentine walks, and so large that the company in our quarter usually come to walk there in the evenings, for which they have my consent—'the more the merrier.'—The house consists of a good *salle à manger* above stairs joining to the very great *salle à compagnie* as large as the Baron D'Holbach's; three handsome bed-chambers with dressing rooms to them—below stairs two very good rooms for myself, one to study in, the other to see company. (183)

From the same landlord[7] Sterne also hired a country house, two miles out of town, 'so that myself and all my family having nothing more to do than to

[5] Quoted by Arthur H. Wilson, *Diderot*, New York, 1972, p. 442.

[6] CURTIS, 175, first suggested his connection with the MacCarthy-Reagh family. but Curtis does not make a convincing case that he was the MacCarthy who pilfered money from Voltaire. The name was a common one. CONNELY, 95–6, identified him as Nicholas MacCarthy of the MacCarthy-Reagh family that had lived in Toulouse for three generations. I have consulted his source, the *Eloge de M. le Vicomte Justin de MacCarthy*, Toulouse, 1864, pp. 10–12; but the passage in question indicates that the abbé Nicholas MacCarthy was only a boy in 1762. Moreover, other sources indicate that the MacCarthy-Reaghs had only recently come to France: see Richard Hayes (ed.), *Biographical Dictionary of Irishmen in France*, Dublin, 1949.

[7] In TRISTRAM SHANDY, Sterne has Tristram say that he is writing Uncle Toby's amours 'in a handsome pavillion

take our hats and remove from the one to the other.' Elizabeth had a cook as well as a 'decent *femme de chambre*', and a 'good looking *laquais*'. The rental for the houses was a mere £30 a year and everything else proportionately cheap (183). By October Sterne was estimating that they would live in the highest style for £250 a year (187). Since the income from his parishes and farms was more than that, they would be able to save – a point which became increasingly important to Elizabeth.

Handling money from a remote region during wartime proved difficult. Sterne banked with the small international firm of Selwin & Foley, as did most of the English who came to France at this time. Money from Yorkshire or from the sale of books in London had to be deposited in London with the senior partner, Charles Selwin; Selwin had to notify Robert Foley in Paris of the credit; and Foley had to inform Sterne in Toulouse. There was a co-operating Toulouse banking firm, MM. Brousse *et fils*, which would accept a 'remittance' – a transfer of credit – or a draft which Sterne could cash. The whole system was so awkward and the mails so unreliable that Sterne several times found himself short. 'When a man has no more than half a dozen Guineas in his pocket—& a thousand Miles from home. . . . You will not envy my Situation—God bless You—remit Me the Ballance due upon the rec^{pt} of this' (189). To another letter, he added,

> *PS*
> ☞ I have not 5 Louis to vapour w^{h}, in this Land of Coxcombs. My Wife & D^{r} greet you. (193)

Sterne grew very fond of Robert Foley, a man of charm and rectitude, and wrote him many affectionate letters. He once got angry with him for not sending £80 which he had been told had been deposited to his account in London; but it turned out his 'noodle of an agent' – Chapman, one supposes – instead of simply depositing the money had requested that a remittance be sent directly to Toulouse; of course, it went astray in the mails. Foley, innocent of any neglect, sent an unsecured remittance as soon as he learned of the situation. 'When I write the history of my travels,' said Sterne,

built by *Pringello*, upon the banks of the Garonne, which Mons. Sligniac has lent me' (622). Pringello we need not take seriously, since Sterne himself added a note which allows us to identify him as Hall's friend Sir William Chambers: see *EMY*, 188–9. But 'Sligniac' suggests the common French name of Salignac. No householder of this name has been identified in the police registers, the *Calendriers de Toulouse*, the *Almanac Royal*, the registers for the capitation tax, or other city archives.

'Memorandum! I am not to forget how honest a man I have for a banker at Paris' (198).

Sterne's finances were sound at this juncture, Elizabeth's anxieties notwithstanding. Foley, who knew more about them than anyone else, was willing to lend him money. A banker in Montpellier by the name of Ray, a friend of Boswell's, voluntarily opened a generous line of credit – £200 (198). Sterne's financial problems in France had to do, not with the ultimate supply of money, but with its management in a far corner of a foreign country.

They were still unpacking when a terrible 'epidemic vile fever which killed hundreds about me' (185) struck Sterne down and nearly took his life. Indeed, this disease, the symptom of which was a fiery throat, killed not hundreds but thousands in the area of Toulouse.[8] After his recovery, Sterne wrote to Hall,

> I drink, dear Anthony, to thy health and happiness, and to the final accomplishments of all thy lunary and sublunary projects.—For six weeks together, after I wrote my last letter to you, my projects were many stories higher [than the moon], for I was all that time, as I thought, journeying on to the other world. . . . The physicians here are the errantest charlatans in Europe, or the most ignorant of all pretending fools—I withdrew what was left of me out of their hands, and recommended my affairs entirely to Dame Nature–She (dear goddess) has saved me in fifty different pinching bouts, and I begin to have a kind of enthusiasm now in her favour, and in my own, That one or two more escapes will make me believe I shall leave you all at last by translation, and not by fair death. (185–6)

He hired a milch ass and a cow and began taking milk from each, three times a day (181). Fortunately, he still could enjoy a bottle of Frontignac (185) and the '*soupe, boulli, roti*—&c. &c.' (187) which the French cook put upon the table.

Since Hall had friends in Toulouse,[9] it has been suggested that Sterne would have been entertained by them. One was a Countess Fumel, who cannot be identified because there were so many of that name and title.[10]

[8] For an eyewitness account of this 'rhume très fort, avec un mal de gorge affreux', see Barthès, *Toulouse*, 233.

[9] Named by Tollot in his letter to Hall-Stevenson, 8 January 1764, in SEVEN LETTERS, 6.

[10] See de la Chenaye-Desbois, *Dictionnaire de la Noblesse*, 12 vols, Paris, 1778.

Another was Anne-Marie d'Aignan, Baron d'Orbessan, a learned man who played host to most of the distinguished visitors. He was Président à Mortier of the Parlement – that is, its presiding judge; *mortier* refers to his mortar-board cap.[11] A third was Alexandre de Requet, Seigneur de Bonrepos, another lawyer and the Procureur-Général of the Parlement.[12] These were members of that bourgeois class called the *noblesse de robe* to distinguish them from the old aristocratic families, the *noblesse d'épée*. Men of this class, more by heredity or purchase than by legal training, dominated the Parlement, which was the centre of their lives. But Sterne, for whatever reason, grew to dislike *parlement* towns (202). He must have been aware that French *parlements* were strictly judicial bodies; so the Parlement of Toulouse had to bear much of the blame for the Calas affair. In any event, Sterne said nothing about these people in his letters to Hall from Toulouse. He did indeed socialize with the French to some degree, as his strictures against the French character indicate – 'little variety, no originality . . . at all' (186) – but it is doubtful whether he saw much of Hall's old friends.

The Sternes' social life was primarily with the handful of English in Toulouse. Some were only passing through. John Wodehouse, the son of the squire of Kimberley Hall, Norfolk, and future Baron Wodehouse, met Sterne there when he stopped on his grand tour (193). But others who were seeking a cure had taken houses. A certain Mrs Meadows had a house in which she entertained the Sternes (188). But most important was a family by the name of Hodges. The husband may have been the Rev. Mr George Hodges, Rector of Woolstanton, Shropshire.[13] Sterne had met them in Paris (152), and after they had gone on to Toulouse they had written to advise him about his arrangements (172). Happily, Elizabeth and Lydia took to them. The Hodges family had also hired both a summer and a winter house. The two families, with four houses at their disposal, began to make visits to each other in one or another place, sometimes for weeks at a time – 'a happy Society living all together like Brothers & Sisters' (190).

As winter came on, the Sternes, the Hodgeses and other British families held nightly gatherings before roaring wood fires (187). 'We begin to live extremely happy, and are all together every night – fiddling, laughing and

[11] *Biographie Toulousaine*, Paris, 1823, II, 112–14.

[12] Chonaye-Desbois, *Dictionnaire*.

[13] If this tentative identification is correct, George Hodges was the son of George Hodges of Shrewsbury, Shropshire. He matriculated at Christ Church, Oxford, in 1739, aged nineteen, and received his BA in 1743: *Alumni Oxonienses*.

singing, and cracking jokes' (191). For the Christmas season Sterne suggested they put on some plays, whereupon they transformed themselves into a 'company of English strollers' and set about making costumes and rehearsing. Sterne probably acted, and certainly he played in the 'grand orchestra'. They put on Mrs Centlivre's *Busy Body*, and *The Provok'd Husband; or, A Journey to London*, by Vanbrugh and Cibber. Sterne had some thoughts about adapting the latter to their situation – and making it the 'Journey to Toulouse'. 'Thus . . . for want of something better we have recourse to ourselves, and strike out the best amusements we can find from such materials' (191).

But Christmas jollity could not banish the spectre of death from these tubercular people. On the first day of March 1763, one of their number died. This was George Oswald, an illegitimate son of a well-known Scottish merchant and diplomat, Richard Oswald. The father, an intelligent, learned man, a friend of Adam Smith and Benjamin Franklin, is remembered as a negotiator of the peace between England and America in 1783.[14] At the moment he was serving as a commissary-general to the English forces and their allies in Germany. Richard Oswald had no children by his wife, but he had reared as gentlemen his two sons by a mistress, Agnes Barr, and may have intended to make them his heirs. The older of these brothers had recently vanished, having quarrelled with his father. He later turned up in Jamaica and was reconciled with his parent.[15]

[14] Richard B. Morris, *The Peacemakers*, New York, 1965; CURTIS, 205.

[15] My account of Sterne and George Oswald is based upon two letters from Sterne to Oswald's father, Richard, and three to the father's business associate, John Mill, all concerning the illness and death. They were published by Archibald Bolling Shepperson, 'Yorick as Ministering Angel', *Virginia Quarterly Review*, XXX (1954), 54–66. The University of Virginia Library provided me with photostatic copies of the original letters, from which I have taken my quotations. The originals are among the family papers of Rear-Admiral J. J. R. Oswald, who kindly shared with me his information about his collateral ancestors. The hypothesis that the sons, Richard and George Oswald, were the illegitimate children of Richard, the diplomat, by Agnes Barr was suggested by Admiral Oswald on the basis of letters in his possession, though he insists that the hypothesis remains unproved. It is unlikely that the brothers were the children of Richard Oswald's only recorded wife, née Margaret (or Mary) Ramsay, of Jamaica, whom he did not marry until 1750. She was, however, aged thirty-three when she married; so a possibility remains that the young men were her children by Oswald before he married her. Young Richard's flight from England to Jamaica after his quarrel with his father suggests that he might have gone back to the home of his childhood. What happened to this son I do not know; but his father died without an heir on 6 November 1784.

The younger son, George, had come to the south of France in a desperate hope of curing his diseased lungs. He had gone first to Montpellier to be treated by the eccentric Dr Antoine Frizès. After a month Dr Frizès announced that the air of Montpellier was too 'sharp' for his lungs and that he should seek the 'soft' air of Toulouse. 'Then you're a sordid villain', cried Oswald, 'for allowing me to stay here till my constitution is irretrievable.' The story was told by Smollett, who heard it from Elizabeth Sterne.[16]

By February Oswald had grown so weak he could not look after himself. Sterne took charge, assisted by a kindly Catholic priest of Irish descent, the abbé O'Leari. In the third week of February they moved the patient to a house in the country which they had taken in his name. They hired a cow to provide him with milk. Sterne had little hope, but, wanting to do everything he could for the young man, he called in a group of doctors from the university, including the Professor of Physic. The doctors declared the case hopeless. On 24 February 1763 Sterne returned to Toulouse to pack a bag, it being now apparent he should begin the death watch.

Unable to discover where in Germany the father was, Sterne wrote to his business associate in London, John Mill, warning him of the young man's danger. George had made a gift to Sterne of his pocket watch, which 'he has desired me to wear for his Sake as long as I live—which be assured I shall do—but only on one Proviso—that I am desired also by his father to do so.' He also asked Sterne to return his sword to his father, but told Sterne to wear it himself until he got to London; and Sterne said he would do that 'because I think it an honour to wear a mark of any good Soul's friendship'. The second and third letters to Mill told the sad story of the young man's death.

> So long as there remain'd the least probability of Life—knowing how much depended upon cheariness of heart, I kept the Danger of his condition from him—but when this management could be of no longer Service to him—I felt I could not answer it either to him or myself, if I did not deal truly with him—a dismal Task indeed! at least so I found it, to be the Messenger of Death to one we love. He rec^{d} the news in such manner as would put philosophy wth all its Cant, to the blush—'God's will be done', my good friend, said he without

[16] *Travels through France and Italy*, Letter XI, in Frank Felsenstein edition, Oxford, 1981, pp. 101–2 and nn. 20, 21.

> any emotion, but that of religion—& taking hold of my hand, he added that he was more grateful for this last act of friends^{p} & thank'd me more for it, than for all the others he had rec[eive]d.

As he neared the end, Oswald asked Sterne the moment he closed his eyes to write his father to return thanks for all his kindnesses, and to beg his pardon for any indiscretions which had caused him pain – a task which Sterne carried out faithfully in his first letter to the father. George wanted his clothes and some money left to the Italian man-servant who had attended him with 'great Assiduity & fidelity—& wth an appearance of great attachment'. He made a donation of ten guineas to the abbé O'Leari, 'a very worthy creature (notwithstanding he is a popish priest)', who had sat for days at the bedside and 'did him every office his Wants required in a Way which shew'd, his Service came from his heart—This Young fellow I shall love & honour for the goodness of his disposition, & the great fellow feeling he shew'd to our friend.'

At eleven o'clock on the night of 1 March, as Sterne sat by his side, George Oswald died without pain. The next morning Sterne went into Toulouse and returned with the Professor of Anatomy and the doctors who had been in attendance to perform an autopsy. Oswald had specifically requested this because a few years before he had been wounded in the abdomen in a duel; he wanted it established beyond any doubt that the wound did not contribute to his death so that the gentleman who had given it would be relieved of any guilt. Sterne attended the autopsy, and reported the findings:

> It appear'd plain the gunshot wound had no Connection with his Malady, which was intirely in the Lungs, the whole of 'em being full of Abscesses—the right Lobe allmost entirely skirrous—& both of 'em adhering to the pleura, to the greatest degree that the Physician & Surgeon had ever seen—so that 'twas a miracle how he has lived at all; these last 3 months.

The doctors departed, and a tax collector appeared to claim the worldly goods of the deceased in accordance with the scandalous law called the *droit d'aubaine*. By this law, which Sterne would satirize in *A Sentimental Journey* (66–7), the Crown, acting through the *fermiers* of the taxes, could seize the goods of any foreigner dying on French soil. Sterne firmly refused. The tax collector disappeared and returned shortly with a 'file of musketters sent to take me in durance'. Sterne escaped by a back way, and walked into Toulouse and to the *hôtel de ville*. Aware that local authorities were embarrassed by the law and often subverted it,[17] Sterne 'made a shift to tell my Story so well, That I marchd back with a 2^{d} File to dislodge the first.' And so for a brief moment Laurence Sterne was able to live out his long dream of being a soldier. One supposes he was wearing Oswald's sword.

His troubles were not yet over. When he went to make arrangements for the burial, he found himself confronted by 'a brace of fiery Ecclesiasticks', who with 'barbarity' and 'insult' denied permission for a Christian burial, 'all cruel actions being *in the name of the Lord*'. Because he could not write all the details, for fear the censor would destroy the letter, we do not know how Sterne overcame these difficulties or what funeral service he conducted. We know only what he told Mill: 'I have conquer'd all, at last, & our friend is laid at rest, in the best Manner our Situations would let me.'

Since Sterne himself had put out the money for the house, the cow, the funeral – a total of £23. 15*s*. 0*d*.—he now had to render an exact account so that he could be reimbursed and to inform Mill of other unpaid debts and obligations. Finally, he wrote a letter of consolation to the father:

> Most gladly would I have saved this al-worthy Creature for the great Love I bore him, and for the pity I bore to those, who I knew must love him still more——But He, my dear Sir, who loved him more than Father or Mother or the tenderest of his Friends, has thought fit to order Things otherwise—his Will be done—it is the only Consolation under the Many heart-felt Losses of this kind we are smit with in this Turbulent Passage—& devoutly do I pray to Him who directs all our Events that you may bear up against this, & recover the wound, if possible, without a Scar. . . . He was a Treasure of all that was good & virtuous in a Young heart—inflexibly honest in his Sentiments—of great Truth and plainness in his words—hated every Thing that look'd like equivocation,—or that was mean or Mean-hearted—He had a just Sense of Religion, with an Abhorrence of Vice & of whatever was debauch'd or savour'd of professed Libertinism. . . . Had God spared him, He had agreed to live with me, so long as he staid in these parts—my House had room enough in it for so good a

[17] See the Chevalier Chastellux's review of Smollett's *Travels* in the *Gazette littéraire de l'Europe*, VIII (1766), 365–84.

> Soul, and my Wife who loved him as if he had been her own Son, would have nursed him with the tenderest care——but Alas!————

Then Sterne himself fell ill. After being up all night four nights in a row, 'with the agitation of Spirits & of Business & the anxieties which the Cure has inhumanly caused me', he turned feverish and began spitting blood. Toulouse had done nothing for his health. Two months later he would write to Archbishop Drummond, describing the unceasing warfare he had carried on with 'agues, fevers, and physicians'. His blood was so thin, he said,

> that the physicians found it necessary to enrich it with strong bouillons, and strong bouillons and soups a santé threw me into fevers, and fevers brought on loss of blood, and loss of blood agues—so that as *war begets poverty, poverty peace*, &c. &c.—has this miserable constitution made all its revolutions; how many more it may sustain, before its last and great one, God knows—like the rest of my species, I shall fence it off as long as I can. (195)

He probably spent a lot of time reading. On his shelves were eighty English books which George Oswald had brought with him. Sterne had asked Mill if he could have the use of them, since English books were rare, and the father had responded by presenting the books to him.[18] He read Rousseau's latest work, *Emile*, which he had bought in Paris when it first came out.[19]

But he was not able to get much done on his own novel. He had written something in Paris (169), and he had arrived in Toulouse in a good frame of mind for work. 'I am in spirits', he had told Hall in August, 'writing a crazy chapter' (181). Even that epidemic fever had not discouraged him: 'I am

[18] I surmise that Richard Oswald gave the books to Sterne, since we find him in July sending books, not to Mill, but to Becket, and instructing him about the duty to be paid (199).

[19] Sterne's copy of this four-volume first edition is now at the Beinecke Library, Yale, presented by L. P. Curtis. Sterne's signature appears on the half-title of Vol. IV, and some money calculations in his hand are on the fly-leaf of Vol. I. CURTIS, 188, commented about the book: 'As the text of the first volume was lacking its concluding pages, the binder added blank leaves which Lydia filled in with the original French for her father'. Curtis subsequently decided he had been mistaken about Lydia's hand, as he informed me in a conversation. But W. G. Day, after comparing the hand with Lydia's in her letters, decided that Curtis's first conclusion was correct: 'Sterne's Books', *Library*, 5th series, XXXI (1976), 245–8.

now stout and foolish again as a happy man can wish to be—and am busy playing the fool with my uncle Toby, who I have got soused over head and ears in love' (186). He was writing, not the narrative which became Volume VII, but the story of Uncle Toby and the Widow Wadman which became Volumes VIII–IX.[20] He was still working on that story in November, despite his poor health. 'I am got pretty well,' he said, 'and sport much with my uncle Toby in the volume I am now fabricating for the laughing part of the world—for the melancholy part of it, I have nothing but my prayers' (189).

He did not get far. He was still tinkering with the Toby story two years later. For the first time since 1759 when he had taken up his writing career, his creativity had failed. His health was poor. He was living in the same house with his wife. He had gone through all the episodes he had planned for the satirical story of Walter's misguided attempts to rear Tristram perfectly. All of these conditions served to depress his creative spirit. He may have told Becket in March 1763 that he would bring home a 'Continuation of Shandy' (191), but he had not written to Becket for months, and he wanted to assure him that Tristram Shandy had not died. He was more candid with his banker, in a letter of 29 March:

> How does Tristram do? You say in Y^{rs} to him—faith but so, so: but the worst of human Maladies is Poverty—tho' thats a . . . Lye,—for Poverty of Spirit is worse than Poverty of Purse, by ten thousand p Cent. (192)

He had 'hints and projects for other works' (186), including a travel narrative. When he was considering going to Spain, he said, 'I shall cross the Pyreneans, and spend a week in that kingdom, which is enough for a fertile brain to write a volume upon.—When I write the history of my travels' (198). After that, for the remainder of his stay in France, Sterne said not another word about writing.

Yet the stay in Toulouse was worth any difficulty, for there Lydia recovered her health. 'I have been fixed here with my family these ten months,' he told Archbishop Drummond in May, 'and by God's blessing it

[20] Volume VIII opens with Tristram's saying that he is writing in France – in a much idealized rural setting: 'in these sportive plains, and under this genial sun, where at this instant all flesh is running out piping, fiddling, and dancing to the vintage' (655).

has answered all I wished for, with regard to my daughter' (195). Understandably, Lydia fell in love with the land which had given her back her life. 'Miss Shandy', Sterne told Hall, 'is hard at it with musick, dancing, and French speaking, in the last of which she does *à marveille*, and speaks it with an excellent accent, considering she practices within sight of the Pyrenean Mountains' (186).

Elizabeth shared her daughter's enthusiasm for France. She was delighted by a style of life more luxurious than anything she had known since her childhood, and she felt at home in the easygoing English society at Toulouse. She began to talk about staying another year. It would save them money, she argued. But Sterne was bored. Although Toulouse was 'as good as any town in the South of France', yet 'for my own part, 'tis not to my taste' (186). He missed his friends at Crazy Castle (181, 185); he missed Paris (194). He wanted to leave: 'A year will tire us all out I trow' (181). So Sterne and his wife were left with an 'opposition of wishes' which was 'not . . . as sour as lemon, yet . . . not . . . as sweet as sugar candy' (186).

But Elizabeth would not quarrel. Sterne wanted to visit the spas at Bagnères-de-Bigorre; she opposed it. 'My dear wife is against all schemes of additional expences—which wicked propensity (tho' not of despotick power) yet I cannot suffer—tho' by the bye laudable enough' (186). He knew they could afford the trip and that Elizabeth was being obsessive about money. Still, she would not quarrel. 'I will do my own way, and she will acquiesce without a word of debate on the subject.—Who can say as much in praise of his wife?' (186).

Finally, they compromised. They would leave Toulouse and go to Bagnères for a summer visit; then they would hunt for another place in which to spend the next winter – perhaps Florence (193). England and France had signed a peace treaty in February, and during the spring a flood of English had come into France. Sterne thought he would find at Bagnères, not only his health, but a 'concourse of adventurers from all corners of the earth' (193).

So Sterne decamped 'like a partriarch with my whole household' (193), arriving in Bagnères late in June. It turned out to be a village, closely surrounded by steep hills. The area was not unlike Halifax, where Sterne had spent his school years. There were public baths on the hills, and a Hôtel d'Angleterre, which still stands. But Sterne found the amenities of the place below those he was used to at Scarborough (227–8), and for good reason. There were few assemblies, card games or balls, and the regular diversion was to walk in the country.[21] Neither the air nor the baths did him any service: 'The Thiness of the pyrenean Air brought on continual breaches of Vessels in my Lungs, & with them all the Tribe of evils insident to a pulmonary Consumption.' He was left no choice 'but gentle change of place & air' (204–5).

The change proved anything but gentle. They returned to Toulouse to pack and then started out for the west. They may have got as far as Nice, which they intended to investigate (194). We know they reached Marseilles, which they rejected out of hand because of 'the dearness of Living & House rent' (200). So they backtracked to Aix, which they did not like, 'it being a parliament town, of which Toulouse has given me a surfeit' (202). They went further back, having decided upon Montpellier. 'I . . . traversed the South of France so often that I ran a risk of being taken up for a Spy' (205).

Elizabeth did not like Montpellier. 'Things are moderate enough—tho' a third dearer than at Toulouse' (201). She began to talk of going back to Toulouse without her husband (202). And Sterne himself had doubts about the climate. 'The air is as cold, by fits, here as w^{h} You,' he told Lord Fauconberg,

> and I'm persuaded, in winter will be more thin and penetrating—but the air is elastic, & the Sky generally clear—& the temptations to get out o' doors more frequent—this place has had a bad Character of late years, as the grave of consumptive people—I see nothing yet to terrifye me upon that score—It may do hurt—but where it does no hurt, I believe it will do a great good—& for my own part, I love to run hazards—rather than dye by inches. (200)

Sterne found rooms 'on the hill' and the family settled in for the winter. Montpellier, a booming commercial town of some 25,000 inhabitants, was built up the sides of a central hill. Englishmen usually thought the houses were unimpressive and the streets narrow, but they admired the aqueduct which brought water to the town, and the citadel and the Parc de Peyreau which crowned the hill, where there were fountains, orange trees, palms and lovely walks with views of distant mountain ranges. Montpellier had no *parlement*, but it was the capital of the states of Languedoc and the site of the governor's office. Immediately around the town was the plain of Languedoc,

[21] CURTIS, 228–9.

an area given over to the cultivation of grapes and the making of wine.[22] Since the Bordeaux grapes had been destroyed by hail that year, the wines of Montpellier were in demand. One of Sterne's first activities was to ship off a hogshead to Lord Fauconberg (200).

Montpellier was also tormented by religious problems. Although a sixth of the citizens professed Protestantism, Protestant worship was strictly forbidden. On Sundays English visitors usually joined the Huguenots and other Protestants, who walked several miles into the countryside where in a field canvas shelters were rigged up on poles, under which several thousand people worshipped in a non-denominational service. The location was changed weekly. Every Sunday the guard at the citadel was ordered out to arrest the worshippers, and every Sunday the soldiers managed to take a wrong turning and so not find the meeting.[23]

Sterne made no friendships that we know of with the citizens of Montpellier, though he must have met some of them. Most of his social life was among the English. He made the acquaintance of a young man from Bath, Charles F. Palmer, who left a story about him in a letter to the Earl of Huntingdon. Palmer found occasion, he said, to compliment Sterne upon *Tristram Shandy* and to say 'that so far from thinking his Bawdy was a Lascivious kind of Bawdy that I had twice in my Life given his Book away to two of the Modestest Women in the World, but they were Women whose Heads were good as well as their Hearts.' One of these modest women was an old flame of Palmer's, Bet Randall, who, alas, had married a 'Paralytic old Mercer'. Sterne left Palmer and went on to join other English company, where he was introduced to the young wife of an old mercer. In their conversation, she told him that a gentleman from Bath had given her *Tristram Shandy*. As Palmer told it, Sterne at once put two and two together:

> Then Madame I know what sort of a woman you are—& said some civil things to her & mentioned my name. The Surprise was too much for her, She could not stand it, & by his Account the Confusion was such as must give me hopes. I have not seen her yet—but some how or other I find myself embarked in a Love Affair without meaning it, & Mr. Stern made the confidant of the two Parties, without either of their consents.[24]

[22] Van R. Baker, 'A French Provincial City and Three English Writers: Montpellier as Seen in the 1760's by Sterne, Smollett, and Boswell', *Eighteenth-Century Life*, II, 54–8; CRADDOCK, II, 189–201.

[23] Baker, 'A French Provincial City'.

[24] Charles F. Palmer to Francis, tenth Earl

Early in November[25] Sterne had the pleasure of a call from Lord Rochford, the newly appointed ambassador to Spain, who was passing through Montpellier on his way to Madrid (208). This was the well-known William Henry Nassau de Zulestein, fourth Earl of Rochford, the powerful Whig who had turned against Pitt to support Bute. At a later date Rochford by his single vote would prevent the repeal of the American stamp duties and thus precipitate the American revolution.[26]

About the same time, there appeared at Montpellier Colonel William Hewett, the eccentric world traveller and member of the Crazy Castle set. And a little later, the Thornhill brothers and their mentor Tollot arrived.[27] Christmas 1763 at Montpellier may not have been as pleasant for Elizabeth and Lydia as at Toulouse, but Sterne probably had a good holiday.

At Montpellier Sterne made the acquaintance of Tobias Smollett. Smollett had come to consult 'the Boerhaave of Montpellier', Dr Antoine Fizès, the physician who had misdiagnosed the case of George Oswald. Smollett soon decided that Dr Fizès was a humbug and discharged him. But he and his wife enjoyed their stay at Montpellier, attending the concerts offered twice a week by the Académie de Musique, mostly for English visitors, seeing plays at the Salle de Spectacles, and visiting many English acquaintances.[28] His meeting with Sterne was probably cool. Although Smollett's *Critical Review* had not been so hard upon *Tristram Shandy* as had its rival, the *Monthly Review*, Sterne had poked fun at Smollett in Volume VI: Yorick had wrapped his funeral sermon for Le Fever in 'a half sheet of dirty blue paper, which seems to have been once the cast cover of a general review, which to this day smells horribly of horse-drugs' (515–16); the *Critical* was issued in blue wrappers and the smell of horse-drugs alludes to Smollett's unsuccessful career as a physician. The squib may have been

of Huntingdon, 4 November [1763], MS at the Huntington Library: HA 9827; published in part in the report by the Royal Historical Manuscripts Commission, *Hastings*, III (1934), 142.

[25] The text of Letter 119 in LETTERS, 208–9, is based upon MEDALLE and bears the date under which she published it, 'Jan. 20', to which Curtis has added the year 1764. The MS has since been found and is housed at the National Library of Scotland (MS 2208, fol. 26). It is dated in Sterne's hand at Montpellier, 5 November 1763. It is hard to account for Lydia's carelessness.

[26] *DNB*.

[27] Tollot to Hall-Stevenson, 8 January 1764, in SEVEN LETTERS, 4–5.

[28] Lewis M. Knapp, *Tobias Smollett, Doctor of Man and Manners*, Princeton, NJ, 1949, pp. 252–4. Sterne's meeting of Smollett is attested to in the SENTIMENTAL JOURNEY and in the fact that Smollett got his story about George Oswald and Dr Fizès from Elizabeth Sterne.

inspired more by the *Critical Review*'s scathing attacks upon Hall's satires than by anything they said about Sterne.[29] Smollett, worried that the social life at Montpellier was damaging both his purse and his health, left after a month.

Sterne was not impressed by the social life. 'I suppose you are full of English,' he wrote to Foley, 'but . . . we are here as if in another world, where unless some stray'd soul arrives, we know nothing of what is going on in yours' (209). It had been a year since Sterne had declared, 'The humour is over for France, and Frenchmen' (181), and he had not changed his mind: he told Lord Fauconberg, 'I am more than half tired of France, as fine a Country as it is—but there is the *Pour* & the *Contre* for every place,—all w[ch] being ballanced, I think Old England preferable to any Kingdome in the world' (201).

So, from the time of his arrival in Montpellier, Sterne had been planning upon a return to England – probably alone.

> My wife and daughter purpose to stay a year at least behind me—and when winter is over, to return to Toulouse, or go to Montaubon, where they will stay till they return, or I fetch them—For myself I shall set out in February for England, where my heart has been fled these six months. (202)

He flirted with the idea of returning via Brussels and Holland, but quickly gave that up when he began thinking about Paris: 'I must stay a little with those I love and have so many reasons to regard' (202). Elizabeth, however, had not been able to get Toulouse out of her mind, 'where the cheapness and plenty of every thing is astonishing'.

> This weighs much with my wife, who being a great Œconomist, has a strong desire to return there, & stay a year behind me, with my daughter—she talks of nothing less than saving as much money in a year, as will equip them in Cloaths &c. &c. for seven. (201)

But a separation, though it might save money in the long run, would put

[29] Suggested by the editors of TS NOTES. Hall's initial quarrel with the *Critical Review* may have been literary. As mentioned in Chapter 1, the periodical chastised him for his 1760 *Two Lyrick Epistles*, and he responded with *A Nosegay and a Smile for Reviewers*. But Hall's continued attacks in subsequent publications were probably for political reasons. He had become a supporter of Wilkes, and Smollett supported Wilkes's enemy, Bute.

a strong immediate demand upon Sterne's financial resources. 'I can neither leave Madame with an empty purse—or travel 800 miles with one myself' (201). He would wait for Chapman and Croft to deposit the income which would fall due at Christmas from his parishes and farms. Candlemas Day, 2 February, would be his departure date.

He had been concerned for some time that Becket still had so many unsold copies of Volumes V–VI of *Tristram*. He had written from Toulouse, asking for a strict accounting: out of 4000 copies printed, 991 remained (192). He calculated that Becket owed him some £20 and asked for it. It did not come and he was annoyed (199). The money finally reached him in Montpellier, whence he wrote a recently discovered letter to Becket:

> It always gives me pleasure to be convinced no wrong was intended me—& a man of common Justice and good nature will ever be satisfyed with it,—& take for granted That some Mistake was the Cause. If I should have Occasion for money before I set out for England, I will draw upon you for 20 Louis'd'ors, with the more willingness, as I trust so much will be in y^r hands.[30]

The sales, however, moved slowly, and Sterne allowed his frustration to spill over into *Tristram Shandy*: 'Is is not enough that thou art in debt, and that thou has ten cart-loads of thy fifth and sixth volumes still——still unsold, and art almost at thy wit's ends, how to get them off thy hands' (663). He would not unload them entirely for another two or three years.[31]

Sterne was beginning to worry. His credit with Foley and the Montpellier banker, Ray, was stretched to the limit. Finally, late in November, he asked for a loan of £50 from John Mill and Richard Oswald. After all, he had himself lent them money without security at the time of young Oswald's death. He wrote to Mill.

> You may be assured dear Sir, my first Visit will be to Philpot Lane, to bring along wth me, (at least) the Interest in ten thousand thanks—& for the Capital, The whole Shandean family will stand bound—You shall be paid the very first Money God sends.—May he send You my

[30] Dated 26 September 1763: Appendix I.

[31] He wrote to Becket from Coxwold ~~on 30~~ August 1766, 'I shall publish the 9th & 10 of Shandy the next winter—but sh^d be glad to know, how many of the 4 last have moved off in the Compass of almost a Year, since We last settled' (288). Sterne published a second edition of Volumes V–VI in 1767: MONKMAN.

dear friend its Blessings, w^{ch} [in] my Computation, are comprehended in Health & peace of Mind (205)

Then, unlooked for, the blessing he had wished for Mill fell upon himself. A young nobleman whom Sterne had met in Paris set up for him, unsolicited, another hundred pounds' credit. Richard, Baron Grosvenor, a dashing bachelor of thirty-two, had a reputation for generosity. A decade before, when he had inherited his father's estate, his mother expressed disappointment that her late husband had left nothing to a younger son; Grosvenor immediately presented his brother with £10,000. He also had a head for politics, had served as mayor and MP for Chester, and in 1761 had been created Baron Grosvenor of Eaton.[32] 'I shall never forget your Lordships great Genteelness to me, as long as I remember any thing in this world,' wrote Sterne;

> '*Poor Sterne! what with sickness and bad Management, has run aground in the furthest part of France—& wants* to borrow fifty pounds—I'll lend him a hundred'—No body but Lord Grosvenor would have thought of such a Thing—
>
> I would not wish to have a better Text than this, for a Sermon upon public Spirit—How should a man, my Lord, have that in the *Gross*, which he has not in the *Detail*? or pretend to be a friend to all Mankind, who has not a Soul to do a kindness to any one Man?—You may take my word, my Lord, That a Man must have a *good* heart before he can have a *generous* one—and that to have a generous one, A Man must live so as to *Afford* to consider this public more than himself. (206)

At last he was ready to depart. 'My wife returns to Toulouse,' he told Foley, 'and purposes to spend the summer at Bagnieres—I on the contrary go and visit my wife the church in Yorkshire.—We all live the longer—at least the happier—for having things our own way' (209).

According to Tollot, who wrote to Hall from Montpellier about Christmas, Sterne had originally intended to take the family back to England, 'but it seems that the two ladies wish to pass yet another year in France to *finish* Miss Sterne.' Sterne was worried. He begged his daughter 'to make no friendships with the French-women—not that I think ill of

[32] *DNB*; NAMIER AND BROOKE; Burke's *Peerage*.

them all, but sometimes women of the best principles are the most *insinuating*—nay I am so jealous of you that I should be miserable were I to see you had the least grain of coquettry in your composition.' He still cherished an ideal of naturalness for his daughter: 'Remember to write to me as to a friend—in short whatever comes into your little head, and then it will be natural' (212). He was interested in her musical accomplishments and sent her a guitar when he got to Paris. But he told her, a little harshly, 'you have no genius for drawing, (tho' you never could be made to believe it) pray waste not your time about it.' From Paris he sent her books for her amusement and a set of *Spectators* for her instruction (212). And so, out of love for Lydia, Sterne began to oppose their intention to remain behind.

But his protests were weak because Elizabeth was driving him mad. He could not work at his writing. His health was not getting better. Tollot saw him as that same 'good and agreeable Tristram' he had known in Paris two years before, but he wanted Hall to understand the plight of their friend:

> He spent a long time in Toulouse, where he would have been amused without his wife, who follows him everywhere and wishes to be everything to him. The disposition of this good woman has given him bad times enough, but he bears these disagreeable moments with the patience of an angel.[33]

Tollot might presume that Hall would know what he meant by the 'disposition of this good woman'. Elizabeth Montagu was constrained to be more specific. Elizabeth Sterne, though she did not quarrel openly with her husband in France, complained of him after he left to her cousins, Elizabeth Montagu and Sarah Scott. When Mrs Scott asked her sister to enlighten her, Mrs Montagu replied,

> I cannot imagine he is of a sort to make a good Husband, & I wish his wife may not often feel the want of money abroad. She is certainly very ill tempered . . . always taking frump at somebody & for ever in quarrels & frabbles. In the South of France she met Miss Townshend & Capt. Orme, & instead of quietly avoiding them she entered into violent quarrels. . . . M[rs] Carter one night met a Lady who from

[33] Tollot to Hall-Stevenson, 8 January 1764, in SEVEN LETTERS, 5; my translation from the French.

thence brought strange stories of her violence & unbalance & as Tristram was in another Kingdom this scrape must be her own seeking. One should hardly think a Woman unhappy from the persecutions of her Husband w^{d} be eternally entering into disputes with strangers yet this has been her case. All people at home & abroad say she is as rude as a bear to those she does not like & indeed it was always her manner, at the same time she has many good qualities, but neither conscious virtue nor superior parts authorize peoples using their neighbours with haughty contempt or bitter sarcasms. She is very absurd if having a domestick enemy she tries to have as many out of her family as she can make, but her Father was of ye same sort.[34]

So Sterne withdrew his opposition when Elizabeth insisted upon staying behind. 'My System is to let her please herself—so I shall return to Coxwould alone, and manage my health & self in my own Country as well as I can' (201). And, when she increased the stakes and began talking about staying two or three years, he consented: 'I have no objection, except that I wish my girl in England' (210). In the end, he maintained a formal position that the family should remain together, but did not insist. To make certain Lydia understood, he wrote to her after he reached Paris:

I acquiesced in your staying in France—likewise it was your mother's wish—but I must tell you both (that unless your health had not been a plea made use of) I should have wished you both to return with me. . . . If your mother's rhumatism continues and she chooses to go to Bagnieres—tell her not to be stopped for want of money, for my purse shall be as open as my heart. (212)

What he did not say to Lydia was that the burden of caring for her mother was going to fall upon her. Lydia was now a young lady of seventeen, perfectly at home in France – where indeed she would spend the rest of her life – and competent in all practical matters of travel and housekeeping. From this point until Elizabeth announced an intention of returning to England in 1767, Sterne ceased writing to his wife: all his letters were addressed to Lydia, the virtual mother in the family.

Sterne remained faithful in his support. He left them £100 in pocket, and

[34] Dated 11 April 1765: Huntington Library, MO 5820.

as soon as he got to England he deposited another £100 that they could draw upon (222). He wrote many letters to Foley or his young associate, Isaac Panchaud, arranging their finances. And he gave Elizabeth moral support when she needed it. When a pip-squeak banker in Montauban insinuated to Elizabeth that she was to be separated from her husband permanently, Sterne sent a firmly worded letter to Foley telling him to set the man straight: 'Now as this is not true in the first place, and may give a disadvantageous impression of her to those she lives amongst—'twould be unmerciful to let her, or my daughter, suffer by it; so do be so good as to undeceive him' (228).

On 5 January 1764 Sterne hired a horse to ride to Pézenas, a small town some fifteen miles to the west much frequented by English people seeking a cure. Halfway there the horse balked and turned about. Sterne was not much of a horseman. He did not know the difference between a canter and a trot (213). The animal 'was as unmoveable as Don Quixote's wooden horse, and my arm was half dislocated in whipping him—This quoth I is inhuman.' A peasant happened along and offered to drive the beast, 'so he laid on his posteriors, but 'twas needless—as his face was turn'd towards Montpellier he began to trot' (207–8). Then this farce very nearly became a tragedy. Sterne began to feel feverish. He got home as soon as he could and took to his bed. He lay ten days in a terrible 'scuffle with death . . . but unless the spirit of prophecy deceive me—I shall not die but live' (208). He allowed himself time to recover some strength and then packed his bags.

Elizabeth had finally given up any idea of returning to Toulouse and had fixed instead upon nearby Montauban. All her arrangements had been made. In late February, Sterne wrote to Mrs Fenton:

> I am preparing, my dear Mrs. F[enton] to leave France, for I am heartily tired of it—That insipidity there is in French characters has disgusted your friend Yorick.—I have been dangerously ill, and cannot think that the sharp air of Montpellier has been of service to me—and so my physicians told me when they had me under their hands for above a month—if you stay any longer here, Sir, it will be fatal to you—And why good people were you not kind enough to tell me this sooner?—After having discharged them, I told Mrs. S[terne] that I should set out for England very soon. . . .

The annual meeting of the states of Languedoc had been convened in

January, and Sterne had witnessed with distaste the elaborate parade and ceremonial.[35] ''Tis a fine raree-shew,' he told Mrs Fenton,

> with the usual accompanyments of fiddles, bears, and puppet-shews.—I believe I shall step into my post-chaise with more alacrity to fly from these sights, then a Frenchman would to fly to them—and except a tear at parting with my little slut, I shall be in high spirits, and every step I take that brings me nearer England, will I think help to set this poor frame to rights (209–10)

[35] For a discussion of a ceremonial procession at Montpellier and its meaning to an eighteenth-century citizen of the town, see Robert Darnton, *The Great Cat Massacre and Other Episodes in French Cultural History*, New York, 1984, pp. 107–43.

A Single Life 1764–1765

In March of 1764 Sterne took his wife and daughter to their new residence in Montauban, said his farewells, and travelled on to Paris. It must have been with a sigh of relief that he sat down in the Hôtel d'Entragues, rue de Tournon, with a new 'family', as he called the coterie which he now formed with Thomas and George Thornhill and Jean-Baptiste Tollot (214). It appears he came as a guest of Thomas Thornhill, who had enticed him to this luxurious hotel with a promise of his own room and a place at their table.[1] 'They are good and generous souls', Sterne wrote to Lydia (212).

He called upon the Baron d'Holbach and the 'joyous sett'. Jean-Baptiste Suard had begun a new journal, the *Gazette littéraire de l'Europe*, which was to prove an important means for bringing English literature to the attention of Frenchmen. It had been inspired by John Wilkes, an old friend of Suard's. Wilkes even contributed nine or ten articles, but they were so carelessly written that Suard had to rewrite them. Most were by Suard and the abbé François Arnaud.[2] Soon after Sterne arrived in Paris, one of the other of these men reviewed his *Sermons* of 1760, the occasion being their reissue in a fifth edition, of 1763. Sterne would have liked reading that his sermons offered 'an entirely new course in morality', but he must have been disappointed to see in the same issue another review, of Churchill's *Poems*, in which Suard mentioned *Tristram Shandy*, as a novel 'more gay than decent'.

According to Joseph Craddock, French enthusiasm for Sterne as a person

[1] Tollot to Hall-Stevenson, 8 January 1764: SEVEN LETTERS, 5–6.

[2] Louis I. Bredvold, *The Contribution of John Wilkes to the 'Gazette Littéraire de l'Europe'*, University of Michigan Contributions in Modern Philosophy, No. 15, 1950; Gabriel Bonno (ed.), *Lettres inédites de Suard à Wilkes*, University of California Publications in Modern Philology, XV, No. 2, 1932, pp. 161–5.

had cooled since 1762. The French, he said, could not bear Sterne because of 'some keen ridicule which he had thrown on the Parisians'.[3] Sterne certainly had said caustic things about polite society in France. One sarcasm he repeated so often that Suard reported it in the *Gazette*,[4] whence it made its way into the *London Chronicle* for 16–18 April 1765:

> They tell us a pleasant anecdote relating to Mr. Sterne when he was at Paris: A French Gentleman asked him, If he had found in France no original characters that he could make use of in his history? '*No*, replied he, *The French resemble old pieces of coin, whose impression is worn out by rubbing*.'

This was repeated word-for-word in the *Annual Register* for 1765. Another man might have denied the story, or at least tried to brush it aside. Not Laurence Sterne. Three years later he put it into *A Sentimental Journey* in a way which reveals much about him as man and author. In the *Journey*, while insisting upon the point, he so qualifies it as to take away its sting. Those who wonder how the early satirical version of *Tristram Shandy* could become the bittersweet story of parson Yorick in Volume I of the novel may contemplate how an insult to Frenchmen could become a part of the tempered sentimental comedy of the *Journey*. Yorick is talking with the Count de B[issy]:

> Should it ever be the case of the English, in the progress of their refinements, to arrive at the same polish which distinguishes the French, if we did not lose the *politesse de cœur*, which inclines men more to human actions, than courteous ones—we should at least lose that distinct variety and originality of character, which distinguishes them, not only from each other, but from all the world besides.
>
> I had a few king William's shilling as smooth as glass in my pocket; and foreseeing they would be of use in the illustration of my hypothesis, I had got them into my hand, when I had proceeded so far—
>
> See, Mons. Le Compte, said I, rising up, and laying them before him upon the table—by jingling and rubbing one against another for seventy years together in one body's pocket or another's, they are

[3] CRADDOCK, II, 277.

[4] In the course of reviewing *Tristram Shandy*, VII–VIII, March 1765, pp. 39–43.

become so much alike, you can scarce distinguish one shilling from another.

The English, like antient medals, kept more apart, and passing but few peoples hands, preserve the first sharpnesses which the fine hand of nature has given them—they are not so pleasant to feel—but in return, the legend is so visible, that at the first look you see whose image and superscription they bear.—But the French, Mons. Le Compte, added I, wishing to soften what I said, have so many excellencies, they can the better spare this—they are a loyal, a gallant, a generous, an ingenious, and good temper'd people as is under heaven—if they have a fault—they are too *serious*.

Mon Dieu! cried the Count, rising out of his chair.

Mais vous plaisantez, said he, correcting his exclamation—I laid my hand upon my breast, and with earnest gravity assured him, it was my most settled opinion. (231–3)

Inevitably, Sterne in 1764 spent most of his time in Paris with English visitors. Since the signing of the Treaty of Paris ending the Seven Years War, a great many English had come to France. In Paris at any one time there were two hundred or more. It was an occasion of great joy when they got an ambassador. Francis Seymour-Conway, first Earl of Hertford, had been appointed in April 1763. When at last he arrived, in October, his embassy became the centre of social life for the English in Paris. Everyone hoped for an invitation to dinner, and, if they did not receive one, came there anyway to services in the ambassador's chapel. The chapel was not a consecrated building or room, but an institution. It was convened in whatever large room was available and it followed the embassy wherever it went. Originally, Lord Hertford had taken over the small Hôtel de Grimbergh, in the rue Saint-Dominique. But his landlord withdrew the lease and he was forced to look for another house. Finally, through the direct intervention of Louis XV, he acquired the Hôtel de Brancas, a magnificent Bourbon palace among beautiful gardens on the left bank of the Seine. When Sterne came to Paris, the English colony was excitedly waiting for the renovations to be completed. Today the Chamber of Deputies stands in what was then the gardens. The house itself serves as the residence of the President of the Chamber.[5]

[5] Harlan Hamilton, 'Sterne's Sermon in Paris and Its Background', *Proceedings of the American Philosophical Society*, CXXVIII (1984), 316–25. As Hamilton points out,

Sterne saw Lord Tavistock again (214), and probably spent some time with Charles James Fox, whom he had expected to find there (202, 209), and his older brother Stephen, the sickly heir to Lord Holland. 'The eldest cub of the *Fox* is here,' John Wilkes commented sourly, 'dissipating the ill-got, fleeting wealth of the father.'[6] George Macartney was probably with them. Lord Holland in London was trying to get Macartney a seat in the Commons. He did not succeed, but got him in 1766 a better plum – ambassador to Russia. Sterne went to see Hall's uncle, Lawson Trotter, and discovered that the old Jacobite had become something of a curiosity and was visited by numerous English, 'as well by In's as Out's' (214). Sterne had dined with him in the company of the ambassador's son, Francis Seymour-Conway, Viscount Beauchamp. Beauchamp was one of the more conspicuous figures in Paris, a young man of twenty-two, handsome and polished – 'the most amiable youth I have seen among all our young Noblemen', said Sir Horace Mann. Despite his youth he had been a member of the Irish Parliament for three years and held some undemanding Irish offices.[7] He had about him a group of former Eton schoolfellows, among them Arthur Lee, Constantine John Phipps and Sir James Macdonald. Another of this circle was William Combe, who would be remembered as the author of *Dr. Syntax* and one of the early editors of *The Times*. Combe, at the age of twenty-one, had come into a small inheritance and set himself up as a fine gentleman. Eventually he would come to hate Lord Beauchamp, whom he would satirize in the *Diaboliad* as greedy and cowardly, but by then he was saddled with Beauchamp's cast-off mistress, whom he had been bribed into marrying. Combe would become a gossipy correspondent of Sterne's and many years later he would turn a penny by snipping up the letters he had received from Sterne and incorporating the pieces in the many letters 'by Sterne' which he forged. But the William Combe whom Sterne saw in 1764 would have suggested none of this: he was a bright youth, a witty companion, well mannered and moderate in his habits.[8]

the house today is popularly called the Hôtel de Lassay after the Duc de Lassay, who built it. But in 1755 it came to be called the Hôtel de Lauraguais after the Comte de Lauraguais, who purchased it. In 1764 it was renamed the Hôtel de Brancas because that man had been created Duc de Brancas.

[6] Wilkes to Churchill, 10 April 1764: BL, Add. MSS 30878, fol. 44ᵛ.

[7] [John] Doran, *'Mann' and Manners at the Court of Florence, 1740–1786*, 2 vols, 1876, II, 132; NAMIER AND BROOKE.

[8] Harlan Hamilton, *Doctor Syntax: A Silhouette of William Combe, Esq.*, Kent, Ohio, 1969, pp. 19, 62–5 and *passim*; and HAMILTON.

Sterne missed Garrick and his wife. They had come to Paris in the autumn, been lionized in the most distinguished salons, and gone on to Italy. At the moment, the two most prominent members of the English colony were David Hume and John Wilkes – a study in contrasts. Hume lived at the embassy as unofficial secretary to Lord Hertford and tutor to Lord Beauchamp. 'His manners were polished,' said Joseph Craddock, 'his conversation correct and guarded.' His round face and ample figure were pleasant to look at, his talk amusing and enlightening. All of Paris, English and French, were enamoured of him. True, Hume had been reared a Presbyterian and become an agnostic – some said atheist – and this led to many jokes: Would the chaplain take him in hand and force him to chapel with the family twice daily? Had the chaplain become 'a Convert to infidelity?' and the like.[9] But the good-natured philosopher and historian was not disturbed. D'Alembert was his closest friend, and the *Encyclopédistes* revered him. Hume had a grudging admiration for Sterne. He would write in a letter of 1773, 'The best Book that has been writ by any Englishman these thirty Years (for Dr. Franklyn is an American) is Tristram Shandy, bad as it is.'[10]

John Wilkes had come to Paris as a political refugee, a non-person to the ambassador. Never invited to the embassy, he defiantly attended the ambassador's chapel – regularly, though he probably was an atheist. The ironies were unmistakable, and in London the *Public Advertiser* of 1 June 1764 reported: 'It is with Pleasure we hear, that the two most constant Attendants upon divine Service in our Ambassador's Chapel at Paris, are David Hume and John Wilkes, Esqrs.' Wilkes was at the nadir of his career. Pursued by creditors, expelled from the Commons, stripped of his colonelcy in the Buckinghamshire militia, rebuked by the Lords for printing a scandalous, obscene satire, the *Essay on Woman*, condemned by both Houses for seditiously libelling the king, and nursing a wound from a duel, he had fled to Paris. His daughter was at school there, and there he had many friends, most notably d'Holbach, with whom he had been intimate since their student days at Leyden. He found himself hailed by French intellectuals as a hero, largely because of a rousing speech he had made the previous May. From the dock of a London courtroom, he had electrified the mob by an eloquent and courageous proclamation of the rights of the

[9] Macartney to Lord Holland, 14 October 1763: BL, Add. MSS 51388, fols 141–5.

[10] *Letters*, 2 vols, ed. J. Y. T. Greig, Oxford, 1932, II, 269.

common man. So the *philosophes* now looked upon him as a great spokesman of their Enlightenment ideals. They dubbed him Gracchus, after two Roman patriot brothers who had united plebs and equites against the Senate. The appellation was apt, for the one power still at Wilkes's command in England was the adoration of the common people. When the hangman had attempted to burn Wilkes's *North Briton*, No. 45, the mob had taken the man in duress and forced him to burn instead a jackboot and petticoat, symbolizing the alleged love affair between Bute and the king's mother, which Wilkes had earlier alluded to in the paper. Eventually, the courts of law would stand behind him in his suit against Lord Halifax and others of the ministry, but at the moment it seemed likely Wilkes would be forced into a permanent, impotent exile.[11]

Sterne had known Wilkes in London before any of this had taken place. Wilkes had been a friend of Hall's for years; he had subscribed to Sterne's *Sermons*; and he had been on the board of governors when they invited Sterne to preach at the Foundling Hospital.[12] It was of some interest in England that the now notorious insurgent and the audacious author should have renewed their friendship in Paris. The *Birmingham Register, or Entertaining Museum* for 19 May carried an account, which it had probably picked up from some London newspaper: 'We hear that Mr. W. and Tristram Shandy, both now in Paris, are going to make a tour of Italy, etc. together.'[13] Perhaps someone had overheard them chatting about some future project; the import lay less in the rumoured journey than in the intimacy it seemed to reveal.

That Sterne and Wilkes were indeed intimate can hardly be doubted. It was at this time that Sterne presented his friend with a volume of recently discovered fragments of classical literature, *Catullus, Tibullus et Propertius. . . . Accedunt Fragmenta Cornelio Gallo inscripta*, handsomely printed in Paris by Joseph-Gérard Barbou in 1753. Wilkes proudly recorded the gift on the front blank: '*Ex dono L. Sterne 1764. Lutetiae Parisiorum.*'[14]

[11] Charles Chenevix Trench, *Portrait of a Patriot: A Biography of John Wilkes*, 1962; Horace Bleackley, *Life of John Wilkes*, 1917.

[12] Wilkes had been treasurer of the Foundling Hospital branch at Aylesbury, which he had helped to establish. But when he fled to Paris he left the books in a disastrous condition, with many unpaid bills: R. H. Nichols and F. A. Wray, *History of the Foundling Hospital*, 1935, pp. 299–301.

[13] CURTIS, 212.

[14] The gift was first noted by John Nichols in ANECDOTES, IX, 754. The issue is listed in Paul Ducourtieux, *Les Barbou Imprimeurs*, Paris, 1896. Wilkes's copy bearing the inscription was put on sale by Blackwell's in 1981 and described in their Rare Books Catalogue A17.

The complete truth about his intimacy with Wilkes, Sterne probably hoped to hide from the world. 'Sterne and I often meet, and talk of you,' Wilkes wrote to Charles Churchill on 10 April. 'We have an odd party for to-night at Hope's, two lively, young, handsome actresses, Hope and his mistress—Ah! poor Mrs Wilkes!!!'[15] Hope was Wilkes's reprobate Dutch landlord and friend. The word 'actress' of course, was a common euphemism for prostitute.

If Sterne thought he could preserve appearances while seeking these pleasures, he was mistaken. Wilkes, hating his own distorted face, had repeatedly made a neurotic display of his sexuality, no doubt to prove to the world his attractiveness to women. He never hid his participation in the scandalous gatherings of the Hell-Fire Club.[16] His brief, unfinished autobiography, written this very year (1764), hardly mentions public events, but dwells upon his lurid love affair with the Italian courtesan, Gertrude Corradini.[17] He had no desire to protect Sterne's image as a clergyman, reading into Sterne his own atheism or Churchill's apostasy or both. It is with perfect misunderstanding that he said about Sterne's preaching, 'Tristram pleads his cause well, tho' he does not believe one word of it'.[18] Such a man was certain not to keep the secret of his and Sterne's adventures with women.

There is no knowing whether the incident with Wilkes was repeated, but Sterne did not became a rake on the cut of Wilkes. This sort of liaison with women was incidental, not something he pursued with a fixed determination. We can best understand his conduct in the light of the Latin letter of 1761: 'what with not sleeping with my wife, I am unbearably horny—and I am done to death by desire—and I am made foolish' (124). His turning to prostitutes was nothing new. As his servant from the early Sutton days said, 'When any thing produced a difference between him & his wife, he would order Richard to bring out his horse, & they would go together to York, where he soon lost all his cares in the arms of some more blooming beauty.'[19] Sterne, however, neither liked nor respected his own

[15] Wilkes to Churchill, 10 April 1764, cited above.

[16] Chenevix Trench, *Portrait of a Patriot*, 55 and *passim*. The club is described by Donald McCormick, *The Hell-Fire Club*, 1958.

[17] *John Wilkes, Patriot: An Unfinished Autobiography*, ed. R. des Habits, 1888.

[18] Wilkes to Suard, 25 March 1764, quoted by Joel Gold, 'Tristram Shandy at the Ambassador's Chapel', *Philological Quarterly*, XLVIII (1969), 421–4.

[19] GREENWOOD; *EMY*, 81–6, 135–6. The Latin letter is translated above, Chapter 2.

sexual passions, a 'lascivious devil' that drove him. He had wanted his marriage to work, and had brought his wife to France determined to patch up their disintegrating relationship. He was unerring in Toulouse and Montpellier – in all probability: it is not the sort of point which can be proved. But the *ideal* he stated in a letter to Foley was to live 'as merrily but *as innocently* as we can' (208). The experiment had failed, and Sterne had lost faith in marriage. Mrs Thrale passed on an anecdote about Sterne in his single life:

> Says a Gentleman who listen'd while Sterne was abusing Matrimony—Come, Come, Jesus Christ once honoured a Wedding with his presence—but between You & I Sir replies Sterne, that was not the *best* thing he ever did.[20]

Sterne wanted something more than a battle of the sexes and more than the gratifications of a night. He wanted love. He wanted it to be with gentlewomen, and he wanted it to be sweet, pleasurable and profound. And because he wanted it to be free of blame, even for a clergyman, he wanted it to be public. To supply these moral rather than sexual needs, he invented his own sort of sentimental love.

In the spring of 1764 Sterne had a sentimental love affair in Paris. It was going on, in fact, at the very time he spent that evening whoring with Wilkes. 'I have been for eight weeks smitten with the tenderest passion that ever tender wight underwent,' he wrote to Hall on 19 May. He was in love with an unidentified English lady who had stopped in Paris on her way to Italy, where no doubt she was seeking a cure. Sterne could never resist consumptive ladies.

> I wish, dear cosin, thou couldest conceive (perhaps thou can'st without my wishing it) how deliciously I canter'd away with it the first month, two up, two down, always upon my hânches along the streets from my hôtel to hers, at first, once—then twice, then three times a day, till at length I was within an ace of setting up my hobby horse in her stable for good an all. I might as well considering how the enemies of the Lord have blasphemed thereupon. (213)

Because he had hidden nothing, he had set wagging the tongues of the

[20] *Thraliana*, ed. Katharine C. Balderston, Oxford, 1942, p. 255.

'enemies of the Lord'. He might as well have gone to bed with the lady, since the gossips would have it so; but he had not. He was more interested in sympathy than sex. He had done nothing 'but mix tears, and *Jouer des sentiments* with her from sun-rising even to the setting of the same.' The essential of sentimental love as Sterne reinvented it was to *jouer des sentiments*, to toss them back and forth, to give and receive expressions of sympathy, the sort of chaste love he would one day document in the *Journal to Eliza*.

This is not the first time Sterne had carried on a sentimental courtship. He had fallen in love with his wife while she languished from consumption and courted her with a sentimental gallantry. But this sentimental affair is the first we know of during his years of fame. There would be others.

But if Sterne attracted some attention, the English ambassador seemed unaware of his love affair or his friendship with John Wilkes. Lord Hertford, faithful in his duty to represent the Crown, persistently snubbed Wilkes;[21] but he paid Sterne the gracious compliment of asking him to preach in his chapel at the opening of his embassy in the Hôtel de Brancas. Sterne was amused by the excitement:

> Lord *Hertford* had just taken and furnished a magnificent *Hôtel*; and as every thing, and any thing gives the fashion of the moment at Paris, it had been the fashion for every one to go to see the English Ambassador's new hotel.—It occupied the curiosity, formed the amusement, and gave a subject of conversation to the polite circles of Paris, for a fortnight at least. (219)

On Sunday, 25 March, the doors were to be opened. Most of the people would arrive in time to attend the service and hear Sterne's sermon. Later there would be a dinner. It has been said that this occasion was the climax of Hertford's brief, uneventful tenure as ambassador to France.[22]

It might also have been the climax of Sterne's preaching career, had he not been physically weak and a little foolish. The invitation was brought to him, he said, 'when I was playing a sober game of Whist with the *Thornhills*' (219) on Saturday, the day before he was to preach. He got to work at once. Casting about in his mind for a text which would allude to Lord Hertford and the Hôtel de Brancas, he hit upon the story of how Hezekiah proudly

[21] Wilkes's letter of 5 June 1764 in *Correspondence*, ed. John Almon, 5 vols, 1805, III, 124–9.

[22] Harlan Hamilton, 'Sterne's Sermon in Paris and Its Background'.

showed his palace to the messengers from Babylon. 'An odd subject your mother will say,' he wrote to Lydia (212). The sermon soon moved beyond the story of Hezekiah and became a discussion of hypocrisy and integrity with interesting moral reflections and psychological insights. Sterne included it among the *Sermons* he published in 1766, adding the note, 'Preached before his Excellency the Earl at Hertford. At Paris, 1763,' (He got the date wrong: it was preached on 25 March 1764.[23]) Sterne insisted that the ambassador had thanked him 'again and again' and '*David Hume* favoured it with his grace and approbation' (218–19).

One difficulty was Sterne's voice, which had grown so weak he could not be heard. The chapel was held in a stately room, the Grande Gallerie, elegant with chandeliers and mirrors and tall windows looking out to the gardens and river. It seated some 250 people. The day turned out to be fine and everyone came – representatives from other embassies, numerous French guests, and virtually the entire English colony. 'My chapel was crowded yesterday', said Lord Hertford, 'to hear Doctor Sterne preach.'[24] Wilkes invited Suard: 'If, for dear variety, you chuse a slice of the Church of England and of Tristram Shandy, I will carry you this morning to the Embassador's Chapel.'[25] Hume may have brought d'Holbach and Diderot and other of the intellectuals. As Sterne later said, he preached to 'a concourse of all nations, and religions too' (212).

Sterne may not have been told how large was the Grand Gallerie. Wilkes, however, was anticipating difficulties with Sterne's voice before the service began: he said in his invitation to Suard, 'Tho' you may not catch every word of Tristram, his *action* will divert you, and you know that *action* is the first, second, third, &c parts of a great orator.' Within the previous two years, Sterne had suffered at least seven life-threatening attacks that had left him with a weak, cracked voice. In a letter to Archbishop Drummond that autumn, Sterne said,

> by long & obstinate coughs, & unaccountable hemorrages in my lungs, & a thorough relaxation of the Organ (or something worse) in consequence of them—I am foretold by the best physicians both in france & here, that 'twill be fatal to me to preach. indeed nature tells

[23] The date was established by Joel Gold, 'Tristram Shandy at the Ambassador's Chapel'.

[24] WALPOLE, XXXVIII, 353.

[25] Quoted by Gold, 'Tristram Shandy at the Ambassador's Chapel', from the MS, at the University of Michigan library.

> me I have no powers—and the last poor experiment I made in preaching at the Ambassador's Chapel at Paris . . . had liked to have fulfill'd their predictions.[26]

Sterne's foolishness on this occasion lay in his doctoring the biblical text for the sake of a joke. As he later explained to William Combe,

> That unlucky kind of fit seized me, which you know I can never resist, and a very unlucky text did come into my head,—and you will say so when you read it.
>
> 'And Hezekiah said unto the Prophet, I have shewn them my vessels of gold, and my vessels of silver, and my wives and my concubines, and my boxes of ointment, and whatever I have in my house, have I shewn unto them: and the Prophet said unto Hezekiah, thou has done very foolishly.'
>
> Now, as the text is a part of Holy writ, that could not give offence; though wicked wits are sometimes disposed to ill-treat it with their own scurvy misrepresentations. (219)

But the text is *not* holy writ, or even a paraphrase; it is a travesty of writ. It contains in outline the story of 2 Kings 20: 12–18, but, in Sterne's rendition, the treasures are more vividly drawn, the prophet's doom more dramatically pronounced. The wives and concubines are entirely Sterne's invention. It was this 'unlucky text', not the sermon itself, which had offended.

Sterne had made this sort of mistake before. In 1743, honoured with an invitation to preach the enthronement sermon for Archbishop Thomas Herring, he had picked a wry text – Genesis 4: 7, which all too obviously evoked the ghost of the late archbishop, Lancelot Blackburne, a prelate who had been egregiously negligent of his duties: 'If thou doest well, shalt thou not be accepted? And if thou doest not well, sin lieth at the door.' Nobody thought it funny.[27] And nobody thought the false text of the Paris sermon funny. Sterne tacitly admitted his fault when in the printed sermon he used a genuine biblical text – 2 Kings 20: 15: 'And he said, What have they seen

[26] LETTERS, 229. I have omitted a phrase which raises questions about the size of the room in which Sterne preached, or about Sterne's candour. In the full quotation Sterne speaks of preaching in the ambassador's chapel, '(tho no larger than y^r grace's dining room)'. I suspect he was reducing the size of the room for rhetorical reasons, the better to make the point about his weak voice.

[27] *EMY*, 152.

in thine house? And Hezekiah answered, All the things that are in my house have they seen; there is nothing amongst all my treasures that I have not shewn them.' It suited the sermon well enough. Not without reason did Sterne depict himself in *Tristram Shandy* as Parson Yorick,

> as mercurial and sublimated a composition,—as heteroclite a creature in all his declensions;——with as much life and whim, and *gaité de cœur* about him, as the kindliest climate could have engendered and put together. With all this sail, poor *Yorick* carried not one ounce of ballast; he was utterly unpractised in the world; and at the age of twenty-six, knew just about as well how to steer his course in it, as a romping, unsuspicious girl of thirteen: So that upon his first setting out, the brisk gale of his spirits, as you will imagine, ran him foul ten times in a day of some body's tackling; and as the grave and more slow-paced were oftenest in his way,——you may likewise imagine, 'twas with such he had generally the ill luck to get the most entangled. (27–8)

At the age of fifty, Yorick still had not learned.

The afternoon or evening at the ambassador's dinner, David Hume, seated at a table with Sterne, began to tease him about the miracle in the story of Hezekiah – the sun's shadow being turned ten degrees back on the dial. Sterne defended the account. Later, as Combe told Sterne, a rumour passed around that they had quarrelled. 'Absolutely false,' answered Sterne.

> Mr. *Hume* and I never had a dispute—I mean a serious, angry or petulant dispute, in our lives—indeed I should be most exceedingly surprized to hear that *David* ever had an unpleasant contention with any man . . . for, in my life, did I never meet with a being of a more placid and gentle nature; and it is this amiable turn of his character, that has given more consequence and force to his scepticism, than all the arguments of his sophistry.—You may depend on this as a truth.
>
> We had, I remember well, a little pleasant sparring at Lord *Hertford's* table at Paris; but there was nothing in it that did not bear the marks of good-will and urbanity on both sides.—I had preached that very day at the Ambassador's Chapel, and *David* was disposed to make a little merry with the *Parson*; and, in return, the Parson was equally disposed to make a little mirth with the *Infidel*; we laughed at one another, and the company laughed with us both—and, whatever

your informer might pretend, he certainly was not one of that company. (218)

In May, Sterne's quixotic affair with the sentimental lady came to an end. He wrote to Hall:

> The last three weeks we were every hour upon the doleful ditty of parting—and thou mayest concieve, dear cosin, how it alter'd my gaite and air—for I went and came like any louden'd carl . . . and now she is gone to the South of France, and to finish the comedie, I fell ill, and broke a vessel in my lungs and half bled to death. Voila mon Histoire! (213)

He must have been desperately ill. Garrick in Rome heard about it and wrote to his colleague George Coleman in London, 'I was told by a Gentleman who is just come from *Sterne*, that he is in a very bad way.'[28]

If the kind Thornhills delayed their departure until Sterne could travel, which seems probable, he gave them no credit: 'We have been talking and projecting about setting out from this city of seductions every day this month,' Sterne grumbled (213). He wanted to get to London before Hall left for Yorkshire (204), but he had committed himself to staying with the 'family'. Finally they were ready. Sterne wrote to Hall, making use of an indecent French word one seldom sees in print:

> On Thursday morning we set out from foutre-land, tho' we ought not to abuse it—for we have lived (shag rag and bobtail), all of us, a most jolly nonsensical life of it, and so dear cosin Antony adieu, in full hopes on my side, that I shall spend many still more joyous deliriums with you over many a pint of Bergundy—so be it. (214)

They reached London on or about 29 May. On 5 June the *Public Advertiser* noticed Sterne's arrival. Hall, alas, had left town. Sterne wrote to try to arrange a meeting at Scarborough. 'Write a line to us at Thornhil's, where I shall be whilst in town' (214). He was still the guest of his generous friend Thomas Thornhill, comfortably situated in his handsome house in Berkeley Square.[29]

Sterne spent a month 'in and about the environs' of London (222). He

[28] *Letters*, ed. David M. Little and George M. Kahrl, 3 vols, Cambridge, Mass., 1963, I, 411.

[29] On the west side, No. 49: ratepayers' list in Hugh Phillips, *Mid-Georgian London*, 1964, p. 287 ff.

must have seen many friends. He would have called on John Mill to discuss or discharge his debt, and upon Richard Oswald to return George's sword. He spent a morning with Reynolds, but not, as has been said, sitting for another portrait: Reynolds entered only one appointment in his book.[30] Sterne, who was interested in the copies made of his portraits,[31] may have wanted to discuss copies or prints of the great 1760 portrait, still in Reynolds's possession. He was still under Reynolds's spell and would compliment him yet again in *Tristram Shandy*, VII (590).

Sterne also made the acquaintance about this time of young Allan Ramsay, who had set up a studio in London in 1761. Soon thereafter Ramsay was made portrait painter to His Majesty and dutifully set about painting the royal family and numerous of the chief ministers and courtiers. Sterne was chatting with him one day in his studio and looking at the paintings. 'Mr Ramsay,' he remarked, 'you paint only Court Cards, the King, Queen, and Knave.'[32]

Sterne missed seeing Mrs Montagu because he put off calling until his last week in London and then found himself 'hurried out of Town on Wednesday to stay a night or two with Lord Ligoniers' (215). He had gone out to Cobham Place, Surrey, to be the guest of Field Marshal John-Louis Ligonier, Baron Ligonier, commander-in-chief of the armies of Great Britain, but commander mostly in name, for the armies during the Seven Years War were managed directly from the cabinet. At eighty-three years, Ligonier was a small, straight, handsome man with an engaging accent. He had been born French. He was notorious, or perhaps admired, for his amours with very young women. Sterne's father and Ligonier had been officers under Marlborough at the battles of Douai, Béthune and Aire, and Ligonier had been in Ireland commanding a cavalry troop when Sterne as a boy went trailing through that country with his mother and brothers and sisters, following his father's regiment. His father and Ligonier had both

[30] Reynolds's appointment book at Burlington House, 11 June 1764; *EMT*, 305–6.

[31] Foley owned a portrait of Sterne, probably a copy of the Carmontelle, which Sterne was anxious to have copied. He knew a copyist in Paris, a Mlle Geneviève Novarre, whom he recommended: 'I really believe, twill be the parent of a dozen portraits to her—if she executes it with the spirit of the Original in y^r hands—for it will be seen by half London—and as my Phyz—is as remarkable as myself———if she preserves the Character of both, 'twill do her honour & service too' (231). For Mlle Navarre: *EMT*, 308.

[32] Alastair Smart, *Life and Art of Allan Ramsay*, 1952, p. 112.

served on the Vigo Expedition in 1719.[33] At such great distance and after such a career, it does not seem likely that Ligonier would recollect Ensign Roger Sterne. He probably loved Sterne as a man who understood and respected soldiers, who had created Captain Toby Shandy and Corporal Trim. One cannot but wonder if Sterne did not have Ligonier in mind when a few years later he drew that engaging sketch of the kindly old French officer in *A Sentimental Journey* (170–81).

Sterne got back to London about 18 June, paused long enough to take leave of the Thornhills, and set out for York. His time with Ligonier may have rekindled his imagination and stimulated in him a desire to complete the story of Uncle Toby. Moreover, he now had an idea how he might continue the story of Walter Shandy. On the road, when he had stopped for the night, he scribbled an exuberant letter to Mrs Montagu:

> I am going down to write a world of Nonsense—if possible like a man of *Sense*—but there is the *Rub*. Would Apollo, or the fates, or any body else, had planted me within a League of M[rs] Montague this Summer, I could have taken my horse & gone & fetch'd Wit & Wisdome as I wanted them—as for nonsense—I am pretty well provided myself both by nature & Travel. (216)

Nature *and travel*: he had the idea for Volume VII.

He reached York on Saturday, 23 June – a fact noticed by the *York Courant* three days later. He stayed at York four or five days, probably with friends, since he no longer had the house in the Minster Yard. No doubt on Sunday he appeared in the vestry of the Minster to greet his colleagues in the Chapter, to walk in procession with them, and to sit in the North Newbald prebendal stall in the choir. And there were practical matters to be taken care of at York. Since Sterne had missed Archbishop Drummond's primary visitation, he reported to the archbishop's deputy registrar, the lawyer Richard Mackley, to whom he 'exhibited' his priest's orders and other papers authorizing various clerical functions. Mackley signed them, and Sterne completed the archbishop's questionnaire for Coxwold.[34]

Toward the end of the month he set out for Coxwold, going no doubt by

[33] Rex [Reginald Henry] Whitworth, *Field Marshal Lord Ligonier*, Oxford, 1958; *DNB*; NAMIER AND BROOKE.

[34] The MS, *Archbishop Drummond's Visitations*, at the Borthwick Institute, contains the questionnaire for Coxwold, reproduced in LETTERS, 217–18. The papers signed by Mackley: BL, Add. Charters 16158–16166.

way of Sutton-on-the-Forest and Stillington. He would have called upon his curate for these parishes, Marmaduke Callis, perhaps in the dilapidated timber parsonage next to the church which had been Sterne's home for twenty years. Callis liked neither the house nor his job, but he had done his duty and the parishes were in good order. Probably Sterne stopped at Stillington Hall to celebrate a reunion with Henrietta and Stephen Croft. Then it was on to the rolling hills of Coxwold. It would hardly be surprising if he felt a certain anxiety as he settled into his 'Philosophical Hut' (228), for this was the first time since he was a very young man that he had lived alone in the stillness of a Yorkshire village.

He had only a few clerical duties that summer and autumn. He had given up preaching entirely (222, 229) and said so in the archbishop's questionnaire: 'I have a residing Curate—and always shall have one, as I fear I shall never be in a condition to do duty myself.' James Kilner, the Coxwold curate, after several stammering attempts to apply for ordination during Sterne's absence, had withdrawn his application in confusion and fear. So Sterne now took care of the matter: he sent formal letters testimonial and a personal note to the archbishop:

> His character in this parish is very good; and . . . the man is well liked as a quiet and an honest man, & withal as a good reader and preacher: I think him so myself; and . . . a good Scholar also—I do not say, a graceful one—for his bodily presence is mean; & were he [to] stand for Ordination before a popish bishop—The poor fellow would be disabled by a Canon in a moment.
>
> . . . as I cannot discharge my duty myself, tis the more incumbent on me, to have it unexceptionally done by others. (229)

Kilner was ordained the next month.[35]

[35] Kilner went personally to the archbishop on 10 May 1762 to deliver a letter of recommendation Sterne had sent from France and to discuss ordination. For Sterne's letter, see LETTERS, 164. The archbishop added a note to Sterne's letter about the conditions of Kilner's employment, which concluded, 'He declined going into Priests orders, for reasons till Mr Sterne came over: but I c^{d} not understand all his reasons': CURTIS, 165. Kilner wrote to the archbishop on 6 September 1762, again declining to be ordained: 'I have been in several poor Places, & in frequent Journeyings, among People who now & then ought to have us'd me more liberally; so that my Pocket has been kept low. For this Reason, a Journey to Brodsworth, & Licencing might embarass me, as my Ability is yet but weakish': Borthwick Institute, R. Bp 5/24. On 10 September 1763 he wrote again saying that he had applied for ordination, but his papers were not yet in order: 'I

Sterne made no appearances in the spiritual courts in 1764. Most were inhibited by the archbishop's primary visitation, and Sterne's own 'peculiar' courts were being handled by substitutes. He signed a nomination for John Stapylton, yeoman, to become parish clerk of Stillington,[36] and no doubt he did other small tasks. And there were the inevitable political obligations of a clergyman. 'Tis the church militant week with me,' he wrote to Hall, 'full of marches, and countermarches—and treaties about Stillington common, which we are going to inclose' (232). Sterne would not benefit personally from the Stillington enclosure, but 18 acres would be granted to the parish in exchange for the small tithes, a move which much improved the living. Stephen Croft got the lion's share of the 1400 acres of enclosed wasteland.[37]

'I am now sat down till December in my sweet retirement,' Sterne wrote to Foley. Not feeling very strong, he got a 'she ass' for its health-giving milk (233). Still he thought of himself as living in the 'lap of contentment', but he added, 'we must bring three parts in four of the treat along with us—In short we must be happy within—and then few things without us make much difference—this is my Shandean philosophy' (234). For all that, he was not particularly happy during the summer and autumn of 1764, and he worked on *Tristram Shandy*, only in a desultory way: 'I go on, not rapidly, but well enough with my uncle Toby's amours' (225).

Sterne was lonely and restless and kept thinking of getting back to the continent. The idea of a trip to Italy got fixed in his mind (232–3, 234). Yet by some mental legerdemain he had completely forgotten how he had suffered so many haemorrhages in France. 'If I get a cough this winter which holds me three days,' he wrote to Foley, 'you will certainly see me at Paris the week following, for now I abandon every thing in this world to health and to my friends' (222). Once he had a fantasy about getting 'some *gros* my Lord', i.e. Fauconberg, to take him to Paris: 'I'll try if I can make him relish the joys of the *Tuileries*, *Opera Comique*, &c' (228). But he was not acting on a pipedream when he took the very realistic precaution of conveying legal control over the Tindal Farm and his other properties to Richard Chapman.

---

perceive I cannot be admitted for Priest's Orders against ye 18th inst.': R. Bp 5/25. Sterne took matters in hand with his letter to the archbishop of 30 October 1764: LETTERS, 229–30. Kilner was ordained at Brodsworth on 5 November: Borthwick Institute, *Act Book (Institutions) 1755–1768*, fol. 285.

[36] Borthwick Institute, D/C Nom. PC. 1764.

[37] *EMY*, 261, n. 2.

There seems no explanation for the deed of conveyance which he signed on 12 July 1764, except that he was giving his property in trust to Chapman in case he should die abroad.[38]

Travel was costly, and he could hardly go to Italy without publishing another instalment of *Tristram Shandy*. He lacked inspiration. 'There is no sitting, and cudgeling ones brains,' he wrote to Hall, 'whilst the sun shines bright' (225). In fact, he would succeed in finishing two more volumes before the winter set in, but only after cheering himself by excursions to the spas at Harrogate and Scarborough, to York races, and to Hall's 'Crazy Castle'.

He decided to make the Harrogate trip upon an impulse that seized him one July evening. No doubt he thought the waters would do him good. But on the road he became anxious lest he find no one there he knew. So he dismounted at Boroughbridge to write a letter to a '*loyal ami*' at nearby Ripon asking if he would join him at the Green Dragon hotel. His friend was a physician, Thomas Kilvington, who often saw clients at the Green Dragon. But Sterne was not writing to ask for a medical consultation, for he asked Dr Kilvington to come 'in Case, the Goddess of Prudence makes it feasable for you to leave Rippon' (221). It sounds as though Kilvington's wife might not have approved.

Race Week at York was held as usual during the third week of August. 'This year', wrote a local historian, 'was the greatest Company at York Races that ever was known in the Memory of Man.' The city had been spruced up: many streets were newly paved, shop windows that protruded too far into the street had been reduced, and rain spouts had been installed on the houses in Stonegate and Coney Street. There were 436 subscribers to the Assembly Rooms, '& one Night that week Mr Baker the Master of the Theatre took £100–18–0.'[39] Hall came with his wife, and Sterne saw him for the first time in three years. The Thornhill brothers were there. Croft brought his family, and Nathaniel Cholmley and his wife appeared.[40] It must have been a gay reunion. Sterne probably danced at the balls. He went to the races. Once he was standing on the stage from which bets were placed, watching horses being brought out, when he heard someone ask a

[38] North Riding Registry of Deeds, AM 741, pp. 553–4. This conveyance was dated 4–5 April 1764, when Sterne was still in Paris, but was registered on 12 July when he was in Yorkshire.

[39] Thomas Beckwith, MS *History of York* at Minster Library.

[40] *York Courant*, 28 August 1764; LETTERS, 223.

lady why she bet upon the smallest horse. 'Because', she replied, quoting Ecclesiastes, 'the race is not always to the swift nor the battle to the strong.' Sterne turned to her and begged the honour of her acquaintance, 'and a good deal of pleasant conversation took place between them to the great entertainment of the surrounding company.' The lady was Elizabeth Graeme, daughter of a Philadelphia physician. Like many other women who interested Sterne, she was a person of intellectual accomplishment, being the translator of the works of Fénelon, Archbishop of Cambrai.[41]

But the woman at York races who most excited Sterne was no bluestocking: Sarah Tuting, who had begun life among the hearty, horsy people of Newmarket, was now wasting with consumption and planning a tour of the continent in search of health. She wanted to know from Sterne how to get the most benefit from her travels. Sterne dissolved in sentimental love – the very passion he had felt for the lady in Paris five months before. Yes, of course he would be glad to teach her how to travel in search of health. The first principle was not to be homesick; 'if you have a Philander—think not about him.'

> If you hunger and thirst like a kindly Soul with too warm an impatience after those You have left behind—You will languish away the little fragment which is left of you to a shadow: The heart must be chearful and free from desires during all this Pilgrimage in search of health—no hard jostlings in your journey must disturb either body or mind one moment. . . . You must smile upon inconveniency and impositons—upon bad inns—& what will hurt you most of all because most contrary to y^{r} nature—upon unfeeling looks.
>
> The gentle Sally T[uting] is made up of too fine a texture for the rough wearing of the world—some gentle Brother, or some one who sticks closer than a Brother, should now take her by the hand, and lead her tenderly along her way—pick carefully out the smoothest tracks for her—scatter roses on them—& when the lax'd and weary fibre tells him she is weary—take her up in his arms——
>
> I despise Mankind, that not one of the race does this for her—You know what I have to say further——but adieu. (224)

[41] Hazard's *Register*, IV, 394, as cited by Katherine M. Jackson in her discussion of Elizabeth Graeme in *Outlines of the Literary History of Colonial Pennsylvania*, Lancaster, Pa., 1906. A more fanciful and romantic version of the story appeared in the *Universal Asylum and Columbian Magazine*, VI (March 1791), 168.

He found her exceedingly attractive, and his sympathetic concerns were mixed with desire in a manner suggestive of Yorick's attachment to the distressed Madame de L*** in *A Sentimental Journey*. 'When you lie down, may your pillow, gentle Sally,' he wrote, 'be soft as your own breast.' He would write to friends in Paris on Sarah Tuting's behalf (222, 227), and he would see her again in Italy (273). But it seems unlikely that they actually had an affair either in York or in Italy.

He returned to Coxwold, perhaps taking with him the visitor he was to have for a week or two – William Combe, the gossipy young man he had met in Paris.[42] Then he heard that Lord Granby was coming to Scarborough. 'What a temptation!' (225).

John Manners, Marquis of Granby, was another glamorous soldier, next in line after Ligonier for the post of commander-in-chief. He had commanded the British troops in Germany during the recent war and by his courage and leadership in the field had won the hearts of the men and indeed the public at large.[43] Sterne could not resist.

> I am going to leave a few poor sheep here in the wilderness for fourteen days—and from pride and naughtiness of heart to go see what is doing at Scarborough—stedfastly meaning afterwards to lead a new life and strengthen my faith. . . . there are dismal months enow after to endure suffocation by a brimstone fire-side. (225)

When Sterne got there he found Colonel William Hewett, who had come to pay his respects to his old pupil Granby.[44] Another of the party was William Petty, Earl of Shelburne, later Marquis of Lansdowne. Shelburne, an Anglo-Irishman not yet thirty, was heir apparent to the faction of Pitt, now Lord Chatham. He was on the verge of a long, convoluted political career in and out of ministries. His house in London, with its fine library and art collection, became in time the centre of London intellectual life. He was a friend to d'Holbach, Diderot, Hume, Johnson and Reynolds, and later became a patron of Priestley, Bentham and Richard Price.[45] Shelburne

[42] HAMILTON. There is a temptation to identify Combe with the 'C——' who visited Sterne that autumn. But, if Lydia's date for Letter 135 is correct, 'C——' was there in November.

[43] NAMIER AND BROOKE.

[44] Smollett, *Humphrey Clinker*, ed. Lewis M. Knapp, 1966, 182–3. CURTIS, 227, points out that Hewett's meeting of Granby at Scarborough could have taken place in either 1764 or 1765; so it is no more than a guess that Sterne met him there.

[45] *DNB*; NAMIER AND BROOKE; Lord Edmond Fitzmaurice, *Life of William, Earl of Shelburne*, 2 vols, 1912.

became Sterne's correspondent and friend. Though only a single letter survives, in it Sterne spoke of 'numberless and unmerited civilities from your lordship' (342). Mlle de Lespinasse said after she met Shelburne in 1774: 'He is a man of spirit; he is the chief of the opposition party; he was the friend of Sterne: he adores his works.[46]

Sterne stayed at Scarborough three weeks.

> I have been drinking the waters ever since the races, and have received marvellous strength, had I not debilitated it as fast as I got it, by playing the good fellow with Lord G[ranb]y and Co. too much. (226)

Hewett is said to have forgotten his age and 'sacrificed so liberally to Bacchus, that the next day he was seized with a fit of apoplexy, which has a little impaired his memory.'

Meanwhile, Sterne worked intermittently on *Tristram Shandy*, but made surprising progress. He had a fair copy of Volumes VII and VIII by 16 November (234). He had begun working on the story of Uncle Toby and the Widow Wadman in France in 1762 and had taken it up again in the current, 1764 summer (225). So one guesses that he had completed the portion of the story he was able to publish as Volume VIII before he set to work on the travel narrative which became Volume VII. Be that as it may, we shall talk about them here in the order in which Sterne finally placed them.

Volume VII brings the most surprising turn of the novel. The focus shifts off the Shandy brothers to Tristram himself, not as a boy, but as an adult, not at his family seat, Shandy Manor, but in France where he is fleeing that '*son of a whore*', Death.

> —You call him rightly, said Eugenius,—for by sin, we are told, he enter'd the world——I care not which way he enter'd, quoth I, provided he be not in such a hurry to take me out with him—for I have forty volumes to write, and forty thousand things to say and do.. . . had I not better, whilst these few scatter'd spirits remain, and these two spider legs of mine (holding one of them up to him) are able to support me—had I not better, Eugenius, fly for my life? 'tis my advice, my dear Tristram, said Eugenius——then by heaven! I will

[46] My translation from *Lettres de Mademoiselle de Lespinasse*, ed. Gustave Isambert, 2 vols, Paris, 1876, I, 158.

lead him a dance he little thinks of—for I will gallop, quoth I, without looking once behind me to the banks of the Garonne. (576–7)

This adult Tristram is strikingly like his author, weak and nearly voiceless (576), but doggedly determined to live. He is restless: 'so much of motion, is so much of life, and so much of joy——and . . . to stand still, or get on but slowly, is death and the devil' (593). He is thin (593), an amateur painter (589), and he delights in pretty women (585). In a letter to a friend, Sterne did not hesitate to call the volume 'a comic account of my journey from Calais thro' Paris to the Garonne' (234). Always pleased when his readers called him Tristram, he had no concern at all to make his protagonist different from himself. He even went so far as to dress him in clerical garb – 'a man with a pale face, and clad in black' (599) – and to make him a writer of sermons (615). Nevertheless, not a single episode of the novel can be shown to have happened to Sterne. He brings Tristram to Paris, but introduces him to no ladies of the salons, no nobles, no writers or *philosophes*. 'I am quite civil to the parisiens,' he told Foley, 'et *per Cosa*,— You know—tis likely I may see 'em again' (231). He was thinking only of his and Foley's friends, for the Paris chapters are full of trite satire of the city – the nasty streets, the obsession with food, and the self-satisfaction of the Parisians.[47] In Tristram's narrative one can find, not adventures which happened to Sterne, but a distillation of his feelings about France. In Tristram himself, he drew another idealized self-portrait, as he had done earlier in the character of Parson Yorick.

Sterne, whose protagonists are always scribbling, conceived of Tristram in Volume VII as a 'travel-writer'. 'As odd a Tour thro' france', Sterne called it, 'as ever was projected or executed by traveller or travell Writer since the world began' (231). Accounts of travel and books of advice to travellers were highly popular in that age,[48] and to such writings Tristram constantly compares his own observations. The one particular book he repeatedly mocked, and from which he paraphrased and plagiarized, was a French book, Jean Aimar Piganiol de la Force, *Nouveau Voyage de France* (1724; reissued in two volumes, 1755);[49] but by implication the satire is directed

[47] TS NOTES.

[48] Charles L. Batten, Jr, *Pleasurable Instruction*, Berkeley, 1978. Batten, in his discussion of Sterne, 79–81, maintains that Sterne modified this tradition by encouraging a more personal narrative than had been popular.

[49] Van R. Baker, 'Laurence Sterne and Piganiol de la Force: The Making of Volume VII of *Tristram Shandy*', *Comparative Literature Studies*, XIII (1976), 5–14.

against travel writers of any nationality. Travellers themselves, English travellers, come in for a knock now and then, usually because they are foolish enough to take this sort of thing seriously, because they would rather have their guidebooks give them the 'length, breadth, and perpendicular height of the great parish church' of Montreuil instead of telling them how beautiful is Janatone, the innkeeper's daughter (589–90).

This Tristram is still of a piece with Tristram the family historian. He still is a raconteur. He makes fun of the Roman church in the story of the abbess of Andoüillets and her novice (606–14). But he does not take himself too seriously: he laughs at his own *naïveté* and romanticism in the story of his headlong dash after the nonexistent tomb of the lovers, Amandus and Amanda (643). He is whimsically sensitive to the plight of an ass that is trying to eat an artichoke stem while stuck in a gate. Tristram feeds him a macaroon. 'With an ass, I can commune for ever' (631). And Tristram's ongoing commentary upon time and duration reaches a climax when he tells about standing in the square of Auxerre reflecting upon his previous visit there with his father, uncle and Trim, for in this 'puzzled skein' of three time-layers alive in one thought he nearly loses himself (621–2).

But, foolish or wise, Tristram the traveller has a particular genius – a nose for adventures in the most unlikely places. Nothing is more terrible to other travel writers, he says, than a plain, 'of little or no use to them but to carry them to some town' (646). But Tristram's plain is full of adventures – with a drum-maker going to a fair, a couple of talkative friars, a gossip trying to sell a basketful of figs without parting with her basket. Some day, says Tristram, adumbrating *A Sentimental Journey*, he will publish his collection of 'PLAIN STORIES' (648).

Yet all the while Tristram is fleeing 'that death-looking, long-striding scoundrel of a scare-sinner, who is posting after me' (585). He begins his flight on 'spider legs' that will scarce support him, but ends it dancing joyfully in a 'carousal' during the grape harvest with 'a sun-burnt daughter of Labour' (649). Death, for the nonce, has given up the chase. The implication is clear: Tristram's 'good spirits' have defeated Death. Indeed, the story had begun when Tristram's spirits rescued him:

> When DEATH himself knocked at my door—ye [his spirits] bad him come again: and in so gay a tone of careless indifference, did ye do it, that he doubted of his commission——
>
> '——There must certainly be some mistake in this matter,' quoth he. (576)

It was then that Death turned back for a moment, giving Tristram a chance to flee. As he rushes across France, the rough roads, bad inns and surly officials tempt him to commit himself to 'SPLEEN' as the best principle upon which to travel. But he discovers that spleen ruins his appetite and gives him a diarrhoea (598, 603–4). So he chooses instead the health-giving principle of good spirits (575, 604). Tristram now 'scampers' on, his appetite for adventure increasing the further south he goes. 'Still he followed,——and still I fled him——but I fled him chearfully' (645).

With this triumph of good cheer over Death, Sterne concluded the first of his two main stories in *Tristram Shandy*, that of Walter's misguided attempt to rear the perfect son. We now see that Tristram has turned out to be everything his father had hoped to avoid – a weakling, unmarried and rootless. He is heroic in a quality for which his father had no admiration – cheerfulness. He will look ridiculous as a squire. Nevertheless, the family virtues have not been lost upon Tristram. He has the satirical wit of his father, the kindness of his uncle, and the good humour of Parson Yorick. The lesson he teaches is how to get through an ironic world cheerfully.[50] We see him as the fit *moral* heir to Shandy Hall.

Sterne turned in Volume VIII to the second of his stories, that of Uncle Toby and his amours with the Widow Wadman. In this eighth volume, Sterne tells how Mrs Wadman wins Uncle Toby; in the ninth, which would not be published until much later, how she loses him.

The story of Mrs Wadman's triumph unfolds with many twists and turns and digressions; but the nub is Mrs Wadman's attack upon Toby in his sentry box, which takes place on the day when Toby and Trim, in accordance with the Peace of Utrecht, blow up the fortifications of Dunkirk upon the bowling green. As Mrs Wadman secretly watches from her arbour, the two old soldiers sit down after their labours to talk. Somehow Trim gets on to the subject of love, and tells how he fell in love with a fair Beguine who had nursed his wounded knee.

> The more she rubb'd, and the longer strokes she took——the more the fire kindled in my veins——till at length, by two or three strokes longer than the rest—my passion rose to the highest pitch——I seiz'd her hand——

[50] See Malcolm Bradbury, 'The Comic Novel in Sterne and Fielding', WINGED SKULL, 124–31. In this discussion of Volume VII, I am also endebted to Melvyn New, *Laurence Sterne as Satirist*, Gainesville, Florida, 1969, pp. 171–84, though I am not certain Professor New would subscribe to my view.

——And then, thou clapped'st it to thy lips, Trim, said my uncle Toby——and madest a speech.

Whether the corporal's amour terminated precisely in the way my uncle Toby described it, is not material; it is enough that it contain'd in it the essence of all the love-romances which ever have been wrote since the beginning of the world.

CHAP. XXIII

As soon as the corporal had finished the story of his amour—or rather my uncle Toby for him—Mrs. Wadman silently sallied forth from her arbour. . . .

CHAP. XXIV

——I am half distracted, captain Shandy, said Mrs. Wadman, holding up her cambrick handkerchief to her left eye, as she approach'd the door of my uncle Toby's sentry-box——a mote——or sand——or something——I know not what, has got into this eye of mine——do look into it—it is not in the white—

In saying which, Mrs. Wadman edged herself close in beside my uncle Toby, and squeezing herself down upon the corner of his bench, she gave him an opportunity of doing it without rising up————Do look into——said she.

. . . I see him yonder with his pipe pendulous in his hand, and the ashes falling out of it—looking—and looking—then rubbing his eyes——and looking again, with twice the good nature that ever Gallileo look'd for a spot in the sun.

——In vain! for by all the powers which animate the organ——Widow Wadman's left eye shines this moment as lucid as her right——there is neither mote, or sand, or dust, or chaff, or speck, or particle of opake matter floating in it——there is nothing, my dear paternal uncle! but one lambent delicious fire, furtively shooting out from every part of it, in all directions, into thine—— (703–7)

From time to time Sterne turned aside from the novel to do some editing or rewriting of sermons. Since 1763 he had been thinking about bringing out another two volumes (192) and probably tinkered with them off and on. One day in November of 1764, while working on the sermons, he was disturbed by two young women who were visiting in the neighbourhood and wanted to meet the famous author. Sterne wrote to Hall:

CHARLES WATSON-WENTWORTH, SECOND MARQUIS OF ROCKINGHAM
By Sir Joshua Reynolds, 1760

THOMAS BELASYSE, FOURTH VISCOUNT, LATER FIRST EARL FAUCONBERG
By Andrea Soldi, *c.* 1755

GARRICK BETWEEN 'TRAGEDY' AND 'COMEDY'
By Sir Joshua Reynolds, 1761

JOHN WILKES
By Robert Edge Pine

ANNE JAMES WITH HER DAUGHTER ELIZABETH ANNE
By Catherine Read, 1768

A detail from A CARICATURE GROUP

Key to identifications – See pp. 369–72

A LADY SURPRISED TO HAVE FOUND HER NAME WRITTEN ON A TREE.
Exhibited under this title by the artist, John Downman, in 1779. It is probably a fanciful portrait of Eliza Draper

I have been *Miss-ridden* this last week by a couple of romping girls (*bien mises et comme il faut*) who might as well have been in the house with me, (tho' perhaps not, my retreat here is too quiet for them) but they have taken up all my time, and have given my judgment and fancy more airings than they wanted.—These things accord not well with sermon making. (233)

Hall wrote asking him to Skelton. Sterne was expecting a house guest, a certain Mr C——, who had been ill in London. In an impulsive act of compassion, Sterne had invited him to come and breathe the clean air of Coxwold. Still, he wanted to get to Skelton before the winter set in. 'I cannot do otherwise', he wrote, 'than to bring him with me—nor can I gallop away and leave him an empty house to pay a visit to from London, as he comes half express to see me' (232). Hall extended the invitation, and in a golden November Sterne and C——travelled over the moors to Skelton. Probably some of the old companions were there. Panty Lascelles lived close by, and Thomas Gilbert was in evidence (225).

Then it was back to Shandy Hall to put the finishing touches to Volumes VII and VIII and then on to London to publish them. He had planned to get there before Christmas (228), but he may have lingered to attend the wedding at Beverley on 1 January 1765 of his young cousin, Richard Sterne of Elvington, the fifth Sterne of that name, the direct heir to Archbishop Sterne's name and fortune. Richard would have wanted his cousin Laurence to attend the wedding, since he was the senior member of the family and the most renowned. Richard would live to oversee the end of the family fortunes, to sell Elvington, and to die childless in 1791, the last of the Sternes in Yorkshire.[51]

Soon after he got to London, Sterne set up in the lodgings which he would keep for the rest of his life.[52] His rooms were on the first floor of a

[51] J. W. Clay, 'The Sterne Family', *Yorkshire Archaeological and Topographical Journal*, XXI (1911), 91–107; *Yorkshire Pedigrees*, 1944, II, 412.

[52] The best authority on Sterne's Old Bond Street lodgings is L. P. Curtis, 'Sterne in Bond-Street', *TLS*, 24 March 1932, p. 217, much of which is repeated in CURTIS, 293. Curtis, however, refused to say that Sterne was lodged in Old Bond Street earlier than January 1767, when the street name appeared in the heading of one of Sterne's letters. But there is evidence he was there earlier in the letter dated 11 June 1765 and addressed to William Combe. This is one of three letters published by Combe which CURTIS (250–2) accepted as genuine. However, he was suspicious of the last paragraph and deleted it. Harlan Hamilton, the expert on Combe, believes that most of the paragraph is genuine, including the following: 'In the beginning,

house in Old Bond Street, the third on the left from Piccadilly, the site of the present No. 48. His landlady, Mary Fourmantel, a widow, was a 'bagmaker', that is, she made the silk bags in which gentlemen who did not shave their heads tied up their hair. She styled herself 'bagmaker to his Majesty' and called her shop on the ground floor the King's Arms. She advertised 'a great Choice of Bags of the newest and most fashionable Taste', as well as gentlemen's linen of all sorts. She washed and repaired lace and ruffles 'to look like new'.[53] Sterne had to pass through her shop to reach the staircase at the back. Mrs Fourmantel, her children and her servants occupied the two top floors. The house was pulled down and replaced in 1904, but we know what it looked like from the next house to the north, which was its twin.

No one knows for sure whether Mary Fourmantel was related to Sterne's former mistress Catherine Fourmantel, but if so it was probably not a near kinship. It is highly unlikely that Mary was Catherine's mother. Mary Dent and the late Charles Fourmantel had been married in 1742, and Mary had borne other children in the two succeeding years. Had Catherine been born to the couple in 1745, her known appearance at Ranelagh Gardens in 1758 would have been at the age of thirteen. It is possible, of course, that Catherine had been the child of Charles or Mary by some previous marriage, or a niece to Charles; but so far no connection has been established.[54] By the

the very beginning of October, I mean to arrive in Bond-street with my *Sermons*; and when I have arranged their publication, then—hey go mad for Italy.' I agree with Hamilton. The repetition, 'the very beginning', sounds like Combe's padding, but the elliptical clause, 'hey go mad for Italy' has a Sterneian ring and sounds not at all like Combe's prose. If the sentence is genuine, it shows that Sterne had established his Bond Street residence before May 1765.

[53] Advertisement in the *Public Advertiser*, 1 May 1767, pp. 2–3. CURTIS, 293, described a similar advertisement in that same newspaper of 16 January 1768. I have not seen all of the documents examined by Curtis, but Mrs Fourmantel's ownership of a house in Old Bond Street is evidenced in a rate book for 1767 in the City of Westminster Library Archives Department – shelf number 1760 [*sic*], fol. 126.

[54] For information about Mrs Fourmantel and her family gleaned from the parish registers of St George's, Hanover Square, see CURTIS, 339. More recently L. Collins of the Society of Genealogists and Professor Van R. Baker have looked into the problem of Catherine's origins, as have I. Mary Dent and Charles Fourmantel of the parish of St James's (probably the church in Piccadilly) were married on 12 August 1742 in St George's chapel in Curzon Street close to Shepherd Market. This chapel lay within and belonged to the fashionable St George's, Hanover Square, but it was notorious for clandestine marriages outside canon law, i.e. without banns or licences, or, in the case of a minor, without the consent of parents. No marriage licence has

time Sterne settled into Mrs Fourmantel's house in Old Bond Street, Catherine, whether by death or marriage, had been removed from the London entertainment world. She is last seen completing a season at the Dean Street concert rooms operated by Mrs Theresa Cornelys: her benefit night was 4 February 1763, a time when Sterne was with his family at Toulouse.[55]

Mrs Fourmantel's was a modest house, and Sterne's apartment probably did not command a high rent; yet it was located in an area in which many wealthy, socially prominent people lived. Around the corner in Hanover Square stood St George's, one of the newest fashionable churches in London. Sterne began to attend services there, and on Sundays might have met Lord Fauconberg, Lord Grosvenor, or any number of nobles and gentlefolk. The Rector, Dr Charles Moss, destined to become Bishop of Bath and Wells, had been at Caius College, Cambridge, when Sterne was at Jesus.

Volumes VII and VIII of *Tristram Shandy* were published on 23 January 1765. Sterne had made no change in his business arrangements. Becket and Dehondt continued as principal booksellers and distributors, and Sterne was still his own publisher. Again he had William Strahan print the volumes, and he himself sat at the bindery signing the copies of Volume VII. As before, 4000 copies were run off. Although the previous two volumes were not yet entirely off Sterne's hands (288), the new set sold very well (235, 239). By the end of the summer Sterne would realize about £400 from his instalment.[56]

The volumes were reviewed forthwith in the January issues of the *Universal Museum* and the *Critical Review*. The *Museum* commentary was

been discovered or is likely to be. A child was born to the couple and baptized in St George's, Hanover Square, on 18 June 1743, and a second on 13 August 1744 (yet another in 1749). There was a certain Mary, wife of George Dent, whose son, John, was baptized at St James's, Piccadilly, on 5 September 1741; it is possible she could have had a daughter by her previous marriage. Charles Fourmantel died intestate in 1763 and was buried out of St George's on 23 June. A grant of administration was made to his widow in May 1764, but the record of this at the Public Record Office reveals nothing about any other member of the family. Mary herself was buried on 21 November 1776.

[55] *London Stage*, Part IV, ed. George Winchester Stone, Jr, 1962, p. 977.

[56] For details of the publication and the finances involved, and subsequent lifetime editions, see MONKMAN. The earliest advertisement announcing publication appeared on 23 January in *Lloyd's Evening Post* for 21–3 January 1765; a similar advertisement appeared in the *London Chronicle* and the *St. James's Chronicle*, both dated 22–4 January.

along the lines which had become trite: though it was proper to use ridicule to correct vice, it was irresponsible for a clergyman to talk bawdy. Tristram, it concluded, evoking a theatrical phrase, was now playing '*to empty benches*'. The *Critical* reviewer liked the volumes no better. He imagined a symposium – Walter Shandy, Toby, the Corporal and Mrs Shandy – in which Trim tells how he paid a man to look into his box to see an invisible cock.

> Then, Trim, said my father, you was not cheated; for if you paid your money for an invisible thing, how couldst thou see it? Aristotle treats upon this subject in his chapter of cocks.—Here my mother took another large pinch of snuff.
>
> We are afraid the purchasers of these two volumes are pretty much in the corporal's situation.

In a similar vein, Ralph Griffiths in the *Monthly Review* for February imagined a dialogue between himself and Tristram as they travel across France and finally settle down in a tavern. He praises Tristram for the story of Uncle Toby's amours and pleads with him to write more 'pathetic' scenes:

> In fine, Mr. Shandy, do, for surely you can, excite our passions to *laudable* purposes—awake our affections, engage our hearts—arouze, transport, refine, improve us. Let morality, let the cultivation of virtue be your aim—let wit, humour, elegance and pathos be the means; and the grateful applause of mankind will be your reward.

Lloyd's Evening Post, 15–17 April, simply subscribed to Griffiths's remarks. Suard, reviewing the volumes in the March issue of the *Gazette littéraire de l'Europe*, called them 'bizarre'. Sterne, he said, teases the reader into finding meanings that are not there: he is like the charlatan who filled the Haymarket with a crowd that had paid to watch him get into a two-pint bottle, but made off with the money, leaving the bottle on the stage.[57] This was the year for reviewers to evoke images of emptiness.

The books off his hands, Sterne plunged into his old London social life. Lady Mary Belasyse, Lord Fauconberg's daughter, wrote to her father on 25 February, 'I saw Mr. Sterne yesterday, he looks rather better than he did,

[57] A translation of Suard's review, heavily cut, appeared in the *London Chronicle*, 16–18 April 1765. For excerpts from these reviews, see HOWES, 159–69.

has prodigious spirits, & leads a life of perpetual Rackett, I wonder how he bears it.'[58] Three weeks later Sterne wrote to Garrick, 'I lead such a life of dissipation I have never had a moment to myself which has not been broke in upon' (234). Helfrich Peter Sturz, the German diplomatist and essayist, enquired about Sterne when he came to London a few years after Sterne's death: 'He degenerated in London, as all my acquaintances assure me, like a plant that has been badly transplanted.' Then he added, with some poetic licence, 'the incense of the great corrupted his head, just as their ragouts did his stomach; he became sick and proud, an invalid in body and spirit.'[59] Sterne's more prudish critics may have thought him an invalid in spirit, but his friends would have said with Lady Mary that his spirits were 'prodigious'. Yet everyone agreed he was abusing his sickly body. Everyone but Sterne.

Sterne was convinced that his health would improve if he could only manage to act like a well man. He was not unrealistic: he was constantly seeking the help of physicians, spas, foreign climates. But he also had a strong faith in his will. In 1767 he would describe to Richard Davenport an illness which '*ought* to have killed me—but that I made a point of it, not to break faith with the world, and in short *would* not die, (for in some cases, I hold this affair to be an act of the will).'[60] In less critical illness, he would force himself into the posture of a man of good health and, evoking his acting abilities, try to believe himself normal. When he was on his way to France in 1762, he travelled like an English gentleman, never admitting his illness to his companions. When he caught Richard Phelps in the act of writing to Henry Egerton that he, Sterne, was failing, he was furious: 'Phelps is a son of a Bitch for saying I was worse . . . for I am ten, nay 15 per Cent better.' We will see in the *Journal to Eliza* how time and again he drove himself out of his sickbed to take the air in Hyde Park or to call upon his

[58] WOMBWELL PAPERS.

[59] *Schriften*, Leipzig, 1786, pp. 129–30. Although Sturz said he was recording a 'conversation' with David Garrick, it is clear from his wording that he also drew from printed or manuscript sources and from the reports of other acquaintances. Sturz's comments on Sterne were known to Isaac D'Israeli, who in an essay published in 1840 spoke of seeing an account of Sterne by Garrick 'preserved in Dr. Burney's collections', a remark which led me to a long and fruitless search among the Burney papers at the British Library. It is now clear that what he had seen was Sturz's account or a translation of it: *Miscellanies of Literature* [first edn 1840], 1884, p. 30.

[60] Letter to Richard Davenport, 9 June 1767, in Earl R. Wasserman, 'Unedited Letters by Sterne, Hume, Rousseau', *Modern Language Notes*, LXVI (1951), 73–80.

friends. So it is hardly surprising that he should have delighted in a new proverb he learned in Paris, 'There is nothing so bad as wishing to be better.' He promptly put it to use, revelling in the life of that city. Now, in the winter of 1765, he threw himself into a 'perpetual round of engagements wherein, every moment of my time has been mortgaged' despite 'Some Days Illness, the natural fruits of so much dissipation.'[61] Sterne may have burnt himself out in the end, but for reasons he had considered well. Certainly he wanted to live fully before death caught him, but he also believed that in driving away the damps of melancholy he would prolong his life.

In late March, feeling himself weakened, in part by the humid, smoke-filled London air (253), he set off to try the waters of Bath – to our knowledge, his first and only visit to that spa. He stayed for some three weeks, bathing in the celebrated Roman Baths, drinking the waters at the Pump Room, ambling through the parks and dancing at the balls. The Ionic façades of the Royal Crescent had only recently been completed, and the last touches were being put to the Circus.

But the visit to Bath was costly to Sterne, for it resulted in the loss or near-loss of his valued friend and patron, Elizabeth Montagu. The difficulties began when Sterne called upon Mrs Montagu's sister, Sarah Scott, the historian and novelist.[62] Mrs Scott, estranged from her husband, the well-known mathematician George Lewis Scott, was living more or less permanently at Bath. She and Mrs Montagu were fond of one another and constantly writing letters. Mrs Montagu wrote to her about Sterne:

> I have sent you the deepest Divine, the profoundest casuist, the most serious (on paper) the reformed Church affords. . . . whatever he may want in seriousness he makes up in good nature. He is full of the milk of human kindness, harmless as a child, but often a naughty boy, and a little apt to dirty his *frock*.[63]

But Mrs Montagu's affection for Sterne was delicately poised, since she did not like *Tristram Shandy*. Moreover, at that very moment she was reading in manuscript the revised version of Mrs Scott's novel, *A Man of*

[61] Letter to Thomas Astle: Appendix I.

[62] Walter M. Crittenden, *Life and Writings of Mrs. Sarah Scott*, Philadelphia, 1932. Sterne's arrival at Bath was noted in neither the *Bath Chronicle* nor the *Bath Journal*.

[63] Dated 23 [March 1765]: Huntington Library, MO 5819.

Sensibility, or the History of Sir George Ellison. Sterne might have a growing reputation as a man of sensibility but he would never measure up to Mrs Scott's standards. A few days later Mrs Montagu replied to a letter she had received from Mrs Scott:

> I am glad Tristram gave you some entertainment, I can never send you such another. The extravagant applause that was at first given to his works turn'd his head with vanity. He was received abroad with great distinction which made him still more vain, so that he realy believes his book to be the finest thing the age has produced. The age has graced him, he has disgraced the age, nothing gives me such contempt for my contemporaries as to see them admire ribbald facts & ribbald witts, it speaks a bold licentiousness that if it was not softend by fribblism might break out very dangerously. I like Tristram better than his book.[64]

Then Sterne took a false step: he began a lighthearted flirtation with Mrs Scott's companion, Mrs Cutts. The women were pleased at first. 'When could Tristram have grace enough to be in love with M[rs] Cutts?' asked Mrs Montagu.[65] And two weeks later:

> I am charmed with M[r] Sterne for thinking if our friend had quitted her single blessedness it w[d] have been for companionship with him. I always thought since I conversed with him that there was something good in him & I am now convinced of it. . . . I am in hopes M[rs] Cutts will do him much good by her conversation, he was design'd for virtue, the softeness of his temper & the levity of his understanding has exposed him to follies.[66]

But difficulties arose, not because Sterne paid too much attention to Mrs Cutts, but because he paid too little. This season there were a great many Anglo-Irish at Bath, and Sterne found himself enjoying the ladies among them – 'the charming widow *Moor*, where, if I had not a piece of legal meadow of my own, I should rejoice to batten the rest of my days;—and the gentle elegant *Gore* with her fine form and Grecian face, and whose lot I trust it will be to make some man happy, who knows the value of a tender

64 Dated 11 April 1764: Huntington Library, MO 5820.

65 Ibid.

66 Dated 20 [April 1765]: Huntington Library, MO 5822.

heart.'[67] As Sterne said to Garrick in a letter, 'I am playing the devil at Bath' (237). No doubt Mrs Scott and Mrs Montagu were displeased.

It also appears that Sterne at Bath was indiscreet in his talk about Bishop Warburton. When he got back to London someone at Bath sent him a letter signed 'Jenny Shandy', a poor imitation of *Tristram Shandy*, the main idea of which was to offer a scatological example of Lockean association psychology. It closes with a request: 'The Shandy-family desire this may be the 2[d] chapter of y[r] next book, and that the original Letter be preserved with the same care, & in the same Cabinet with the Bishop of Glocester's Letter.'[68] Why would the writer or writers say such a thing unless Sterne at Bath had been making fun of Warburton publicly, perhaps even showing his letters? If so, it is not unlikely that these pleasantries would be repeated to Warburton, whose country estate was only a few miles away at Prior Park. And his friend Bishop Newton was only a few miles further, at Bristol. If either heard of such joking at Warburton's expense, they would have reported it to Mrs Montagu, who at this moment was exchanging letters with Newton about her ward, Elizabeth Botham, a niece of Elizabeth Sterne, whom she was sending to Newton and his wife so that the girl could take the waters of Bristol.[69]

For these or similar reasons, Mrs Montagu cooled toward Sterne. On 30 April, days after Sterne returned to London, she wrote to her sister:

> I have not seen y[e] great Tristram since his return except at y[e] Drawing Room where he told me he left you pretty well. To tell you y[e] truth I was ashamed to hold long converse there with y[e] author of a tawdry book. He has since calld at my door but I am obliged to reserve many mornings for business or quiet.[70]

[67] LETTERS, 250. Sterne said this in the course of protesting against a rumour that he had cast ridicule upon his Irish friends at Bath. Mrs Montagu spoke in her letters of the unusual number of Irish at Bath in 1765. The woman named Gore is probably the Letitia Gore who subscribed to *Sermons*, III–IV, V–VI, and *A Sentimental Journey*. In this passage Sterne also mentions Mrs Vesey as another admired Irishwoman, but the way he does so suggests that she came into his mind as an afterthought. Since Mrs Montagu makes no mention of Mrs Vesey in her letters to Mrs Scott of this period, I doubt that Mrs Vesey was at Bath.

[68] At the Morgan Library; published by CURTIS, 241–2.

[69] Dated 20 [April 1765]: Huntington Library, MO 5822. Prior Park was Warburton's rural residence, though he had not yet inherited it. It still belonged to the widow of Ralph Allen, but at her death was to pass to Warburton and his wife, who had been Allen's favourite niece. Mrs Allen died the following year.

[70] Huntington Library, MO 5823.

But Mrs Montagu, always concerned to keep up appearances, did not cut herself off absolutely. She would subscribe to Volumes III–IV of Sterne's *Sermons*, and she would come forth to play a cousinly role in the events surrounding Sterne's death. Her behaviour toward Sterne was not unlike her later behaviour toward Dr Johnson, keeping up a public appearance of regard even when the friendship had ceased.[71] But we know of no further correspondence between Mrs Montagu and Sterne until the period of his final illness. After his death she was embarrassed to talk about her friendship with him and constrained to make excuses. In a letter to Leonard Smeldt she maintained, 'By many humble addresses, he forced me to take some kind of civil notice of him, I assure you his witt never attoned with me for the indecency of his writing.' In that same letter she laid out a literary theory to explain her rejection of Sterne's books which was probably shared by Mrs Scott and others in her circle, like Mrs Vesey and Bishop Newton.

> The Lowest animal in society is a Buffoon. He willingly degrades himself in the rank of rational Beings, assumes a voluntary inferiority of soul, defaces the Divine image in his mind to put on the monkey & the Ape, & is guilty of spiritual bestiality. . . . & the great who encouraged such writings are most to blame, for they seduce the frail witt to be guilty of these offences, but we are now a Nation of Sybarites who promise rewards only to such as invent some new pleasure.[72]

Her opinion was not quite as impersonal as this seems, for she added, 'I used to talk in this severe manner to him, & he would shed penitent tears, which seem'd to shew he erred from levity & not malice.' Mrs Montagu may not have been fully aware of Sterne's acting ability.

Mrs Montagu and her friends would probably have withdrawn their objections had Sterne 'cleaned up' Volumes VII–VIII, but he did not. He insulted their intelligence by having Tristram set the ephemeral beauty of a chambermaid above the hard-won, durable productions of art (588–90). If he was less teasing of the reader's embarrassing propensity toward the sexual meanings of words, he offered a scene such as is seldom found in literature – the narrator-protagonist standing with his garters in his hand before his beloved Jenny, confessing to the reader his impotence (624). If he

[71] BOSWELL, IV, 64 and n. 1; *passim*.
[72] Undated: Huntington Library, MO 4999.

stopped the naughty play upon the phallic meaning of the nose, he went one step further by imputing a vaginal meaning to a furred cap (669–71).

Sterne himself was getting a reputation for talking bawdy in social gatherings. Henry Fuseli, the Swiss painter who had recently settled in England, was shocked when he met Sterne by Sterne's use of strong language, though Fuseli himself soon became adept at such communication.[73] Garrick described Sterne, said Sturz, as a '*lewd companion*, even wilder in society than in his writings, usually driving away all the women through his obscenities.' Sturz was probably heightening the colour of what Garrick had told him, but his remark may contain an essential truth. Few in that age would have thought twice about bawdy talk among men, even from a priest; it was what was said before women that mattered. Although our evidence is limited, it does appear that Sterne sometimes approached the limits of decency when he spoke with women. According to one anecdote, 'An old Dowager asked Sterne how old he was. He answer'd Quatre Fois, Madame, shewing her that he knew she meant to find whether he was able to gratify her.'[74] Then there is a letter in Sterne's hand written in the spring of 1765 replying to an unidentified 'Mrs. F' who had sent him a letter from Bath after his return to London. Mrs F. had enquired whether Tristram Shandy were a married man.

> Such fair advances from so fair a Princess—(freer & freer still) are not to be withstood by one of Tristram Shandy's make and complexion—Why my dear Creature (—we shall soon be got up to the very climax of familiarity)—If T. Shandy had but one single spark of galant[r]y-fire in any one apartment of his whole Tenement, so kind a tap at the dore would have call'd it all forth to have enquired What gentle Dame it was that stood without—good God! is it You M^rs F——! what a fire have You lighted up! tis enough to set the whole house in a flame. (240)

When conversation between them runs out, he foresees they will enter into 'Satyre & sarcasm—scoffing & flouting—rallying & reparteeing of it,—thrusting & parrying in one dark corner or another' (241). It is a funny, naughty letter – in which Sterne says that he is forty-four years old when he

[73] Peter Tomory, *Life and Art of Henry Fuseli*, New York, 1972, p. 15.

[74] Told by John Scott, later Earl of Clonmell (1739–96): Kenneth Monkman, 'An Annotated Copy of Sterne's *Sentimental Journey*', *ABA Annual* (1952), 36–9.

was actually fifty-one. It has no cover and no address; so we cannot know whether it is a copy of a letter Sterne actually posted or some literary exercise or fantasy. Nevertheless, it gives us a notion of the comic pruriency of which he was capable, and the incident of his showing the pornographic picture to Dr Johnson and the company at Sir Joshua Reynolds's reveals how uninhibited Sterne could be in a social gathering.

Paradoxically, Sterne liked himself as a bawdy talker and writer, though he was unhappy with himself when his sexual urges became strong and explicit. The ribald joke in the drawing room probably made him feel that he had objectified his passions and set them at further distance. In his fiction he sometimes used bawdry for elevated, intellectual purposes, as the chapter on Whiskers, used to comment upon the puzzles of linguistic communication (409–15). But none of this served to banish sexual desire, which continued to plague him: ''tis my vile errantry, as Sancho says, and that is all that can be made of it' (233).

We have one letter in which Sterne offers himself as a lover to a lady of rank, and a gloomy lover he seems. The woman was probably Lady Anne Stuart, Lady Warkworth, daughter of the Earl of Bute and wife of Hugh Percy. Her husband, the future Count Percy, at this time styled himself Lord Warkworth.[75] Lady Warkworth, a beautiful nineteen-year-old, was a

[75] The tentative identification was made originally by CROSS, 362–3, who called her 'Lady Percy', and accepted by CURTIS, 243–4, who called her 'Lady Warkworth'. Lady Anne Stuart styled herself Lady Warkworth from her marriage in July 1764 until October 1766, when her husband was created Count Percy; she called herself Lady Percy from that date until her husband divorced her in 1779. Lydia Sterne Medalle, who collected her father's letters in the spring of 1775, would have known her as Lady Percy. In MEDALLE, the letter bears the heading 'To Lady P——'. The identification by Cross rests only upon this cryptic heading. The history of the lady's affairs and intrigues, much expanded by Curtis, serves to encourage the identification.

The date of the letter is also uncertain. In Lydia's edition, it is dated on 'Tuesday 3 o'Clock'. Cross assigned the date of 23 April 1765, and this was accepted by Curtis. Cross first rejected various years, narrowing the field to 1765 and 1768. Then, he argues, 'If he cannot make an engagement with Lady Percy, Sterne says that he is going to Miss *******'s benefit. No unmarried actress had a benefit on a Tuesday in the spring of 1768 before March 18, the date of Sterne's death. But on Tuesday, April 23, 1765, benefits were given to Miss Wright at Drury Lane, and to Miss Wilford at Covent Garden. The seven stars correspond to the letters in the name of Miss Wilford' (363n.). Cross was particularly concerned with the date, since Thackeray had asserted that the letter was written on Tuesday, 21 April 1767, and then berated Sterne for having made love to another woman while he was making love to Eliza Draper. Thackeray made a show of dating the letter by looking at possible benefit concerts, but his facts were wrong;

notorious adulteress whose affairs would eventually lead her husband to divorce her. She would remarry, but would abandon her second husband for another man. To Sterne she must have looked available. His letter to her has a sad tone, remarkably different from the gay, carefree letters he had written to Catherine Fourmantel. Yet, unhappy as he was, he could not pull free of the vortex, as he called it, of Lady Warkworth's charms.

> There is a strange mechanical effect produced in writing a billet-doux within a stone-cast of the lady who engrosses the heart and soul of an inamorato—for this cause (but mostly because I am to dine in this neighborhood) have I, Tristram Shandy, come forth from my lodgings to a coffee-house the nearest I could find to my dear Lady [Warkworth]'s house, and have called for a sheet of gilt paper, to try the truth of this article of my creed—Now for it—
>
> O my lady—what a dishclout of a soul hast thou made of me? . . . Would not any man in his senses run diametrically from you—and as far as his legs would carry him, rather than thus causelessly, foolishly, and fool-hardily expose himself afresh—and afresh, where his heart and his reason tells him he shall be sure to come off loser, if not totally undone?—Why would you tell me you would be glad to see me?—Does it give you pleasure to make me more unhappy—or does it add to your triumph, that your eyes and lips have turned a man into a fool, whom the rest of the town is courting as a wit?—I am a fool, the weakest, the most ductile, the most tender fool, that ever woman

more important, he never questioned the year 1767, in which the letter was traditionally placed in editions of his time: 'A Roundabout Journey: Notes of a Week's Holiday', *Cornhill Magazine*, 11 (July–December 1869), 623–40. Cross correctly pointed out that Thackeray's date had to be wrong, since the *Journal to Eliza* reveals that Sterne was quite ill during that period. But Cross made little attempt to rule out other, earlier periods; his excluding of 1766 on the argument that Sterne was abroad is inconclusive, since Sterne passed through London in June; and he gave no consideration at all to the dates of 1760 and 1761, though both are possible, even if one assumes the correspondent was Lady Warkworth, since Sterne could have known her before her marriage. I would agree with Cross on one point only, that 1768 is unlikely because none of the benefit plays or concerts before Sterne's death would suit the wording in the letter. But any other period when Sterne was in London beginning with March 1760 is a possible time for the letter. The task of searching out all the known benefits given on Tuesdays during those periods and correlating them with the letter would be enormous and no doubt inconclusive. We know this letter was written after Sterne was famous because he says that the town is courting him as a wit. Beyond that, we have no idea when it was written.

tried the weakness of—and the most unsettled in my purposes and resolutions of recovering my right mind.—It is but an hour ago, that I kneeled down and swore I never would come near you—and after saying my Lord's Prayer for the sake of the close, of not being led into temptation—out I sallied like any Christian hero, ready to take the field against the world, the flesh, and the devil; not doubting but I should finally trample them all down under my feet—and now am I got so near you—within this vile stone's cast of your house—I feel myself drawn into a vortex, that has turned my brain upside downwards, and though I had purcheased a box ticket to carry me to Miss ******* benefit, yet I know very well, that was a single line directed to me, to let me know Lady [Warkworth] would be alone at seven, and suffer me to spend the evening with her, she would infallibly see everything verified I have told her. . . . If I hear nothing by that time I shall conclude you are better disposed of—and take a sorry hack, and sorrily jogg on to the play—Curse on the word. I know nothing but sorrow—except this one thing, that I love you (perhaps foolishly, but)

most sincerely,

L. Sterne (242–3)

Whether or not she admitted him, we do not know.

But Sterne's racy conversation and misbehaviour with women had no appreciable effect upon his popularity among the gentlemen and ladies who regularly bought his books and whose company he sought. At this very time, the winter of 1765, he began to collect subscriptions for two more volumes of sermons. He had been planning this edition for two years (192) and had begun sifting through his manuscripts the previous autumn (233). Though the volumes would not appear for another year, by March of 1765 he was bent upon sending them into the world 'with a prancing list of *de toute la noblesse*' (235). On 15 April he wrote to Foley, 'Almost all the nobility of England honour me with their names, and 'tis thought it will be the largest, and most splendid list which ever pranced before a book, since subscriptions came into fashion' (239). In the end Sterne would fulfil most of his ambitions. The final list contains 693 names, thirty-six more than the list for the 1760 *Sermons*. This is quite remarkable when we consider that the subscriptions of 1760 were collected when Sterne was the rage of London. The new list did not name 'almost all the nobility', but it did include some fifty – about the same number as in 1760. There were thirty-five clergymen on the list – the same number, give or take one or two, as for the 1760 *Sermons*.[76] But there is one notable exception: in 1760 there were six bishops among the clergy, in 1766 none. Sterne must have been disappointed that Archbishop Drummond did not subscribe. But subscription lists for Sterne's books were highly imperfect: Drummond's name would appear among the subscribers to *A Sentimental Journey*.

Sterne lost another patron in the spring of 1765 – David Garrick. The difficulty arose over the £20 which Sterne had borrowed from Garrick when he went abroad in 1762. Garrick and his wife had also gone abroad, the following year, and were sojourning in Italy during the early months of 1764, when Sterne stopped in Paris on his way back to England. When a gentleman brought Garrick the news that Sterne was seriously ill in Paris, Garrick got worried about the money owed him. He wrote to George Coleman from Rome on 11 April 1764, 'I hope *Becket* has stood my Friend in regard to what he ought to have receiv'd from me, some time ago—I had a draught upon him from Sterne for 20 p[ds] Ever since he went abroad—pray hint this to him, but let him not be ungentle wth Sterne.' [77] Hearing nothing, Garrick, now in Paris, wrote several times to Sterne in London. The letters miscarried, said Sterne. When one finally reached him, Sterne was so offended by the tone that he scribbled an angry reply. Garrick shot back that Sterne was scalping him. Then Sterne tried to retreat: 'I scalp You!—my dear Garrick! my dear friend!—foul befall the man who hurts a hair of y[r] head!' (236). He begged pardon for his 'false delicasy', telling himself that Garrick's nerves were 'as fine and delicately spun' as his own, 'his Sentiments as honest & friendly—thou knowest, Shandy, that he loves thee—why wilt thou hazard him a moment's pain? Puppy! Fool, Coxcomb, Jack Asse &c &c' (236). Sterne probably had no new chance to discharge the debt until Garrick got back to London a month later. There is no proving that he took care of the matter then, but it seems likely. That summer he was scolding Foley for not paying off another debt (to Lord Grosvenor?): he would see Foley's face 'with more pleasure', he said, 'when I am out of debt'

[76] My estimates of the numbers of nobles and clergy are necessarily rough. Is a nobleman's wife to be counted as a noble? His sons or daughters? In the end, I have tried to count only noble families, whether represented by one or several members. A lot of guesswork was involved. Similar guessing went on in counting clergy. The title of 'Doctor', for instance, might be used by a clergyman, a physician or a lawyer.

[77] *Letters of David Garrick*, I, 411.

(254), a phrasing which suggests that his other debts had already been paid.

Garrick, like Mrs Montagu, kept up a public appearance of friendship with Sterne. Sterne saw him when he returned to London in the autumn of this year;[78] Garrick's name appeared among the subscribers to *Sermons*, III–IV; and he was helpful to Elizabeth and Lydia after Sterne's death. Nevertheless, he and Sterne ceased writing to one another, so far as we know, and no further compliments to Garrick appeared in Sterne's books. The friendship, such as it was, had grown cold. But in truth the friendship had never been so important to Garrick as it had to Sterne. In modern biographies of Garrick, Sterne figures hardly at all. And we have already seen how in 1760 Garrick quietly betrayed Sterne to Bishop Warburton, whose friendship and patronage he *did* value. There is a possibility, of course, that Sterne was at fault in some degree in the matter of the debt, but Garrick did not have the affection for him which would assuage his anger.

Sterne left London precipitately in May 1765, a departure he described in a comic letter addressed to an unidentified lady.[79] She had sent him a 'Letter de Cachet' and he wrote to apologize for not obeying her summons. He would not forget her 'past kindnesses', and he looked forward to 'future ones', but he had been forced to 'escape' to Yorkshire in the company of a militia captain, 'not from Principles of rebellion,—but of virtue'.

> The Goddess of Prudence and Self-denial bears witness to our Motives—We ran headlong like a Telemachus and a Mentor from a Calypso & her Nymphs, hastening as fast as our members would let us, from the ensnaring favours of an enchanting Court, the delights of which, we forefelt in the end, must have un-*captain'd* the Captain—& dis-*Order'd* the Priest. (244–5)

In all probability Sterne's companion, the militia captain, was the distinguished parliamentarian and MP for Yorkshire, Sir George Saville, Bart, of Thornhill. Because rank in the militia was determined by the

[78] Kitty Clive, the leading lady at the Drury Lane Theatre, mentioned Sterne in a letter she wrote to Garrick on 14 October 1765 in a way that indicated Sterne and Garrick had been talking about her: quoted by CONNELY, 149, without documentation, but taken from *Garrick's Private Correspondence*, 1831–2, Vol. I.

[79] CURTIS's identification of Sterne's correspondent as Lady Warkworth is not convincing, since it rests solely upon the similarity of style in this letter to that which he had previously argued was to Lady Warkworth, cited above (No. 143). I find little similarity. Sterne is here slightly flirtatious and quite playful; in the letter to Lady Warkworth, he is deadly serious and candid about his desires.

officer's wealth, Saville held the rank of colonel in the West Yorkshire militia, but he performed the duties of a captain and may have dressed as one. His regiment had been ordered on 'Manoeuvers' to Leeds. In other northern towns, such as Norwich and Manchester, the silk weavers had been rioting in protest at the government's encouragement of imports from France. The restlessness may have spread to the woollen mills of Leeds. The ironies of such a military assignment were not lost on Sterne, who explained in his letters that his friend was preparing

> to plunge himself into dangers, to forget himself—his friends—& think only of his country—now does the drum beat—& the shril Fife shriek in his ears—his pulse quickens—mark how he girds on his sword—for heaven's sake! where will this end?
>
> he is going, with his whole Batallion to Leeds—to Leeds?—yes M^{dm} he is going to root out the manufactures—to give the spinsters & Weavers no elbow room—to compliment Industry with a Jubilee—by all that is good! He will do the State some service; & they shall know it. (245)

It is amusing to think of these mock-heroic lines being written about Sir George Saville – if indeed it was he – for Saville was universally admired for his high-minded politics and personal kindness.[80]

Unfortunately, Sterne did not go directly to Coxwold where he could rest. He had found Hall at York, so naturally he stayed on and continued the merrymaking – for one day too many. The luck which had remained with him throughout the London stay left him, and he began bleeding from the lungs. Then Hall belied the image which Sterne had given him and abandoned his bedridden friend. Sterne grumbled about him in a letter to Lord Effingham: 'Hall left me bleeding to death at York, of a small vessel in my lungs—the duce take these bellows of mine; I must get 'em stop'd, or I shall never live to *persifler* Lord Effingham again' (248).

[80] For Saville's career, see *DNB* and NAMIER AND BROOKE. The identification of Sterne's companion as Saville was argued convincingly by CURTIS, 246–7, who also showed that Saville's regiment was dispatched to Leeds. That Sterne's companion might have been someone other than Saville remains, however, a possibility, since Sterne knew many men who were active in northern militia regiments. Lord Grosvenor, for instance, belonged to the Cheshire militia, and Thomas Scrope (*EMY*, 187–8) was a captain in the Lincolnshire militia. It was a common practice to use militia regiments to quell industrial riots, and not at all uncommon for regiments to be sent for that purpose into neighbouring counties: see R. B. Turton, *North Yorkshire Militia*, Stockton-on-Tees, 1973.

6 Italy 1765–1766

Sterne went to Coxwold as soon as he had strength enough, arriving late in May 1765. It would be a short stay, for he was now determined to try the air of Italy. But no search for health was ever, in his mind, separate from work or play. He would 'saunter philosophically for a year or so, on the other side the Alps', but his efforts would also be 'in the service of the world, in a tour round Italy, where I shall spring game, or the duce is in the dice', that is, he would collect materials for his fiction (235).

And, of course, he wanted to see Elizabeth and Lydia. He had never been out of touch and had supplied what they needed, whether money (231, 238) or copies of the latest volumes of *Tristram Shandy* (254). Once he had acted the role of protector-father when a French 'gentleman of fortune' took it upon himself to write asking, not for Lydia's hand, but an accounting of the dowry and inheritance she would eventually receive. Sterne replied, 'Sir, I shall give her ten thousand pounds the day of marriage—my calculation is as follows—she is not eighteen, you are sixty-two—there goes five thousand pounds', and so on (256).

In August Sterne wrote to a friend: 'At this moment am I sitting in my summer house with my head and heart full, not of my uncle Toby's amours with the widow Wadman, but my sermons' (256). He did not attempt a single chapter of *Tristram Shandy* this year, but concentrated his efforts upon the forthcoming two volumes of the *Sermons of Mr. Yorick*. 'Was I to tell you the subject of the first sermon,' he wrote to Lord Effingham, '. . . you would think it so truly Shandean, that no after-wit would bring me off' (247). The subject was the character of Shimei. 'Nothing venture nothing have,' he added.

He decided to offer twelve sermons in two volumes, though he had manuscripts for more and had once told prospective subscribers there would be sixteen (239). Though he spoke of 'composing' sermons (254), he probably meant rewriting or editing. Of the twelve, three were recent sermons which some of his public had heard him preach. 'National Mercies Considered' he had delivered at Coxwold upon the occasion of King George III's accession to the throne; 'The Parable of the Rich Man and Lazarus Considered' was his charity sermon for the Foundling Hospital; and 'The Case of Hezekiah and the Messengers' he had preached in Paris at the ambassador's chapel. He also included the sermon read by Trim in the second volume of *Tristram Shandy*, 'The Abuses of Conscience, Considered'. This publication of Sterne's favourite sermon would be, in fact, its third, for the 'Abuses' had previously been published by itself, in 1750. All or most of the others had probably been written years before for delivery at York Minster.[1]

Sterne was restless and yearned after a young countess he had recently met in London or York. One day he sat down and wrote her a love letter.[2]

[1] I shall not undertake the risky business of trying to date the writing of Sterne's sermons. An attempt was made by Lansing van der Heyden Hammond in *Laurence Sterne's 'Sermons of Mr. Yorick'*, New Haven, Conn., 1948; but see the criticism in *EMY*, 220–1, and James Downey, '*The Sermons of Mr. Yorick*: a Reassessment of Hammond', *English Studies in Canada*, IV (1978), 192–211.

[2] I date this letter 18 June 1765, disagreeing with CURTIS, who dated it 1767. Sterne had originally written 'Coxwould June 18', and one begins with the assumption that this is correct. (When he revamped and readdressed the letter to Eliza Draper, he erased the word *June*, but it can still be made out.) Sterne was in Coxwold in mid-June in the years 1760, 1761, 1765 and 1767. I rule out 1760 and 1761 on the ground that such an interesting figure as the ghostly Cordelia would have appeared in the numerous letters we have between 1761 and 1766. In fact, the only other place we find her is in the *Journal to Eliza*. The first time Sterne mentions her in the journal is under the date of 16 April 1767, written while Sterne was still in London. As CONNELY pointed out, the entry implies that Sterne had been telling Eliza about Cordelia in the winter months of 1767; therefore, he must have had the fantasy during or before the summer of 1766. But 1766 is not a possible date because Sterne had not reached Coxwold by 18 June of that year. So that reduces the choices to 1765 or 1767. CURTIS, 362–3, opted for 1767 upon the following argument: 'Certain it is that Sterne's waggish and erotic devotion to the "Countess" is nearer the spirit of certain letters written in 1765, than to those of 1767. But since the material of the letter, namely Sterne's whimsical communion with the ghostly Cordelia, was especially occupying his thoughts and leisure during the spring and summer of 1767, I can see no alternative other than to assign this letter to the month of June in that year.' This is not convincing. There are few grounds for saying that Cordelia was 'especially occupying' Sterne's thoughts in 1767. She is named in the *Journal* four times. Two references to her are very brief – 16 April

That the countess was young we surmise from the condescending advice into which he slipped when asking her to write: 'Dear Lady write anything and write it any how, so it but comes from y^r^ heart, twil be better than the best Letter that ever came from Pope's head' (362).[3] When he had met her, he had chatted about the walks he sometimes took to the ruins of Byland Abbey near Coxwold and had confessed that he sometimes conjured up visions of nuns who, he wrongly supposed, once lived there and lay buried there. Now, in his letter, he set about expanding upon that conversation, unfolding a long fantasy about a ghostly nun named Cordelia, *vis-à-vis* whom Sterne (as the figure in the fantasy) behaves more like the poet in Gray's *Elegy* than Tristram or Yorick.

> in no time or place, dear Lady, do I call your figure so strongly up to my imagination and enjoy so much of y^{r} good heart and sweet converse as when I am in company with my Nuns: tis for this reason, since I have got down to this all-peaceful and romantick retreat, that my Love and my Devotion are ever taking me and leading me gently by the hand to these delicious Mansions of our long-lost Sisters: I am just now return'd from one of my nightly visits; & tho' tis late, for I

(323) and 1 August (386). The other two passages are similar to but shorter than the passages in the letter (12 June, 356; 27 July, 382). When one takes account of the *Journal to Eliza* as a whole, with its hundred entries, approximately, one finds little reason for saying that Cordelia played a prominent part in Sterne's thoughts during 1767. Moreover, it does not seem likely that Sterne would have been making sentimental love to two women at the same time. Certainly I have no desire to exonerate him from Thackeray's charge that he made love to two women at one time (Thackeray thought, or pretended that he thought, that Letter No. 142, addressed, probably, to Lady Warkworth, had been written during the period of the *Journal to Eliza*). On the contrary, I have argued above, in Chapter 5, that Sterne in Paris spent an evening with Wilkes and the 'actresses' at the very time he was carrying on a daytime sentimental courtship of an unidentified lady. It is not hard to conceive of Sterne paying this sort of court to a woman during the day while whoring at night, but to carry on simultaneously two public sentimental courtships with well-bred women is out of keeping with his character as I understand it. So I rule out 1767 and date the letter 18 June 1765.

[3] Cf. Sterne's letter of 23 February 1767 to Lydia: 'never let your letters be studied ones—write naturally, and then you will write well' (302). CONNELY, 232, identifies the countess as the Comtesse de Vair, Sterne's host near Dijon in 1766, but his reasoning is unconvincing. He lists as candidates various countesses Sterne knew, including Lady Fauconberg, who had died in 1760, and then opts for de Vair. But Sterne must have met numerous noble ladies about whom we have no knowledge. Moreover, there is no hint in the letter that the countess was French.

was detain'd there an hour longer than I was aware of, by the sad silence and breathlessness of the night, and the subject (for it was yourself) which took up the conversation—yet late as it is, I cannot go to bed without writing to you & telling you how much, and how many kind things we have been talking abou[t] you these two hours—Cordelia! said I as I lay half reclined upon her grave—long—long, has thy spirit triumphed over these infirmities, and all the contentions to wch human hearts are subject—alas! thou hast had thy share—for she look'd, I thought, down upon me with such a pleasurable sweetness—so like a delegated Angel whose breast glow'd with fire, that Cordelia could not have been a stranger to the passion on earth—poor, hapless Maid! cried I—Cordelia gently waved her head—it was enough—I turn'd the discourse to the object of my own disquietudes—I talk'd to her of Lady ******: I told her, how kindly nature had formd you—how gentle—how wise—how good—Cordelia, (me thought) was touchd with my description, and glow'd insensibly, as sympathetic Spirits do, as I went on—This Sisterly kind Being with whose Idea I have inflamed your Love, Cordelia! has promised, that she will one night or other come in person, and in this sacred Asylum pay your Shade a sentimental Visit along with me—when?—when? said she, animated with desire—God knows, said I, pulling out my handkerchief & dropping tears faster than I could wipe them off—God knows! said I, crying bitterly as I repeated the words—God knows! but I feel something like prophetic conviction within me, which says, that this gentlest of her Sex will some time take sanctuary from the cares and treachery of the world and come peacefully & live amongst You———and why not sleep amongst us too?—O heaven! said I, laying my hand upon my heart—and will not you, Yorick, mix your ashes with us too?—for ever my Cordelia! and some kind Swain shall come and weed our graves, as I have weeded thine, and when he has done, shall sit down at our feet and tell us the Stories of his passions and his disappointments.

My dear Lady, tell me honestly, if you do not wish from your soul to have been of this party—aye! but then as it was dark and lonely, I must have been taken by the hand & led home by you to your retired Cottage—and what then? But I stop here—& leave you to furnish the answer.—*a propos*—pray when you first made a conquest of T. Shandy did it ever enter your head what a visionary, romantic, kind of

> a Being you had got hold of? When Lady ****** suffered so careless and laughing a Creature to enter her roof, did she dream of a man of Sentiments, and that, She was opening the door to such a one, to make him prisoner for Life—O Woman! to what purpose hast thou exercised this power over me? or, to answer what end in nature, was I led by so mysterious a path to know you,—to love You,—and fruitlessly to lament and sigh that I can only send my spirit after you, as I have done this night to my Cordelia—poor! spotless Shade! the world at least is so merciful as not to be jealous of our Intercourse—I can paint thee blessed Spirit all-generous and kind as hers I write to—I can lie besides thy grave, and drop tears of tenderness upon the Turf w[ch] covers thee, and not one passenger turn his head aside to remark or envy me—(360–1)

Curiously, Sterne appears to court Cordelia more than the countess. As we have observed, Sterne made sentimental love to women who were sickly – his wife in 1740–1, the woman he courted in Paris in 1764, and Sarah Tuting. All were suffering from Sterne's own disease, consumption. Sterne, desirous of these women, but not wanting to admit his sexual yearnings either to them or to himself, hid them behind the feelings of sympathy which he also strongly felt. But the mechanism broke down before the countess who, so far as we can make out, was in very good health. Sterne must have felt that he could not come close to this woman, having no reason to offer her sympathy. But Cordelia was the perfectly approachable love object, being dead.

This artificiality of the role in which Sterne cast himself as sentimental lover appears clearly in a letter he wrote this very summer, 1765, to a friend, John Wodehouse. Wodehouse had written to tell Sterne he had fallen in love. 'I am glad that you are in love,' Sterne replied,

> 'twill cure you (at least) of the spleen, which has a bad effect on both man and woman—I myself must ever have some dulcinea in my head—it harmonises the soul—and in those cases I first endeavour to make the lady believe so, or rather I begin first to make myself believe that I am in love—but I carry on my affairs quite in the French way, sentimentally—'*l'amour*' (say they) '*n'est rien sans sentiment*'—Now notwithstanding they make such a pother about the *word*, they have no precise idea annex'd to it—And so much for that same subject called love—(256)

How unappealing this role must have seemed to the women before whom it was played. A lover who courts a woman, not out of passion, but for her medicinal qualities, who begins by trying to convince himself he is in love and then proceeds in a style of lovemaking he has picked up in France, is not apt to win his lady. In fact, none of Sterne's sentimental affairs lasted very long – except, of course, that with Elizabeth Lumley, with whom he made a woeful marriage. The countess did not long remain a correspondent. Two years later, when Sterne was making sentimental love to Eliza Draper, he went through his copy of the letter to the countess, making erasures and substitutions so as to readdress it to Eliza. Cordelia, we suppose, was too engaging a creature to be wasted.

Ultimately, what Sterne was seeking in sentimental love was not love at all, but health. If love cures the spleen and harmonizes the soul, as Sterne told Wodehouse, anyone in any state of health would want to fall in love, and, if he were sick and fearful of his life, he would not wait to fall, but would pursue love in all haste. Sterne drove himself to this sort of lovemaking, believing it would make him whole.

He was not talking about moral wellbeing alone, but about a health that was at once moral and physical. The concept of spleen, of course, derives from the ancient humour psychology which was also a physiology; it designated a condition which was mental and physical at one and the same time. Sterne treated it so in Volume VII of *Tristram Shandy*: Tristram is saved by the good spirits which Sterne set in opposition to spleen, a deathly principle which gives Tristram diarrhoea. In *A Sentimental Journey* he would describe the 'spleen and jaundice' which 'discoloured or distorted' everything that Smelfungus sees. 'I'll tell it, cried Smelfungus, to the world. You had better tell it, said I, to your physician' (118). The health which is the opposite to this illness must also be at once physical and mental.[4]

[4] To explain Sterne's notions about humour psychology, the editors of TS NOTES, 41, turn to Robert Burton's *Anatomy of Melancholy*, citing the general definitions of spirits and humour in I, i, 2 (2), but then pointing out that other of Sterne's favourite source books take a view of the humours and spirits modified by the new science – Ephraim Chambers in the *Cyclopaedia* and George Cheyene in *The English Malady*, 1753. I am uncertain just where to place Sterne's ideas about the humours and spirits. What he says suggests Burton when he gets very specific (e.g. TRISTRAM SHANDY, 1–2, or 360); but in these passages he is usually seeking some comic effect. In more serious comments, he tends to leave the notions of 'spleen' and 'good spirits' vague. On the other hand, he obviously assumes that the balance or condition of humours and spirits in the body affects one's mental state, and in this he seems closer to Burton's old-fashioned view than the more recent view of, say,

Sterne had spent the past few years of his life, as he said in the dedication to William Pitt, endeavouring 'to fence against the infirmities of ill health, and other evils of life, by mirth; being firmly persuaded that every time a man smiles,—but much more so, when he laughs, that it adds something to this Fragment of Life' (vii). He had sought to banish spleen in the writing of comedy and in his laughter in the drawing room. Sentimental lovemaking was yet another way in which he tried to 'harmonize' his soul, to evoke his good spirits, to drive away the spleen, thereby to regain his health.

In time Sterne would decide that this experiment was a failure, for in *A Sentimental Journey* he would turn sentimental lovemaking into a comedy. Yorick, the narrator-protagonist, is another sickly parson with a penchant for frail women, who believes that love is a cure for the spleen:

> having been in love with one princess or another almost all my life, and I hope I shall go on so, till I die, being firmly persuaded, that if ever I do a mean action, it must be in some interval betwixt one passion and another: whilst this interregnum lasts, I always perceive my heart locked up—I can scarce find in it, to give Misery a sixpence; and therefore I always get out of it as fast as I can, and the moment I am rekindled, I am all generosity and good will again. (128–9)

But then he adds a line which undercuts what he has been saying: 'I am all generosity and good will again; and would do any thing in the world either for, or with any one, if they will but satisfy me there is no sin in it.' The deft 'or with' suggests that it is sex after all and not benevolence that is generated by love. Sterne treats the drummer's letter to the corporal's wife as the archetypal love letter, including in it the very aphorism which he had quoted to Wodehouse, 'l'amour n'est *rien* sans sentiment'; but in the novel he adds a second part, 'Et le sentiment est encore *moins* sans amour' (153), which acknowledges that sex has a proper place in love. By the time Sterne wrote *A Sentimental Journey*, his eyes had been opened to the artificiality of his theory of sentimental love and he no longer would allow himself to mask his desires behind a façade of sympathy. But in 1765, when he sat in his summerhouse explaining his notions to John Wodehouse, he conceived of a sentimental love, the essence of which was not sex but tenderness and

Boerhaave, whose modified humour theory was more physiological than psychological: see the explication of Boerhaavian theory in Lester S. King, *The Medical World of the Eighteenth Century*, Chicago, 1958, Ch. III.

sympathy, and the physical and moral wellbeing they brought with them.

In June Sterne was away from Coxwold for a week, probably staying at Stillington with Stephen Croft. He appeared at the archdeaconry of Cleveland visitation at Thirsk on 12 June, and attended a meeting of Stillington landowners on 17 June, signing a petition for the enclosure of Stillington common. The following day he presided over the Alne and Tollerton Peculiar Court – the last time he would don the robes of a dignitary of the spiritual courts.[5]

Coxwold parish demanded little of Sterne's attention in 1765 because his curate, James Kilner, now in holy orders, was officiating at the services and looking after the flock. But he might have done well to take a greater interest in the parishes of Sutton-on-the-Forest and Stillington, where his other curate, Marmaduke Callis, was growing restless.

On the afternoon of Friday, 2 August, 'an affrighted messenger, on a breathless horse, . . . arrived to acquaint me, that the parsonage house at [Sutton] was on fire, when he came away, and burning like a bundle of faggots.'[6] A story about the fire appeared in the *London Chronicle* of 8–10 August. On the first day of the month,

> in the afternoon, the end of the parsonage house of Sutton in the Forest, next the church, was discovered to be on fire; but by timely assistance, it was extinguished without much damage, and some men sat up all night to watch it. Next day everything was thought to be safe, but in the afternoon the other end of the house was found to be on fire, which burnt so furiously, that its progress could not be stopp'd, and the whole building was consum'd, but the greatest part of the furniture was saved. How these fires happened is not known.

Since the house caught fire at opposite ends on two successive days, its origins are suspect. But Sterne charitably attributed the fires to 'the carelessness of my curate, or his wife, or some one within his gates'.

> The matter, however, that concerns me most in the business, is the strange unaccountable conduct of my poor unfortunate curate, not in

[5] Borthwick Institute, *Alne and Tollerton Court Book*, 1748–61, fol. 22; *Cleveland Court Books*, 1734–74; *EMY*, 261, n. 2; *York Courant*, 28 May 1765.

[6] Putting to use the general argument advanced by HAMILTON, I accept as authentic the passage on the fire from William Combe's Letter IX in *Original Letters of the late Reverend Mr. Laurence Sterne*, 1788, though not the entire letter. This passage, which occurs on pp. 45–8, sounds not at all like Combe.

> *setting fire* to the house, for I do not accuse him of it, God knows, nor any one else; but in *setting off* the moment after it happened, and flying like *Paul* to *Tarsus*, through fear of prosecution from me.[7]

Poor Callis had some cause to be fearful, for circumstantial evidence was piling up against him. He had tried unsuccessfully to get free of his obligation to Sterne while Sterne was abroad.[8] Now, in 1765, he had received an invitation to become the assistant curate of Walsby and Wellow, Nottinghamshire, at a salary higher than Sterne paid him. He had gone so far as to get testimonial letters from the neighbouring clergy.[9] Sterne, no doubt, had declined to release him. Given this history, most people were going to suppose – as indeed we too suppose – that Callis or his wife or both, their patience worn out, had set fire to the house.

Callis did not literally run off, for his entries continue in the parish registers until the end of the year. But Sterne had seen the writing on the wall. On 20 August, the archbishop granted Callis the licence to serve Walsby and Wellow.[10] Sterne, unable to find a properly qualified replacement in the short time before leaving for Italy, arranged for a temporary curate, Lancelot Colley, the twenty-five-year-old parish clerk of Alne, a man of good local reputation but not in holy orders. Careful not to repeat his error, Sterne gave him a salary £6 above that which he had been giving Callis.[11]

[7] *Original Letters*, p. 48. In LETTERS, 256, he spoke of the carelessness only of the wife.

[8] Nomination, signed by John Rakes, Vicar of Well, and note from Callis to the archbishop's scribe, Richard Clapham: Borthwick Institute, R. Bp. 5, No. 255.

[9] File of 'Curates Nominations' at Borthwick Institute, R. IV. L, 1765. The testimonials were signed by Richard Mosley (the younger), Rector of Wigginton; John Armistead, Curate of Easingwold; and Richard Hawxwell, Vicar of Sheriff Hutton.

[10] Archbishop's *Act Book, 1755–1768*, at Borthwick Institute.

[11] Since Colley took up his duties on 1 January 1766, when Sterne was abroad, one presumes Sterne had made the arrangement before he left but failed to complete the formalities. The nomination of Colley in a scribal hand but signed by Sterne is at the Borthwick Institute (R.IV.A, 1766); the archbishop granted the licence on 20 October of that year (*Act Book [Institutions] 1755–1768*, fol. 355). Colley left in June 1767 to become assistant to Sterne's friend Thomas Mosley at Strensall (Minster Library: *Subscription Book*, 13 February 1770). CURTIS, 145, who first brought to light the information about Colley, was mistaken in one detail: he thought that, between the services of Callis and Colley, Sterne had yet another curate, John Armistead. Armistead was serving as Curate of Easingwold when he signed the testimonial letter for Colley cited above. His name does appear from time to time in the Sutton registers, but I believe he was no

The fire was costly. Some books and furniture were burned, but they were not the major loss. Sterne was now responsible for rebuilding the house. Should he die before it was replaced, his widow might be sued for dilapidations. He suggested to Archbishop Drummond a plan whereby he would set aside every year a sum of money toward this expense. But he did not do it, and made matters worse by ordering the salvaged timbers and wood to be taken to the Tindal Farm to be used for building sheds. Elizabeth was indeed threatened with a suit after Sterne's death.[12]

In August, Sterne went to York races and the Assembly Room balls. Many old friends were there – the Crofts and Thornhills, Sir George Saville, Henry Egerton.[13] Lord Rockingham came as usual to preside over the opening ceremonies, but this year his Yorkshire friends had special cause to cheer Rockingham. The month before, when the ministry of Grenville had collapsed, he had formed the new government.

Sterne was in good form as a wit during Race Week: he himself told the story:

> A sensible friend of mine, with whom not long ago, I spent some hours in conversation, met an apothecary (an acquaintance of ours)—the latter asked him how he did? why, ill, very ill—I have been with Sterne, who has given me such a dose of *Attic salt* that I am in a fever—Attic salt, Sir, Attic salt! I have Glauber salt—I have Epsom salt in my shop, &c.—Oh! I suppose 'tis some French salt—I wonder you would trust his report of the medicine, he cares not what he takes himself—(258)

When Sterne got back to Coxwold he was pleased to find a package from Lord Spencer. The fortunes of Sterne's friend had continued to wax, and he was to be advanced from his rank of baron to that of earl. The creation would not be announced until October, but the lord was preparing a general celebration and giving out memorial gifts in advance. He had sent Sterne a

more than a neighbouring cleric who was filling in temporarily. Callis's hand last appears in the Stillington register on 15 December 1765; Colley's first appears on 1 January 1766 (and in the Sutton registers, 25 February 1766).

[12] Archbishop Drummond to Mrs Montagu, 26 March and 17 June, 1768, in LETTERS, 433–7. On the laws covering dilapidations, see G. F. A. Best, *Temporal Pillars*, Cambridge, 1964, pp. 18–19.

[13] *York Courant*, 27 August 1765.

silver ink standish, which became one of Sterne's most cherished possessions.[14]

In September Sterne suffered 'the most violent spitting of blood that ever mortal man experienced', and suddenly his projected trip to Italy had become another flight from death. He set off for York about 2 October 'to recruit myself', probably under the care of his old friend Doctor John Dealtary, 'because I had rather (in case 'tis ordained so) die there, than in a post-chaise on the road' (257–8).

He could not have lingered at York long, for on 7 October he was in London and writing to Foley in Paris to ask him to get his neighbour Madame Requière to make him a wig – 'a terrible thing to be in Paris without a perriwig to a man's head!' (260). Wigs had begun to go out of fashion since George III did not wear one. And Sterne, who still had a head of dark brown hair,[15] may have ceased to wear one in England. He stayed in London only a few days – time enough to make the final arrangements with Becket about the publication of the sermons. He had not written a preface, but told Becket he would do that when he was abroad. He did in fact write one in Paris, but decided not to use it: 'tis better the Sermons go into the world without Apology—let them speak for themselves' (261).

The Sermons of Mr. Yorick, III–IV, did not appear until 18 January 1766, when Sterne was in Naples.[16] William Rose, who reviewed them for the *Monthly Review* of March 1766,[17] disapproved of the 'air of levity in some of

[14] At this time, 1 October 1765, Sterne thanked Lord Spencer for a gift made of either gold or silver, but he did not say in the letter what the item was (LETTERS, 258–9). I am presuming it was the ink stand of which CROFT spoke when he gossiped about Sterne's pluming himself upon presents from the nobility, 'particularly a Silver Ink Standish from Earl Spencer which he boasted of'. Later, on 13 June 1767, Sterne spoke in the JOURNAL about presents he had received, especially 'a grand Ecritoire of 40 Guineas' from Lord Spencer (357). The word can mean either a writing desk or an ink stand. True Sterne said he was talking about presents received 'this' year, but I think he probably stretched the point and included the earlier present from Lord Spencer.

[15] The only portrait which shows his hair is the John Hamilton Mortimer portrait. See Appendix II.

[16] Advertisements announcing the publication 'this day' appeared in the *St. James's Chronicle*, 16–18 January; *Lloyd's Evening Post*, 17–20 January; the *Public Advertiser*, 18 January; and the *Gazetteer and New Daily Advertiser*, 18 January. The price was 5*s.* sewn, 6*s.* bound. Most of the advertisements also offered complete sets in four volumes and *Tristram Shandy* in eight volumes. A pirated Dublin edition of *Sermons*, III–IV, appeared in 1766.

[17] For the attribution to Willam Rose, see NANGLE, N. 385.

them'. 'Serious subjects, indeed, seem but little suited to Mr. Sterne's genius. . . . He is possessed, however, of such a fund of good humour, and native pleasantry, and seems, at the same time, to have so large a share of philanthropy, that it is impossible, for us at least, to be long displeased with him.' The reviewer for the *Critical Review* of January–February said:

> The author of *Tristram Shandy* is discernible in every page of these discourses. . . . the same acute remarks on the manners of mankind, the same striking characters, the same accurate investigation of the passions, the same delicate strokes of satire, and the same art of moving the tender affections of nature. But the author sometimes forgets the dignity of his character, and the solemnity of a christian congregation, and condescends, on the most interesting topics of religion, to excite a jocular idea, or display a frivolous turn of wit.

Sarah Scott was offended by the sermons. She wrote to her sister Elizabeth Montagu, 'surely such stuff never was published. . . . He has the most cavalier way of treating the Patriarchs that ever I met with.'[18] But Mary Wollstonecroft thought well enough of these sermons to include an excerpt from 'The Case of Hezekiah' in her *Female Reader*.[19] The most perceptive comment that comes down to us was made by William Cowper, who puts the finger precisely upon the difference between his own Christ-centred evangelicalism and Sterne's man-centred philosophy.

> He is a great master of the pathetic; and if that or any other species of rhetoric could renew the human heart and turn it from the power of Satan unto God, I know no writer better qualified. . . . But alas! . . . the evil of a corrupt nature is too deeply rooted in us all to be extirpated by the puny efforts of wit or genius. The way which God has appointed must be the true and only way to virtue, and that is faith in Christ. . . . though I admire Sterne as a man of genius, I can never admire him as a preacher. For to say the least of him, he mistakes the weapon of his warfare, and fights not with the sword of the Spirit for which only he was ordained a minister of the Gospel, but with that wisdom which shone with as effectual a light before our

[18] Dated from Bath, 30 January 1766: Huntington Library, MO 5319.

[19] Published 1789 under the pen-name of 'Mr. Cresswick'. Excerpt printed pp. 300–1 under the subheading 'A Portrait of Mankind Influenced by Vanity'.

Saviour came as since, and which therefore cannot be the wisdom which He came to reveal to us.[20]

On or about 10 October 1765, Sterne set forth upon his journey to Italy. At Calais he stayed at the hotel newly opened by Pierre Quillacq, the celebrated innkeeper whom Sterne in the *Journey* called 'Dessein', but everyone else called 'Dessin'. The Lyon d'Argent, where Sterne had stayed in 1762, had burned down in a fire probably set by Dessin who did not own the building. By then Dessin had become the pet of many English travellers coming to France after the peace. So with the help of these English friends, especially Lord Shelburne, he had raised a subscription in London with which he had purchased and revamped another hotel – the Hôtel d'Angleterre, which he opened in March 1765. It was this hotel which figured in the imaginations of Sterne's first readers when they looked at the opening passages of *A Sentimental Journey*. Dessin profited enormously from Sterne's use of his name in the *Journey*. Years later he told Frederick Reynolds, 'Your countryman, Monsieur Sterne, von great, von vary great man, and he carry me vid him to posterity. He gain moche money by his Journey of Sentiment—mais moi—I—make more through de means of dat, than he, by all his ouvrages reunies——Ha, ha!'[21]

In Paris, though 'much recovered' (261), Sterne probably consulted the physician to the British Embassy, Dr Richard Gem, a man who had been at Cambridge when Sterne was there but had made Paris his home for many years. Sterne would later write to him from Italy.[22] Sterne may have stayed at the Hôtel de Modène in the rue Jacob on the left bank – the hotel at which Yorick stays in *A Sentimental Journey*.[23] But this is only a guess, for he might have stayed there during any of his four visits to Paris, or might never have stayed there at all, but simply used it in his fiction.

Social life among the English visitors was pretty much as he had known it in 1764, except that Lord Hertford, the ambassador, had left. However,

[20] Cowper to Joseph Hill, 3 April 1766, in *Correspondence*, ed. Thomas Wright, 1904, I, 64–5, as quoted in HOWES, 172–3.

[21] Quoted from Frederick Reynolds, *Life and Times*, I, 179–81, by CROSS, 384. For the story of Dessin's hotels, see CURTIS, 177–8. I have but one small detail to add to the account: an advertisement for Dessin's subscription in the *Public Advertiser*, 9 March 1765, includes a letter by Shelburne and lists twenty-nine subscribers, including Lord Spencer.

[22] W. P. Courtney, 'Richard Gem', *N&Q*, 11th series, II (1910), 121–3; CURTIS, 275–6.

[23] For a discussion of the hotel, now vanished, and its probable location, see SENTIMENTAL JOURNEY, 162 n.

David Hume was serving as chargé d'affaires, and so popular was the historian-philosopher that the embassy's function as the centre of social life continued unbroken. Among Hume's companions was Horace Walpole. Walpole wrote to a friend on 19 October 1765, 'You will think it odd that I should want to laugh, when Wilkes, Sterne, and Foote are here; but the first does not make me laugh, the second never could, and for the third, I choose to pay five shillings when I have a mind he should divert me.'[24]

Foote, of course, was Samuel Foote, the actor, whom Sterne had met in 1760, now grown such a friend that Sterne, in anticipation of seeing him in Paris, had sent from London his 'kind love' (260). He saw Wilkes (262). Though still a banished man, Wilkes's hopes had risen because the Rockingham ministry was friendly to him. They had given him a pension made up from the salaries of the ministers, but on the stipulation that he remain abroad.

Sterne had been looking forward to seeing d'Holbach and 'the rest of the joyous sett' (258), and had offered to bring over any books which d'Holbach or Diderot wanted (254). Since he would continue to send greetings to them (275), we know that he was happy with his reception. But the Anglophilia of this circle was cooling. D'Holbach had just returned from his first and last visit to England, where he found the common people distant, the aristocrats cold and proud, the buildings bizarre and the food unpalatable.[25] And Suard had lost enthusiasm specifically for Sterne. In the previous March he had printed in the *Gazette littéraire de l'Europe* that unfriendly review of *Tristram Shandy*, VII–VIII, which we have already noted.

Sterne also called upon the other English visitors, as was the custom, and struck up a friendship with three lively and witty young men of leisure. Lord William Gordon was a brother to the mad Lord George Gordon who would lead the shameful Gordon riots of 1779. John Fitzpatrick, second Earl of Upper Ossory, not yet twenty-one, would later purchase from Reynolds the great 1760 portrait of Sterne. The third of this triumvirate was John Craufurd, son of the Laird of (among other places) Errol, in Perth. 'Fish' Craufurd, as he was called for his restless inquisitiveness, was an extravagent gambler and lively talker: he became a great favourite of Madame du Deffand.[26]

[24] WALPOLE, XL, 386.

[25] C[harles] Avezac-Lavigne, *Diderot et la société du Baron d'Holbach*, Paris, 1875, p. 135.

[26] *EMT*, 301. Ossory, who became in 1773 a member of Johnson's circle, is mentioned frequently in BOSWELL. All three men are noticed by NAMIER AND BROOKE. For

Craufurd appears to have told Sterne an amusing story about having to share a room in a crowded inn with a gentlewoman, which Sterne transformed into 'The Case of Delicacy', which concludes *A Sentimental Journey*. We know Craufurd's story because it was recorded by his footman, John Macdonald, in his amusing memoirs. It is by no means identical with Sterne's story. The woman and Craufurd, in this tale, gamble for the one regular bed; the loser is to take a cot in the closet. The lady loses. When she is put to bed by her maid, she gives strict orders for the door to the closet to be bolted, though the bolt is on Craufurd's side.[27] Sterne in his version kept the general outline, but dropped the main point of Craufurd's story – the location of the bolt – for Sterne designated the cot for the maid and put his protagonist and the lady in beds that stood side by side. Out of this situation Sterne drew a highly complex comedy about people trying to keep their chaste agreements (285–9) and reason themselves out of temptation.

Toward the end of October 1765, Sterne made the 'agreeable journey' to Lyons (262). Probably he took the main route as far as Auxerre, but then branched off to the west on a road that carried him through Moulins and Tarare. It is at Moulins that Tristram in the ninth volume (780–4) and Yorick in *A Sentimental Journey* (268–76) meet the mad girl, Maria, and it is the badness of the road over Mount Tarare which leads Yorick to the family of peasants who celebrate their devotion to God in dance (280–4).[28]

Sterne was no stranger to Lyons, which he had passed through with his family in 1762 and written about in Volume VII of *Shandy*. The comic scene with the chaise-vamper's wife is laid in that city, as is Tristram's frustrated attempt to visit Lippius's clock, the Jesuit library, and the tomb of the lovers Amandus and Amanda (622–43). But, in fact, Sterne seems to have taken all his information about these curiosities from guidebooks. Actually, Sterne in 1765 had 'a joyous time there; dining and supping every day at the commandant's' (262). Sterne seems to have most enjoyed 'Lord F. W.', the

Craufurd, see also Norman Pearson, '"Fish" Craufurd', *The Nineteenth Century and After*, LXXV (January–June 1914), 389–401; and J. C. Hilson and John Valdimir Price, 'Hume and Friends, 1756 and 1766: Two New Letters', *Yearbook of English Studies*, VII (1977), 121–7.

[27] *Memoirs of an Eighteenth-Century Footman* [1790], ed. Sir E. Denison Ross and Eileen Power, 1927, pp. 86–7.

[28] For travellers going south, the two routes separated at Auxerre and rejoined at Lyons. Since in Volume VII of *Tristram Shandy* Sterne sent Tristram on the main route via Dijon (615), and in Volume IX places him in the secondary, western route via Moulins, one guesses that Sterne himself went via Moulins after he had written Volume VII, i.e. going to or coming from Italy.

second Earl Fitzwilliam, Rockingham's nephew, heir to his political interests.

Among the dozen English at Lyons was a brilliant young intellectual, John Horne, who would be remembered by the name of John Horne-Tooke. (He later took the name of a friend who made him his heir.) Horne was in holy orders, though he disguised the fact by dressing in elegant, colourful suits which he regularly left in Paris when he returned to England. He would eventually resolve his doubts by resigning his holy orders. Horne would have a brilliant but stormy career as a radical populist. Imprisoned for his activities in support of the American cause and barred from the practice of law upon his release, he became nevertheless the greatest constitutionalist of his age. The theory of language which he published in the *Diversions of Purley* is often hailed today as the earliest work of English philology.[29] But Horne, though rich, was the son of a poulterer, and as a young man was full of insecurities. Though he boasted that he 'passed a Week with Sterne at Lyons', he was not above using Sterne to try to get closer to his idol, John Wilkes. He would soon write to Wilkes from Montpellier telling him about Sterne, and adding:

> Forgive my Question, and do not answer it, if it is impertinent. Is there any Cause for Coldness between you and Sterne? He speaks very handsomely of you, where it is absolutely necessary to speak at all; but not with that Warmth and Enthusiasm that I expect from every one that knows you. Do not let me cause a Coldness between you if there is none. I am sensible my Question is at least imprudent, and my Jealousy blameable.[30]

[29] Alexander Stephens, *Memoir of John Horne-Tooke*, 2 vols, 1813; James E. Thorold Rogers, *Historical Gleanings, Second Series*, 1870; and Minnie Clare Yarborough, *John Horne Tooke*, New York, 1926.

[30] BL, Add. MSS 30689, fols 4–5. In this same letter Horne included an indiscreet comment upon his priesthood which Wilkes would later use against him: 'You are entering into a Correspondence with a *Parson*, and I am a little apprehensive lest that Title should disgust you: But give me Leave to assure you I am not ordained a hypocrite. It is true I have suffered the infectious Hand of a Bishop to be waved over me: whose Imposition like the sop given to Judas, is only a Signal for the Devil to enter. . . . But I hope I have escaped the Contagion: And if I have not, if you should at any Time discover the BLACK Spot under the Tongue, assist me kindly to conquer the prejudices of Education and Profession.' After years as Wilkes's ardent supporter, Horne quarrelled with him over the management of funds for the Society of the Bill of Rights, and Wilkes published the letter.

It was indeed an impertinent question and might have sown the seeds of distrust in a man more cautious than Wilkes. But it seems to have had no effect. Lydia Sterne, after her father's death in 1768, looked upon Wilkes as one of her father's closest friends.

Sterne left Lyons on or about 6 November and immediately ran into rainy weather and flooded roads. He reached Pont-de-Beauvoisin before he and a small group of travellers were stopped and held in 'vexatious captivity' by two rivulets swollen from the mountain run-off. The travellers could neither advance nor retreat. Two days later he crossed Mt Cenis Pass, probably carried by porters, which was the usual method. The porters also dismantled the chaises and carried them over in pieces.[31] When Lady Holland made the trip the following autumn, she told how 'The greatness, solemnity, and singularity of the views exceed all one can imagine, hills far beyond the clouds, immense falls of water, rapid torrents, great rivers, vast groves of spruce.'[32] But such scenes were of no interest to Sterne, and he described them in neither letters nor novels. In all, he spent eight days getting from Lyons to Turin, where he decided to stay for a few more days since the road ahead was inundated.

Turin, the capital of the kingdom of Sardinia, was a pleasant city famous for its hospitality. The buildings were laid out in a neat grid with long avenues, the whole dominated by the palace. Visitors were regularly taken on tours of the palace art collection. Sterne's erstwhile companions, George Pitt and Richard Phelps, were no longer at the English embassy. But Sterne, needing no introduction, was soon invited 'into a dozen houses . . . tomorrow I am to be presented, to the King—and when that Ceremony is over, have my hands full of Engagements' (263). Charles Emmanuel III was a soldier, diplomat and gallant. He hunted almost every morning, and visitors were welcome to join in; but, said Peter Beckford, the writer of books on hunting and travel, hunters were expected to follow a strict convention of never overtaking His Royal Highness. In the evenings the

[31] We are assured this was the usual way of traversing the pass by Joseph-Jérôme Le Français de Lalande, *Voyage d'un Français en Italie, Fait dans les Années 1765 & 1766*, 8 vols, Paris, 1769, I, 20–30. Wilkes was carried across with his dismantled carriage in January 1765: *Correspondence*, ed. John Almon, 5 vols, 1805, II, 120–1. But when Lady Holland made the crossing in October 1766 her carriage was dragged over by horses, but at a very slow pace: see below, next note.

[32] *Correspondence of Emily, Duchess of Leinster, 1731–1814*, ed. Brian Fitzgerald, 3 vols, Dublin, 1949–57, I, 474–6.

king danced at all the balls. 'It was there in the year 1765', wrote Beckford in his account of Turin,

> I met that eccentric genius STERNE—Alas, poor YORICK! many a merry hour have I passed in thy company, admired thy wit, and laughed at thy vagaries!—hours that might have been more profitably employed, but never more agreeably.[33]

At Turin, Sterne struck up a friendship with the youthful Sir James Macdonald, Laird of Skye, whom he had met in Paris in 1764. Sir James, a great favourite of Mrs Montagu and her circle, was universally admired for his broad knowledge and keen intellect – 'The Marcellus of the North', Boswell called him. Indeed, Macdonald does seem like a young Scottish Johnson, if such a notion can be entertained at all, for he too had a scarred and ugly face and a too heavy figure, the disadvantages of which he quickly overcame by his brilliant talk.[34] Macdonald became Sterne's companion for the rest of the journey southward and for the stay in Naples.

'I am just leaving this place with Sir James Macdonald for Milan, etc.', Sterne wrote on 28 November; 'We have spent a joyous fortnight here, and met with all kinds of honours, and with regret do we both bid adieu' (265). In their company was another man whom Sterne called 'Ogilby', probably the person listed as 'Ogilvy' in the subscribers' list for *Sermons*, III–IV. Sterne, always uninhibited in pushing his own books, had continued to solicit subscriptions during his travels. He had obtained d'Holbach's and Diderot's names in Paris, Horne's in Lyons, and those of Ogilvy and Beckford in Turin – and sent them back to Becket promptly, for the volumes were published only six weeks after Sterne left Turin. No doubt other names on the list represent persons Sterne met during this journey, but they are not so readily identified.

Sterne wrote no letters from Milan – none that survives – but he and his friends must have stopped there several days. Sterne was entertained by the

[33] Peter Beckford, *Familiar Letters from Italy to a Friend in England*, 2 vols, Salisbury, 1805, I, 68. Beckford, cousin of the author of *Vathek*, was the squire of Steepletown Iwerne, Dorset. He is noticed in the *DNB* and NAMIER AND BROOKE.

[34] But Macdonald's pretence to knowledge had its weakness. Elizabeth Carter, knowing he had taught himself Erse, asked his opinion of MacPherson's *Ossian*, to which he answered that it was 'Inferior to the original': *Series of Genuine Letters between Mrs. Elizabeth Carter and Miss Catherine Talbot from the year 1741 to 1770*, ed. Montagu Pennington, 4 vols, 1809, III, 87. For a biographical sketch of Macdonald, see CURTIS, 264.

Austrian minister, Count Firmian, and at his house met Gian Carlo Passeroni, the priest-poet. On another occasion he was entertained by Allessandro Verri, the historian, who was president of the city's leading literary society.[35]

Curiously, Milan is the scene of one of the few incidents in *A Sentimental Journey* which is laid in Italy. Yorick, explaining how he 'translates' the actions of people into their feelings and motives, tells what happened to him as he was entering Martini's concert in Milan. At the door he and a lady got into one of those laughable situations where they each kept trying to let the other pass but only succeeded in getting in each other's way. Yorick then begged to hand her to her coach:

> Upon my word, Madame, said I when I had handed her in, I made six different efforts to let you go out—And I made six efforts, replied she, to let you enter—I wish to heaven you would make a seventh, said I—With all my heart, said she, making room—Life is too short to be long about the forms of it—so I instantly stepp'd in, and she carried me home with her—And what became of the concert, St. Cecilia, who, I suppose, was at it, knows more than I.
>
> I will only add, that the connection which arose out of that translation, gave me more pleasure than any one I had the honour to make in Italy. (173)

The lady was identified in 1789 by Arthur Young as the Marchesa Fagnani, erstwhile mistress of George Selwyn and later of the fourth Duke of Queensbury, but the identification is doubtful, as are all identifications of Sterne's characters when Sterne himself did not leave a hint.[36]

[35] The account of these meetings was passed on by Giulio Garcano in his *Memorie di Grandi*, 2 vols, Milan, 1869, I, 202, and reported in Giovanni Rabizzani, *Sterne in Italia*, Rome, 1920, pp. 29–37; and by Paul Kirby, 'Sterne in Italy', WINGED SKULL, 210–26. Passeroni later said that Sterne, by his own account, had taken the design of *Tristram Shandy* from his satire of Roman life, *Il Cicerone*; but CROSS, 399, sensibly points out that Sterne is unlikely ever to have heard of the man or his work before their meeting. The information on Verri's literary society from Lalande, *Voyage d'un Français en Italie*, I, 374–5.

[36] Emilio Legnani, 'L'Avventura Milanese di Sterne con la "Marquesina di F***" fu "fabbricata di pianta"', *English Miscellany*, VI (1955), 247–57, raises an elaborate but inconclusive argument that Sterne got the story from Alessandro Verri when Verri visited him in London in 1767 – a story which Verri fabricated to discredit the name of the countess. See Stout's summary and evaluation in SENTIMENTAL JOURNEY, 343–4.

By 18 December Sterne and his friends had reached Florence, having passed through Parma, Piacenza, Bologna, 'with Weather as delicious, as a kindly April in England' (265–6). 'I stay here three days to dine with our Plenipo—Ld Tit[c]hfield & Cowper' (266). Other people might plan a stop in Florence to see the Duomo or Michelangelo's *David*, but so social a creature was Laurence Sterne that he was planning nothing but visits with three Englishmen he had not yet met. In fact he was mistaken about Lord Titchfield, who was not in Europe; he may have confused him with his younger brother Lord Charles Edward Bentinck.[37] The men were cousins of his friends the Egertons. Earl Cowper was an eccentric man so infatuated with his Florentine mistress that he did not leave that city for ten years, even when his father died and he came into his title and estates.[38]

The 'Plenipo' whom Sterne looked forward to meeting was the remarkable Sir Horace Mann, Bart, Envoy Extraordinary and Minister Plenipotentiary to the Court of Florence from 1740 until his death in 1786. Mann made the acquaintance of virtually every Englishman who came to Italy and corresponded with many of them. His many letters to Horace Walpole are justly admired. He possessed an unusual set of qualities: he was at once an astute diplomat and a man beloved for his sincerity, wisdom and kindness. 'When his carriage passed,' wrote Louis Dutens, 'people stopped, as before that of their sovereign, to salute him, and to obtain one of his kind looks; and I saw, with inexpressible pleasure, the joy which his presence diffused over the countenances of all the good people of Florence.'[39] Horace Walpole had sent Mann the first two volumes of *Tristram Shandy* in 1760, and Mann had replied,

> You will laugh at me, I suppose, when I say I don't understand Tristram Shandy, because it was probably the intention of the author that nobody should. It seems to me *humbugging*, if I have a right notion of an art of talking or writing that has been invented since I left England. It diverted me, however, extremely.[40]

[37] CURTIS, 266–7, reported his correspondence with the librarian of the then current Duke of Portland which indicated that Lord Titchfield was not abroad but his brother was. Lord Charles Edward Bentinck is noticed in NAMIER AND BROOKE.

[38] CURTIS, 267; DUTENS, II, 131; NAMIER AND BROOKE, II, 265–6.

[39] DUTENS, IV, 88. For Mann's life and career, see John Doran, *'Mann' and Manners at the Court of Florence, 1740–1786*, 2 vols, 1876; and I[sabel] Giberne Sieveking, *Memoir of Sir Horace Mann*, 1912.

[40] WALPOLE XXI, 446, 520.

After reading the third and fourth volumes, he gave up: 'Nonsense pushed too far, becomes unsupportable.' But Mann in 1765 did not fail to play the host to Sterne. As we shall see, he sent him off to Rome with a letter of introduction to Cardinal Alessandro Albani.

During this visit to Florence or his return to the city on his way back or both, Sterne sat for a portrait – the amusing caricature in oil of Sterne and Death which now hangs in Jesus College.[41] The artist was Thomas Patch, who made his home in Florence. Patch was a favourite of Mann, frequently visited his house, and often made cartoons of the English guests – but always with their permission. One cannot but wonder whether Sterne himself suggested that Patch might paint him as Tristram Shandy greeting Death with such urbanity that Death went away, that key scene in Volume VII of *Tristram Shandy* (576). Patch rendered Death as a skeleton holding a scythe and an hourglass flanked with bat's wings. Sterne, in clerical black with white bands, but curiously wearing a sword, bows with hands folded across his breast to Death while still looking at him in the face – so to speak. Patch kept his painting of Sterne and later made a line engraving based upon it, but much elaborated: about the room are many symbols of Sterne's life and work, jackboots, a map of Namur, a pen and, for some curious reason understood by Patch, a machine for shredding paper. Still later Patch did an etching, this time without the symbols and with only the hand of Death showing, made for his book, *Twenty-Five Caricatures* (1769).

Sterne stayed in Florence a day or two longer than he had planned, but he and Macdonald were on the road again about 22 December. They reached Rome on Christmas Day or the day after. Since Sterne had intended to 'tread the Vatican, and be introduced to all the Saints in the Pantheon' (266), one supposes that he saw the Sistine Chapel, walked through St Peter's and visited the Vatican Museum. In *A Sentimental Journey* he made use of the Pantheon to ridicule Tobias Smollett – the second Italian incident of the novel. 'I met Smelfungus in the grand portico of the Pantheon—he was just coming out of it—*'Tis nothing but a huge cock-pit*, said he' (117). The notorious Cockpit in St James's Park, London, was a domed structure, and

[41] In *EMT*, 310–11, I maintained that the painting was done between 18 December 1765 and 1 January 1766, the day I then thought Sterne left Florence, and was misdated on the frame, 1766. I now think it likely that Patch finished the cartoon at his leisure after Sterne's departure; so the date of 1766 is not incorrect. Moreover, I now think the period of Sterne's stay in Florence was more probably 17–22 December 1765, or thereabouts. On Patch, see the *DNB*.

Smollett had indeed said in his *Travels* that the Pantheon looked like a cockpit. But, of course, Sterne never met Smollett on the steps: Smollett was in England.

On 28 December 1765, an old man in scarlet robes sat down in the magnificent Villa Albani in the suburb of Porta Solaria, and dictated a letter to Sir Horace Mann:

> Monsieur
>
> I have had the pleasure of entertaining Mr. Sterne, who brought me the letter which you had the goodness to write me on the 17th. The conversation was not very long because we are so busy these days, but that did not keep me from noting his great wit. If he were not in such a hurry to get on to Naples, I would have had the pleasure of seeing him on other occasions and enjoying his learning and sallies. I have offered my services to him, and I will give them to him whenever he seeks me out again. Pray accept my thanks for your care to make me acquainted with a countryman of such worth and fame. I have the honour to be, Sir
>
> Alessandro Albani[42]

Cardinal Albani, one of the most wealthy men in Rome, was a consummate politician, an astute diplomat, and a shrewd dealer in antique art. He had built his magnificent villa primarily to show off his collection of ancient Roman statues and pottery to the buyers who came from all over Europe. He was also the unofficial envoy for Great Britain. Nations which would have no official diplomatic relations with the Pope – who at that time was the absolute ruler of the Roman state – pursued their diplomatic ends through one cardinal or another who was known as their 'protector'. As protector of Great Britain, Albani worked primarily with Sir Horace Mann in Florence. He also was the protector for Sardinia and the Holy Roman Empire. He was paid no stipend for his servcies, but sold his information. To develop this part of his enterprise, he built up an elaborate private spy network. He was now seventy-three years old and almost completely blind.

At the time Sterne called upon the cardinal, Rome was buzzing with rumours about the imminent death of James Francis Edward Stuart, the

[42] My translation from Albani's original letter, written in French; MS at the PRO: SP 105/316, fol. 352. The letter, one of many by Albani in the PRO, was brought to light by Leslie Lewis in her study, *Connoisseurs and Secret Agents in Eighteenth-Century Rome*, 1961, p. 232. I depend upon Lewis for information about Albani.

'Old Pretender'. Letters were racing back and forth between the cardinal and Mann, between Mann and Westminster. James Francis Edward, who was recognized by the Pope as the king of Great Britain, had lived since 1717 in the Muti Palace in Rome, displaying the royal arms of the Stuart kings above its door. The situation had become intolerable to George III and his ministers, and Sir Horace Mann had been told to see that Rome put a stop to the recognition of the house of Stuart when James Francis Edward died. Cardinal Albani daily took his long frame to the Vatican Palace for a conference with Innocent XIII. He prevailed, largely on the argument that Rome must no longer antagonize a Protestant king who had been lenient to his Catholic subjects. When the Old Pretender died on 1 January 1766, the Pope's servants came in the night and removed the arms from over the door. Albani himself wrote to the Young Pretender, Charles Edward, the very man who in 1745 had led his Highland army as far south as Derby and very nearly captured the throne, to explain that when he returned to Rome he must no longer expect to be treated as royalty: he would henceforth be only Mr Stuart. In time Charles Edward destroyed his own cause by leading a life of drunken debauchery, abandoning his wife, and dying childless.[43]

Sterne met another dealer in antique art at Rome – Joseph Nollekens, an Englishman of Dutch descent. Nollekens came from a line of painters and in his youth had won a series of prizes for sculpture from the Society of Arts. He had settled early in Rome and taken to dealing in antique statues which he had restored. He had given up thinking of himself as an artist until David Garrick, who came to Rome in 1764, recalling the prizes Nollekens had won, talked him into making a sculpture portrait. Putting to work the skills he had developed as a restorer, Nollekens made a sculpture bust of Garrick which Sterne and everyone else much admired. Sterne became his second subject. The lifesize bust he executed was an exact likeness made from precise measurements of Sterne's head and face – except for the hair, which he rendered in the ancient Roman convention.[44] 'With this performance,' wrote J. T. Smith, his biographer, 'Nollekens continued to be pleased even to his second childhood.' He even had his friend, John Francis Rigaud, make

[43] Lewis, *Connoisseurs and Secret Agents*, 211–18; Doran, *'Mann' and Manners*, II, 156–66.

[44] When Sterne's remains were exhumed in London in 1969 for reburial in Coxwold, the skull was identified, in part by location, in part by an anatomist's demonstration that the skull perfectly matched the Nollekens bust: below, Chapter 9.

an oil painting of him leaning on the bust of Sterne.[45] Later he brought it to London, exhibited it at the Society of Arts show of 1767, and commenced making and selling copies in plaster or marble.[46] The busts of Garrick and Sterne and a third, of the Duke of York, made Nollekens's reputation as a portrait sculptor; in a short time he found himself the most sought-after portraitist in England – after Reynolds. In person Nollekens was a grotesque, a bowlegged dwarf with a large ugly head, uncouth in his habits and crude in his manner. Some found him illiterate, gluttonous and filthy, but Fanny Burney liked him – 'as jolly, fat, lisping, laughing, underbred, good humoured a man as lives'.[47] One cannot but wonder whether Nollekens figured in Sterne's imagination when he wrote the plea for dwarfs in *A Sentimental Journey* (174–9).

Among the handful of Englishmen at Rome, Sterne found an old acquaintance, Henry Errington, squire of Sandhoe, Northumberland. Errington turned out to be another Thomas Thornhill: he thought it such a privilege to be in Sterne's company that he was willing to pay the bills for most of Sterne's travel expenses. 'A good hearted young gentleman', Sterne called him (269). Errington now joined Sterne and Macdonald, and the three set out for Naples about 10 January 1766.

Naples, a great amphitheatre opening toward the sea, was beautiful from a distance, but upon near inspection proved to be a teeming mass of some 330,000 people – almost twice the size of Rome. Vast numbers of impoverished *lazzaroni* milled through the streets and slept on the banks of the canals at night. In 1764 thousands had died of starvation, and another famine was beginning when Sterne arrived. Street violence was common and riots were frequent. Wealthy families kept private police forces and were escorted everywhere. Nevertheless, Neopolitan culture flourished. Sterne was treated to 'a little comedy acted . . . with more expression and spirit, and true character than I shall see one hastily again' (269). He probably was talking about the theatrical performance for carnival put on by the Celestine Monks. He went often to concerts, for music was the glory

45 William L. Pressley, 'A Portrait of Joseph Nollekens Reattributed to John Francis Regaud', *Connoisseur*, CXCVII (1978), 110–15.

46 Further details in *EMY*, 311–13.

47 *Early Diaries*, ed. Annie Raine Ellis, 2 vols, 1907, II, 145. John Thomas Smith, who was disappointed when he found he had not been made rich by Nollekens's will, drew a highly unflattering portrait in *Nollekens and His Times*. I use the edition by Edmund Gosse, 1894; the Sterne portrait is discussed on pp. 34, 51–2. See also Joseph Farington, *Diary*, ed. James Greig, 8 vols, 1922–8, I, 124–6; and *DNB*.

of Naples. Everyone of any education was knowledgeable about music; there were numerous conservatories, and concerts, public and private, were given almost every night. Visitors travelled to Pompeii and Herculaneum, where the famous archaeological excavations were already under way.[48] On 24 January, some two weeks after Sterne and his friends arrived, they were treated to a spectacular display as Mount Vesuvius erupted once more, belching fiery gases and shooting sparks high into the sky.[49]

Sterne shared his lodgings with Errington and Macdonald. They must have gone together to call upon William Hamilton, the British envoy to the Court of Naples, who regularly entertained visitors and kept an open house for their pleasure. Sterne would later send his thanks to Hamilton and his beautiful but asthmatic wife (273). The couple were lovers of art and music, and he was an amateur archaeologist. Mrs Hamilton, whose maiden name was Barlow, is not to be confused with Hamilton's second wife, born Emma Lyon, who became notorious as the mistress of Admiral Nelson. Among the twenty-five Englishmen in Naples that winter (272) was John Symonds, soon to be appointed Professor of Modern History at Cambridge, for whom Sterne wrote a letter of introduction to Dr Richard Gem in Paris (275–6). Another was Sir William Stanhope, the younger brother of Lord Chesterfield, a man who had the reputation of being less polite than his brother. He was a wit and a gambler, and Sterne liked him very much and became his correspondent.[50] Sterne met some local gentry. He later sent greetings to the Countess Rougé, wife of Gabriel-François, Comte de Rougé, and to the Countess Mahong, born in England Lady Anne Clifford, now the widow of Count Joseph James Mahony or Mahong, a soldier of fortune who had served the Sicilian Crown (274).

Sterne's health improved. On 3 February he wrote to Lydia, 'I find myself infinitely better than I was—and hope to have added at least ten years to my life by this journey to Italy—the climate is heavenly, and I find new principles of health in me, which I have been long a stranger to' (267). And to Hall he wrote a few days later, 'and here I am, as happy as a king after all, growing fat, sleek, and well liking—not improving in stature, but in breadth' (269).

Sterne enjoyed himself thoroughly. 'We have a jolly carnival of it,' he

[48] Lalande, *Voyage d'un Français en Italie*, VI, 313–49, VII, 88–109; DUTENS, II, 154.

[49] *St. James's Chronicle*, 22–5 February 1766; William Hamilton to Sir Horace Mann, 24 December 1765: PRO, SP 105/316, fols 342–3.

[50] NAMIER AND BROOKE; CURTIS, 395.

told Hall, 'nothing but operas—punchinellos—festinos and masquerades' (269). A story was being passed around among the English visitors at Naples which captures at least a part of the atmosphere of this city:

> At *Naples* there is a place called the *Largo del Castello*, not unlike our *Tower-Hill*, the resort of the idle populace. Here, every afternoon, Monks and Mountebanks, Pickpockets and Conjurors, follow their several occupations. The Monk (for I never saw more than one at a time) holds forth, like our itinerant field-preachers, to what congregation he can collect; the Mountebank, by means of Punch, and his fellow comedians, endeavours to gather as great an audience as he can. It happened one day, that Punch succeeded marvellously, and the poor Monk preached to the air, for not a living creature was near him: Mortified and provoked that a puppet-shew within thirty yards of him, should draw the attention of the people from the Gospel to such idle trash, with a mixture of rage and religion he held up the crucifix, and called aloud, *Ecco il vero Pulcinello*;—'*Here is the true* Punchinello,—*come here,—come here*!'[51]

The phrase became a joke between Sterne and Hall. The following summer Sterne tried to tempt Hall to Scarborough: 'If you would profit by y[r] misfortunes & laugh away misery there for a week—ecco lo il vero Punchinello! I am your man' (281).

Social frivolities in Naples were less frequent than in London, but not entirely absent. Sterne wrote to Hall, 'We (that is nous autres [foreigners]) are all dressing out for one [a masquerade] this night at the Princess Francavivalla, which is to be superb.—The English dine with her (exclusive) and so much for small chat—'(269). Small chat indeed; but how we wish he had described his costume! This masked ball, a celebration of Shrove Tuesday, was held on 11 February at the magnificent Palazzo Cellamare, near the Porta Chiaia, a villa famous for its gardens. They were guests of Michele Imperiali, Principe di Francavilla, and Principessa Eleanora Borghese, the leading host and hostess of Naples.[52] The

[51] Samuel Sharpe, *Letters from Italy*, 2nd edn, 1767, pp. 183–4.

[52] CURTIS, 270. Louis T. Milic, 'A Sterne Letter Re-dated', *N&Q*, CCI (January–June 1956), 212–13, demonstrated that the Principessa's ball was given on Shrove Tuesday, 11 February. Consequently, Milic pointed out that Sterne's letter to Hall (No. 158) should be dated 11 February 1766 instead of 5 February as Lydia Sterne's edition of *Letters* gave it.

Principessa was something of an Anglophile: her guests for the dinner were, as Sterne said, exclusively English, and at the ball everyone danced English country dances.[53] Sterne may have danced that night with Sarah Tuting, that attractive consumptive with whom he had been so sentimentally smitten at York in 1764. But the greeting he sent to her through Hamilton after he left Naples does not suggest an intimacy: 'When You see Miss Tuting pray present my most friendly good wishes for her—as well as respects to her' (273).

Another guest at the dinner and ball was Garrick's friend, Dr Samuel Sharp, the physician who wrote *Letters from Italy, Describing the Customs and Manners of the Country, in the Years 1765 and 1766*. Since the book appeared late in 1766, it is little wonder Sharp was identified as Sterne's 'Mundungus' in *A Sentimental Journey*, another travel writer whom Sterne linked to 'Smelfungus' (Tobias Smollett).

> Mundungus, with an immense fortune, made the whole tour; going on from Rome to Naples—from Naples to Venice—from Venice to Vienna—to Dresden, to Berlin, without one generous connection or pleasurable anecdote to tell of; but he had travell'd straight on looking neither to his right hand or his left, lest Love or Pity should seduce him out of his road. (119)

But the identification is doubtful. It has been pointed out that Dr Sharp did not have an immense fortune and did not travel to Vienna, Dresden or Berlin. Moreover, Sterne made no specific allusion to Sharp's *Letters* in the way he alluded to Smollett's *Travels*.[54] Mundungus may well be a composite figure, for Sterne probably met other writers of travel books. He might, for instance, have known a French writer, Joseph-Jérôme Le Français de Lalande, whose book, *Voyage d'un François en Italie, Fait dans les Années 1765 & 1766*, in eight volumes, was to be published in Paris in 1769. Lalande was the sort of writer of whom Sterne was most contemptuous, one who spends his time measuring buildings and courtyards and gathering statistics about

[53] So reported the following year by the youthful Earl of Offaly, later second Duke of Leinster, to his mother: *Correspondence of Emily, Duchess of Leinster*, 1949–57, III, 435–6.

[54] The argument, made originally by Louis T. Milic in an unpublished Columbia master's degree thesis, is reported and subscribed to by Stout in SENTIMENTAL JOURNEY, 119, note. On Sharpe's friendship with Garrick, see George Winchester Stone, Jr, and George M. Kahrl, *David Garrick*, Carbondale and Edwardsville, Ill., 1979, pp. 118–19.

the numbers of inhabitants of towns. Though Sterne could not have known Lalande's book, which appeared after Sterne's death, he might well have observed this busy researcher in action.

Though he continued to think he had 'received much benefit from the air' (272) and to predict he would return home fat (271–2), Sterne grew tired of Naples itself. A few weeks later in Paris he found occasion to tease the abbé Galiani about his native city: 'It is better to die in Paris', said Sterne, 'than to live in Naples.'[55] Besides, Sterne and Errington wanted to see the pageantry of Holy Week in Rome. So in mid-March they took leave of Macdonald. Sir James had been ill during much of the stay, but Sterne thought he was 'just recovering' from 'a long and most cruel fit of the rheumatism' (272). He never did recover. He lingered for a while at Naples and then dragged himself to Frascati, where on 26 July the poor young man died.

Sterne and Errington left Naples travelling by horseback. 'My friend and self', Sterne later wrote from Rome, 'had a voyage of it by Mount Cussino, full of cross accidents; but all was remedied along the road by sporting and Laughter' (273). They 'dined and supped and lay' at the celebrated Benedictine Abbey of Monte Cassino, the traditional stopping place for travellers making the Rome–Naples journey via Capua. Some fifty years earlier the monks had added a handsome wing to the monastery in which they housed guests 'of distinction'. Meals were excellent and the monks themselves waited at table. 'We were rec^{d} and treated like Sovereign Princes' (273). They reached Rome on Saturday, 15 March, 'without bodily hurt except that a Dromedary of a beast fell upon me in full Gallop, and by rolling over me crushed me as flat as a Pankake—but I am growing round again' (273).

At Rome they found Samuel Sharp, who had also come for Holy Week. Sharp recorded in his *Letters* much of what he and we suppose Sterne saw. They went to the Pope's chapel on Palm Sunday to watch His Holiness present imitation palm branches to the cardinals, and to follow the procession to St Peter's, the Pope carried in a chair. On Holy Thursday, the Pope blessed the people from a balcony of St Peter's. Sharp understood that the prayers read by two cardinals were curses on heretics like himself. Then the Pope pronounced a benediction, 'and wipes off all the efficacy of the

[55] My translation from Galiani's *Correspondence*, 2 vols, Paris, 1881, II, 328.

Curse.' Sharp was impressed with the robes and the handsome uniforms of the papal guard, but the processions he thought all 'mummery' and 'farce'.[56]

'I am much recover'd in my health, by the Neapolitan Air,' Sterne wrote to Dr Gem from Rome;

> I have been here in my return 3 Weeks, seeing over again wt I saw first in my way to Naples. . . . We have pass'd a jolly laughing winter of it—and having changed the Scene for Rome; We are passing as merry a Spring as hearts could wish. I wish my friends no better fortune in this world, than to go at this rate—haec est Vita dissolutorum. (275)

Sterne and Errington parted company at Rome, and early in April Sterne set out to find his family in France. Elizabeth and Lydia had written that Tours was an unhealthy town, so they were thinking of Bourg. Sterne was against the plan – 'a vile place for agues', he wrote.

> But trust me, my Lydia, I will find you out wherever you are, in May. . . . if I live, the produce of my pen shall be yours—If fate reserves me not that—the humane and good, part for thy father's sake, part for thy own, will never abandon thee!—If your mother's health will permit her to return with me to England, your summers I will render as agreeable as I can at Coxwould—your winters at York—you know my publications call me to London. (267–8)

Sterne's letter to Lydia was written from Naples on 3 February 1766. Five days later he had changed his mind and was planning to return without seeing them. He would travel via 'Venice, Vienna, Saxony, Berlin, and so by the Spaw, and thence through Holland to England' (269). It was Errington who had planned this trip and invited Sterne to accompany him, offering to pay his expenses. Sterne wrote to Foley on 8 February explaining that he would travel 'with a gentleman of fortune', and so would have little need of money; Foley was to see that Elizabeth got 'what cash she wants' (271). Two days later he repeated the instructions to Panchaud and made arrangements to draw money from a banker in Venice, which would be on the new route (272). But the plan fell through.[57] Errington seems to have

[56] *Letters from Italy*, 191–203 (Letters XLI and XLII).

[57] CONNELY, 168, expressed the view that Sterne went as far as Venice, but I do not find sufficient evidence of such a visit.

had a friendship with the ambassador to the imperial court at Vienna, Lord Stormont. But Lady Stormont died on 16 March, and Errington decided not to make the journey.[58]

One must not jump to the conclusion that Sterne was betraying Lydia and planning to return without seeing her when she expected him. It is more likely that he had received a letter telling him they were on the move and it would not be practicable for him to find them until they settled upon some location. What we know for sure is that in the end Sterne went to a great deal of trouble to find them. As he later told Hall, 'Never man has been such a wildgoose chace after a wife as I have been—after having sought her in five or six different towns, I found her at last in *Franche Comté*' (277) on the Swiss border. If he had wanted to avoid seeing his family, it would have been easy enough to give up the search and go on to Paris.

We do not know exactly where Sterne met his family or how long he stayed with them. Elizabeth, he said, was 'very poorly' (279). 'Poor woman!' he wrote to Hall, 'she was very cordial, &c. and begs to stay another year or so—my Lydia pleases me much—I found her greatly improved in every thing I wish'd her' (277). Despite his relatively improved health, Elizabeth thought he looked very ill, 'but I shall live these ten years, my Antony, notwithstanding the fears of my wife, whom I left most melancholy on that account' (277).

Sterne went on, but stopped near Dijon to visit Marguerite, Comtesse de Vair,[59] at her 'delicious Chateau', where, as he told Hall,

[58] Reported by CURTIS, 270–1, on the basis of a passage in the journals of Lady Mary Coke.

[59] One presumes Sterne's hostess was the Comtesse de Vair, also known as the Comtesse de la Noüe, because Miss Trist dated the letter cited below from '*Lanoüe near Dijon*' and because Sterne spoke of his hostess as a countess. MEDALLE rendered the name 'Countess of M——', but that was probably a careless error. CURTIS, 278, first identified the countess and correctly described her as the wife of Gabriel-François de la Noüe-Vieuxpont (1714–79), Comte de Vair, Comte de la Noüe. Then Curtis goes on to say that la Noüe was occupying the house of a friend at Fontette, near Dijon, citing as his source Henri Carré, *La Charlotais et le duc d'Aiguillon*, Vol. XV of *Mémoires de la Société des Antiquaires de l'Ouest*, 1893. This source establishes that there was indeed a house called Fontette near Dijon, owned by Jean-Baptiste-Antide Fevret, Chevalier de Fontette, but not that la Noüe was occupying the house. A month before Sterne's visit, Fevret wrote a letter, dated 18 April 1766, in which he says that la Noüe has arrived from Versailles 'gros et gras', to give them the court news. A footnote identifies him as Gabriel-François de la Noüe-Vieuxpont, Comte de Vair, 'dit la comte de la Noüe', infantry colonel, commandant of the coastguard militia of Brittany, Chevalier de Saint-Louis, and Minister Plenipotentiary to the Elector of

> I have been patriarching it these seven days with her ladyship, and half a dozen of very handsome and agreeable ladies—her ladyship has the best of hearts—a valuable present not given to every one.—Tomorrow, with regret, I shall quit this agreeable circle, and post it night and day to Paris. . . . This is a delicious part of the world; most celestial weather, and we lie all day, without damps, upon the grass—and that is the whole of it, except the inner man (for her ladyship is not stingy of her wine) is inspired twice a day with the best Burgundy that grows upon the mountains. (277)

Among the guests of the countess was a daughter or daughters of Browse Trist, recorder of Totnes, in Devon.[60] Trist had three daughters, one or more of whom were abroad, not with their mother, who was in England, but with their father or some relative – some of the 'handsome and agreeable ladies' whose company Sterne was enjoying. One day one of the Misses Trists – be it Agnes, Elizabeth or Susanna, for we do not know which – was writing to her mother that 'the famous Doctor' was a 'pleasing, agreeable man as well as the most sensible that I ever was in company with'; she happened to leave this half-finished letter upon the table where Sterne found it. He promptly turned it over and wrote on the other side:

> Miss Triste having gone out of the room (but upon what occasion God knows) Tristram Shandy has thought meet to profit by her absence and the temptation this void has laid in his way, of sending his best respects to the mother, not altogether for the sake of the daughter (for that wd. be uncivil), but in testimony of his esteem for Mrs. Triste and her worthy character, and at the same [time] in Homage to the Graces of her fair offspring, which appear so lovely in the eyes of Tristram Shandy, that 'tis well for the fair Goddesse that he is under a slight pre-engagement—indeed 'tis only marriage. (276)

Miss Trist, continuing her letter, explained how 'Tristram Shandy took up

Cologne; married to Marie-Marguerite Chevalier (pp. 152–3 and n.). I would guess that la Noüe and his lady had a house in the neighbourhood of Fontette, that Sterne and the Trist family were guests there, and that the heading of Miss Trist's letter indicates, not a village, but the house.

[60] He had served as Member of Parliament for Totnes until he sold out to Henry Fox when Fox set about clearing Parliament of all members opposed to George III's peace policy. Trist sold out for £1600 and the promise of a captain's commission in the army for his son: NAMIER AND BROOKE; CURTIS, 276.

my pen & wrote what you see on the other side; he goes to England to-morrow, and takes this letter to put in the office in London' – which indeed he faithfully did.

Sterne arrived in Paris during the last week of May. On the 27th of the month a certain Rev. Mr Garland saw him attending mass at the Church of Saint-Roch in the rue Saint-Honoré. He had heard a monk preach there, Garland wrote in his diary, 'who seeing me approach him and knowing (I suppose) by my manner I was not a Roman began to exclaim & to show that the Hereticks wou'd be all damn'd; near me, I discover'd Tristram Shandy (Mr Sterne) who seemed to be very attentive to the Monk's rant'[61] – a rare picture of Sterne the novelist observing men and manners. The only documentary evidence of Sterne's presence in Paris in the spring of 1766 is Garland's diary entry and the recollection of the abbé Galiani that Sterne had told him it was better to die in Paris than to live in Naples. Yet the week or two he spent at Paris may well have given shape to the rest of his writing career.

The *philosophes* and other English-speaking Parisians were talking about a book which had appeared in London on 8 May, Tobias Smollett's *Travels through France and Italy*. One imagines they were incensed at Smollett's constant complaints about French customs and manners and his facile condemnations of French society. They seem to have chosen a spokesman for their view, a newcomer to the d'Holbach set, François-Jean Chastellux, soldier, historian and friend of Wilkes, who is usually remembered today as 'le Chevalier de Chastellux'. Chastellux's review of Smollett appeared in the *Gazette littéraire de l'Europe* for 15 February, but antedated and printed no earlier than the middle of May.[62] Sterne, who had been pondering the possibility of another travel book, may have had the idea of *A Sentimental*

[61] Quoted by CURTIS, 156.

[62] Two writers on Smollett have kindly advised me about Chastellux's review, the date of its appearance and its significance for French thinking about Smollett – Professor Paul-Gabriel Boucé of the Sorbonne Nouvelle and Dr Frank Felsenstein of Leeds University. Dr Felsenstein pointed out that the review was later reissued in a somewhat changed form under the title 'La Lettre critique sur le voyage de M. Smollett en France', in *Recueil Amusant de Voyages*, Paris, 1784. The review of the *Recueil* in *L'Année littéraire*, XXXI (1784), ii, 114–20, also makes many references to Smollett's *Travels*. These suggest that the hostility toward the *Travels* in France was not short-lived. Chastellux's authorship of the review, notwithstanding it was later claimed by Suard (*Variétés littéraires*, 4 vols, [Paris,] 1804, III, 182–203), was demonstrated by Eugène Joliat, *Smollet et la France*, Paris, 1935, pp. 147–8.

Journey as he listened to his French friends and perused Chastellux's review.

Probably Sterne did not reach London as early as 4 June, the king's birthday, which he had hoped to celebrate with Hall (277); his arrival was not noticed until 17 June, in the *St. James's Chronicle*:

> Before the celebrated Tristram Shandy returned from France, his Laundress brought home his Shirts complete in Number, but when he came to his Lodging in Town, and was going to dress, the Servant putting one to air, behold both the Laps were cut off. On Examination the Whole were found deficient in the same Manner. Now . . . is it not likely that the Laundress, being far advanced in her Pregnancy, might take it in her Head, that such soft Linen would make excellent Baby-Clothes to wrap the little dear Creature in, and by this Kind of fortunate Circumstance would inherit the same Wit and Humour as that renowned Author?

Sterne would soon make use of this story in the ninth volume of *Tristram Shandy*, but would place the incident at Milan and give it an indecent twist. Tristram says nothing at all about a baby, but emphasizes that the theft was done by a 'cunning gypsey of a laundress', but 'with some consideration', since they were fore-laps and Tristram was just returning out of Italy – i.e. they bore the evidence of recently acquired clap (780).[63]

By 28 June Sterne was in York (278) and home to Shandy Hall a few days later. He had seen Hall somewhere on this journey, at York or London, and presumably Hall had found Sterne in the mood he had described in his letter from Dijon: 'I am most unaccountably well, and most accountably nonsensical—'tis at least a proof of good spirits, which is a sign and token given me in these latter days that I must take up again the pen.—In faith I think I shall die with it in my hand' (277).

[63] TS NOTES; the editors quote from 'A Panegyrick upon Cundums' in the *Works of Rochester, Roscommon, and Dorset*, 1731, II, 225: 'For now tormented sore with scalding Heat / Of Urine, dread fore-runner of a Clap! / With Eye repentant, he surveys his Shirt / Diversify'd with Spots of yellow Hue, / Sad Symptom of ten Thousand Woes to come!'

7

Eliza 1766–1767

Sterne took up his pen 'in good earnest' on 15 July 1766 (281). He had decided to publish only a single volume of *Tristram Shandy* before turning to a new work. He wrote to a friend[1] on 23 July,

> I am in my peaceful retreat, writing the ninth volume of Tristram—I shall publish but one this year, and the next I shall begin a new work of four volumes, which when finish'd, I shall continue Tristram with fresh spirit.—What a difference of scene here! But with a disposition to be happy, 'tis neither this place, nor t'other that renders us the reverse.—In short each man's happiness depends upon himself—he is a fool if he does not enjoy it. (284)

Perhaps he was thinking of Smelfungus.

As always when he first arrived at Coxwold, 'A thousand nothings, or worse than nothings, have been every day snatching my pen out of my hands' (281). He had a house guest too, William Combe.[2] Combe was soon going abroad (294) and so decided to leave his post-chaise with Sterne. The

[1] In MEDALLE the correspondent is called only 'Mr. S.' CURTIS, 284–5, suggested that he may have been Edward Stanley, FRS (1718–89). When Curtis wrote, it was generally believed that Sterne had once owned a portrait of himself painted by Reynolds which he had presented as a gift to Stanley. In *EMY*, 305–6, I argue that there is no evidence for this family tradition among Stanley's descendants and that the portrait is not an original Reynolds but a copy of the 1760 Reynolds made after Sterne's death. I believe 'Mr. S.' has not been correctly identified.

[2] Sterne wrote that '—B— has left me his post chaise' (281); CURTIS, 282, identified the visitor as Combe, since Sterne in the manuscript had written 'Combes', then scratched it out and substituted 'B'.

gesture forced Sterne to 'reform' his 'cavalry' (281), which he did by purchasing two long-tailed horses (353, 392). He was 'tormented to death and the devil' (291) by meetings about the Stillington enclosure, which dragged on and on.[3] And there were other meetings of the gentry to discuss how to extend the road from York through Sutton and Stillington and whether to make it a turnpike.[4] And Lord Fauconberg kept summoning him to Newburgh Priory for dinners or other social occasions which gave Sterne no joy (290).

He also read for the first time the satire Hall had published in London on 7 April, *The First Chapter of Prophecies of the Prophet Homer. With a letter to the B[ishop] of G[loucester]*.[5] About half of this pamphlet was taken up with a 'translation' of a transparently pseudo-Homeric poem, 'The Nativity', about the birth of Apollo – an olio of classical myths, Judaic imagery and

[3] Sterne was complaining about meetings with the commissioners for purposes of apportioning the land. The Enclosure Act itself had passed through Parliament. The petition, bearing Sterne's signature among others, was submitted to the Commons on 17 January 1766; the Act was read in the Commons for the third time on 3 March and passed to the Lords, where it was read for the third time on 17 March; it received the royal assent and became law on 18 March 1766 (*Journal of the House of Commons*, *Journal of the House of Lords*, *Private Acts of Parliament*, 6 George III, c. 16). The commissioners, named in the Act, were Robert Bewlay, a York lawyer; Richard Clapham, a lawyer and registrar for the spiritual courts of York; and the Rev. Mr John Dealtary, Rector of Acaster Malbis and Vicar of Bishopthorpe, Sterne's friend and correspondent of younger years. Such a commission would be certain to serve the interests of Stephen Croft, which indeed it did. Most of the land was granted to Croft, some to William Stainforth, Esq., a neighbour, some to the prebendaries of Stillington. Nothing was granted to Sterne in his own right, but 18 acres went to the vicars of Stillington in lieu of small tithes. The deed conveying ownership was recorded 27 February 1768, a few days before Sterne's death: North Riding Registry of Deeds, AH. 38, pp. 167–214.

[4] LETTERS, 292. John Croft and Nathaniel Cholmley were among those who opposed the plan; they lost to the proponents, including Thomas Mosley and John Harland, brother and heir to Sterne's old neighbour at Sutton, Philip Harland, who had died on 26 November 1766 (*Public Advertiser*, 5 December). The petition for the turnpike was read a third time in the House of Commons on 9 February 1768, and a third time in the House of Lords on 2 March; it received the royal assent on 8 March 1768: *Journal of the House of Commons*; *Journal of the House of Lords*.

[5] CURTIS, 280, was the first to suggest Hall-Stevenson's authorship. HARTLEY, while admitting that Curtis had a good argument, rejected it on the grounds that the pamphlet has a style and wit which, as Curtis admitted, is 'rather above than below the excellence of Hall-Stevenson's writings'. Moreover, the pamphlet does not appear in Hall's collected *Works*, 3 vols, 1795. However, since I have not been able to find any evidence, in reviews or elsewhere, of any other pamphlet which might have been the subject of Sterne's and Hall-Stevenson's discussion, I accept Curtis's suggestion.

Christian theological concepts. This was prefaced by a long letter to Bishop Warburton, purportedly explaining the religious meanings of the poem: Apollo was 'a Type of the Messiah' and a 'true Son of Glory', Artemis was 'Faith', and the like. It ridiculed Warburton for his discussion of the *Aeneid* and the Eleusinian mysteries in the *Divine Legation of Moses*. The pamphlet is a bit mad, as indeed Hall was mad on the subject of Christianity. But it was not unclever and might have won some acclaim had it not been for a calumny which Hall cast upon Warburton and his wife. He had compared Gertrude Warburton to the Virgin Mary, 'a perfect Virgin' in regard to her husband, who was not the father of her child. But the bishop, 'like *Joseph*', was warned by an angel to put up with the situation because of the great riches she would inherit. Hall was alluding to a current rumour that Mrs Warburton had been having an affair with Thomas Potter, son of the late Archbishop of Canterbury.[6] Understandably, the slander put off the critics. In the April 1766 issue, a writer for the *Critical Review* condemned the performance for attacking a prelate 'at the expence of the regard that every Christian ought to entertain for the sacred truths of religion'. The *Monthly Review* for May printed a sizeable excerpt, but arraigned the author for his 'illiberal allusion to a scrap of domestic scandal . . . which . . . must necessarily render the Author an object of detestation and abhorrence to every generous reader, as it evidently shews him to be void of every delicate feeling, and an utter stranger to the first principles of decency and good-breeding.' When Sterne told his friend he had read the satire, Hall replied, 'the Reviewers have had a stroke at me, and in good truth not without cause.—and so I am very contrite for my bestiality with the bishop of G[loucester] but there is no help for it; so lend me some assistance to set me well again with myself.'[7] Sterne wrote back affectionately,

[6] EVANS, 131–2, discussed the rumour, but concluded that it was false. Gertrude Warburton was a sprightly, mischievous woman who probably conducted herself in a manner which gave rise to false rumours. She was, as we have noted already, the niece and heiress of Ralph Allen, whom Hall-Stevenson alludes to as the interdicting angel. Benjamin Boyce in his life of Allen, *The Benevolent Man*, Cambridge, Mass., 1967, pp. 231–2 and n. 57, also rejects the story, as a slander spread by Wilkes and Churchill.

[7] Sterne's copy of Hall's letter, dated 13 July 1766, survives: LETTERS, 279–80. Sterne's reply, also a copy, is dated 15 July (280–1). Since Sterne speaks of getting back to Coxwold and setting to work on his novel, we cannot doubt the dates of these letters. Hence it appears that Sterne and Hall did not discuss this matter when they saw each other in London or York during Sterne's trip home from Italy (281), that Sterne read Hall's pamphlet when he got back to Shandy Hall and that he then opened a correspondence about it.

> Thou hast so tender a conscience my dear Cosin Antonio, and takest on so sadly for thy sins, that thou wast certainly meant and intended to have gone to heaven—if ever Wit went there—but of that, I have some slight mistrusts, inasmuch as we have all of us (accounting myself, thou siest, as one) had, if not our good things, at least our good sayings in this life; & the Devil thou knowest, who is made up of spight, will not let them pass for nothing. (280)

Sterne was only too glad to point out that he too had been guilty of such a slur – of Dr Richard Mead, as 'Kunastrokius'. In the same passage he had also made an oblique reference to the sexual appetite of Solomon.[8] 'But every footman and Chamber maid in town knew both their Stories before hand—& so there was an end of the matter.' He advised Hall to let the 'poor Devils' the reviewers 'stop their own mouths' (280–1). Sterne signed the letter with a blessing – 'may god give you grace'. That autumn, though he did not write frequently, Sterne treasured the thought of Hall: 'I consider thee as a bank-note in a corner drawr of my bureau—I know it is there . . . tho' I seldome take a peep at it' (290). A mutual friend had stopped at Shandy Hall, and Sterne wrote for no reason other than to say he was glad of the accounts he had received of Hall. Sterne the priest is even more evident in the benediction with which he concluded this letter, setting it out thus:

> and the blessing of God the Father
> Son
> &
> holy ghost be with you
> *Amen*

He had not been working many days on Volume IX of *Tristram* when he received a letter from a man he had never met, Ignatius Sancho, a black who had been rescued from slavery by the Montagu family, which he now served in the capacity of butler. Sancho had educated himself, became a writer of sorts, and developed friendships among the artists and intellectuals of London.[9] He had recently read Sterne's sermon, 'Job's Account of the

[8] TRISTRAM SHANDY, 12; see *EMY*, 295, n. 3.

[9] *DNB*; ANECDOTES, VIII, 109; CURTIS, 283. One of Sancho's sons, a bookseller, published his father's letters in 1782; for the frontispiece, he reproduced Sterne's letter to Sancho in facsimile.

Shortness and Troubles of Life, Considered', and was deeply moved by the passage on slavery (I, 169). 'Of all my favourite writers, not one do I remember, that has had a tear to spar[e] for the distresses of my poor moorish brethren, Yourself, and the truely humane author of Sr George Ellison [Sarah Scott, Mrs Montagu's sister] excepted.' He begged Sterne to give some attention to slavery:

> that subject handled in your own manner, would ease the Yoke of many, perhaps occasion a reformation throughout our Islands—But should only *one* be the better for it—gracious God! what a feast! very sure I am, that Yorick is an Epicurean in Charity—universally read & universally admired—you could not fail.[10]

Sterne replied in a letter which reveals how much he had thought about the subject of slavery and the distinctions of race:

> There is a strange coincidence, Sancho, in the little events, as well as the great ones of this world; for I had been writing a tender tale of the sorrows of a friendless poor negro girl, and my eyes had scarse done smarting, When your Letter of recommendation in behalf of so many of her brethren and Sisters came to me—but why, *her brethren*?—or yours? Sancho,—any more than mine: it is by the finest tints and most insensible gradations that nature descends from the fairest face about St James's, to the sootyest complexion in Africa: at which tint of these, is it, Sancho, that the ties of blood & nature cease? and how many tones must we descend lower still in the scale, 'ere Mercy is to vanish with them? but tis no uncommon thing my good Sancho, for one half of the world to use the other half of it like brutes, and then endeavour to make 'em so.
>
> For my own part, I never look westward, (when I am in a pensive mood at least) but I think of the burdens which our brethren are there carrying. . . .

[10] LETTERS, 282–3. Sancho quoted from the sermon in his letter, citing the passage as 'p. 78 Vol. 2^d'. The passage actually occurs on p. 98 of the second volume, 1760 edition. Kenneth Monkman believes that Sancho's '78' was a slip of the pen. CURTIS, 284, says that Sancho was quoting from 'a reprint by Dodsley', but Monkman knows of no edition by Dodsley that would fit the reference. However, the sermon was reproduced in an anthology, the *Practical Preacher*, 4 vols, ed. W. W. Rose, published by Becket and Dehondt, 1762.

> If I can weave the Tale I have wrote, into what I am about, tis at the service of the afflicted. (286–7)

Sterne never found a way to work the pathetic story of this gentle black girl into his narrative, but Trim's recollection of her, attending the butcher's shop and shooing the flies instead of swatting them, sets off a dialogue which must have pleased Ignatius Sancho:

> A Negro has a soul? an' please your honour, said the Corporal (doubtingly).
>
> I am not much versed, Corporal, quoth my uncle Toby, in things of that kind; but I suppose, God would not leave him without one, any more than thee or me——
>
> ——It would be putting one sadly over the head of another, quoth the Corporal.
>
> It would so; said my uncle Toby. Why then, an' please your honour, is a black wench to be used worse than a white one?
>
> I can give no reason, said my uncle Toby——
>
> ——Only, cried the Corporal, shaking his head, because she has no one to stand up for her——
>
> ——'Tis that very thing, Trim, quoth my uncle Toby,——which recommends her to protection——and her brethren with her; 'tis the fortune of war which has put the whip into our hands *now*——where it may be hereafter, heaven knows!——but be it where it will, the brave, Trim! will not use it unkindly.
>
> ——God forbid, said the Corporal.
>
> Amen, responded my uncle Toby, laying his hand upon his heart. (747–8)

In July Sterne was writing about the black girl and pondering how to weave the story into what he had already written. He must have had a sizeable manuscript of Volume IX by that time. It has been said that he did not begin the volume until August – because in the first chapter we find Tristram declaring that he is writing on 12 August 1766 (737). Sterne may well have written that passage on 12 August, perhaps the entire chapter. But, if so, he added it to the front of the manuscript he had previously written. Indeed, one wonders whether he did anything that summer and autumn but polish a narrative he had written long before. He had begun working on the story of Uncle Toby's amours four years earlier (186).

The only other passage in the volume which can be fixed in the summer or autumn of 1766 is Sterne's 'advertisement' for *A Sentimental Journey*, and the transitional passage leading to it – Chapter 24. Though Tristram sets out to invoke the spirit of Cervantes to help him tell the story of Maria, he soon wanders into a digression on the good and bad experiences of travelling. Yes, the laundress cut the laps off his shirt; yes, his tinderbox was stolen and he was overcharged for this or that; still, 'I do not think a journey through France and Italy, provided a man keeps his temper all the way, so bad a thing as some people make you believe' (780–1). It would have been obvious to most of his readers that he was alluding to Smollett's *Travels*, which had appeared in the previous spring. 'Unless you pay twelve sous for greasing your wheels, how should the poor peasant get butter to his bread? . . . who would embroil their philosophy for it? for heaven's and for your own sake, pay it' (781). The passage strongly suggests that Sterne was preparing a work which would answer Smollett. To whet the reader's appetite for more, Sterne moved on to the sentimental story of Tristram's meeting with the mad peasant girl, Maria, sitting on the roadside near Moulins.

As in every other August, he set aside his work to go to York for Race Week. It was an especially colourful festival in 1766 because the Duke of York was present. 'Never were the races so numerously or so respectably attended,' wrote the local historian, '. . . the splendid retinues of the nobility which had resorted to meet the duke, gave additional brilliancy to the scene, and contributed much to the hilarity of the meeting.'[11] Hall, Ossory, Errington and numerous other friends and acquaintances were there. The duke arrived on Tuesday and was taken to the house of Sterne's old associate, John Clough, proctor of the ecclesiastical courts. 'The Lord Mayor, Recorder, Alderman, and Sheriffs waited on his Royal Highness the Duke of York in their Formalities, to congratulate him on his Arrival.'[12] The week was brought to a close with a service at the Minster. At the request of the duke,[13] Sterne preached the sermon:

[11] William Hargrove, *History and Description of the Ancient City of York*, 2 vols, York, 1818, I, 238.

[12] This and the following quotation from the *York Courant*, 26 August 1766. The story was repeated in a somewhat abridged form in the *St. James's Chronicle*, 26–8 August, and the *Annual Register* for 1766, p. 130.

[13] My speculation. It had been years since Sterne had had anything to do with the cathedral chapter; he had fallen out with Dean Fountayne; and William Mason, the precentor, disliked him and disapproved of his writing. I cannot imagine their asking him to preach upon this occasion for any reason other than the duke's request.

On Sunday his Royal Highness went to the Minster, where he was received at the West Door by the Residentiary and Choir, the Lord Mayor, Recorder, and Aldermen, who usher'd him up to the Archbishop's Throne, where he heard an excellent Discourse from the Rev. Mr. Sterne.

This was the last sermon Sterne would ever preach. Probably it was a mistake to attempt it. His voice was now very weak, and most of those in attendance would have heard little of what he had to say. The duke probably had no trouble because he and Sterne faced one another from the pulpit and the archepiscopal throne about forty feet apart and high above the benches and prebendal stalls of the choir. The officials, dignitaries and honoured guests who were seated in the choir would have heard fairly well, but the ladies and gentlemen, to say nothing of the common folk, who had to stand beyond the screen in the cavernous transept and nave, probably heard little or nothing. It may well have been this sermon which gave rise to the mistaken notion that Sterne was a poor preacher.[14]

Sterne came home to Coxwold in good spirits, to put the finishing touches to the story of Uncle Toby and the Widow Wadman. As we have already seen, in Volume VII Sterne had brought to a conclusion the first of his two major stories – that of Walter Shandy's frustrated attempts to rear the perfect child. Now Sterne completed his second story – that of Uncle Toby's attempt to heal himself after being wounded at Namur. Toby's physical wound, whatever its nature, is less important to the story than his mental trauma. We first see him in a state of deep depression lying in his brother's London house; out of a need to talk about what had happened to him, he develops an interest in the history and geography of the battle of Namur – a therapeutic hobby, which eventually takes the form of the

[14] CROSS, 245, who cites CROFT, the source of this notion. In VOICES SONOROUS AND CRACKED, I speculate that John Croft, recently returned from a long stay in Portugal where he had gone as a youth to learn the family wine business, was among those who were present but could not hear Sterne's sermon before the duke. It would have been, in fact, the only opportunity he would have had to hear Sterne preach at the Minster in his adult years. He wrote: 'When it was Sterne's turn to preach at the Minster half of the Congregation usually went out of the Church as soon as he mounted the Pulpit, as his Delivery and Voice were so very disagreeable.' People may indeed have left the church on the occasion of this sermon. Nevertheless, anyone who looks at the whole of Sterne's preaching career will conclude that Croft was wrong in suggesting that Sterne had never been a successful preacher.

miniature battles he and Corporal Trim play out on the bowling green. Volume VIII had told the story of how the Peace of Utrecht had affected the Manor of Shandy. It had put a stop to the little wars on the bowling green, caused the Widow Wadman to launch her own attack, and resulted in Uncle Toby's falling in love, a love which promised complete recovery, a return to reality, an adult life, perhaps even fatherhood.[15] Volume IX tells the story of how this promise came to naught. Poor Mrs Wadman, grown impatient during her long years of enforced celibacy watching through her hedge Uncle Toby at his war games, is not delicate enough in her enquiries about the state of her lover's wound. Toby, in his naïve sense of propriety, is shocked to discover her sexuality and turns for advice to the one person least qualified to give it – his brother. Walter, hating women and hating love, opens an attack upon sex which tips the balance and fixes Uncle Toby, as Tristram had said in Volume III, 'in a resolution, never more to think of the sex,——or of aught which belonged to it' (245).[16]

There are no villains in the novel. Walter Shandy is full of rage, but he is not malicious and he has the grace of wit. Uncle Toby and Mrs Wadman are good people, but the one is unworldly, the other tactless.[17] Their stories end, not in happiness, but in stasis. Mrs Wadman must give up her dreams

[15] See Jean-Jacques Mayoux, 'Variations on the Time-sense in *Tristram Shandy*', in WINGED SKULL.

[16] Sterne's major mistake in the writing of *Tristram Shandy* was his founding of this story on what proved to be a false footing: in the first volume Toby is said to suffer 'a most extream and unparallel'd modesty of nature' (74), which he got by a blow from a stone fragment during the battle of Namur (75) – a history which leaves the impression that Toby was rendered impotent. Sterne changed the story in the second volume by insisting that Toby's modesty arose from the shock Mrs Wadman had given him (117). But the original impression probably stayed with most readers; so Sterne began in Volume VIII to correct it: he had Toby explain that the purpose of love is to 'make a man marry, and love his wife, and get a few children', to which Walter replies that were he a monarch he would require Toby to beget him a child every month (718–19). In Vol. IX, Sterne had three other people declare categorically that Toby was not incapacitated by his wound – Dr Slop (791–2), Trim (797) and Tristram (777). Tristram's pronouncement is often misunderstood because many editions of the novel, including James Work's edition, 1940, 626, repeat an old typo in that passage: the word *defeated* (the correct reading) is misprinted as *defended* – which suggests the opposite of what Sterne had originally said. Mark Sinfield, in 'Uncle Toby's Potency: Some Critical and Authorial Confusions in *Tristram Shandy*', *N&Q*, CCXXIII (1978), 54–5, comes independently to a similar conclusion.

[17] For a comment upon Sterne's underlying optimism about human nature, see A. E. Dyson, 'Sterne: The Novelist as Jester', *Critical Quarterly*, IV (1962), 309–20.

of marriage. Toby must return to the childish world of the bowling green;[18] Walter will have no heir beyond Tristram; and the Shandy family must come to an end[19] – except for their story. What we have finally is Tristram in his purple jerkin and yellow slippers writing for posterity the story of his family: 'I say . . . Posterity—and care not, if I repeat the word again—for what has this book done more than the Legation of Moses, or the Tale of a Tub, that it may not swim down the gutter of Time along with them?' (754). Lest the bantering tone of these allusions to Warburton and Swift mislead us, Sterne had Tristram continue with perhaps the most serious lines in the novel, lines which make clear that the only villain of Tristram's piece is Death.

> I will not argue the matter: Time wastes too fast: every letter I trace tells me with what rapidity Life follows my pen; the days and hours of it, more precious, my dear Jenny! than the rubies about thy neck, are flying over our heads like light clouds of a windy day, never to return more——every thing presses on——whilst thou art twisting that lock,—see! it grows grey; and every time I kiss thy hand to bid adieu, and every absence which follows it, are preludes to that eternal separation which we are shortly to make.——
>
> ——Heaven have mercy upon us both! (754)

Sterne was so pleased with what he had done that he began to have second thoughts about publishing only a single volume this time. At the end of August he told Becket – and we can hardly doubt his intention, since he was writing to his chief bookseller – that he would publish '9th & 10 of Shandy the next winter' (288). But, beset by illness and anxiety, he never wrote a tenth volume.

Elizabeth, in France, was 'poorly', and grew worse as the autumn wore on. She and Lydia had decided to winter in Chalon, but had got no further than Avignon, where Elizabeth could have reasonable medical care. In September her symptoms grew so alarming that Sterne began making plans to return to France. A young nobleman would take him as far as Paris, and

[18] Often readers fail to notice that the campaigns Toby and Trim were enacting in 1718 when Tristram was born are distinct from and later than the campaigns that were terminated in 1713 by the Peace of Utrecht. Sterne himself was not confused: see Tristram's explanation in Volume III, 247.

[19] William Bowman Piper, in *Laurence Sterne*, New York (Twayne's English Authors Series, No. 26), 1965, argues that this disappointed ambition of the Shandy brothers unifies the novel.

from there, if she grew worse, he could go to her. 'I cannot think of her being without me—and however expensive the journey would be, I would fly to Avignon to administer consolation to both her and my poor girl' (288). On 25 October he wrote to Foley to arrange to send them additional money. 'My daughter says her mother is very ill—and I fear going fast down by all accounts—'tis melancholy in her situation to want any aid that is in my power to give' (289). Elizabeth rallied, and Lydia was able to take her away from Avignon. They went, not to Chalon after all, but to Vaucluse, where they engaged a large house for the winter. But Elizabeth sickened once more, and by the end of the year Sterne was again convinced she was 'going the way of us all' (291). She would actually outlive her husband by five years.

Then Sterne himself suffered a 'severe attack'[20] followed by a violent fever (294). In Chapter 24, which he wrote in the summer or autumn of 1766, he spoke about losing 'some fourscore ounces of blood this week in a most uncritical fever which attacked me at the beginning of this chapter' (779). He had not recovered by December when he wrote to Hall, 'I have had my menses thrice this month, which is twice too often' (290).

Although it was hard to give up, he came to realize, as the autumn faded, that he could not publish two volumes this time. 'I shall be in London by Christmas week,' he wrote to Panchaud on 25 November; '. . . I am going to ly in of another child of the Shandaick procreation' (289–90). Yet in mid-December he was still trying to work at the novel. 'So Tristram goes on busily,' he told Hall, '—what I can find appetite to write, is so so' (290).

Today most students of Sterne believe that *Tristram Shandy* as we have it is a completed novel.[21] The stories of Walter's childrearing and Toby's failure to marry complete intentions declared in the first volume. Volume IX ends with a 'cock and bull story' – a conventional signal that the book is

[20] Lord Fauconberg's son, Henry, Lord Belasyse, wrote to his father from London on 4 November, responding to news which Lord Fauconberg had sent about Sterne's health: 'I am concerned for Mr Sterne, who has I thought for some time looked very ill, but hope he will overcome this severe attack': WOMBWELL PAPERS.

[21] See Wayne C. Booth, 'Did Sterne Complete *Tristram Shandy*?', *Modern Philology*, XLVIII (1951), 172–83. Booth maintains that Sterne knew how his novel would end before he began writing it. R. F. Brissenden, in what he called a 'corrective footnote' to Booth, argues cogently that Booth has overstated his case in respect of the first volume, which contains many false starts, unfinished promises, and indications of directions not taken in the rest of the novel: '"Trusting to Almighty God": Another Look at the Composition of *Tristram Shandy*', in WINGED SKULL.

finished. And certain key passages in the final volume echo others in the first: 'All I wish is, that it may be a lesson to the world, "*to let people tell their stories their own way*," ' says Tristram, quoting what he had said in the first volume (9, 785). Tristram in his study on 12 August 1766 dressed in his purple jerkin and yellow slippers is pondering the fact that he has fulfilled his father's prediction in the opening pages of the book, 'That I should neither think nor act like any other man's child' (4, 737). But internal evidence that Sterne finished the novel does not preclude the possibility that he would have taken it up again had he felt inspired. He may have kept the possibility in mind for months. Not until September of the following year, 1767, do we find external evidence that he had finally given up *Tristram Shandy*. At that time Sterne made the acquaintance of a minor writer, Richard Griffith, who recorded their conversation:

> *Tristram* and *Triglyph* [Griffith's narrator] have entered into a League offensive and defensive, together, against all Opponents in Literature. We have, at the same Time, agreed never to write any more *Tristrams* or *Triglyphs*. I am to stick to *Andrews*, and he to *Yorick*.[22]

Sterne left Coxwold on the first or second of January 1767. It was snowing when he reached York, and by the time he set out for London the next morning, sharing a coach with a captain of the 'Blues', the Yorkshire militia, a blizzard was blowing. The storm, which was moving south with them, turned into

> such a terrible Hurricane of Wind & snow as no one but a Captain of the *blues*, & a Parson of the *true blues* [as the old-fashioned Whigs called themselves], would have ventured out in—'twas one continued storm all that way, & many stages had we to plough through Snow up to the horses bellies, so that with the utmost perseverence (or obstinacy if y^{r} Lordship pleases) We could get but to Barnet the third night. (292)

He reached London the fourth day, so impatient for a taste of urban life that he went that very evening to the theatre. He wrote to Lord Fauconberg later that night from his Bond Street rooms, promising to keep his daughters posted upon 'what kind of Weather there is in the theatrical

[22] *A Series of Genuine Letters between Henry and Frances*, augmented edition of 1786, 6 vols, Letter DXCVIII, dated 10 September 1767, pp. 86–8.

World'. The snow came down as fast as the streets were cleared, and a 'dead stagnation' lay over everything. Though others took to their beds, the cold had the opposite effect upon the wiry limbs of Sterne. 'It has set in, now, with the most intense cold—I could scarse lay in bed for it' (295). He went to church and to court, finding few people in either place; he dined with 'the duke of York's people' and other friends; he bought a season subscription to the Soho concerts; and he returned to the theatre night after night. At the Drury Lane Theatre he saw the king at a command performance of Garrick's new dramatic romance, *Cymon*. But at Covent Garden Theatre 'No body . . . but the Citizen's children & apprentices' (295). The most interesting theatrical news he sent the ladies was about an amateur:

> The Duke of York was to have had a play house of his own, & had studied his part—in the fair penitent and made Garrick act it twice on purpose to profit by it—but the King 'tis said has desired the Duke to give up the part & the project with it— ☞ (all this is for the Ladies). (295)

The duke's people actually fitted out a small theatre for him in Petty France, near the south entrance to St James's Park, and that winter and spring the duke and his friends put on performances of Rowe's *Fair Penitent*. They were to be his last public appearances. The duke had become enamoured of his leading lady, Anne Delaval Stanhope, sister of Sterne's acquaintance Sir Francis Delaval and wife of his friend Sir William Stanhope. The alarmed king hurried him off to France. He fell ill at Toulon, 'having danced too much' in the house of a French nobleman.[23] He was carried to Monaco, where on 14 September 1767 he died.

On 13 or 14 January 1767, the snows began to melt. 'Garrick's Cimon—fills his house brim full every night,' wrote Sterne (297). 'It thaw'd the concert at Soho top full—& was (This is for the Ladies) the best assembly, and the best Concert I ever had the honour to be at' (296). Mrs Theresa Cornelys, who since 1760 had conducted lavish assemblies and balls at Carlisle House in Soho Square, had added in 1765 a series of concerts conducted by Karl Friedrich Abel, the great master of the viola da gamba, and Johann Christian Bach. Which man conducted on this particular night we do not know.[24] Lord Fauconberg's youngest daughter was there – Anne,

[23] John Charnock, *Biographia Navalis*, 6 vols, 1794–8, VI, 382–5.

[24] Admission was by subscription only. At a later date the assemblies, especially the

wife of Francis Talbot. 'Lady Anne', reported Sterne, 'had the goodness to challenge me, or I had not known her, she was so prudently muffled up.' She was in the company of her brother Henry, Lord Belasyse, the heir, who had become a father only days before. 'Lord Bellasyse—I never saw him look so well—Lady Bellasyse recovers *a marveille*—& y^{r} little neice I believe, grows like flax' (296–7). *Niece*, or *neice* as Sterne spelled it, was a standard term for granddaughter.[25]

His own family in France was doing well. Elizabeth had improved, and they had gone to Marseilles for Christmas. There Lydia received an offer from a gentleman with a considerable fortune. 'I suppose Md^{lle} with Madame ma femme will negociate the Affair,' Sterne told Panchaud (300). Nothing came of it. When they got back to Vaucluse, Elizabeth and Lydia were entertained by the abbé Jacques-François-Paul-Alphonse de Sade, retired from clerical duties and devoting himself to his eccentric memoir of Petrarch, in which he attempted to demonstrate that Laura had married into his family. Lydia met there the abbé's mad nephew Donatien-Alphonse-François, Marquis de Sade. 'I am out of all patience with the answer the Marquis made the Abbé,' wrote Sterne, commenting upon something Lydia had told him; ' 'twas truly coarse, and I wonder he bore it with any christian patience' (301). Later in the year Lydia was enjoying '*les fêtes champêtres* of the Marquis de Sade' (391). Lydia had begun a translation of her father's sermons into French. Sterne sent her a guitar to replace her old one, which had broken, and to Elizabeth some of Huxham's Tincture of the Bark, a popular nostrum.

He busied himself preparing for the publication of Volume IX. 'I miscarried of my tenth Volume by the violence of a fever, I have just got thro',' Sterne wrote to William Combe; 'I have however gone on to my reckoning with the ninth, of wch I am all this week in Labour pains' (294). Advertisements for the forthcoming volume commenced in the *London Chronicle* for 8–10 January 1767 and the *Public Advertiser* of 9 January. Not

masked balls, acquired an unsavoury reputation, but that was after the opening of Almack's, in 1768, which attracted most of the wealthy subscribers as well as Abel and Bach. See the advertisement on the first page of the *Public Advertiser*, 2 January 1768; CURTIS, 297; and Hugh Phillips, *Mid-Georgian London*, 1964, p. 233.

[25] This child, born 10 January 1767 and baptized Charlotte, was destined to inherit the family estates from her father. She married Thomas Wynn, who took her name, but she died childless. The estates passed to her nephew, Sir George Wombwell, Bart.

wanting his readers to think he might take them on another continental journey, Sterne included the statement: 'This Volume contains the Amours of my Uncle Toby.' On 21 January, he settled his accounts with Becket, signing a receipt for £205. 17*s*. 0*d*.[26] When Volume IX appeared, the advertisements would also offer the previous volumes of *Shandy* and the *Sermons of Mr. Yorick*; Sterne and Becket had reached an agreement with Dodsley whereby they could sell the first four volumes of the novel and the first two of the sermons, in which Dodsley held the copyright. They also found they had run short of copies of Volumes V–VI of *Shandy*, which were among those still in Sterne's control; so they quietly brought out a second edition.[27]

Sterne was still being pestered by spurious volumes of the novel. In 1766 T. Durham and T. Caslon had published a false Volume IX, and in 1767 they brought out a so-called Volume X, which named as its author, 'Hatspen Barnvelt'. This 'Volume X' was no more than a reissue of the false Volume IX with the first fifteen pages rewritten. Nevertheless, Sterne set about signing the copies of the genuine Volume IX.

Finally, he wrote a dedication to the new prime minister. Rockingham's ministry had collapsed in July of 1766, and William Pitt, who had waited restlessly in the wings for his second chance, had at last been invited to form another government. But the ministry was rapidly becoming a disaster, in part because Pitt had lost the leadership of the Commons when he accepted a peerage as Viscount Pitt and Earl of Chatham. He was in ill health and frequently absent from the cabinet when Sterne dedicated the volume to him. A few weeks later he would suffer an attack of manic-depressive insanity which would force the king to remove him from office.[28] Sterne's dedication 'To a Great Man' playfully avoids naming him: 'HAVING, *a*

[26] The receipt, 'being in ful ballance of al Accounts to this day as paid', is housed in the autograph file at the Houghton Library, Harvard. It is impossible to say which book sales this profit represented.

[27] MONKMAN, who says that the second edition of Volume VI is of no particular significance; but the second edition of Volume V is puzzling because it 'exists in three completely different settings, all equally proclaiming themselves to be the second edition'. All three carry the additional Latin motto mentioned above, Chapter 2, as well as two additional sentences. Sterne signed the copies of one setting only, no doubt the earliest. Melvyn New, in the textual notes to TRISTRAM SHANDY, 835, says that only the signed setting should be considered as the true second edition: 'it is found in sets only with the second edition of volume VI. The other two settings (which are rarer) always appear in collected sets with a "New Edition", dated 1769, of volume VI.'

[28] NAMIER AND BROOKE, III, 298.

priori, intended to dedicate *The Amours of my uncle Toby* to Mr. ***——I see more reasons, *a posteriori*, for doing it to Lord *******.' This passage, in which Sterne compliments Pitt for his integrity and then alludes to his absence from office between 1761 and 1766, may be, as is usually said, 'graceful', but the second half of the dedication is eccentric, a sort of mirror image of what Sterne intended to convey to Chatham. 'No ideas are so totally different as those of Ministers and innocent Lovers' (i.e. Uncle Toby and Mrs Wadman); so in the future, when Sterne will write a volume on statesmen and patriots, he will dedicate *that* volume to 'some gentle Shepherd'. Thereupon he moves into a parody of Pope's famous lines about the poor Indian, in the first epistle of the *Essay on Man*: 'Whose Thoughts proud Science never taught to stray, / Far as the Statesman's walk or Patriot-way', and so forth. Sterne seems to have intended to emphasize his point that the ideas of statesmen and lovers differ in the extreme, a contrast which particularly recommends the book to a statesman after his 'labour and sorrow'. 'Nothing is so perfectly *Amusement* as a total change of ideas.' It has been suggested that he may have been expressing the popular theory that diversion and amusement were useful for the treatment of mental illness.[29] Was the town talking about Lord Chatham's psychological breakdown, and was Sterne alluding to it? The dedication is odd.

Advertisements announcing the publication 'this day' of *Tristram Shandy*, IX, appeared in the *Public Advertiser* for 30 January 1767 and the *London Chronicle* for 29–31 January. The printer had run off 3500 copies instead of the 4000 of earlier volumes.[30] Sterne may have been worried that he was offering only one volume, and the shortest yet. The price remained the same, two shillings, sewed and bound in boards.

'Have you got the 9th V. of Shandy?' Sterne asked of Panchaud on 25 February;[31] '—tis liked the best of all here' (300). But one must doubt. No further editions appeared during Sterne's lifetime, and there are few comments about the volume in private letters. Warburton, of course, would

[29] TS NOTES, 528–9. See the discussion of diversion as therapy in Michael V. De Porte, *Nightmares and Hobbyhorses: Swift, Sterne, and Augustan Ideas of Madness*, San Marino, Calif., 1974, p. 137 ff.

[30] MONKMAN.

[31] The MS of Letter No. 182 is now in the Robert H. Taylor collection, Princeton University Library. The date is 25 February [1767] and not 20 February as given in MEDALLE. There is no signature, and there is a second postscript which she did not print: it reads, 'my best Comp^s^ to B. D'Holbach and all friends——.'

be expected to dislike anything Sterne wrote. He replied to a letter from William Mason, saying,

> All you say I *know*, and all you think I believe of that agregious Puppy who has received of me the most friendly services and has repaid them as all such men do. Not but that I deserved as much, for tho' Nature sowed in him the seeds of *Puppybility*, yet I cultivated them when I brought him out into the world.[32]

The volume won no plaudits in the press, though the *London Chronicle* printed the story of Maria. The writer for the February *Critical Review* attacked Sterne for his failure to 'accommodate to the ear of innocence', but compared him to Rabelais in a way that acknowledged his genius. Ralph Griffiths in the *Monthly Review* of February said that Sterne should be compared, not to Rabelais or Cervantes, but to Harlequin, for his book was the very 'pantomime of literature'.[33] Griffiths, whose puritan sensibilities Sterne had so often shocked, was offended by the story of the parish bull. A writer for the February *Gentleman's Magazine*, maintaining that the volume was harmless but tasteless, wrote,

> It tends as little to inflame the passions as *Culpepper's Family Physician*. . . . Perhaps he will be found to deserve the thanks of virtue no better than he, who, to prevent gluttony, should prohibit the sale of any food till it had acquired a taste and smell that would substitute nausea for appetite.

The argument did not prevent 'Censor' from writing to *Lloyd's Evening Post* a letter which they published on 13–16 March: 'The same hand, that one day gives us the most *pathetic* Sermons, the next gives us . . . compositions, to rouse our sensitive appetites; to inflame with lust, and debauch and corrupt our youth of both sexes.' And on 30 March a letter from 'Davus' in the *Public Ledger* called upon the church to intervene. So well did 'Davus' argue his case that a group of laymen petitioned Archbishop Drummond to censure the author and put a stop to this book, written to the 'disgrace of his sacred order and the detriment of society; of which surely many fathers and mothers can testify, whose daughters have not thereby been mended, but most probably corrupted, of which there may be given instances.'[34]

[32] BL, Add. MSS 32563, fol. 17, as quoted by EVANS, 231. Also in CURTIS, 96.

[33] Griffiths identified by NANGLE.

[34] Percy Fitzgerald, *Life*, 2 vols, 1864, II, 331–2. Fitzgerald saw the petition 'among the Archbishop's papers'. CROSS, 423–4,

Not everyone was so humourless. The March issue of the *Gentleman's Magazine* excerpted a passage from a recent anonymous work entitled, *Adventures of an Author*:

> Oct. 2. Wait upon Lady L——, and find *Tristram Shandy* upon her toilet—She desires me to explain the stars. I excuse myself, by telling her I have not read it, and ask her what she thinks of *Locke*?—She blushes—is confused—'and is surprised I should put so indecent a question to her.'

Sterne had already turned his mind to his new book, which he had now named. It was to be published by subscription. He began at once pressing his friends. 'Im going to publish a *Sentimental Journey* through *France & Italy*,' he wrote to Panchaud; 'the undertaking is protected & highly encouraged by all our *Noblesse*—& at the rate tis subscribed-for, will bring me a thousand guineas (au moins)—' (300). The reality was not quite that. In the end, he succeeded in obtaining 334 subscriptions – about half the number for the third and fourth volumes of the *Sermons of Mr. Yorick* – which at ten shillings each (he had increased the price over that for *Shandy* by *6d.* per volume) brought in 159 guineas. Even if he had managed to get as many subscribers as he had for the sermons, he still would have taken no more than 315 guineas. But in the winter of 1767 he kept talking about the thousand guineas he would collect before a word of the book was written – so reported Alessandro Verri, the Italian historian, who saw him that January.[35] No doubt in the end Sterne was disappointed that he had not done better, but his health was so bad during the spring of 1767 that he could not personally solicit many subscriptions. He got as far as he did largely through the good offices of friends. Isaac Panchaud got twenty subscriptions in Paris, though he failed to get the names to the printer in time to include them on the list. Another friend, a 'Mr. Crew', was listed for twenty sets. Other friends, like Richard Davenport, solicited subscriptions; but because they sent in lists which went to the printer there is no record of how many they collected.[36] Sancho, who was still serving the Duke and

also tells the story without documentation. CURTIS, 300–1, adds the information that the petition once belonged to Mrs K. C. Braithwaite of Bath.

[35] Giovanni Rabizzani, *Sterne in Italia*, Rome, 1920, pp. 34–7.

[36] Sterne to Richard Davenport, 9 June 1767, in Earl R. Wasserman, 'Unedited Letters by Sterne, Hume, Rousseau', *Modern Language Notes*, LXVI (1951), 73–80.

Duchess of Montagu as a butler, was asked to beg their subscriptions and another from their son.

> But you have something to add, Sancho, to what I owe your good will also on this account, and that is to send me the subscription money, which I find a necessity of duning my best friends for before I leave town—to avoid the perplexities of both keeping pecuniary accounts (for which I have very slender talents) and collecting them (for which I have neither strength of body or mind) and so, good Sancho dun the Duke of M[ontagu] the Duchess of M[ontagu] and Lord M[onthermer] for their subscriptiions, and lay the sin, and money with it too, at my door— (340)

A person has to be quite secure of his position to ask and receive such favours, especially from a man who could not afford a subscription himself.

Sterne had taken up his wonted social life once more. Verri reported seeing him in January 1767 at some assembly of fashionable ladies and gentlemen. He was dressed, not in black, but in a grey suit and wearing a close-cut wig. Sterne was beloved of everyone, said Verri, and his friends paid his way wherever he went. He also frequented less fashionable circles. He had fallen in with a group of artists, antiquarians and theatrical people who met for dinners or parties in Covent Garden. John Hamilton Mortimer, a young painter of twenty-five years, who may have been the organizer of this group, painted a group caricature of them during this spring, in which Sterne figures prominently in a jolly set of men enjoying a wine and oyster party. Among others, one recognizes Dr Thomas Arne, the genius composer of theatrical music; Giovanni Cipriani, the Italian painter who had settled in London; his countryman and friend, Francesco Bartolozzi, painter and engraver and later librarian to George III; Captain Francis Grose, antiquary and draughtsman; John Ireland, the first biographer of Hogarth; and Mortimer himself.[37]

Some time during the early weeks of 1767, Sterne made the acquaintance of Commodore and Mrs William James. Sterne, who had always loved military men, felt an easy admiration for this retired commander-in-chief of the marine forces of the East India Company, and Mrs James fulfilled all of his ideals as a woman of sensibility. He seems to have loved them on first sight. Certainly, he treasured their friendship as one of his closest during

[37] Appendix II.

the few months of life remaining to him. He was soon writing to Lydia.

> I wish I had you with me—and I would introduce you to one of the most amiable and gentlest of beings . . . a Mrs. J[ames] the wife of as worthy a man as I ever met with—I esteem them both. He possesses every manly virtue—honour and bravery are his characteristicks, which have distinguished him nobly in several instances—I shall make you better acquainted with his character, by sending Orme's History, with the books you desired—and it is well worth your reading; for Orme is an elegant writer, and a just one; he pays no man a compliment at the expence of truth.—Mrs. J[ames] is kind—and friendly—of a sentimental turn of mind—and so sweet a disposition, that she is too good for the world she lives in—Just God! if all were like her, what a life would this be!—Heaven, my Lydia, for some wise purpose has created different beings—I wish my dear child knew her—thou art worthy of her friendship, and she already loves thee; for I sometimes tell her what I feel for thee. (301–2)

William James, some eight years younger than Sterne, was said to have been the son of a miller of Bolton Hill, near Haverfordwest. He went to sea as a boy, quickly won a reputation, and was commanding a ship in the Virginia trade before he had reached his majority. In 1747 he joined the navy of the East India Company, rose in the ranks and in 1751 was made commander-in-chief. He distinguished himself in two battles against the pirate king, Angria, at Severndroog and Gheria, and took part in the wars in Bengal and Bombay province. He was all that Sterne saw in him, a brilliant naval strategist and a sailor of great personal courage. Robert Orme, in his *History of the Military Transactions of the British Nation in Indostan*, had every reason to devote several pages to him. He retired to England in 1759 with a large fortune taken in loot, purchased an estate at Eltham, Kent, and a house in London. In 1765, at the age of forty-four, he married an heiress, Anne Goddard, daughter of Edmond Goddard of Hartham, Wiltshire, who had been a well-known soldier at Bombay. Their child, Elizabeth Anne, was a baby in her sixth month when Sterne met them. A son would be born in 1774. Their house in Gerrard Street, Soho, soon become the centre of social life for the servants of the East India Company who were in London.[38]

[38] William James served as a director of the East India Company from 1768, chairman in 1779, when he became a close supporter of Lord Sandwich. He served as governor of

In the early weeks of January 1767, Sterne fell in love with a woman of this group, Eliza Draper.[39] She and Anne James were the best of friends. Eliza was twenty-three years old,[40] Anne about the same age. They were both of small stature and frail constitution, but the world accounted them pretty. Eliza in their circle was often called the 'Belle Indian'. She was an intelligent woman, widely read, and a good writer with ambitions to be recognized as a bluestocking. Anne was bright, but had, said Sterne, only one pursuit, 'that of pleasing her husband' (403). Both were women of sensibility, and sometimes their romantic ideas bordered upon the foolish. They were perfect objects for Sterne the sentimental lover, and he was smitten with both. But Anne was with a husband whom he admired. Eliza, at the moment, was alone. Sterne let himself fall in love.

Actually, Eliza was married to Daniel Draper, currently at his post in Bombay, where he served as secretary and Portuguese secretary to the Bombay government. Eliza had been born in India, at the Anjengo factory on the south Malabar coast, where her father, May Sclater, was serving as secretary to the chief, Charles Whitehill. He had married Whitehill's daughter, Judith, who bore him Eliza and a younger daughter, Mary. The children were orphaned at an early age[41] and taken by their grandfather to

Greenwich Hospital, deputy master of Trinity House, and Fellow of the Royal Society. He was defeated in a by-election for New Shoreham in 1770, but was returned for West Looe in 1774 and represented that borough until his death. He was created a baronet in 1778. See *DNB*; NAMIER AND BROOKE; CURTIS, 302–3; Robert Orme, *History of the Military Transactions of the British Nation in Indostan*, 3 vols, 4th edn, Madras, 1861, I, 407–14; [George Edward Cokayne], *Complete Baronetage*, 1906, V, 199; Burke's *Landed Gentry*, 1862, Pt I, 560, on 'Goddard of Wilts'; Charles Rathbone Low, *History of the Indian Navy*, 2 vols, 1877, I, 125–39; Charles C. Prinsep, *Record of Services of the Honourable East India Company's Civil Servants*, 1885, xiv–xxi; James Douglas, *Bombay and Western India*, 2 vols, 1893, I, 416–33.

[39] Unless otherwise documented, the following account of Elizabeth Draper, née Sclater, usually called Eliza, and her husband Daniel Draper is taken from WRIGHT AND SCLATER *as corrected* by Mr Sclater in his later article, 'Letters Addressed by Eliza Draper to the Strange Family, 1776–1778', *N&Q*, CLXXXVI (January–June 1944), 201–4, 220–4; CLXXXVII (July–December 1944), 7–13, 27–33, 48–54. The family history by C. E. L. Sclater, *Records of the Family of Sclater*, Newport, Isle of Wight, 1966, makes use of the corrections in the article but adds nothing new. I will note separately my own research at the India Office Library.

[40] Eliza herself said she was born on 5 April 1744: WRIGHT AND SCLATER, 122. *Ecclesiastical Returns, Bombay, 1709–57* (India Office Library, N/3/1) contains no record of her birth, but it is a highly imperfect document.

[41] Their father died, probably, in 1746; their mother remarried, to Captain Samuel

his large house in Bombay, where they spent their early childhood. When they were seven or eight, Whitehill sent them to England to be educated under the care of their father's sister, Elizabeth, wife to Thomas Pickering, Vicar of St Sepulchre's, which stood next to Newgate Prison. Eliza during this period became fast friends with her cousin, Thomas Limbrey Sclater, with whom she began a correspondence that lasted her lifetime. On 9 March 1757, the council at Bombay gave permission for Eliza and Mary to return to their relatives in Bombay.[42] On 28 July 1758, when she was fourteen years old, Eliza married Daniel Draper at Bombay.[43] Her sister married at the age of fifteen and died in childbirth two years later. Eliza, within four and a half years of her marriage, had borne a son and two daughters.[44] In 1763, when the youngest was less than a year old, the family undertook the arduous journey to England, leave having been granted Daniel Draper to go there 'for the recovery of a spasmatic complaint of [the] right hand'.[45] Though his leave was extended twice, he was forced in March 1766 to set out for India leaving his family behind.[46] Eliza placed her children in school at Salt Hill, near London, and was preparing to join him. On 21 January 1767, about the time she met Sterne, the East India Company governors in London granted her permission to take to India her English servant, Elizabeth Mihil or Mitchell.[47] Eliza, though deeply distressed at having to leave England, was determined to keep the agreement she had made with her husband. The story that Daniel Draper ordered his wife home when he heard about Sterne is manifestly impossible, since it took a minimum of six months for mail to reach India.

Eliza hated her husband. He was thirty-nine years old,[48] exceedingly

---

Hough, bore him a daughter, and died soon after: Louisa H. Bullock, 'Sterne's Eliza', *N&Q*, CXCIX (1954), 474–5.

[42] *Court Minute Records*: India Office Library, B/74, fols 281, 290.

[43] *Ecclesiastical Returns, 1757–1773*, N/3/2, fol. 21.

[44] William, born 11 February 1760; Elizabeth, born 25 October 1761; and Anne, born 30 December 1762: *Ecclesiastical Returns, 1757–1773*, N/3/2, fols 67, 93, 116. The son died in England at the house of his grandfather Whitehill, Warfield, Shropshire, in 1769. The youngest, Anne, died at an early age, but when and where we do not know.

[45] MS letter of Daniel Draper to the governors dated at London, 29 February 1764: India Office Library, Home Correspondence: Miscellaneous Letters Received, E/1/46.

[46] India Office Library, Bombay Dispatches, E/4/997, fols 466, 654, 847.

[47] Bombay Dispatches, B/82, fol. 364.

[48] He died on 20 March 1805 at the age of seventy-seven; so he was born in 1727 or 1728. No birth record is to be found in the *Ecclesiastical Returns, 1709–57*, but he had

ugly, as we know from an existing portrait, and a man who knew nothing of the world except the colonial service to which he had been born. His father had been chief at Gambroon and Mayor of Bombay. Draper was determined to make a great fortune in the service, and to this end was brutally aggressive. He no sooner arrived in Bombay after his English stay but he picked a quarrel with William Hornby, marine paymaster, whose post he coveted. He got rid of Hornby, but failed to get his position.[49] He then attacked John Horn, governor of Tellicherry, and this time succeeded in ousting the man and taking his lucrative post.[50] Eliza, on the high seas in her journey back to India, often consoled herself with the thought that at least she would be able to take up life in Draper's luxurious residence in Bombay, Belvedere House, but found when she arrived that she would have to follow her husband to a backwater community where there were no diversions and no companions but Daniel Draper. She wrote to her cousin Thomas,

> Not that I think I should have any aversion to the Idea of being secluded from the World, if my Husband had those Companionable Virtues which are requisite, to banish the Dull severe [*sic*], in a very retired Situation; but He has not. . . . by Nature cool, Phlegmatic, and not adorned by Education with any of those pleasing Acquirements which help to fill up the Vacuums of time agreeably, if not usefully—added to which, Methodically formed, in the Extreme, by long Habit, and not easily roused into Active measures by any Motive Unconnected with his sense of Duty.[51]

Like most men of his station, Draper had Indian concubines – pitiful creatures literally enslaved – and by them several children. At a later date

brothers born on 29 December 1726 and 2 January 1729/30 (I, fols 118:61; 126:65). His father was William Henry Draper, who married first Theodosia Sutton on 10 January 1722/3 (fol. 77:40) and, second, Ann Pack on 17 December 1725 (fol. 99:52). Daniel Draper joined the company as a writer at least as early as 1749: *Bombay Civil Servants, 1750–1859*, India Office Library, BGB/CH, fol. 124. He is said by an anonymous Indian historian to have held the posts of Secretary and Portuguese Secretary during this period: 'An Age of Progress in Bombay, 1740–1762', *Bombay Quarterly Review*, V (January 1857), 189–96.

[49] MS letter from Samuel Court to the Council, 16 September 1766, in General Correspondence, 1766, E/1/48. The quarrel is discussed by Douglas, *Bombay and Western India*.

[50] Bombay Dispatches, E/4/998, fols 125–9.

[51] WRIGHT AND SCLATER, 131–2.

he took into 'public keeping' an Englishwoman by the name of Leeds, a servant of Eliza's. Eventually, in 1773, Eliza would make an escape from her husband and India, never more to return to a place and a life she detested. But in January of 1767 she had made up her mind firmly to return to Draper, 'whose humour, I now am resolved to Study and if possible conform to. . . . Honour, prudence and the interest of my beloved Children demand the necessary sacrifice'.[52]

When Sterne got home after meeting Eliza, he bundled up a complete set of his books and sent them to her – as he had once sent Catherine Fourmantel his sermon 'The Case of Elijah and the Widow of Zerephath, Considered'. To Eliza, a woman of sensibility, he thought it best to play down his novels and appear proudest of his sermons. The novels, he wrote, 'came from the head', but the sermons 'all hot from the heart'. And with no more introduction than that, he declared his love – but guardedly: 'I know not how it comes in—but I'm half in love with You.—I ought to be *wholy so*—for I never valued, (or saw more good Qualities to value,)—or thought more of one of Y^r^ Sex than of You' (298). Eliza was not displeased. She soon grew so trusting as to ask him to take her five-year-old daughter, Elizabeth, back to Salt Hill after some family affair in town, probably the birthday of her son, which fell on 11 February. Eliza's picture, he said much later, was 'the best Company I ever took a Journey with', but then he added, 'excepting a Journey I once took with a friend of Y^rs^ to Salt hill, & Enfield Wash'. And there seems to have been more than one: 'The pleasure I had in those Journies, have left *Impressions* upon my Mind, which will last my Life—You may tell her as much when You see her' (364). Eliza and Sterne were soon calling each other by the pet names of 'Bramin' and 'Bramine'. He began a campaign to encourage her to think well of herself: 'Reflect, Eliza, what are my motives for perpetually advising thee? . . . I think you are a very deserving woman; and that you want nothing but firmness, and a better opinion of yourself, to be the best female character I know' (309). In the way typical of their age, they wrote to each other even though separated by no more than a dozen London streets. She sealed her letters with a signet ring he gave her (381). Since neither was in good health, they easily fell into those exchanges of sympathy over pains and anxieties – for Sterne the *sine qua non* of sentimental love.

[52] WRIGHT AND SCLATER, 65.

> Best of all good girls! the sufferings I have sustained the whole night on account of thine, Eliza, are beyond my power of words.—Assuredly does Heaven give strength proportioned to the weight he lays upon us! Thou has been bowed down, my child, with every burden that sorrow of heart, and pain of body, could inflict upon a poor being; and still thou tellest me, thou art beginning to get ease;—thy fever gone, thy sickness, the pain in thy side vanishing also.—May every evil so vanish that thwarts Eliza's happiness, or but awakens thy fears for a moment! (305)

He presented her with his picture, probably one of the Fisher mezzotints of the 1760 Reynolds, which she mounted above her writing table. He was pleased – 'Yorick smiles contentedly over all thou dost' (305). She in turn sat for a miniature portrait for him. He enjoyed contrasting it with the painting of Eliza made for the Jameses, probably by Richard Cosway:[53]

> She has got your picture, and likes it: but Marriott and some other judges, agree that mine is the better, and expressive of a sweeter character. But what is that to the original? yet I acknowledge that hers is a picture for the world; and mine is calculated only to please a very sincere friend, or sentimental philosopher.—In the one, you are dressed in smiles, with all the advantages of silks, pearls, and ermine;—in the other, simple as a vestal—appearing the good girl nature made you;—which to me, conveys an idea of more unaffected sweetness, than Mrs. Draper, habited for conquest, in a birthday suit, with her countenance animated, and her dimples visible.—If I remember right, Eliza, you endeavoured to collect every charm of your person into your face, with more than *common* care, the day you sat for Mrs. James.—Your colour too, brightened; and your eyes shone with more than usual brilliancy. I then requested you to come simple and unadorned when you sat for me—knowing (as I see with *unprejudiced* eyes) that you could receive no addition from the silk-worm's aid, or jeweller's polish. (312)

[53] In the JOURNAL, 356, Sterne spoke of a Cosway portrait of Eliza – presumably that reproduced in WINGED SKULL, about which Kenneth Monkman, 309, reports 'the provenance is good but not certain'. It is in a private collection. True, Sterne said that when Eliza sat for Anne James's picture she dressed in 'silks, pearls, and ermine', but there are neither pearls nor ermine visible in the painting. But Sterne, who did not have the picture before him when he wrote, must have been speaking loosely.

This wording might suggest that Sterne himself made the painting, but that is unlikely. Although he was an amateur painter and was at this very time preparing to give lessons to Anne James (324, 412), he probably did not know the highly specialized craft of miniature portraiture. Moreover, in the *Journal to Eliza* he spoke of the miniature as 'a present' (357). As Verri reported, Sterne's friends often paid his expenses. One guesses that the Jameses insisted upon paying for the miniature but, since it was to be a gift to Sterne, allowed him to direct the painting.

> You are not handsome, Eliza, nor is yours a face that will please the tenth part of your beholders,—but are something more; for I scruple not to tell you, I never saw so intelligent, so animated, so good a countenance; nor was there, (nor ever will be), that man of sense, tenderness, and feeling, in your company three hours, that was not (or will not be) your admirer, or friend, in consequence of it; that is, if you assume, or assumed, no character foreign to your own, but appeared the artless being nature designed you for. A something in your eyes, and voice, you possess in a degree more persuasive than any woman I ever saw, read, or heard of. But it is that bewitching sort of nameless excellence, that men of nice sensibility alone can be touched with. (312–13)

Sterne was uncommonly proud of his little portrait of Eliza and began to show it about wherever he went.[54] He showed it so often it became something of a joke. In the Mortimer caricature group we see a grinning Sterne pulling open his shirt to display to his tipsy friends a large heart-shaped locket hanging against his bony chest. Actually, Mortimer invented the locket: Sterne had the picture mounted in a snuffbox.[55]

[54] He showed it, we know, to Lady Spencer (339), Archbishop Drummond (346), twice to the company at Skelton Castle (365, 379), and to the Turners (379). There must have been dozens of other times of which we have no record.

[55] JOURNAL, 27 June, p. 365. A snuffbox would hardly have served Mortimer's purposes: a picture of Sterne opening his box for his friends would have seemed like a man offering snuff. Sterne too, for his own fictional purposes, created a locket for Eliza's picture when he wrote the opening section of the SENTIMENTAL JOURNEY: speaking of the *droit d'aubaine*, Yorick says, 'all must have gone to the King of France—even the little picture which I have so long worn, and so often have told thee, Eliza, I would carry with me into my grave, would have been torn from my neck' (66–7). If the passage represents the original draft, Sterne wrote it about 13 June (JOURNAL, 357, 358), a time when the picture was still in the snuffbox. Perhaps

To make a public show of affections was part and parcel of sentimental love for Sterne. Probably it reassured him that there was nothing shameful in what he was doing. The nabobs who associated with the Jameses knew all about Sterne and Eliza; and, when he went among his more highly placed friends and patrons, Sterne talked about her to anyone who would listen.

> I got thy letter last night, Eliza, on my return from Lord Bathurst's, where I dined, and where I was heard (as I talked of thee an hour without intermission) with so much pleasure and attention, that the good old lord toasted your health three different times; and tho' he is now in his eighty-fifth year, says he hopes to live long enough to be introduced as a friend to my fair Indian disciple, and to see her eclipse all other nabobesses as much in wealth, as she does already in exterior and (what is far better) in interior merit. I hope so too. . . . there was only a third person, and of sensibility, with us.—And a most sentimental afternoon, 'till nine o'clock, have we passed! But thou, Eliza, wert the star that conducted and enliven'd the discourse.—And when I talked not of thee, still didst thou fill my mind, and warmed every thought I uttered; for I am not ashamed to acknowledge I greatly miss thee. (304–5)

Though Eliza's letters to Sterne do not survive, those she addressed to others amply demonstrate her talent and intelligence. Sterne was very proud and did not hesitate to show her letters 'to half the literati in town'.

> You shall not be angry with me for it, because I meant to do you honour by it.—You cannot imagine how many admirers your epistolary productions have gained you, that never viewed your external merits. I only wonder where thou couldst acquire thy graces, thy goodness, thy accomplishments—so connected! so educated! Nature has, surely, studied to make thee her peculiar care— (321)

Sterne was doing no more than projecting his intentions, for he did not like the mounting, as he said in the entry of 14 July: 'I verily think my Eliza I shall get this Picture set, so as to wear it, as I first proposed—ab[t] my neck—I do not like the place tis in—it shall be nearer my heart' (379–80). Whether he actually reset it or not, we do not know. However, in August he received the gift of 'an elegant gold Snuff[box] fabricated for me at Paris' in which he was thinking of mounting Eliza's picture (388).

Sterne was in love, but he had tested the waters in his first letter when he had declared himself 'half in love'. Not getting an encouraging response, he ceased to speak candidly of his passion while Eliza was in London. Instead, he addressed her as 'my child' and talked about her reunion with her husband – in prose somewhat too highly coloured – and encouraged her writing as though she were his pupil (306). Not until she had left London and was waiting with her ship for a wind did he screw up his courage:

> Talking of widows—pray, Eliza, if ever you are such, do not think of giving yourself to some wealthy nabob—because I design to marry you myself—My wife cannot live long . . . and I know not the woman I should like so well for her substitute as yourself.—'Tis true, I am ninety-five in constitution, and you but twenty-five—rather too great a disparity this!—but what I want in youth, I will make up in wit and good humour.—Not Swift so loved his Stella, Scarron his Maintenon, or Waller his Sacharissa, as I will love you, and sing thee, my wife elect! (318–19)

When the ship sailed and there was no longer a chance of being rejected, Sterne, as we shall see, declared his love without inhibition.

Early in the relationship, Eliza was discreet in her conduct. Once when she was ill – as she often was – she would not let her servant admit Sterne to her bedroom. He was annoyed. 'Remember, my dear,' he scolded, 'that a friend has the same right as a physician. The etiquettes of this town (you'll say) say otherwise.—No matter! Delicacy and propriety do not always consist in observing their frigid doctrines' (299). Eliza grew more confident, and they began to have intimate dinners tête-à-tête before the fire in the Bond Street rooms, served by Molly, Mrs Fourmantel's servant, who was titillated by the scene and enamoured of Eliza.[56]

So the gossips talked. On 23 February he wrote to Lydia:

> I do not wish to know who was the busy fool, who made your mother uneasy about Mrs. [Draper;] 'tis true I have a friendship for her, but not to infatuation—I believe I have judgment enough to discern hers, and every woman's faults. I honour thy mother for her answer—'that she wished not to be informed, and begged him to drop the subject.' (301)

[56] These dinners are mentioned frequently in the JOURNAL: 323, 333, 336, 341, 352.

The talk spurred certain busy people into trying to separate Eliza from Sterne. Charles Boddam, a director of the East India Company, whose brother was the widower of Eliza's late sister Mary, kept urging upon Eliza the necessity of returning according to plan. 'I like not his countenance,' said Sterne. 'It is absolutely killing.—Should evil befal thee, what will he not have to answer for? I know not the being . . . that I shall hate more' (317).[57] Indeed, when it came to Eliza, Sterne's wonted indulgence towards the faults of those around him vanished completely. A family of London merchants, lawyers and politicians named Newnham[58] seems to have acted in concert in trying to turn Eliza away from him.

> The [Newnhams]s, by heavens, are worthless! I have heard enough to tremble at the articulation of the name.—How could you, Eliza, leave them, (or suffer them to leave you rather,) with impressions the least favourable? . . . For God's sake write not to them; nor foul thy fair character with such polluted hearts.—*They* love thee! What proof? Is it their actions that say so? or their zeal for those attachments, which do thee honour, and make thee happy? or their tenderness for thy fame? No—But they *weep*, and say *tender things*.—Adieu to all such for ever. (309)

But because Anne James continued to accept them Sterne was unable to effect a separation while Eliza remained in London. Once she had left town, he accomplished it by the simplest of stratagems – a blatant lie. He told her that Anne had rejected the Newnhams because 'She knows they are not her friends, nor yours; and the first use they would make of being with her, would be to sacrifice you to her (if they could) a second time' (313). Then he had the temerity to talk openly about what he had done. To a friend who had been thinking about seeking an acquaintance with the Newnhams, he wrote,

[57] The will of Daniel Draper, proved at London 1805 (PRO: fol. 168/Nelson) names Rawson Hart Boddam, Eliza's brother-in-law, as an executor.

[58] CURTIS's information on the family, 314, has been superseded by that of NAMIER AND BROOKE. The head of the family was Nathaniel (*c.* 1699–1778) of Newtimber Place, Sussex. He had a son, George Lewis (*c.* 1733–1800), and a younger son, Nathaniel (*c.* 1741–1809). All were London merchants who sat in the Commons at various times for various constituencies. Several members of the family subscribed to *A Sentimental Journey*.

> I think I have effected my purpose by a falsity, which Yorick's friendship to the Bramine can only justify.—I wrote her word that the most amiable of women reiterated my request, that she would not write to them. I said too, she had conceal'd many things for the sake of her peace of mind—when in fact, L—e, this was merely a child of my own brain, made Mrs. J[ames]'s by adoption, to enforce the argument I had before urged so strongly.—Do not mention this circumstance to Mrs. J[ames], 'twould displease her—and I had no design in it but for the Bramine to be a friend to herself.— (369)

Sterne's friends were not disapproving. His infatuation was obvious to all, but they thought it harmless enough. 'There was nothing in the Affair worth making a Secret of,' wrote Richard Griffith. 'The World, that knew of their Correspondence, knew the worst of it, which was merely a simple Folly. Any other Idea of the Matter would be more than the most abandoned Vice could render probable. To intrigue with a Vampire! To sink into the Arms of *Death alive*!'[59] We may discount this imagery, since Griffith met Sterne for the first time in September 1767 after Sterne's long and debilitating illness. As we know from the Mortimer painting, he looked much healthier when Eliza knew him.

It seems unlikely that Eliza and Sterne ever consummated a physical union. Once, in a gathering of Yorkshire friends, where one would expect Sterne to be at his most candid, he was delicately asked about this matter. He had gone to see Hall at Skelton in July 1767, and from there he and Hall had driven to nearby Kirkleatham to dine with their old friends Charles and Elizabeth Turner. He recorded the conversation in the *Journal to Eliza*:

> Dining & feasting all day at Mr Turner's—his Lady a fine Woman herself, in love wth your picture—O my dear Lady, cried I, did you but know the Original[.]—but what is she to you, Tristram[?]—nothing; but that I am in Love with her[.]—et ceetera[?]——said She—no I have given over dashes—replied I—(379)[60]

Eliza, in all probability, was less in love with Sterne than he with her, and she may not have been fully aware of his desires. She was not herself much

[59] *A Series of Genuine Letters*, V, 199–200.
[60] Professor Melvyn New thinks my inserted punctuation is unwarranted tampering and that the passage as Sterne left it might be used to demonstrate the opposite of what I maintain. See his use of it in TS NOTES, 147–8.

driven by sexual passion. In the years after she left her husband, she never took a lover, but passed her days presiding over the homosexual household of her uncle, Charlet Whitehill, who was quite devoted to her. Her cousin, Thomas Limbrey Sclater, a confirmed bachelor, was perhaps the person she most loved, but it was a love of friendship. Friendship meant a great deal to her,[61] and it is possible that she never thought of Sterne in any other way. In one letter to her cousin, she spoke of him as 'my best friend',[62] and she copied at least one of his letters to send to Sclater. To Anne James she emphasized her admiration of Sterne: 'I was almost an Idolator of His Worth, while I fancied Him the Mild, Generous, Good Yorick, We had so often thought Him to be.'[63] Eliza was not a sophisticated woman, but a self-educated colonial in love with England, with its polite society, and with men of letters. Sterne's attentions deeply gratified her and, as she later said, turned her head.[64] In her hunger for his attention, she may have manipulated Sterne, or she may have allowed herself more freedom than was wise. It is doubtful that she intended to cause him pain.

The dreaded day finally arrived, and Sterne handed Eliza into her coach (355). He later wrote, 'How oft have I smarted at the Idea, of that last longing Look by wch thou badest adieu . . . twas the Separation of Soul & Body—& equal to nothing but what passes on that tremendous Moment' (374). John Croft said that Sterne accompanied her as far as the Downs, but not so. Eliza took her carriage to Gravesend, where she met her boat, the *Lord Chatham*. She may have boarded at Gravesend or, as Sterne hoped, gone on by carriage to Deal, in the Downs, and boarded there. Sterne and the Jameses had agreed to take a coach to Deal should the ship be delayed very long (312), but it was not. On 30 March the *Public Advertiser* reported, 'The Lord Chatham East Indiaman, Captain Morris, stationed for Bombay, is arrived in the Downs from Gravesend, and will proceed on her Voyage the first fair Wind.'

Sterne began to get letters written from the *Lord Chatham* as it bobbed at anchor. Eliza had fallen ill again. ''Tis melancholy indeed, my dear,' he

[61] See her 'essay' on friendship contained in her letter to Anne James dated from Bombay, 15 April 1772, edited by Wilbur Cross for the Sterne *Works*, 12 vols, New York, 1904, VIII, 173–268, specifically 217–29. Portions of this letter appear in WRIGHT AND SCLATER and in LETTERS, but only Cross gives the full text.

[62] WRIGHT AND SCLATER, 86.

[63] *Works*, VIII, 182.

[64] Eliza to John Wilkes, 22 March [1775?], in *Works*, VIII, 277–8.

wrote back, 'to hear so piteous an account of thy sickness! Thou art encompass'd with evils enow, without that additional weight!' (308–9). He wrote from the Jameses' house, where he and Anne had 'mixed their tears a hundred times' talking of Eliza – as they would do almost daily until the boat sailed. Eliza's next contained some practical requests, and Sterne was delighted that there was something he could actually do. 'To whom should Eliza apply in her distress, but to her friend who loves her? why then, my dear, do you apologize for employing me?' (310). He got her a special hammer and pliers with which to tune her pianoforte 'from the brass middle string of your guittar, which is C'. He bought her 'ten handsome brass screws, to hang your necessaries upon: I purchased twelve; but stole a couple from you, to put up in my own cabin, at Coxwould.—I shall never hang, or take my hat off one of them, but I shall think of you' (310) – and a pair of globes, celestial and terrestrial, to help her trace her course. These he packaged and entrusted to a Deal pilot who was just setting off. And he gave the man money with which to purchase an armchair for the cabin, 'the best that Deal could afford'.

The *Lord Chatham* was transporting soldiers, and Eliza was thrown into the company of their captain; the man seemed to be 'susceptible of tender impressions,' she wrote. That put Sterne into a rage: 'Five months with Eliza; and in the same room; and an amorous son of Mars besides! . . . The sun, if he could avoid it, would not shine upon a dunghill; but his rays are so pure, Eliza, and celestial,—I never heard that they were polluted by it.—Just such will thine be.' As to the crew, 'If they are decent, and distant, it is enough' (315). Fortunately, she had a cabin mate, Hester Light, who was returning to marry a man in the company's service.[65]

Sterne wrote daily, encouraging, instructing, fretting, grieving letters. He composed a verse on hope, which 'shortens all journies', and told her to sing it 'with the devotion of an hymn, every morning when thou arisest' (321). And, Christian that he was, again and again he blessed her: 'Heaven watch over my Eliza!' (310); 'May the God of Kindness be kind to thee, and approve himself thy protector, now thou art defenceless!' (311). 'Gracious and merciful God!—consider the anguish of a poor girl.—Strengthen and preserve her in all the shocks her frame must be exposed to. She is now

[65] Their story is told by E. A. Greening Lamborn, 'Great Tew: A Link with Laurence Sterne', *N&Q*, CXCIII (1948), 512–15.

without a protector, but thee! Save her from all accidents of a dangerous element, and give her comfort at the last (312).

A north-east wind began to blow, and Sterne, over-agitated, fell ill.

> I have been within the verge of the gates of death. . . . this poor, fine-spun frame of Yorick's gave way, and I broke a vessel in my breast, and could not stop the loss of blood till four this morning. I have filled all thy India handkerchiefs with it.—It came, I think, from my heart! I fell asleep through weakness. At six I awoke, with the bosom of my shirt steeped in tears. I dreamt I was sitting under the canopy of Indolence, and that thou camest into the room, with a shaul in thy hand, and told me, my spirit had flown to thee in the Downs, with tidings of my fate; and that you were come to administer what consolation filial affection could bestow, and to receive my parting breath and blessing.—With that you folded the shaul about my waist, and, kneeling, supplicated my attention. I awoke; but in what a frame! Oh! my God! 'But thou wilt number my tears, and put them all into thy bottle.' (320)

This would be the last letter he could expect her to receive before sailing.

> Cherish the remembrance of me; think how I esteem, nay, how affectionately I love thee, and what a price I set upon thee! Adieu, adieu! and with my adieu—let me give thee one streight rule of conduct, that thou hast heard from my lips in a thousand forms—but I concenter it in one word,
>
> REVERENCE THYSELF.
>
> Adieu, once more, Eliza! . . .
>
> Blessings, rest, and Hygeia go with thee! May'st thou soon return, in peace and affluence, to illumine my night! I am, and shall be, the last to deplore thy loss, and will be the first to congratulate, and hail thy return.—
>
> FARE THEE WELL!

Lloyd's Evening Post, 3–6 April, reported under 'Port News, Deal, April 3':

> Wind N.E. Came down and sailed with his Majesty's ship Tweed, Merlin sloop, and all the outward bound, the Lord Chatham East

Indiaman; Susannah, Hays, for Cadiz; and Beaver, Hamstrom, for Venice.

Three days later, on 9 April, Sterne sat down and wrote to Lydia.[66] He had been fleeced of nearly £50. 'But what is that loss in comparison of one I may experience?' Anne James, his great comfort in distress, had herself fallen ill. 'She has a tender frame, and looks like a drooping lily, for the roses are fled from her cheeks—I can never see or talk to this incomparable woman without bursting into tears. . . . she talks to me of quitting this world with more composure than others think of living in it.' He had written her an epitaph:

Columns, and labour'd urns but vainly shew,
An idle scene of decorated woe.
The sweet companion, and the friend sincere,
Need no mechanic help to force the tear.
In heart felt numbers, never meant to shine
'Twill flow eternal o'er a hearse like thine;
'Twill flow, whilst gentle goodness has one friend,
Or kindred tempers have a tear to lend. (308)

'I am unhappy—thy mother and thyself at a distance from me,' he wrote, 'and what can compensate for such a destitution?—For God's sake persuade her to come and fix in England, for life is too short to waste in separation. . . . I want thee near me, thou child and darling of my heart!' (307). How different would the last year of Sterne's life have been had his wife and child heeded this plea. As it turned out, Anne James recovered, and Elizabeth and Lydia declined the invitation.

Several weeks before they were separated, Sterne began writing a journal for Eliza, a diary of their days together and his love for her. Eliza's 'counterpart' (322), if she ever wrote it, is lost. Sterne first spoke of the journal in his fifth letter to Eliza, while she was on the boat, and it appears

[66] CURTIS was probably mistaken in dating this letter, No. 186, 9 March 1767. Lydia Sterne Medalle's date for it, 9 April 1767, should be retained. See Rufus D. S. Putney, 'Alas, Poor Eliza!', *Modern Language Review*, XLI (1946), 411–13. Sterne spoke in the letter of seeing two days before a 'dear friend', an 'incomparable woman' who is in danger of dying. Curtis took the woman to be Eliza Draper, and was therefore forced to reject Lydia's date. Putney argued convincingly that the woman was Anne James, citing Sterne's letter to the Jameses of 2 August in which he spoke of Anne's alarming illness during the spring (385).

that he was sending her what he had written so far (310). In the next he tells about beginning a 'new journal' that morning: 'if I live not till your return to England, I will leave it you as a legacy. 'Tis a sorrowful page' (311). But he changed his mind about retaining it and sent this second portion to Eliza by a certain Mr Watts, who was sailing for Bombay on 12 April (322). On that same day,[67] he commenced what he entitled the 'Continuation of the Bramines Journal' – the document which we have come to call the *Journal to Eliza*.[68]

The *Journal* opens with a curious preface written for eyes other than Eliza's:

> This Journal wrote under the fictitious Names of Yorick & Draper—and sometimes of the Bramin & Bramine—but tis a Diary of the miserable feelings of a person separated from a Lady for whose Society he languish'd—

[67] The first entry is dated 13 April, but, as Cross pointed out, the entries for 13–20 April should be set back by one day. Otherwise, the dates in the JOURNAL are never off more than a day or two, so far as I can make out, except for the last eight entries, some or all of which have fictional dates, as we shall see later in this chapter.

[68] BL, Add. MSS 34527, fols 1–40; 40 leaves, about 8 × 14 inches, written on both sides, with many alterations. For convenience, I take my quotations from Curtis's edition included with LETTERS. The original edition, by Wilbur L. Cross, in *Works*, VIII, 51–152, is good, but not readily available. A more accurate and readable edition (though lacking the record of Sterne's emendations) is that by Ian Jack: published with his editions of *A Sentimental Journey* and *A Political Romance* in the 'Oxford English Novels' series, 1968; and revised for the 'World's Classics' series, 1984.

The JOURNAL was lost from sight for many years and was found only by accident. It was discovered in a house in Bath by an eleven-year-old boy playing in a room where his family used to store old papers 'to cut up into spills to light candles with'. This bright boy, Thomas Washbourne Gibbs, recognized Sterne's name and carried off the MS as his treasure. Many years later, after he had made himself an expert on Sterne, he revealed his discovery to a meeting of the Bath Literary Institution. His lecture, also published as a pamphlet, *Some Memorials of Laurence Sterne*, Bath, 1878, was the best biographical account of Sterne to that date. Much of it appeared in the *Athenaeum*, 30 March 1878. Gibbs, dying in 1894, bequeathed the MS and other papers to the British Museum (now the British Library).

With the *Journal* at the British Library are two letters to Gibbs from Thackeray, to whom Gibbs had sent the *Journal*. The second contains a condemnation of Sterne, perhaps the beginning of Thackeray's vicious and unscholarly public assaults upon Sterne's image in his lectures (published in *English Humourists of the Eighteenth Century* [Vol. XXVI of *Works*], 1853, reissued in New York, 1904) and his article, 'A Roundabout Journey: Notes of a Week's Holiday', *Cornhill Magazine*, II (July–December 1860), 623–40. Thackeray's letters are published along with Cross's discussion of how Thackeray abused the *Journal* in the Cross edition of *Works*, VIII, xxxiii–xli.

> The real Names—are foreigne—& the Acc^{t} a Copy from a french Mans^{t}—in M^{r} S[terne']s hands—but wrote as it is, to cast a Viel over them—There is a Counterpart—which is the Lady's Acc^{t} what transactions dayly happened—& what Sentiments occupied her mind, during this Separation from her Admirer—these are worth reading—the translator cannot say so much in fav^{r} of Yoricks—which seem to have little Merit beyond their honesty & truth— (322)

We need not take too seriously Sterne's compliment to Eliza at his own expense – the talk of a man in love. More puzzling is his reversal of a literary tradition: instead of passing off a fictional diary as a real one, Sterne seemed to be passing off a real diary as a fiction. Obviously, it was not a serious attempt at disguise, since he guaranteed its failure when he used the names 'Draper' and 'Yorick'. The very use of a literary tradition, however, has led a number of Sterneians into thinking he wrote the *Journal* for publication.[69] But that seems unlikely given the fact that he sent the first two parts to Eliza when he was too ill to make a copy. Nevertheless, in another way the *Journal to Eliza* is a public document. Sterne's sentimental love affairs had always been public, and that with Eliza especially so: he had shown her picture and letters all over town. The preface was a gesture in the direction of modesty, a pretence of reluctance to expose an intimate document when he actually hoped it would be seen and become part of his image as a man of sensibility.

Sterne did have one fear, that Daniel Draper might also see it. Early on, he twice used the word 'wife' to refer to Eliza, but erased it both times (323, 338). Finally, after a long passage in which he figured forth his and Eliza's marriage, he wrote, 'This last Sheet has put it out of my power, ever to send you this Journal to India' (359). Thereafter he used 'wife' freely (366). He had decided to send no more instalments abroad, but to leave the document with Anne James (356), which he eventually did. An odd letter he addressed to Daniel Draper, which was found with the *Journal*, was probably another attempt to protect Eliza from her husband. He gave it to Anne along with the *Journal*, and the two stayed together until they were brought to light. 'I fell in Love with y^{r} Wife,' Sterne wrote, 'but tis a Love, You would honour me for—for tis so like that I bear, my own daughter' (349). In the early

[69] Including the present writer, who no longer takes the position he expressed in the 'Appendix on the *Journal to Eliza*', STERNE'S COMEDY, 133–9.

letters to Eliza, he had often associated her with Lydia, but never in the *Journal* proper. It was not a very practical scheme, to pacify Draper with this letter. Sterne probably wrote it in a feverish state, and Draper surely never laid eyes on it.

The *Journal to Eliza* is the work of a man gripped by an obsession:

> I am absolutely good for nothing, as every mortal is who can think & talk but upon one thing!—how I shall rally my powers, alarms me; for Eliza thou has melted them all into one—the power of loving thee—& with such ardent affection as triumphs over all other feelings—(324–5)

The style is highly elliptical, especially in the early parts. There are occasional flashes of brilliant writing, but most entries seem rather empty. Though Sterne continues to urge Eliza to 'reverence' herself, there is little point in giving advice to someone so distant. The *Journal* abounds in descriptions of Sterne's feelings of love, but contains almost no analysis of the passion. He says nothing about India and little about his own society. He tells Eliza when he is working at his new novel, but says maddeningly little about his writing problems. He passes on virtually no gossip. The descriptions of himself are colourless, since he sees himself as an innocent, victimized by love: 'in all this Storm of Passions, I have but one small anchor, Eliza! to keep this weak Vessel of mine from perishing—I trust all I have to it—as I trust Heaven, which cannot leave me, without a fault, to perish' (351). Again, as in the letters, there are many prayers and ejaculations and expressions of faith:

> the hand of Providence . . . watches over thee for most merciful purposes——Let this persuasion, my dear Eliza! stick close to thee in all thy tryals—as it shall in those thy faithful Bramin is put to—till the mark'd hour of deliverance comes. I'm going to sleep upon this religious Elixir—may the Infusion of it distil into the gentlest of hearts. (337)

The *Journal to Eliza* is a humourless work: 'I could sometimes be wise—& often Witty—but I feel it a reproach to be the latter whilst Eliza is so far from hearing me—& What is Wisdome to a foolish weak heart like mine!' (354). Sterne aptly describes it as 'a Diary of . . . miserable feelings' (322). But his expressions of love are often sweet:

> I shall trace thy track every day in the Map, & not allow one hour for contrary Winds, or Currents—every engine of nature shall work together for us—Tis the Language of Love—& I can speak no other. & so, good night, to thee, & may the gentlest delusions of love impose upon thy dreams. (325)

He no longer hesitates to call his passion 'love', but there is an air of unreality throughout because of the way he implies or says openly that Eliza returns his love – something which he did not and could not know for certain:

> O My Eliza, had I ever truely loved another (wch I never did) Thou hast long ago, cut the Root of all Affection in me—& planted & water'd & nourish'd it, to bear fruit only for thyself—Continue to give me proofs I have had and shall preserve the same rights over thee—my Eliza! (335)

This is addressed to a woman thousands of miles away, and one who probably had never given 'proofs' of her love. Indeed, he admits to being tormented by doubts, turning all night in his bed in dreams 'that Eliza is false to Yorick, or Yorick is false to Eliza' (326), or that she has married the captain of the ship (366). Of course he bolsters his hopes as best he can: 'Doubt! did I say—but I have none—and as soon w^d I doubt the Scripture I have preach'd on—as question thy promises' (372). How could she have made promises when she had not declared her love for him? 'I sh^d not be astonish'd, Eliza, if you was to declare, "You was up to the ears in Love with Me"' (355), he wrote, implying that she had said no such thing. He sometimes imagines Eliza and himself abandoning their mates to take up a life together (367, 373, 378). At others, he dreams of marriage and without much compunction wishes for the deaths of Daniel Draper and Elizabeth Sterne (366, 370–1).

> I have brought your name *Eliza*! and Picture into my work—where they will remain—when You and I are at rest for ever—Some Annotator or explainer of my works in this place will take occasion, to speak of the Friendship wch Subsisted so long & faithfully betwixt Yorick & the Lady he speaks of—Her Name he will tell the world was Draper—a Native of India—married there to a gentleman in the India Service of that Name—, who brought her over to England for the recovery of her health in the Year 65—where She continued to April

> the year 1767. It was ab[t] three months before her Return to India, That our Author's acquaintance & hers began. M[rs] Draper had a great thirst for Knowledge——was handsome—genteel—engaging—and of such gentle disposition & so enlightened an understanding,—That Yorick (whether he made much Opposition is not known) from an acquaintance—soon became her Admirer—they caught fire, at each other at the same time—& they w[d] often say, without reserve to the world, & without any Idea of saying wrong in it, That their Affections for each other were *unbounded*—M[r] Draper dying in the Year xxxxx—This Lady return'd to England, & Yorick the year after becoming a Widower—They were married—& retiring to one of his Livings in Yorkshire, where was a most romantic Situation—they lived & died happily.—and are spoke of with honour in the parish to this day—— (358–9)

Talk about sickness takes up almost as much space in the *Journal* as talk about love. As we have seen earlier, Sterne pursued his sentimental affairs largely for their restorative powers.

> I know to what an amount thou wilt Shed over Me, this tender Tax—& tis the Consolation springing out of that, of what a good heart it is which pours this friendly balm on mine, That has already, & will for ever heal every evil of my Life. and What is becoming, of my Eliza, all this time!—where is she sailing?—what Sickness or other evils have befallen her? I weep often my dear Girl, for those my Imagination surrounds thee with— (331)

He labours under a practical difficulty, having to imagine her illness, but her very absence has an advantage for him. Were she with him, his personal ethic would demand that he accept his own illnesses in the stoic silence he presented to the world: 'My friends . . . Swear I shew more true fortitude & eveness of temper in my Suffering than Seneca, or Socrates' (339). Were she near, 'thy Yorick would not let the Winds hear his Complaints', but since she will not read about them until he has been restored, he says hopefully, he can get relief by sharing his troubles (326).

For a week or ten days after the *Lord Chatham* sailed, Sterne kept to his room, writing his journal and a few letters. He was very ill. Hall came on 12 April to take him to the Brawn's Head Tavern to dine with their old

Yorkshire friends – 'the whole Pandamonium assembled'. He went to Hall's for supper and then home, 'worn out both in body & mind, & paid a severe reckoning all the night' (322). On the fifteenth he commenced taking Dr James's Powder, a severe diaphoretic, which is generally thought to have occasioned the death of Oliver Goldsmith. 'Leand the whole day with my head upon My hand; sitting most dejectedly at the Table with my Eliza's Picture before me.' In the afternoon Molly laid his table for dinner –

> one solitary plate—one knife—one fork—one Glass!—O Eliza! twas painfully distressing—I gave a thousand pensive penetrating Looks at the Arm chair thou so often graced on these quiet, sentimental Repasts—& Sighed & laid down my knife & fork,—& took out my handkerchiff, clap'd it across my face, & wept like a child. (323–4)

The next day he dragged himself to the Jameses to deliver his present to Anne of colours and apparatus for painting. She, in a moment of weakness, told him what Eliza never had – how brutal a person was Daniel Draper. Two days later he returned to dine with them, and after dinner, while the commodore sat reading a pamphlet upon Indian affairs, Sterne and Anne began talking about Eliza. 'I burst into tears a dozen different times after dinner, & such affectionate gusts of passion, That She was ready to leave the room,—& Sympathize in private for us——I weep for You both, said she (in a whisper)' (325).

On Easter Sunday, he was awakened by a severe pain in his testicles (325, 329), which continued unabated for two days. He finally called in a physician 'to satisfy my friends'. The man took twelve ounces of blood 'in order to quiet what was left in me' (326). As we now know, such treatment quieted the patient by putting him in shock and bringing him to the verge of death. On Wednesday morning he was bled a second time. Lying fainting in bed, the bandage slipped, and 'my arm broke loose, & I half bled to death in bed before I felt it' (326). Yet on Thursday he managed to make an entry in his journal. Word had got around of his condition, and friends began pouring into the sickroom – forty of them in one day, he said in the *Journal* (329). Little wonder that the next day he very nearly died. 'So ill, I could not write a word all this morning—not so much, as Eliza! farewell to thee;—I'm going——' (329). But his strength returned, though his pains continued. So he called in 'an able Surgeon & with him an able physician (both my friends)':

> —tis a venerial Case, cried my two Scientifick friends.—'tis impossible, at least to be that, replied I—for I have had no commerce whatever with the Sex—not even with my wife, added I, these 15 Years—You are [poxed] however my good friend, said the Surgeon, or there is no such Case in the world—what the Devil! said I without knowing Woman—we will not reason ab[t] it, said the Physician, but you must undergo a course of Mercury,—I'll lose my life first, said I. (329)

It is certainly untrue that Sterne had not known a woman for fifteen years. He did go ahead with the dangerous mercury cure. His willingness to risk it indicates that he thought the diagnosis was correct. Nevertheless, the physician and surgeon were probably wrong. It is impossible, of course, to say categorically that Sterne did not have syphilis, for the disease was endemic in eighteenth-century England. But painful testicles are not a symptom of it. On the other hand, it is obvious to twentieth-century physicians who have looked at the facts in his case that Sterne suffered from tuberculosis of the fibrocaseous type, as evidenced by the recurrent bleeding of his lungs (haemoptysis, to use their term). Moreover, tuberculosis often attacks other organs besides the lungs, among them the genitals and the vocal chords. In short, one can unify all of Sterne's known symptoms, including his shocking weight loss during his last year, under a diagnosis of tuberculosis. To postulate any other disease would be unjustified in modern medicine.[70]

Sterne promptly sent an account of the diagnosis to his wife (343) and told it all to Eliza in the *Journal*. He may have felt that he could not make a secret of the dangerous cure he was to undergo. Corrosive mercury, he explained, 'in itself, is deadly poyson, but given in a certain preparation, not very dangerous' (347), though 'I shall be sublimated to an etherial Substance by the time my Eliza sees me' (332). He had hardly started on the treatment when he began to suffer terrible 'cholicks' in the stomach and bowels and was forced to give it up. When he got back to Yorkshire, he would begin the treatment again. His friends continued to call: 'my room

[70] In coming to this conclusion, I have had the advice of Dr Maureen Strafford of Harvard Medical School. For discussions of Sterne's tuberculosis, see Walter Radcliffe, 'Dr. John Burton and His Whimsical Contrivance', *Medical Bookman and Historian*, II (1948), 349–55; and Sir Arthur MacNalty, 'Laurence Sterne: A Witty Consumptive', *British Journal of Tuberculosis*, LII (1958), 94–7.

allways full of friendly Visiters—& my rapper eternally going with Cards & enquiries after me' (330).

Despite the seriousness of the cure, he could not help but laugh at so Shandean a situation. He told the whole story in the *Journal*, and then he copied much of it into a letter he was writing to Lord Shelburne.

> Thus, my dear lord, has your poor friend with all his sensibilities been suffering the chastisement of the grossest sensualist.—Was it not as ridiculous an embarrassment as ever Yorick's spirit was involved in? . . . which by the bye would make no bad anecdote in Tristram Shandy's life. (343)

Fortunately, Sterne had the comfort of those he most loved. Hall kept looking in on him. Distressed to find that his friend had been taking only water gruel, Hall coaxed him to try a meal of chicken and fish, and stayed to eat it with him (331). On 28 April Sterne managed to take himself to Gerrard Street to see Anne James.

> Tears ran down her cheeks when She saw how pale & wan I was—& never gentle Creature sympathiz'd more tenderly—I beseech you, cried the good Soul, not to regard either difficulties or expences, but fly to Eliza directly—I see you will dye without her—save y^{r}self for her—how shall I look her in the face? What can I say to her, when on her return, I have to tell her, That her Yorick is no more?—Tell her my dear friend, said I, That I will meet her in a better world—& that I have left this, because I could not live without her. (334)

Two days later, he took an outing to Hyde Park in the carriage. Among those riding about the ring was a woman, an old lover whom Sterne called 'Sheba', perhaps Lady Warkworth.[71]

> Pass'd twice by her without knowing her—she stop'd the 3^{d} time—to ask me how I did—I w^{d} not have askd You, Solomon! said She, but y^{r} Looks affected me—for you'r half dead I fear—I thank'd Sheba, very kindly, but wthout any emotion but what sprung from gratitude—Love alas! was fled with thee Eliza!—I did not think

[71] CURTIS, 339, hypothesized that she was Lady Warkworth, and that does not seem unlikely if in fact Lady Warkworth was Sterne's correspondent in Letter No. 141. In the following March, Lady Warkworth was discovered in an affair with a certain 'Mr. F' – perhaps the lover of whom Sheba speaks (CURTIS, 244).

> Sheba could have changed so much in grace & beauty—Thou hadst shrunk poor Sheba away into Nothing,—but a good natured girl, with out powers or charms—I *fear* your Wife is dead, quoth Sheba——no you don't *fear* it Sheba said I—Upon my Word Solomon! I would quarel with You, was you not so ill—If you knew the Cause of my Illness, Sheba, replied I, you w[d] quarrel but the more with me—You lie, Solomon! answered Sheba, for I know the Cause already—& am so little out of Charity with You upon it—That I give You leave to come & drink Tea with me before You leave Town—you're a good honest Creature Sheba—no! you Rascal, I am not—but I'm in Love, as much as you can be for y[r] Life—I'm glad of it Sheba! said I—You Lie, said Sheba, & so canter'd away. (335)

Sterne felt himself recovering during the week of 3 May. He spent much of the time writing a long letter to Eliza, no doubt mainly copied out of the *Journal*. On Wednesday he dined out and went in the evening to hear Johann Christian Bach conduct a concert at Mrs Cornelys's rooms (338). He began to talk about going home to Yorkshire. The next week he had 'Cards from 7 or 8 of our Grandees to dine with them before I leave Town—shall go like a Lamb to the Slaughter' (339). He also dined with Lord and Lady Belasyse, and on Saturday, 16 May, with Lord and Lady Spencer. 'Drove at night to Ranalagh—staid an hour—returned to my lodgings, dissatisfied' (339). On Sunday he went to a very grand court at which the king, queen and most of the royal family made an appearance. On 20 May he wrote, 'Taking Leave of all the Town' (341). He, or more likely his servant, called on Sir Joshua Reynolds to pick up some copies of the Fisher print of his portrait, no doubt to give as gifts.[72] His friends, finding him so frail, were worried about his attempting even a short journey, but he was determined. Only Lord and Lady Spencer could prevail upon him to delay, and that only because they gave him a farewell dinner party (341).

'My chaise stands at my door', Sterne wrote to John Talbot Dillon on the morning of Friday, 22 May, 'to take and convey this poor body to its legal settlement', that is, Coxwold; 'I am ill, very ill' (344–5). At ten o'clock he set out, but made slow progress. 'Bear my Journey badly—ill—& dispirited,' he wrote in the *Journal* the next day (346). In the space of three days, during which he normally would have reached home, he had got no

[72] In Reynolds's *Account Book* at the Fitzwilliam Museum, under the date 6 May 1767 is the following entry: 'M[r] Stern for 10 Prints 2/15/0.'

further than Newark – 'conveyed thus far', he wrote to Hall, 'like a bale of cadaverous goods consigned to Pluto and company—lying in the bottom of my chaise most of the rout, upon a large pillow which I had the *prevoyance* to purchase before I set out' (346). At Doncaster he was forced to turn aside to seek help from Archbishop Drummond at his estate, Brodsworth, some five miles off the road. 'Staid two days on the road at the A-Bishops of Yorks,' he wrote in the *Journal*; 'shewd his Grace & his Lady and Sister y^{r} portrait—wth a short but interesting Story of my friendship for the Original—kindly nursed & honourd [by] both—arrived at my Thatchd Cottage the 28th of May' (346). Shandy Hall was roofed with slates, but Sterne often provided the more romantic thatch.

For at least a week, he lay in bed, looking, he said in the *Journal*, 'so emaciated, and unlike what I was, I could scarse be angry with thee Eliza, if thou Coulds not remember me, did heaven send me across thy way—Alas! poor Yorick!' (346). On 31 May he dutifully began the course of mercury which he had been forced to give up in town. 'These Gentry have got it into their Nodelles, That mine is *an Ecclesiastick Rhum* as the french call it—god help em!' (347).

Yet he was able to carry on with at least some practical matters. On 30 May he signed a contract with a new curate for Sutton-on-the-Forest and Stillington – John Walker, son of Sterne's predecessor at Sutton. Although young Walker was not a university graduate, he had attained priest's orders in 1762. Sterne allowed him £40 per year and the use of Stillington vicarage, because the house at Sutton, in which Walker had spent most of his childhood, had been lost in the fire. Walker made his first entry in the parish registers on 1 June 1767.[73]

Early in May, Sterne began directing extensive repairs and renovations of Shandy Hall. Most of the upstairs rooms were remodelled in 1767, including the large south-west bedroom, which must have been Sterne's. There were many changes, including the refurbishing of three upstairs fireplaces, each furnished anew with handsome grates from the Carron foundry in Scotland. But the most extensive work was the two-storey brick extension some six feet deep and topped by a parapet which was added to the western end so

[73] The signed agreement is now housed at the John Rylands Library, Manchester: Ryl. Eng. MS 343/32. The will of Sterne's predecessor, John Walker, Vicar of Sutton-on-the-Forest, at the Borthwick Institute, names a son John, presumably Sterne's curate. Further details about his childhood, *EMY*, 68, 117; and his career, CURTIS, 348–9.

that from the garden the house would have a modest Georgian look. Sterne must have borne the noise and chaos of building all that summer. The architects were the well-known John Carr and his assistant, Peter Atkinson, who were in the area working on Newburgh Priory and Coxwold church.[74] Lord Fauconberg, who owned Shandy Hall, may have initiated the project – and that may explain why it was undertaken at a time so inconvenient for Sterne. When Sterne had built the stable, in 1761, he had bargained with Fauconberg to reimburse him for the cost at twelve pence for every pound cost to be added to the rent.[75] He may have made a similar arrangement this time. But Sterne directed the work, as we know from his talk about it in the *Journal*.

Then he learned that his wife and daughter were returning. Before he had left London he had received 'hints' that they might soon come back, but the full import of their intention did not become clear until 2 June, when he received another letter from Lydia. To his surprise and delight, Elizabeth was proposing a formal separation. And how busy these women had been planning the details! They would return to Shandy Hall, but when winter came would go to York, where Sterne was to get them a house. In the spring they would return to France where they would settle permanently. Sterne was to sell the Tindal Farm and his other smaller properties[76] and lay out the money in annuities for them. 'By this they will obtain 200 p^{ds} a year, to be continued to the longer Liver—and as it rids me of all future care—& moreover transfers their Income to the Kingdom where they purpose to live—I'm truely acquiescent—tho' I lose the Contingency of surviving them—but 'tis no matter—I shall have enough' (347–8). He wrote at once, agreeing to everything. He even declared that he would add another hundred guineas a year to their income while Elizabeth was alive (348). What he did not like was their coming home. Why not settle it by correspondence? A visit now would put an end to the *Journal* and hamper his work on the new novel. He wrote to Richard Davenport on 9 June:

[74] A detailed report on the house, including the identification of the architects, made by Dr E. A. Gee, investigator for the Royal Commission on Historical Monuments, is housed at Shandy Hall. Carr and Atkinson are both noticed in Robert H. Skaife, *Civic Officials of York and Parliamentary Representation*, 3 vols, a manuscript housed at the York Public Library.

[75] Chapman to Fauconberg, 6 August 1761, in WOMBWELL PAPERS.

[76] In 1744, Sterne and his wife had purchased the Tindal Farm and three smaller pieces of land – about 200 acres in all. See *EMY*, 146–7.

> This very morning that I set about writing my Sentimental Journey through France,—have I received a letter from my wife, who is at Marseilles, advertising, that she is going . . . to make a Sentimental Journey through France, and post it a thousand miles, merely to pay me a visit of three months.—The deuce take all Sentimental Journeys!!—I wish there had never been such a thing thought of by man or woman—tres menses! cum uxore neque leni neque commodâ!—quid faciam?—quo me vertam?[77]

– the Latin of which may be translated, 'three months! with a wife neither pliant nor accommodating!—what am I to do?—where am I to turn?' He was angered by the thought, not of the money, but of the material possessions they would carry off – 'Provisions of all sorts of Linnens—for house use—Body Use—printed Linnens for Gowns—Magazeens of Teas—Plate. . . . In short I shall be pluck'd bare' (348). Nevertheless, he began negotiating for the sale of his estate, 'to purchace peace to myself—& a certainty of never having it interrupted by Mrs Sterne' (355).

He wanted to get started on his new novel, but found it difficult. 'Cannot write my Travels, or give one half hours close attention to them,' he wrote in the *Journal* under the date of 3 June, 'upon Thy Acc^t^ my dearest friend—Yet write I must, & what to do with you, whilst I write—I declare I know not—I want to have you ever before my Imagination . . . now I must shut you out sometimes' (350). Two days later he wrote, 'I Sit down to write this day, in good earnest—so read Eliza! quietly besides me—I'll not give you a Look——except one of kindness.—dear Girl! if thou lookest so bewitching once more—I'll turn thee out of my Study' (351). How he managed to work in his study is hard to imagine, for the renovations had commenced in the room directly over it. Perhaps he worked at night. In any event, he seems to have begun writing, as he told Davenport, by 9 June. A few days later he had decided to speak about Eliza's portrait in the book (357), and on 17 June he had finished the opening section. It had taken a week to write three pages, but he was full of confidence.

The country air did wonders for his health, and he was soon going out in his chaise. His first visit was to Byland Abbey, 'that sweet Recesse, I have so often described to You', he called it in the *Journal* for 6 June; ''tis sweet in itself—but You never come across me—but the perspective brightens up—& every Tree & Hill & Vale & Ruin ab^t^ me—smiles as if you was

77 Wasserman, 'Unedited Letters'.

amidst 'em . . . but Eliza! Eliza is not with me!' (351–2). Work went forward rapidly on the house, and by 7 June he could describe in the *Journal* what has since come to be known as 'Eliza's room', in the south-east corner of the first floor.

> I have this week finish'd a sweet little apartment which all the time it was doing, I flatter'd the most delicious of Ideas, in thinking I was making it for you—Tis a neat little simple elegant room, overlook'd only by the Sun—just big enough to hold a Sopha,—for us—a Table, four Chairs, a Bureau—& a Book case,—they are to be all y^rs^, Room & all—& there Eliza! shall I enter ten times a day to give thee Testimonies of my Devotion. (352)

A week later the workmen began a carriage house. 'My Chaise is so large—so high—so long—so wide—so Crawford's like,—That I am building a coach house on purpose for it' (358).[78] For company he had Lord Fauconberg, though his duty seemed at times like a 'Bondage' (358), and his cat:

> —eating my fowl, and my trouts & my cream & my strawberries, as melancholly & sad as a Cat; for want of you—by the by, I have got one which sits quietly besides me, purring all day to my sorrows—& looking up gravely from time to time in my face, as if she knew my Situation.—how soothable my heart is Eliza, when such little things sooth it! for in some pathetic sinkings I feel even some support from this poor Cat—I attend to her purrings—& think they harmonize me— (376–7).

Then, hearing the hammering in some corner of the house he added, 'They are *pianissimo* at least, & do not disturb me.' By 19 June, three weeks after his arrival, he felt himself perfectly recovered: 'I never was so well and alert, as I find myself this day—tho' with a face as pale & clear as a Lady after her Lying in' (363).

The thought of his wife's return continued to torment him, 'but tis the last Trial of conjugal Misery—& I wish it was to begin this moment, That it might run its period the faster—for sitting as I do, expecting sorrow—is suffering it' (357). Yet he felt strong enough to do something about his mood: he would go to Hall, 'to be philosophizd with'. He had an errand in York, where he went first. Then it was to Thirsk for the archdeaconry

[78] Still to be seen at Shandy Hall.

visitation. Presiding at the court was his old friend, the portly, high-minded Archdeacon of Cleveland, Dr Francis Blackburne, who had recently attracted the attention of the nation by his powerful arguments that the church should abolish the old requirement for priests and other clerical officers to subscribe to the Thirty-Nine Articles of Religion.[79] By his side sat the proctor, none other than Dr Francis Topham, the lawyer whom Sterne had pillaried in *A Political Romance* and as Didius in *Tristram Shandy*. A less likely team than Blackburne and Topham would be hard to imagine, and never could have come about were it not for the corrupt laws and practices which Sterne had satirized. From Thirsk Sterne was driven over the moors to 'Crazy Castle', where he arrived the next day. Hall was so overjoyed at his friend's recovery that he wrote 'an affecting little poem upon it' (371). But the rest of the company turned out to be too boisterous for Sterne in his present state. 'What a stupid, selfish, unsentimental set of Beings are the Bulk of our Sex' (364). He especially disliked 'Bombay Lascelles', Peter Lascelles, recently retired as a sea captain for the East India Company to an estate he had purchased near Hall's. Lascelles frightened him by telling him about the terrible dangers that ships encountered in Indian waters, things which Sterne did not even want to set down on paper – pirates probably (366, 377). But Hall knew how to cheer him up.

> I am going to ride myself into better health . . . with Hall—whose Castle ly[i]ng near the Sea—We have a Beach as even as a mirrour of 5 miles in Length before it, where we dayly run races in our Chaises, with one wheel in the Sea, & the other on the Sand— (366)

Sterne stayed only a few days.

> June 29. am got home from Halls—to Coxwould—O 'tis a delicious retreat! both from its beauty, & air of Solitude; & so sweetly does every thing ab^{t} it invite y^{r} mind to rest from its Labours—and be at peace with itself & the world—That tis the only place, Eliza, I could live in at this juncture—I hope one day, you will like it as much as y^{r} Bramine—It shall be decorated & made more worthy of You—by the time, fate encourages me to look for you—I have made you, a sweet

[79] 23 June 1767, *Archdeaconry of Cleveland Court Book, 1762–74*, at Borthwick Institute: R.VI.F. 4. Blackburne sparked a national debate with his book, *Confessional*, 1766. The controversy culminated in the Feathers – Tavern Petition of 1771, signed by many prominent clergy. The debate continues today.

> Sitting Room (as I told You) already—and am projecting a good Bed-chamber adjoin[in]g it, with a pretty dressing room for You, which connects them together—& when they are finished, will be as sweet a set of romantic Apartments, as You ever beheld—the Sleeping room will be very large—the dressing room, thro' w[ch] You pass into y[r] Temple, will be little . . . but if it ever holds You & I, my Eliza—the Room will not be too little for us—but We shall be *too big* for the Room. (366–7)

He had come home to work on *A Sentimental Journey*, but still found it hard to get up any momentum. 'I ought now to be busy from sun rise, to sun set,' he wrote to a friend, 'for I have a book to write—a wife to receive—an estate to sell—a parish to superintend, and what is worst of all, a disquieted heart to reason with' (369). In an unusually pessimistic comment to Ignatius Sancho, he wrote, 'I would only covenant for just so much health and spirits, as are sufficient to carry my pen thro' the task I have set it this summer.— But I am a resign'd being, Sancho, and take health and sickness as I do light and darkness, or the vicissitudes of seasons—that is, just as it pleases God to send them' (370). The work went on but slowly, 'my head . . . too full of other Matters' (373). The *Journal to Eliza* continued to distract him (372), and he was increasingly anxious about Elizabeth's return, her choler high, her bowels inconstant (363).

> am tortured from post to post, for I want to know certainly *the day & hour of this Judgment*. . . . I'm pitied by every Soul, in proportion as her Character is detested—& her Errand known—She is coming, every one says, to flea poor Yorick or slay him . . . Spare my Life, & take all I have—if She is not content to decamp with that—One kingdome shall not hold us—for If she will not betake herself to France—I will. (372–3)

It is remarkable that in the midst of this agitation he could write to the Jameses on 6 July, 'I am now beginning to be truly busy at my Sentimental Journey—the pains and sorrows of this life having retarded its progress—but I shall make up my lee-way, and overtake every body in a short time' (375). But he never did make up the leeway, and the *Journey* was to go to press an unfinished work.

By 4 July Sterne's negotiations to sell his estate had brought an offer of £2000 (373) – a fair price considering that six years earlier he had estimated its worth at £1800 (147). He was in the mood to sell, especially since he had learned that he might soon win a 'fine' for the renewal of the lease on his prebendal estate.[80] Then Elizabeth raised the price of freedom.

> Sooth me—calm me—pour thy healing Balm Eliza, into the sorest of hearts—I'm pierced with the Ingratitude and unquiet Spirit of a restless unreasonable Wife whom neither gentleness or generosity can conquer—She has now enterd upon a new plan of waging War with me, a thousand miles off—thrice a week this last month, has the quietest man under heaven been outraged by her Letters—I have offer'd to give her every Shilling I was worth, except my preferment, to be let alone & left in peace by her—Bad Woman! nothing must now purchace this, unless I borrow 400 p^{ds} to give her & carry into france more—I w^{d} perish first, my Eliza! 'ere I would give her a shilling of another man's, wch I must do—if I give her a Shill^{g} more than I am worth.—How I now feel the want of thee! my dear Bramine—my generous unworldly honest Creature—I shall die for want of thee. . . . I think she will send me to my grave. (378)

He retreated into dreams of Eliza. 'I have been all day making a sweet Pavillion in a retired Corner of my garden,' he wrote:

> What a Paradice will I plant for thee—till then I walk as Adam did whilst there was no help-meet found for it, and could almost wish a days Sleep would come upon me till that Moment When I can say as he did—'*Behold the Woman Thou has given me for Wife*' She shall be call'd La Bramine. (377)

Hall's hospitality at Skelton Castle had begun to attract attention. A newspaper reported:

> A Correspondent writes, that Skelton-Castle is, at present, the place of rendezvous of the most celebrated wits: The humourous author of Tristram Shandy, and Mr. G——, author of several ingenious pieces,

[80] Sterne's annual income from the lease of North Newbald prebendal estate was about £12 per year, but he, as all prebendaries, counted upon the rare occasion when he would receive a fine, often £150 or more, for the renewal of the lease. Leases were granted for the lifetime of the longest living of the two or three persons named on the lease. Sterne had probably heard that the last person named on Alderman John Read's lease of North Newbald estate was ailing. See *EMY*, 76–8, 114–15, 118.

> have been there some time: some other persons of distinguished rank and abilities in the literary world, are daily expected.[81]

Hall sent a carriage for Sterne on the morning of 13 July. That evening Eliza's picture went round the table at Skelton Castle and her health after it (379). This too was to be a short visit because Hall and Sterne were going to Harrogate. On Thursday, 16 July, they returned to Coxwold together. While Hall was admiring the renovations, Sterne 'stole away to converse a few minutes' with Eliza. 'Hall is come in in raptures with every thing,' he wrote further down the page, 'so I shut up my Journal for to day & tomorrow for I shall not be able to open it where I go' (380). They were going to York first and on Friday out to Bishopthorpe, where they were to be entertained by Archbishop and Lady Drummond. Sterne wrote in the *Journal* for the next day:

> This good Prelate . . . shews in his treatment of me, what he told me upon taking my Leave—that he loves me, & has a high Value for me—his Chaplains tell me, he is perpetually talking of me—& has such an Opinion of my head & heart that he begs to stand Godfather for my next Literary production. (380)

The following day, 18 July, Sterne spent in York looking for a house he could rent for Elizabeth and Lydia,[82] but so distasteful was the thought, so compelling his dream of Eliza, that he transformed what he was doing into a fantasy. He wrote in the *Journal*, recalling the story of Elisha and the Shunammite woman (2 Kings 4: 8–10),

> at York—where I want to be employd in taking you a little house, where the prophet may be accomodated with a Chamber *in the Wall apart, with a stool & a Candlestick*—where his Soul can be at rest from the distractions of the world, & lean only upon his kind hostesse, &

[81] *Public Advertiser*, 20 July 1767. One supposes that the *Advertiser* had picked up the story from some other newspaper published early in the month: Sterne, in the JOURNAL for 12 July, quoted or paraphrased the original version (379). Sterne seems to have filled out the name of the guest called 'Mr. G.', turning the name into 'Mr Garrick'. It is not impossible for Garrick to have visited Hall, but I rather think Sterne evoked his name only to impress Eliza. I cannot believe that a newspaper account would allude to David Garrick only as the 'author of several ingenious pieces'.

[82] From the first, Elizabeth had demanded a house in York (347), and Sterne later said he had hired it for her (395, 408). So there can be no doubt what Sterne was doing in York on Saturday, 18 July 1767.

> repose all his Cares, & melt them *along with hers* in her sympathetic bosom. (381)

Sterne and Hall went on to Harrogate, only a short trip from York, whence Sterne wrote that he would be drinking the waters for a week. The ladies at the spa, he found, gave him no pleasure at all. 'I Love thee Eliza, more than the heart of Man ever loved Woman's—I even love thee more than I did, the day thou badest me farwel!' (381). Nevertheless, he had begun to tire of writing every day, for he made no entries during his stay – the first large gap one finds in the *Journal*.

On 27 July he started home, but stopped for a night's stay at York. 'I had not been 2 hours before My heart was overset with a pleasure, wch beggard every other, that fate, could give me—save thyself.' He had received a packet of letters, or perhaps a journal, from Eliza. Her boat had put in at St Jago or Santiago, in the Cape Verde Islands west of Africa, and from there she had sent letters to Sterne and other friends and relatives.[83]

> I instantly shut the door of my Bed-Chamber, and orderd myself to be denied—& spent the whole evening, and till dinner the next day, in reading over and over again the most interesting [i.e. moving] Acc^t^—& the most endearing one, that ever tried the tenderness of man—I read & wept—and wept and read till I was blind—then grew sick, & went to bed—& in an hour calld again for the Candle—to read it once more—as for my dear Girls pains & her dangers I cannot write ab^t^ them—because I cannot write my feelings or express them any how to my mind—& O Eliza! but I will talk them over with thee with a sympathy that shall wo[o] thee, so much better than I have ever done—That we will both be gainers in the end— (381)

At this juncture, when one might have expected him to return to the *Journal* with new inspiration, he ceased making entries for three weeks. He went home to Coxwold, worked on *A Sentimental Journey* and returned to York for Race Week, which was held on 16–23 August.[84] During this holiday, he took up the *Journal* again. He began with a new paragraph added to his last: 'I now want to have this week of nonsensical Festivity

[83] WRIGHT AND SCLATER, 60–1. She sent letters to her cousin Thomas Limbrey Sclater from Santiago and shortly after by way of a Dutch vessel.

[84] The *York Courant*, 25 August, listed among those attending the Assembly Rooms ball, Sterne, Cholmley and his wife, Stephen Croft and Mrs Croft, the Turners, the Thornhills and Hall.

over—that I may get back, with thy picture wch I ever carry ab^{t} me—to my retreat and to Cordelia' (382). Then he became worried about having said this with so little preparation. He went back to his entry for 19 July written from Harrogate, and doctored it by adding a single word, 'Races', so that the last line read 'I'm going from hence to York. Races.' He had no worries about placing Race Week in July, for Eliza, who would not see the *Journal* for years, would not be likely to raise any question. In that confidence he wrote three more entries during Race Week and possibly a fourth, antedating them in July and early August so as to make a sequence from the Harrogate entry, though a slightly broken one. Probably he had no hope of writing so many entries as would be needed to fill in three blank weeks, but it seemed important to continue antedating the entries to give Eliza the impression that he had not lapsed in his promise to write daily.[85]

Then during Race Week he received a second set of letters, and lost heart again. Some two weeks after the *Lord Chatham* had left Santiago, she had met a returning Dutch ship; a boat was put down and the vessels exchanged mail. Sterne wrote under the date of 1 August, 'what a sad Story thou hast told me of thy Sufferings & Despondences, from St Iago, till thy meeting wth the Dutch Ship—twas a sympathy above Tears—I trembled every Nerve as I went from line to line' (384). Eliza had done as Sterne had urged: she had written unstintingly about her illnesses – 'rhumatism', 'fever', 'fits', 'Delirium'. He copied some of her description for Anne James (388). Certainly he felt much sympathy. But he had not found in her letters what he longed to see, a declaration of her love for him.

By the time he got back to Coxwold after Race Week, he was thinking realistically about himself and Eliza. If he could no longer dream of marrying

[85] There are two ways to reconcile the discrepancy between the dates Sterne assigned these entries – 27 July–2 August – and the actual dates of Race Week in 1767, 16–23 August. One could assume that Sterne wrote on the dates he assigned, in which event he would have been making up out of his imagination events to come; or one can assume that he wrote during Race Week but antedated the entries. The latter, which seems the more probable, is assumed in this reconstruction.

In the item dated 2 August, Sterne speaks of Dr Jemmett Browne, Bishop of Cork and Ross, who has made him 'great Offers in Ireland'. Sterne would spend some time with Bishop Browne in Scarborough in September, but CURTIS is probably right that Sterne first met him at York during Race Week. So I assume the item was also written during Race Week. If so, the previous item, dated 1 August, also must have been composed during that period. That dated 3 August may or may not belong to the Race Week series: it is impossible to know, since it contains no datable materials.

her, he could still be of some help. She had been so very ill and was returning to such a miserable situation – it went against the grain to think of breaking off the *Journal* for good. He kept it by him as he worked on his novel. Late in September when he was preparing Shandy Hall for the arrival of his family, he made another hasty entry: 'Hurried backwards & forwards ab^{t} the arrival of Madame, this whole weak.' Writing in the *Journal* while Elizabeth was in the house would be impossible: 'something will jarr within me as I do it'. He told Eliza he would write one general account of all *his* sufferings to give her, 'but not in Journals—I shall set my wounds a-bleeding every day afresh by it' (386–7). He then assigned a date of 4 August to this entry, little dreaming that a future annotator, assuming that he wrote on that date, would use the entry to demonstrate that Sterne had grown 'tired of his bondage' to Eliza and 'lied for his liberty'.[86] After all, he did know the family would be back about the end of September (378, 389). They actually arrived on 1 October. Certainly Sterne lied about *something*: the question is, what? Did he say that his wife was arriving when he knew she was not due back for two months? Or did he antedate the entry to continue a sequence with the previous item? The latter is much more probable.

One of the first things Sterne did after Elizabeth and Lydia moved to York at the end of October was to take down the *Journal* and make another entry, this time under the correct date, 1 November.[87] He told Eliza what had happened about the settlement, and then made an attempt to get back into the sort of writing he had done before:

> —And now Eliza! Let me talk to thee—But What can I say, of What can I write—But the Yearnings of heart wasted with looking & wishing for thy Return—Return—Return! my dear Eliza! May heaven smooth the Way for thee to send thee safely . . . (400)

Here he reached the bottom of a leaf. He continued on the next, a clean leaf (folio 40), but wrote in small letters in the top right corner, 'to us, & soj[ourn] for Ever'. It was an odd manipulation. He probably thought that the sentence was not very good and by writing the words in this fashion he

[86] Rufus Putney, 'The Evolution of *A Sentimental Journey*', *Philological Quarterly*, XIX (1940), 349–69. See also Putney, 'Sterne's Eliza', *TLS*, 9 March 1946, p. 115.

[87] The entry appears to be historically accurate except in one detail. Sterne doctored the date of his family's return so as to make what he wrote agree with the previous entry: he said they had been home for two months when they had actually been there only one.

could more easily erase them. If so, something in him wanted to continue the *Journal*. He never did. But he was as reluctant to give it up as he had been to give up *Tristram Shandy*.

In the weeks which followed, while he finished *A Sentimental Journey*, he came to realize that he would not again take up the *Journal*. Still, he continued to talk about Eliza to Anne James (408), and when he went to London that winter he gave the *Journal* to Anne to keep until Eliza returned.[88] He must have continued to feel some tenderness toward her, but the obsession which he had called love was over.

[88] As mentioned above, Sterne speaks in the JOURNAL of leaving the MS with Anne James (356). With the *Journal*, Gibbs found two of Sterne's letters to the Jameses (LETTERS, Nos 208, 226), his draft of a letter to Daniel Draper (No. 199), and the long letter from Eliza to Anne James dated at Bombay, 15 April 1772, cited above. CROSS pointed out that such a collection must have been in the hands of Anne James and constitutes *prima facie* evidence that Sterne left the *Journal* with her. Why she did not give it to Eliza when Eliza came to London in 1777 we do not know.

8

Two Journeys 1767–1768

Race Week in 1767 was plagued with difficulties. Sterne, who no longer rode horseback, was 'set-aground' by an accident to his postillion. The man had 'bursten' two fingers when one of Sterne's pistols went off in his hand: he immediately fell to his knees and said the Lord's Prayer as far as 'hallowed be thy Name', at which point 'like a good Christian, he stopped, not remembering any more of it' (390). Perhaps Hall took Sterne to York for the races. But it was not much of a holiday. In the evenings after the balls and entertainments, he struggled, uninspired, to write entries in the *Journal*. Though he had begun the festivities boasting that he had not been so well since he left college (390), on Friday, 21 July, he began spitting blood again. When he failed to keep some appointment, one of his fox-hunting acquaintances burst into his bedchamber:

> that unfeeling brute ******* came and drew my curtains, and with a voice like a trumpet, halloo'd in my ear— z—ds, what a fine kettle of fish have you brought yourself to, Mr. S[terne]! In a faint voice, I bad him leave me, for comfort sure was never administered in so rough a manner. (392)

But the clear air of Coxwold, when he got back, soon had him on his feet. He would report in October, 'Since I got home to quietness, and temperance, and good books, and good hours, I have mended—and am now very stout' (397).

Inwardly he was less quiet. When he had first heard of Elizabeth's and Lydia's plan to return, he had written a letter welcoming them – he said – on 2 June. Now, on 24 August, when he returned from Race Week, we find him writing again and explaining, 'I am truly surprised, my dear Lydia, that my last letter has not reached thy mother, and thyself.' Their not hearing from him 'looks most unkind on my part' (391). But Sterne had learned about his letter going astray at least as early as 5 July – something he spoke about in the *Journal* (373) and in letters to the Jameses (385) and Hall (389). How are we to explain a seven-week gap between the day he knew the letter had miscarried and the day – 24 August – when he wrote another letter of welcome to replace it?[1] Something in him did not want to welcome them. In fact, so distasteful was the thought that he could not bear to talk about it: he did not speak of it to the Jameses until 2 August, even though he had written to them in July when he was fully informed of his wife's intent. He was anxious about Lydia, fearing that Elizabeth had 'debauch'd her affections',[2] and that French society had turned her into a coquette. 'I will shew you more real politesses than any you have met with in France,' he wrote, 'as mine will come warm from the heart. . . . Another thing I must desire—do not be alarmed—'tis to throw all your rouge pots into the Sorgue before you set out—I will have no rouge put on in England' (391–2). As to Elizabeth, he was in less doubt. He wrote to Anne James:

> Mrs. Sterne & my daughter are coming to stay a couple of month[s] with [me], as far as from Avignion—& the[n] return—Here's Complaisance for you [:] I went 500 Miles the last Spring, out of my Way, to pay my Wife a weeks Visit—and She is at the expence of coming post a thousand miles to return it—What a happy pair!—however, *en passant*, She takes back sixteen hundred p^{ds} into france with her——and will do me the honour, likewise to strip me of everything I have— (389)

[1] It is tempting to theorize that this seeming discrepancy might be explained by some misdating of letters, but in fact the dates of the letters to the Jameses and to Lydia can be reasonably confirmed from internal evidence, and there is no reason to question the date of that to Hall. The pertinent entries in the JOURNAL cannot be dated from internal evidence but they appear in the context of others that can be; so there is no reason to doubt the dates Sterne gave them.

[2] The phrase is erased from the JOURNAL, but legible (384). In Eliza's letter to Anne James dated from Bombay 15 April 1772, in the course of summarizing a letter of Sterne's, she says, 'the Visit Mrs Sterne meditated some time Antecedent to his Death, he most pathetically lamented, as an adventure that would wound his Peace, and greatly embarrass his Circumstances, the former on account of the Eye Witness He should be, to his Childs Affections having been Alienated from Him by the Artful Misrepresentations of her Mother': Sterne's *Works*, ed. Wilbur Cross, 12 vols, New York, 1904, VIII, 209; the entire letter on pp. 173–268.

But he had his work to keep his mind off these troubles. 'My *Sentimental Journey* goes on well,' he wrote to Becket on 3 September, 'and some Genius[e]s in the North declare it an Original work, and likely to take in all Kinds of Readers—the proof of the pudding is in the eating' (393). Actually, he had barely finished the Calais scenes.[3] The next day he packed up the manuscript and took it off to Scarborough, where he was to enjoy a brief holiday with a party of Anglo-Irishmen. He went as the guest of Dr Jemmett Browne, Bishop of Cork and Ross, who had taken a house there. Dr Browne, who would eventually be elevated to the archbishopric of Tuam, was said by Elizabeth Carter to have 'a disposition that finds a cure for grief amidst the dissipation of a gay party. . . . Never surely was there so perfectly anti-sublime a dignitary!'[4] Sterne thought of him as 'one of the best of our Bishops' (397). Sterne may have hoped to see Elizabeth Vesey at Scarborough, for she had been one of the bishop's party; but she seems to have left before he arrived. There were still two women in the party when he got there, one unidentified, the other Lady Anne Dawson, widow of Mrs Vesey's cousin Thomas Dawson. And there was a gentleman, Richard Griffith of Millicent, near Nass, County Kildare, an Irish customs official and the author of a novel, the *Triumvirate* (1764), which had been set in Scarborough.[5] They made 'so good a party', said Sterne, that 'we kept much to ourselves' (397). They drank and bathed in the health-giving waters at the top of the cliff, and then climbed down to plunge into the icy North Sea.

Sterne, who associated with few writers on the English side of the Channel, much enjoyed the company of Griffith. He had known Griffith's wife in Paris in 1762. She was the erstwhile actress, Elizabeth Griffith, now a translator of French drama. In fact, she was again in Paris at this time, making a translation of Diderot's *Père de famille* in the hope that Garrick would produce it.[6] The Griffiths made capital out of their way of living so much apart: in 1757 they had published *A Series of Genuine Letters between*

[3] Richard Griffith, whose meeting with Sterne at Scarborough is described below, said about the MS he saw, 'There is but about a Half a Volume wrote of it yet.' If this is taken literally, we would say that by 4 September Sterne was writing about Yorick in Montreuil.

[4] *Series of Letters between Mrs. Elizabeth Carter and Miss Catherine Talbot from the year 1741 to 1770*, ed. Montagu Pennington, 4 vols, 1890, III, 319–20.

[5] The identifications were made by J. M. S. Tompkins, 'Triglyph and Tristram', *TLS*, 11 July 1929, p. 558. Mrs Vesey, argued Tompkins, had left Scarborough by the time Sterne arrived. If she had been a member of the party when Sterne was there, he would have named her in his letter to the Jameses of 3 October (397–8).

[6] See Garrick's letter to her, No. 472 in the *Letters*, ed. David M. Little and George M. Kahrl, 3 vols, 1963, II, 582–3.

Henry and Frances, letters they said were written during their separations. When they brought out another edition in 1786, it contained three new letters by 'Henry' written from Scarborough in September of 1767.[7]

As Griffith described his meeting with Sterne, in these letters, there was some tension at first because Griffith had made 'strictures' upon *Tristram Shandy* in the preface to the *Triumvirate*: 'Loose expressions, in a woman, are a double vice,' he had written, 'as they offend against decency, as well as virtue; but in a clergyman, they are treble; because they hurt religion also.' But Sterne, goodnatured man that he was, had decided after reading the novel that Griffith had 'no *Inimicability*' in his nature. They were soon conversing in intimate tones. Sterne came every morning into Griffith's 'bower' and claimed the privilege of looking into his manuscripts. He dropped a tear upon reading Griffith's personal memoirs. And he showed his new friend what he was working on:

> He has communicated a Manuscript to us. . . . It is stiled a Sentimental Journey through Europe, by Yorick. It has all the Humour and Address of the best Parts of Tristram, and is quite free from the Grossness of the worst. There is but about Half a Volume wrote of it yet. He promises to spin the Idea through several Volumes, in the same chaste Way, and calls it his *Work of Redemption*; for he has but little Superstition to appropriated Expressions.

Sterne would have never dreamed how, after his death, Griffith would make use of his name. Griffith published anonymously in 1770 a work called the *Posthumous Works of a late Celebrated Genius*. He then planted the idea that it was written by Sterne: his device was to name most of the booksellers of London and to assert that they had all told him that Sterne was the author. Consequently, the book, usually under another title, *The Koran*, was included in many editions of Sterne's works. And this Griffith did, he confessed, to satisfy a wager.[8]

When Sterne had visited Harrogate in July, his thoughts had been so taken up with Eliza that he could not enjoy the company of the ladies there

[7] Augmented edition, 6 vols, 1786, V, 71–4, 82–8.

[8] Griffith planted the false attribution in the 'editor's' preface to the *Posthumous Works* (HOWES, 212), reinforced it in *Something New*, 2 vols, 1772, II, 64–70, and then confessed it on pp. 152–8: see CROSS, 520; *N&Q*, first series, VIII, 418; Alan B. Howes, *Yorick and the Critics*, New Haven, Conn., 1958, pp. 47–8. Griffith is noticed in *DNB*. The *Posthumous Works* has been reissued by the Garland Press in the series *Sterneiana*, X–XI, New York, 1975.

(381). At Scarborough in September, he enjoyed it very much. Indeed, a rumour went around London that, when the party broke up at Scarborough, Sterne had gone with them all to London. 'I dare say charity would add a little to the account,' Sterne commented drily to the Jameses, 'and give out that 'twas on the score of one, and perhaps both of the ladies—and I will excuse charity on that head, for a heart disengaged could not well have done better' (398). Sterne had grown much cooler about love. When a lovelorn friend wrote to him in November, he had replied, 'time will wear off an attachment which has taken so deep a root in your heart' (402).

With the passing of his obsession, Sterne's mood lightened. At Coxwold, when he got back, he was handed an amusing letter from a woman in London, who signed herself only 'Hannah'. He was at Newburgh Priory awaiting dinner when he sat down and whipped off a Shandean reply.

> Ever since my dear H[annah] wrote me word she was mine, more than ever woman was, I have been racking my memory to inform me where it was that you and I had that affair together.—People think that I have had many, some in body, some in mind, but as I told you before, you have had me more than any woman—therefore you must have had me, H[annah], both in mind, and in body.—Now I cannot recollect where it was, nor exactly when—it could not be the lady in Bond-street, or Grosvenor-street, or——Square, or Pall-mall.—We shall make it out, H[annah], when we meet—I impatiently long for it—
>
> Tis no matter, Hannah! I cannot stand writing to you to day—Ill make it up next post—for Dinner is upon the Table—& if I make stay L[d] F[auconberg] wont frank this—how do you do?—which parts of Tristram do you like best?—
>
> god bless you,
> Y[rs] aff L. Sterne (393)

In a letter which he wrote a few days later to Sir William Stanhope, Lord Chesterfield's brother whom he had met in Naples, we see Sterne torn between his laughter-loving, Shandean self and his self as sentimental lover. He told Stanhope about his letter to Hannah, justifying it as innocent 'badinage': 'The sporting of my pen is equal, just equal, to what I did in my boyish days, when I got astride of a stick, and gallop'd away— The truth is this—that my pen governs me—not me my pen' (394). He had not been able to resist writing a jocular letter to Hannah or telling Stanhope about it, even though it projected an image somewhat different from that of sentimental lover, of which he was proud. Sterne had written to Stanhope to advise him about whether to go to Scarborough in the off season and had talked about his visit there with the bishop's party. 'Why do you banter me so about what I wrote to you?' he now asked. 'Tho' I told you, every morning I jump'd into Venus's lap (meaning thereby the sea) was you to infer from that, that I leap'd into the ladies beds afterwards?—The body guides you—the mind me.' Stanhope had made some coarse comment about Sterne's past, to which Sterne responded, 'The past is over—and I can justify myself unto myself—can you do as much?—No faith!—"You can feel!" Aye so can my cat, when he hears a female caterwauling on the house top—but caterwauling disgusts me. I had rather raise a gentle flame, than have a different one raised in me' (394).

On 1 October Sterne took his long-tailed horses and gigantic carriage to York, where he met his wife and daughter, and brought them to Coxwold. That very day he sat down to write a letter of thanks to Panchaud for his kindness to Elizabeth and Lydia: 'my Lydia seems transported with the sight of me.—Nature, dear P[anchaud], breathes in all her composition; and except a little vivacity—which is a fault in the world we live in—I am fully content with her mother's care of her' (396). To the Jameses he wrote, 'My wife and daughter arrived here last night from France.—My girl has return'd an elegant accomplish'd little slut—my wife—but I hate to praise my wife—'tis as much as decency will allow to praise my daughter' (398).

Shandy Hall seems to have remained peaceful during the month they stayed there. In the final entry of the *Journal*, written after Elizabeth and Lydia had moved to York, Sterne bragged that he had conquered his wife 'by humanity & Generosity—& she leaves me, more than half in Love wth me.' Lest this displease Eliza, he tacked on a small lie: 'her age, as she now confesses [is] ten Years more, than I thought—being on the edge of sixty' (399). Elizabeth had just celebrated a birthday at Shandy Hall in October: she had turned fifty-three and was a year younger than her husband.

Lydia had bloomed. She would be twenty in December, a 'dear good creature—affectionate, and most elegant in body, and mind—she is all heaven could give me in a daughter' (400). So attractive was she that sometimes, when talking about her, phrases from the *Journal to Eliza* came into his head, Lydia having replaced Eliza. 'My heart bleeds', he told a friend, '. . . when I think of parting with my child—'twill be like the separation of body—and equal to nothing but what passes at that tremendous moment' (406) – the very words he had used to describe his parting from Eliza.[9] Actually, Lydia, who had been caring for her mother in a foreign country since she was sixteen, was a strong woman, a bit vain, and prone to fits of temper. It was she, probably, who negotiated the financial agreement Sterne reached with his wife and child.

He was to give Lydia £2000 from the sale of his estate for the purchase of an annuity (399–400), no doubt a joint annuity with rights to the survivor, as he had said earlier (347, 355). The income from the annuity he estimated, perhaps too optimistically, would be £200 per annum. Beyond that, he would give to Elizabeth during her lifetime an alimony, but for how much is in doubt. At one point, in the *Journal*, he had said he was prepared to give her 100 guineas (348). Now, in the final entry to the *Journal*, he spoke of 300 guineas (399). One is forced to question this. The income from all of Sterne's preferments, after the expenses of curates and substitutes, which he could not do without, came to something like £250. It seems unlikely that Sterne, who had always taken the gentlemanly position that he wrote not to be fed, but to be famous,[10] would make himself dependent upon his writing. So one guesses that the alimony agreed upon was £100 or £150. Whatever it came to, Sterne concluded his talks about money without any anger. He set to work collecting and bundling up his old letters and copies of letters to make it easier for Lydia when she came to publish them.[11] And he told a sentimental story about her generosity. When she and her mother were preparing to move to York, he pulled out his purse,

> and offered her ten guineas for her private pleasures—her answer was pretty, and affected me too much. 'No, my dear papa, our expences of

[9] JOURNAL, 6 July (374). On 7 December, he also wrote, 'I live for the sake of my girl, and with her sweet light burthen in my arms, I could get up fast the hill of preferment, if I chose it—but without my Lydia, if a mitre was offered me, it would sit uneasy upon my brow' (406), a paraphrase of what he had written to Eliza in the JOURNAL for 3 August: 'with thy sweet light Burden in my Arms, I could get up fast the hill of preferment, if I chose it' (386)

[10] LETTERS, 90; repeated in TRISTRAM SHANDY, 446.

[11] The bundle came to light at Montpellier in 1895 or 1896 and was purchased by J. P. Morgan, who had the letters bound in a guardbook along with some others in his collection – a volume which has since come to be called the Sterne *Letter Book*. It is housed at the Morgan Library. Sterne's wrapper for the original bundle bore a note listing for his wife and daughter the friends to whom he had sent other letters – published as No. 225 in LETTERS, 407–8.

coming from France may have straiten'd you—I would rather put an hundred guineas in your pocket than take ten out of it'—I burst into tears— (406–7).

In any event, Sterne took no immediate steps to sell his estate, but put the whole matter off until he had published his book.

With the family settled in York, Sterne went back to *A Sentimental Journey*. 'I am in earnest at my sentimental work,' he told a friend in November, 'and intend being in town soon after Christmas' (402).

A Sentimental Journey is no more a record of Sterne's travels on the continent than was Volume VII of *Tristram Shandy*. To be sure, one can find some links with Sterne's known experiences. Yorick crosses into France without a passport during wartime, as did Sterne (192). He stays at Dessin's inn at Calais (87), sits at table with David Hume (122), and is entertained in Paris by Popelinière, the *fermier général* (262). The two *Encyclopèdistes* of the Paris scenes are readily recognizable as Sterne's friends Diderot and Morellet (265). But we do not know whether the specific details of these incidents have any basis in Sterne's history. We *do* know that Sterne could fictionalize an experience so as to make of it something new: in 1761 he borrowed £20 from David Garrick before leaving for France; in the book, Yorick has the money thrust upon him by 'Eugenius', that is, by Hall (195).

Yorick, a sickly parson with a weakness for distressed women, is but another of Sterne's idealized self-portraits. Sterne had, of course, painted himself as Yorick in Volume I of *Tristram Shandy*, and this narrator lays claim to that identity. But it has frequently been pointed out that the personalities of the two Yoricks do not cohere at all points, the Yorick of Volume I being much closer to a tragic figure than the cheerful narrator of the *Journey*.[12]

The controlling idea of *A Sentimental Journey*, as we have seen, may have come to Sterne in the spring of 1766 when he called upon d'Holbach and his philosophical friends. They must have been talking about a book which had just appeared in London, Tobias Smollett's *Travels through France and Italy*, which had stringently criticized French culture. Sterne would have read the

[12] Stout in a note to SENTIMENTAL JOURNEY, 192, points out that the *Journey* takes place in 1762, whereas Yorick in Volume I dies in 1748. Stout raises the question whether Sterne intended the reader to see in this discrepancy 'a wild, Shandean jest'.

review of it in the *Gazette littéraire de l'Europe* written by a newcomer to the group, François-Jean, called the Chevalier Chastellux.[13] Chastellux attacked Smollett for 'exposing our nudity in the eyes of the nations with an unexampled inhumanity'. (Sterne would borrow the image for the *Journey*, 216–17.) He took Smollett to task for his remarks on the *droit d'aubaine*, the *petit-maîtres*, the Venus de Medici, and numerous other matters which reappear in Sterne's book. Sterne would have been particularly struck with Chastellux's comment that Smollett had set out on his journey 'consumed with humour and spleen',[14] for Sterne had recently, in Volume VII of *Tristram Shandy*, been writing about the effects of spleen upon travellers in France.

So in *A Sentimental Journey* Sterne painted Smollett as

> The learned SMELFUNGUS, [who] travelled from Boulogne to Paris—from Paris to Rome—and so on—but he set out with the spleen and jaundice, and every object he pass'd by was discoloured or distorted—He wrote an account of them, but 'twas nothing but the account of his miserable feelings. (116)

By contrast, we have Yorick,

> who interests his heart in every thing, and who, having eyes to see, what time and chance are perpetually holding out to him as he journeyeth on his way, misses nothing he can *fairly* lay his hands on.—
>
> . . . the pleasure of the experiment has kept my sense, and the best part of my blood awake, and laid the gross to sleep.
>
> I pity the man who can travel from *Dan* to *Beersheba*, and cry, 'Tis all barren—and so it is; and so is all the world to him who will not cultivate the fruits it offers. I declare, said I, clapping my hands chearily together, that was I in a desart, I would find out wherewith in it to call forth my affections. (144–15)

[13] Vol. VIII, 365–84. The antedating of this issue, Chastellux's authorship, the reissue of the review and the evidence for continued French anger with Smollett are discussed above in the text and notes to Chapter 6.

[14] Chastellux's assumption that Smollett's narrator can be identified with Smollett the author, while understandable for his time, is not acceptable in modern criticism. Robert D. Spector, 'Smollett's Traveler', in *Tobias Smollett: Bicentennial Essays Presented to Lewis Knapp*, ed. G. S. Rousseau and P.-G. Boucé, New York, 1971, pp. 231–46, argues convincingly that Smollett's narrator is a persona.

Sterne's two travel narratives differ in one important respect: Volume VII of *Tristram Shandy* represents a quest for health; the *Journey* a quest for understanding. Yorick seeks to understand cultures and people, but ultimately himself. He has come, he explains to the Count de B****, not to be well fed or entertained, but 'to spy the *nakedness* of their hearts, and through the different disguises of customs, climates, and religion, find out what is good in them, to fashion my own by.' He will not bother to look at French art or architecture, for he conceives 'every fair being as a temple, and would rather enter in, and see the original drawings and loose sketches hung up in it, than the transfiguration of Raphael itself (217–19).

It may seem strange that this should be written by a man who had begun to complain about French manners within months of his first arrival in France in 1762 and who, while he was writing his new novel, was filled with anxieties that his daughter might have been corrupted by French *politesse*. But the *Journey*, being a work of the imagination, need not reflect the likes and dislikes of the author. Besides, the discrepancy is not as great as appears on the surface. Sterne distrusted the French upper classes, the polite world. He made one clear exception: he continued to feel much affection for the d'Holbach circle. The novel reflects his preferences: Sterne is hard on the ladies and gentlemen of the Paris salons, but compliments the urbanity and generosity of the Count de B****, who represents Claude de Thiard, Comte de Bissy, a man of letters and member of the Academy. The gentlewoman Yorick most admires, Madame de L***, is from Brussels. Moreover, the novel is primarily concerned with Yorick's relationships with common folk, toward whom Sterne may have been less critical.

There is much sweetness in *A Sentimental Journey*, in the trust with which Madame de L*** accepts Yorick's advances, in the exchange of snuffboxes with the monk in token of their friendship, in Yorick's concern for his servant, La Fleur, and La Fleur's loyalty to him, in his sympathy with the mad peasant girl, Maria, and the lesson about worship he learns from a generous family of peasants. While Sterne was working on the novel, he wrote to Sir William Stanhope, 'my Sentimental Journey will, I dare say, convince you that my feelings are from the heart, and that that heart is not of the worst of molds—praised be God for my sensibility!' (395–6).

But the *Journey* is also a comedy. While he was writing it, Sterne seems to have been carrying on a correspondence with the elusive Hannah, the woman whose letter from London had sparked such a playful reply. In November, Sterne sent some sort of parcel to Hannah and her sister, Fanny, together with this comment on his new book:

> —but I have something else for you, which I am fabricating at a great rate, & that is my Journey, which shall make you cry as much as ever it made me laugh—or I'll give up the Business of sentimental writing—& write to the Body
>
> —that is Hannah! what I am doing in writing to you—but you are a *good Body*, & that's worth half a Score *mean Souls*. (401)

Again and again, Yorick, in his sentimental quest, falls into one ridiculous posture or another. On his first day in France, his initial hostility toward a mendicant monk serves to demonstrate that he is more taken with the idea of 'sentimental commerce' than with the reality of it. He gets past the difficulty, but manœuvres the situation so that a pretty woman he has seen will notice him. Instead of giving generously to the beggars who await him outside an inn, he ends up buying their flattery. Time and again the story turns out to be, not a simple demonstration of the goodness of the human heart, not sentimentality, but a sentimental comedy in which a cheerful English parson bungles through France trying to demonstrate an article of his creed, the goodness of mankind, but finding altogether too much flattery, greed and lust in himself and others.[15]

There is, moreover, a vein of comic eroticism that runs through *A Sentimental Journey*. Yorick becomes a sentimental lover to Madame de L***, only to have the falsity of his position exposed by La Fleur. He tries to flirt with the mistress of a Parisian glove shop, who makes a fool of him. He is almost seduced by a *fille de chambre*. The entire story ends in a fabliau, 'The Case of Delicacy', in which Yorick must share a room in an inn with a gentlewoman and her maid. Sterne wrote to George Macartney, his companion from Parisian days, now Sir George, Knight, envoy to Russia:

> I am going to ly-in; being at Christmas at my full reckoning—and unless what I shall bring forth is not *press'd* to death by these devils of printers, I shall have the honour of presenting to you a *couple of as clean brats* as ever chaste brain conceiv'd—they are frolicksome too, *mais cela n'empeche pas*— (405)

Yet Sterne thought of his new book as his 'work of redemption', as he told Richard Griffith. To Anne James he wrote in November,

[15] A full development of this argument is in STERNE'S COMEDY.

> My Sentimental Journey will please Mrs. J[ames], and my Lydia—I can answer for those two. It is a subject which works well, and suits the frame of mind I have been in for some time past—I told you my design in it was to teach us to love the world and our fellow creatures better than we do—so it runs most upon those gentler passions and affections, which aid so much to it. (400–1)

The problem for modern students is how to reconcile such a statement with scenes of Yorick feeling the pulse of the *grisette* or buckling the upheld shoe of the *fille de chambre*.

The answer probably lies in the attitude which Sterne's public took toward its clergy. The original readers of the novel, already familiar with the figure of Yorick, from *Tristram Shandy*, did not have to be told that he was in holy orders. The half-dozen shirts and one extra pair of black silk breeches which Yorick packs – 'the coat I have on, said I, looking at the sleeve, will do' (65) – told them that he would travel in the garb of his profession and not follow the practice of John Horne-Tooke and other clergymen who as soon as they were across the Channel shed their black to put on the colours of the gay world.[16] Yorick will be recognized as a *ministre* and must maintain the role. Indeed, he thinks like a low-church Anglican: the monk's horn snuffbox he will use 'as I would the instrumental parts of my religion, to help my mind on to something better' (101). Biblical phrases spring easily to his lips, as well as one aphorism which is not biblical, but sounds so authentic that it has served as text for numerous incautious sermonists: '*God tempers the wind*, said Maria, to the shorn lamb' (272).[17] The 'ironic benediction', as it has been called, which Yorick pronounces upon the two travel writers, Smelfungus and Mundungus, not only sounds like a sermon but in fact was paraphrased from one of Sterne's, 'Our Conversation in Heaven'.[18]

> Peace be to them! if it is to be found; but heaven itself, was it possible to get there with such tempers, would want objects to give it—every

[16] In a letter to Wilkes, 25 May 1767, Horne-Tooke spoke about his elegant coats and suits which he wore abroad but left in Paris when he returned to England: BL, Add. MSS 30869, fol. 124.

[17] CROSS, 476–70. Gerald P. Mander, 'The Shorn Lamb', *TLS*, 17 July 1937, p. 528, suggests that Sterne took the line from a French proverb, one which was used in a children's card game. For the numerous biblical phrases and images in SENTIMENTAL JOURNEY, see Stout's index under 'Bible'.

[18] See Stout's note in SENTIMENTAL JOURNEY, 338–42.

> gentle spirit would come flying upon the wings of Love to hail their arrival—Nothing would the souls of Smelfungus and Mundungus hear of, but fresh anthems of joy, fresh raptures of love, and fresh congratulations of their common felicity—I heartily pity them: they have brought up no faculties for this work; and was the happiest mansion in heaven to be allotted to Smelfungus and Mundungus, they would be so far from being happy, that the souls of Smelfungus and Mundungus would do penance there to all eternity. (120)

In the salons of Paris among deists and atheists, Yorick champions orthodoxy (265), but among the Bourbonnais peasants, when he sees '*Religion* mixing in the dance', he admits the inferiority of traditional forms: 'A chearful and contented mind', explained the old man, 'was the best sort of thanks to heaven that an illiterate peasant could pay——Or a learned prelate either, said I' (284). Yorick may think of God in romantic terms as the 'great SENSORIUM of the world' (278), but his Christianity is traditional in that he believes all virtues are the gift of God, the 'eternal fountain of our feelings' (277). Humour too is a grace; though Sterne did not say so in the *Journey*, he said it in a letter written while the novel was in press. 'It is not in the power of any one to taste humor,' he wrote to Dr John Eustace, 'however he may wish it—'tis the gift of God' (411). Paradoxically – but the paradox lies at the heart of Christianity – though a man cannot acquire virtues by his own effort, but must accept what God sees fit to grant, yet he will be judged for the use of them. Much as Yorick would like to attribute his faults to the tides of the passions and say that the outcome had to do with the phases of the moon, he must take responsibility for his actions (70), even the action of writing a travel book: 'God is my record (before whose tribunal I must one day come and give an account of this work)' (84).

The eroticism which runs through *A Sentimental Journey* did not offend Sterne's public because it did not expect its clergy to be free of sexual desire: it asked only that a parson *try* to do the right thing. Most of the comedy arises from Yorick's attempts to overcome temptation or at the least to respond to a situation in a way worthy of his profession. Almost every adventure involves him in debate with himself. Should he give alms to the monk when his own church disapproves? Is it right to pay court to Madame de L*** when he has sworn fidelity to Eliza? To which of sixteen beggars is he to give one of the eight coins he has in his hand? Should his servant have

Sundays free? Does his flirting with a woman who keeps a glove shop and has actually allowed him to count her pulse oblige him to buy a pair of gloves? Even when none fits? Yorick does not always come off well in these debates, but then no member of the Church of England ever thought there was such a thing as a Christian free from sin. 'But what were the temptations, (as I write not to apologize for the weaknesses of my heart in this tour,—but to give an account of them)—shall be described with the same simplicity, with which I felt them' (90).[19]

Sterne had a knack for intimacy, in his letters, his life and his fiction. His letters to his bankers, Robert Foley and Isaac Panchaud, read as though written to brothers. His behaviour to a comparative stranger, Alessandro Verri, the Italian historian, was described by Verri after he had called upon Sterne at Bond Street in January 1767. 'He gave me some chocolate, and a thousand caresses,' Verri told his brother; 'he took off my coat wet with the rain and spread it over a chair; he embraced me, he pressed my hand and led me to the fire.' When Sterne saw Verri again a few days later at a public assembly, he stepped up to him, embraced him, and began a conversation whispered in his ear.[20] This amicable, familiar manner Sterne passed to his creation, Parson Yorick, not only in the way he candidly opens his heart, his mind and his bedroom door, but in his very speech. 'The jerky, disconnected sentences are as rapid and it would seem as little under control as the phrases that fall from the lips of a brilliant talker.' So said Virginia Woolf in her memorable commentary upon the style of *A Sentimental Journey*:

> The very punctuation is that of speech, not writing, and brings the sound, the associations, of the speaking voice in with it. The order of the ideas, their suddenness and irrelevancy, is more true to life than to literature. There is a privacy in this intercourse which allows things to slip out unreproved that would have been in doubtful taste had they been spoken in public. Under the influence of this extraordinary style the book becomes semi-transparent. The usual ceremonies and

[19] Robert Uphaus, 'Sentiment and Spleen: Travels with Sterne and Smollett', *Centennial Review*, XV (1971), 406–21, argues that Sterne's acceptance of and resignation to life is a Christian attitude and a valid criticism of Smollett's misanthropy. But Smollett, Uphaus argues, learned a lesson from Sterne and wrote in *Humphry Clinker* a book about acceptance and love.

[20] Giovanni Rabizzani, *Sterne in Italia*, Rome, 1920, pp. 34–7.

conventions which keep reader and writer at arm's length disappear. We are as close to life as we can be.[21]

Sterne was quite confident *A Sentimental Journey* would redeem his reputation. 'I have long been a sentimental being,' he wrote to a nobleman at the end of November, 'whatever your Lordship may think to the contrary.'

—The world has imagined, because I wrote Tristram Shandy, that I was myself more Shandean than I really ever was . . . I hope my book will please you, my Lord, and then my labour will not be totally in vain. If it is not thought a chaste book, mercy on them that read it, for they must have warm imaginations indeed! (402–3).

Constant interruptions had delayed Sterne's progress with the work. As he told Macartney on 3 December, 'My wife is come to pay me a sentimental visit as far as from Avignon—and the *politesses* arising from such a proof of her urbanity, has robb'd me of a month's writing, or I had been in town now' (405). Within days of writing this, he fell sick again. He told the Jameses at the end of the month, 'I was cast down myself with a fever, & bleeding at my lungs, which had confined me to my Room three weeks' (408). He lost all hope of finishing the two other volumes he had planned. He had said in the summer that it would be unscrupulous 'to break faith with the world' and not publish all he had contracted for with his subscribers. 'Great Authors make no scruple of it—but if they are great Authors—I'm sure they are little men' (373). But his condition had deteriorated terribly in December: 'I am worn down to a Shadow.' When he would reach London and come to Gerrard Street, he warned the Jameses, 'Youl[l] see me enter like a Ghost—so I tell you before hand, not to be frighten'd (408–9). He must have decided to wait no longer, but to publish what he had, because he feared he might die.

By 28 December he was in York to meet Hall, so weak 'both in body & mind' that he could write nothing better than a 'sad Scratch of a Letter' to tell the Jameses he was on his way to town. The friends set off on 30 or 31 December and toasted the new year, 1768, in some inn along the road.

Hall was coming to town to see another book through the press. His

[21] Introduction to the 1928 World's Classics edition of *A Sentimental Journey*, vi–vii.

Makarony Fables appeared in late February and was reviewed in the *Critical Review* and *Monthly Review* for March. Most of these fables, more of less in the mode of Aesop, are political satires, but one, 'The Black Bird', satirizes the church. Its hero is Sterne. Hall, who usually explained his allegories in the body of his poems, indicated that the owl who is engaged in gloomy vespers represents primarily the church of Rome, but not exclusively, for 'Even here there are some holy men / Would fain lead people by the nose.' Both branches of the church, then, are implicated in Hall's profane treatment of the Eucharistic rite as a ragout tossed up by a 'a sacerdotal Cook' 'to fill the belly of your soul'. Sterne is seen as a blackbird who interrupts the vespers of the owl by his singing and whistling which 'set nature in a gayer light'. The poem concludes:

My good Lord Bishop, Mr. Dean,
You shall get nothing by your spite;
Tristram shall whistle at your spleen,
And put Hypocrisy to flight.

No doubt Sterne would rather not have been put in such a light. His quarrels with the church had long been laid to rest. He was about to publish *A Sentimental Journey*, in which he would represent himself as Yorick, the quiet champion of religion, and in the story of Yorick's friendship with the monk make a moving plea for religious tolerance. Sterne seems to have made it a principle never to interfere with Hall's writing career, but he may have been getting back at his atheistic friend in the *Journey* when he represented Eugenius's love for Yorick as divinely inspired. In the passage about God as the 'great SENSORIUM of the world! which vibrates, if a hair of our heads but falls upon the ground,' he said, 'Touch'd with thee, Eugenius draws my curtain when I languish—hears my tale of symptoms, and blames the weather for the disorder of his nerves' (278). Only days after this would appear, Hall would weep by his friend's beside for the last time.

In London Sterne began the old round of business arrangements and social engagements. He had hardly settled himself in Bond Street when he had a note from Anne James asking if he was going to use his ticket for the Soho concert on Sunday. He was not a subscriber this year, but he would see what he could do. Thereupon he went on a search: 'I have been at a Secretary of State to get one [Lord Shelburne]—have been upon one knee to my friends Sir G[eorge] M[acartney], Mr. Lascelles—and Mr. Fitzmaurice—without mentioning five more—I believe I could as soon get you a place at court' (410). He saw the Jameses often and, when their invitation clashed with other arrangements he had made, he felt free to 'glide like a shadow uninvited to Gerrard Street' (409). He took up again the lessons in painting he had begun to give Anne the year before and begged from a mutual friend an engraving of cows for her to copy (412).

He seems to have been able to serve Anne James, but he was not at first strong enough to enter fully into the old life. Lord Belasyse wrote home to Coxwold on 12 January, 'Poor Sterne, I was with [him] this morning, he looks more miserable than ever, complains, & his spirits tho' better, than one would imagine, not so lively as they are in general.'[22] But he rallied, and a month later was keeping several engagements in one day: when he wrote to a friend, probably Laurence Sulivan of the East India Company, to arrange for them to go together to the Jameses, he explained that he would be having breakfast that day with Topham Beauclerk and was then 'engaged for an hour' with Lord Ossory (412). By mid-February he was 'tyed down neck and heels' with engagements every day and 'exhausted with a room full of company every morning till dinner' (414). He knew he was running a risk. In a letter thanking Sulivan for some prints, he said, 'if I recover from my ill state of health, and live to revisit Coxwould this summer, I will decorate my study with them' (412). Suffering from no specific complaint, but a general weakness, he decided to ask Elizabeth Montagu for a bottle of some sort of tonic he knew she kept. She obligingly sent it round by a servant – the first known contact between Sterne and Mrs Montagu in three years. 'Thanks, thanks—my dear and kind Cosin, for the domestick supply—it is all I wanted—and this bottle alone will be enough to restore me to what I have lost—w^{h} is a little strength—which I usually regain in as short time, as I lost it.' He assured her he was 'absolutely this morning free from every bodily distemper that is to be read of in the catalogue of human infirmities' (414). So the round of social visits continued, as did the hospitality at Bond Street.

Sir Joshua Reynolds noted in his appointment book engagements with Sterne at 9 a.m. on 23 February on and 4 p.m. on 1 March, and it is usually supposed Sterne began sitting for another portrait. But in the dead of winter 9 a.m. and 4 p.m. are not good hours for light in London. These may have been engagements for breakfast and dinner: Reynolds in his book did not

[22] Lord Belasyse to Lord Fauconberg, 12 January 1768, in WOMBWELL PAPERS.

distinguish between business and social appointments. In any event, no second portrait of Sterne has been convincingly identified.[23]

In the midst of Sterne's busy preparations for the book, which he hoped to get out in mid-February, there arrived a letter from America which reminded him of his status as an international figure. Dr John Eustace, a physician who so admired *Tristram Shandy* that he had named his house in Wilmington, North Carolina, 'Shandy Hall', had sent Sterne a curious walking stick, once the property of the governor, Arthur Dobbs. The odd feature of this stick was its several handles: 'a piece of Shandean statuary', Dr Eustace called it (404).

> Your walking stick is in no sense more *shandaic* [wrote Sterne] than in that of its having *more handles than one*—The parallel breaks only in this, that in using the stick, every one will take the handle which suits his convenience. In *Tristram Shandy*, the handle is taken which suits their passions, their ignorance or sensibility. (411)

For the first time Sterne complained about his reading public – 'the *herd* of the *world*.. . . It is too much to write books and find heads to understand them.' The praise of *Tristram Shandy* which most pleased him came from unusually intelligent readers at home and abroad:

> The world, however, seems to come into a better temper about them, the people of genius here being, to a man, on its side, and the reception it has met with in France, Italy and Germany, hath engag'd one part of the world to give it a second reading, and the other part of it, in order to be on the strongest side, have at length agreed to speak well of it too. (411)

Perhaps it was not very generous of Sterne to categorize those who held out against the book as 'Hypocrites and Tartufe's', but his appraisal of his place as a favourite of intellectuals and men of genius anticipates two centuries of reception of *Tristram Shandy*. And it is curious that Sterne should have been told how men of letters in Germany appreciated the book.[24] He had not visited that part of the world, yet he seems to have known how much the

[23] Reynolds's appointment book, Burlington House; *EMY*, 305–6, 315–16.

[24] Bernhard Fabian, 'Tristram Shandy and Parson Yorick among some German Greats', WINGED SKULL, 194–209. The study of Sterne's reception in Germany is thorough: Fabian cities four book-length studies written in the twentieth century.

book was admired by such men as Moses Mendelssohn, Herder, Wieland and Lessing.

Sterne concluded his letter to Dr Eustace with one of his rare comments outside the novels about his philosophy as a writer and humorist: the 'true feeler' of humour 'always brings half the entertainment along with him. His own ideas are only call'd forth by what he reads, and the vibrations within, so entirely correspond with those excited, 'tis like reading *himself* and not the *book*' (411).

At the time he wrote to Dr Eustace, Sterne was busily engaged in reading and revising the printer's proofs of *A Sentimental Journey*. He was a meticulous editor, making hundreds of small changes – as one sees by comparing the holograph manuscript, from which the printer set up the proofs, with the book as finally printed.[25]

The day before the new novel appeared, Sterne in a state of high excitement was at the bindery getting a few advance copies and scratching off hasty notes to the friends he was sending them to, among them Elizabeth Montagu (415). These volumes, he said in a final comment, made to Sulivan, 'will take with the generality—the women will read this book in the parlour, and Tristram in the bed-chamber' (412)

Publication was announced by an advertisement in the *Public Advertiser* for 27 February 1768:

This Day is Published,
(The First and Second Volumes, Price 5s sewed)
A SENTIMENTAL JOURNEY through France and Italy.
by Mr. YORICK.
Printed for T. Becket and P. A. DeHondt, in the Strand.
Subscribers Books will be delivered as above.
Of whom may be had, 1. The Life and Opinions
of Tristram Shandy, 9 vols, 18s sewed. 2. The Ser-
mons of Mr. Yorick. 4 vols. 10s sewed.

When subscribers came to pick up their books, they found a loose page at the front of the first volume which carried the following notice:

[25] Sterne's holograph for Volume I survives at the BL: Egerton MS 1610; that for Volume II is lost. Before he left York or shortly after arriving in London, Sterne had a copy made of his MSS for both volumes, and the copy survives at the Morgan Library. A close study of these MSS reveals much about Sterne's late revisions. See Stout's discussion in SENTIMENTAL JOURNEY, 49–57, 295–307, and his textual notes.

'Advertisement.

The Author begs leave to acknowledge to his Subscribers, that they have a further claim upon him for Two Volumes more than these delivered to them now, and which nothing but ill health could have prevented him, from having ready along with these.

'The Work will be compleated and delivered to the Subscribers early the next Winter.'

Sir Joshua Reynolds erased and wrote over an appointment with Sterne for 9 March. Sterne had fallen ill and was confined to his bed. The next day he was bled three times, and on 11 March was blistered (418). A nurse was brought in, and Mrs Fourmantel's girl, Molly, must have helped. 'The people ab^t me oppress me but with their attention' (416). He wrote to Lydia, 'The want of health bows me down . . . this vile influenza—be not alarm'd, I think I shall get the better of it—and shall be with you both the first of May, and if I escape 'twill not be for a long period, my child—unless a quiet retreat and peace of mind can restore me' (417).

Some busybody had written to Lydia and Elizabeth telling them that Sterne was preparing a new will in which he was going to leave Lydia, should Elizabeth predecease him, in the custody of Eliza Draper. Sterne was 'astonish'd'; it was not to Mrs Draper he would leave her, but to Mrs James.

No, my Lydia! tis a lady, whose virtues I wish thee to imitate, that I shall entrust my girl to—I mean that friend whom I have so often talk'd and wrote about—from her you will learn to be an affectionate wife, a tender mother, and a sincere friend—and you cannot be intimate with her, without her pouring some part of the milk of human kindness into your breast, which will serve to check the heat of your own temper, which you partake in a small degree of. . . .But I think, my Lydia, that thy mother will survive me—do not deject her spirits with thy apprehensions on my account.—I have sent you a necklace, buckles, and the same to your mother.—My girl cannot form a wish that is in the power of her father, that he will not gratify her in—and I cannot in justice be less kind to thy mother. . . . I wish tho' I had thee to nurse me—but I am deny'd that.—Write to me twice a week, at least.—God bless thee, my child, and believe me ever, ever thy

Affectionate father,

L. S. (417–18)

Since he talked in the future tense about what arrangements he would make in a will, he clearly had none as yet.

A letter arrived from Elizabeth Montagu,[26] the 'seasonable benignity' of which 'extorted, what neither Sickness or Affliction have ever had force to do, from me—need I tell you,—that this was a couple of tears' (415).

> The Account, dear Lady, which has interested You so humanely, is a point I cannot contest or deny—tho' I ever make a mystery of these evils—I am ill—very ill—Yet I feel my Existence Strongly, and something like revelation along with it, which tells, I shall not dye—but live——& yet any other man w^{d} set his house in order—(416)

What he wanted to be thinking about was nothing so serious. 'When I die,' he told Mrs Montagu in French, 'They will put my name on the list of those heroes who [like Scarron] died joking.' He had begun again to write—a 'romance', perhaps something to include in the next volume of the *Journey*.

> O! I envy Scarron—tho' I lye most abominably—for when y^{r} kind Billet came in—I was writing a Romance, in truth, & which, as it is most comic—if my Sickness continues but 7 days—I shall finish——tell me the reason, why Cervantes could write so fine and humourous a Satyre, in the melancholly regions of a damp prison—or why Scarron in bodily pain—or why the Author of the Moyen de parvenir (a vile,—but Witty book)—under the bondage of a poor *Canonical*— [27] (416)

His words re-echo what he had written to Lord Rockingham eight years before when he had sent him copies of the first two volumes of *Tristram Shandy*; he had told Rockingham how his comic book had been written 'in affliction; & under a constant uneasiness of mind', and had spoken of

[26] Curtis places this letter before that to Lydia, but I would argue that they should be reversed. Lydia speaks of the reception of the book in York, where it was advertised on 1 March. She could hardly have written earlier than the third; so Sterne's reply may have been written about 6 March. A later date is unlikely because in the letter to Anne James, dated by Curtis, I think correctly, 15 March, Sterne speaks of having written this particular letter to Lydia 'a fortnight ago' (419). Though eleven days is not a fortnight, it might seem like one to Sterne. The letter to Elizabeth Montagu, however, seems to have been written under a threat of death and therefore later.

[27] François Béroalde de Verville, author of *Le Moyen de parvenir* (1599), held a canonry at Saint-Gratien de Tours. Dr John Ferriar knew of a copy of his book in which Sterne had written, '*L. Sterne, a Paris, 8 livres*': CURTIS, 417.

Cervantes writing from a prison and Scarron in the 'pain & Anguish' of illness.[28] He went on to Mrs Montagu, 'there is either an Obliquity in Nature or some unknown Spring only sufferd to act within us, when, we are thus in the house of Bondage——excuse a weak brain for all this—and to strengthen this poor Machine, send me, gentl[e] Lady, at Y^{r} Leisure a very few Jellies.'

On 15 March he wrote to Anne James, having to stop and rest his hand a dozen times to get through the letter. 'The physician says I am better—God knows, for I feel myself sadly wrong, and shall, if I recover, be a long while of gaining strength.' Commodore James had been to see him the day before, and he had asked him to come again, 'for perhaps I have not many days, or hours, to live—I want to ask a favour of him, if I find myself worse.' Perhaps he was preparing a will.

> —my spirits are fled—'tis a bad omen—do not weep my dear Lady—your tears are too precious to shed for me—bottle them up, and may the cork never be drawn.—Dearest, kindest, gentlest, and best of women! may health, peace, and happiness, prove your handmaids.—If I die, cherish the remembrance of me, and forget the follies which you so often condemn'd—which my heart, not my head betray'd me into. Should my child, my Lydia want a mother, may I hope you will (if she is left parentless) take her to your bosom?—You are the only woman on earth I can depend upon for such a benevolent action.—I wrote to her a fortnight ago, and told her what I trust she will find in you.—Mr. J[ames] will be a father to her—he will protect her from every insult, for he wears a sword which he has served his country with, and which he would know how to draw out of the scabbard in defence of innocence—Commend me to him—as I now commend you to that Being who takes under his care the good and kind part of the world.—Adieu—all grateful thanks to you and Mr. J[ames].
>
> Your poor affectionate friend,
>
> L. Sterne (419)

After that he was too weak to write.

But his room was still full of company. 'I am never alone,' he had said in his letter to Lydia; 'The kindness of my friends is ever the same' (418). On

[28] Appendix I.

16 March an unidentified Yorkshire parson called. As he went through the bagmaker's shop, two young women came down the stairs—laughing, one imagines, since one of them was probably Hannah. In any event, when he entered Sterne's room, a lady withdrew to the window. Sterne spoke to her from the bed, using the name of Hannah's sister: 'Do not go out, Fanny; this is an old friend.' 'I am glad you are so carefully attended,' said the parson. 'Had you come sooner,' Sterne replied, 'instead of three, this lady and the two you met on the stairs, you might have seen thirteen.'[29]

'Mr Hall', Lord Belasyse wrote to Lord Fauconberg, 'attended him throughout his illness.'[30]

Sterne died on Friday, 18 March 1768, at 4 p.m. In all probability it was a painless death: his disintegrated lungs had filled with fluid, bringing oxygen starvation, often a euphoric condition, and finally heart failure.[31] The death was witnessed by John Macdonald, the servant of John Craufurd, whose memoir we have had occasion to cite.

> About his time Mr. Sterne, the celebrated author, was taken ill at the silk-bag shop in Old Bond Street. He was sometimes called 'Tristram Shandy' and sometimes 'Yorick'—a very great favourite of the gentlemen's. One day my master had company to dinner who were speaking about him; the Duke of Roxburgh, the Earl of March, the Earl of Ossory, the Duke of Grafton, Mr. Garrick, Mr. Hume, and a Mr. James. 'John,' said my master, 'go and inquire how Mr. Sterne is to-day.' I went, returned, and said: 'I went to Mr. Sterne's lodging; the mistress opened the door; I inquired how he did. She told me to go up to the nurse. I went into the room, and he was just a-dying. I waited ten minutes; but in five he said: "*Now it is come.*" He put up his hands as if to stop a blow, and died in a minute.' The gentlemen were all very sorry, and lamented him very much.[32]

'I find Mrs. Montagu, has undertaken Mr Sterne's affairs,' wrote Lord Belasye. She did not do so personally, of course, but sent a man who had

[29] Eight years later this clergyman told his experience to Daniel Watson, Vicar of Leake in the North Riding, and Watson in turn wrote about it on 15 June 1776 to George Whately, treasurer of the Foundling Hospital: published in the *Monthly Repository of Theology and General Literature*, III (1808), 12.

[30] Dated 19 March 1768: in WOMBWELL PAPERS.

[31] Dr Maureen Strafford of Harvard Medical School has advised me about the probable causes of death.

[32] *Memoirs of an Eighteenth-Century Footman*, [1790], ed. Sir E. Denison Ross and Eileen Power, 1927, pp. 91–2.

frequently acted as her secretary and assistant, the Reverend Mr John Botham, seemingly an appropriate choice, since he was the widower of Elizabeth Sterne's late sister, Lydia. One presumes Botham made the funeral arrangements.

The obituary in the *St. James's Chronicle*, 17–19 March, was insensitive and unworthy of its subject:

> Yesterday, at Four o'Clock in the Afternoon, died the *Reverend Mr. Sterne*, Author of *Tristram Shandy*, four Volumes of Sermons, and the Sentimental Journey.
>
> Alas, *poor Yorick*! I knew him well, a Fellow of infinite Jest, most excellent Fancy, &c. Wit, Humour, Genius, *hadst thou*, *all agree*; *One Grain of* Wisdom *had been worth the Three*!

This was repeated entire in the *Public Advertiser*, 21 March, and in part in the *Gentleman's Magazine* for April. Only the obituary in the *York Courant*, 22 March, was respectful: it carefully named all Sterne's preferments as well as his two novels.

The funeral was held on Tuesday, 22 March, at St George's Church, Hanover Square. The service was conducted by the rector, the Rev. Dr Charles Moss, recently made Bishop of St David's.[33] The *Account Book of Burial Fees* at the Church records the funeral fees paid to the rector, clerk, sexton, grave maker, bearers, and costs such as those for candles. A man of little wealth was buried the same day as Sterne at a total cost of 2*s*. 6*d*. Also buried on that day was the infant Lord George James Montagu, son of Sancho's patron and master, the Duke of Montagu; the funeral of this aristocratic child cost £3. 4*s*. 0*d*. Sterne's funeral cost 16*s*. 6*d*., a modest celebration, but suitable to his status as a clergyman and writer. There is no record of who attended, but, St George's being the most fashionable church in London, many of Sterne's wealthy and titled friends were probably there. Hall, still adamantly atheist, stayed away.[34]

A tradition grew up that Sterne was 'buried' by only two or three people, and that may have been literally true, for the interment took place some distance from St George's. The grounds around the church being full, the

[33] *Burial Register*, 1768, at the church, fol. 119. Dr Moss is noticed in *Alumni Cantabrigienses* and *DNB*.

[34] According to Isaac Reed, 'Mr. Stevenson Hall, the Author of *Crazy Tales*, was applyed to but refused to attend or give himself the least concern about his deceased friend's body': *Diaries*, ed. Claude E. Jones, Berkeley and Los Angeles, 1946, p. 156.

vestry had purchased another burial ground in 1764, a plot lying on a low, bare hill in Tyburn Fields, but west of the place of execution, in the manor of Paddington close to the corner of Edgware and Oxford roads. In an age when the dead were usually buried in the churchyard, there was no tradition of a funeral procession to a distant burial site. Few people, in all probability, followed the hearse to Paddington. Becket was one of them,[35] as was the lawyer Samuel Salt.[36] Tradition says Commodore James made up a third: there is no evidence, but it seems likely. Becket declared an intention of marking the grave with a headstone, and Garrick, hearing of it, wrote an epitaph.[37] Whether it was ever carved on the stone, or whether the stone was ever set in place, we do not know; no stone was to be found a year later. But Garrick's epitaph survives in his own hand:

> Shall Pride a heap of Sculptur'd Marble raise,
> Some unmourn'd, worthless, titled Fool to praise?
> And shall we not by one poor Grave-stone learn,
> Where *Humor*, *wit* and *Genius* sleep with Sterne?

[35] Reed, *Diaries*, 156: 'I remember Becket the Bookseller once told me that he, and I think another, were the only persons who attended the Funeral.'

[36] According to John Thomas Smith, Samuel Salt of the Inner Temple 'informed me that he was one of the few who buried Sterne': *Book for a Rainy Day*, ed. Wilfred Whitten, 1905, p. 100. I have conjectured in the first chapter that Salt was Sterne's London lawyer.

[37] Holograph at the Folger Library: MS W.b.464, fol. 58v, headed, in Garrick's hand, 'An Inscription for a Stone which Becket The Bookseller has put upon *Sterne's* Grave'. MEDALLE published it, following her dedication to Garrick.

Postscript

The new burial ground of St George's, lying at the edge of town, was an easy target for grave robbers. A story about them had appeared in the *St. James's Chronicle*, 24–6 November 1767:

> The Bur[y]ing-Ground in Oxford-Road, belonging to the Parish of St. George's Hanover-Square, having been lately robbed of several dead Bodies, a Watch was placed there attended by a large Mastiff Dog, notwithstanding which, on Sunday Night last some Villains found Means to steal out another dead Body, and carried off the very Dog.

Grave robbers, who were usually medical students, seldom left evidence of their visit. Their method was to dig a shaft at the head of the grave large enough to admit one of them, who would break a hole in the coffin lid, through which the body could be pulled head-first. They would then stop the hole with sacks, fill up the shaft, and be gone without a trace in about an hour.[1]

Sterne's body was stolen from the grave, probably during the night after the interment, and taken to Cambridge to be anatomized before the medical students. Although the story of the theft was probably told quietly around London, not until a year later did anything appear in print, and that was an account in the *Public Advertiser*, 24 March 1769, full of lurid, fanciful details:

> It has been whispered about some Time in great Confidence, that the Skeleton of the famous Yorick has been exhibited in one of our English Universities, and it seems now to be put beyond all Doubt by a

[1] James Moores Ball, *Sack-'em-up Men*, 1928, pp. 151–3.

Gentleman's having applied in Town to search for the Body, and it could not be found. Another Gentleman is well assured of the Identity of his Skull by two or three of the Teeth being remarkably prominent, which were well remembered by those who knew the Deceased. The Curiosity of having Yorick's Scull was, no doubt, the Inducement, and to be able to say

'This same Scull, Sir, was Yorick's Scull.'

'Alas, poor Yorick! I knew him well, Horatio—a Fellow of infinite Jest and most excellent Fancy:—Here hung those Lips!—Where are your Gibes now?——not one to mock your own Grinning! — — —quite Chop-fallen!'[2]

A few weeks later the story in general outline was confirmed by the anonymous author of *Yorick's Sentimental Journey Continued*.[3] He located the anatomy lesson at Oxford.[4] The notes of two sound scholars, Isaac Reed and Edmond Malone, placed the dissection at Cambridge. According to Reed, the body was 'recognized by sevr. persons who knew him'.[5] Malone said that he personally talked to a man who 'was present at the dissection', who 'told me, he recognized Sterne's face the moment he saw the body'.[6]

The anatomy amphitheatre at Cambridge stood at that time in Queens' Lane opposite the entrance to Queens' College and close to Silver Street. There Dr Charles Collignon, Professor of Anatomy, regularly conducted a course of twenty-eight lectures during the Lent term. No doubt Sterne's body was used in one of them. Sterne, who was always interested in

[2] The *Public Advertiser* story seems to have become the gossip among Sterne's parishioners. GREENWOOD told his interviewer that he had 'heard & it was generally believed in the village [Sutton] that his corpse became a subject for the surgeon's knife[.] a gentleman viewing the skeletons or subjects in some of the London Hospitals, challenged one for Sterne by the number of teeth in each jaw.'

[3] The longstanding tradition that Hall-Stevenson wrote this fourth-rate imitation was exploded by Lodwick Hartley, '*Yorick's Sentimental Journey Continued*: A Reconsideration of the Authorship', *South Atlantic Quarterly*, LXX (1971), 180–90.

[4] As did the Rev. Daniel Watson, Vicar of Leake, in his letter to George Whately, 15 June 1776, in *Monthly Repository of Theology and General Literature*, III (1808), 12.

[5] *Isaac Reed Diaries*, ed. Claude E. Jones, Berkeley and Los Angeles, 1946, p. 156.

[6] 'Maloniana', in Sir James Prior, *Life of Edmond Malone*, 1860, pp. 373–4. We need not take too seriously the anecdote passed on in *Willis's Current Notes* (1854), p. 31, from a note in an old copy of the *Journey*, in which the dissection is interrupted when the friend who recognizes the body faints; the lesson then continues: 'That heart whose pulsations were benignity itself, and the hand never extended but in the act of benevolence, were each laid open to the gaze of inhuman curiosity. Each fibre of the heart, it was remarked, seemed relaxed and wrung with sorrow.'

medicine and had attended the autopsy of George Oswald, would not have objected. He would have approved of the direction of Collignon's endeavours in *Medica Politica* (1765) and *Inquiry into the Structure of the Human Body, relative to its Supposed Influence on the Morals of Mankind* (1763). On the other hand, Collignon was a dull lecturer and is said to have been a third-rate practitioner of medicine. When his *Works* appeared in 1787, a reviewer wrote of his poetry, 'With such sacred poems as the Messiah of Collignon may the God of Verse never suffer us to be visited again!'[7]

Once Collignon knew whose body was on his table, he did the best thing he could: he sent it back to be reburied at Paddington. In the confusion which the incident caused, no proper marker was set on the grave. A year later,[8] two Freemasons erected a laughable headstone. They were not certain they had the right grave – 'Alas! Poor Yorick,' begins the inscription, 'Near to this Place / Lyes the Body of / The Reverend Laurence Sterne, A. M.' They got the date of the death wrong and miscalculated the age of the deceased, to say nothing of his temperament: 'This monumental Stone was erected to the memory of the deceased, by two BROTHER MASONS; for although he did not live to be a Member of their Society, yet all his incomparable Performances evidently prove him to have acted by Rule and Square.' In 1893 Captain Frederick H. Carrol of Mundiff, County Wicklow, owner of Woodhouse in Halifax and through his Lister ancestors a distant relative of Sterne's cousin Richard, set up a footstone and handsome border rail.[9]

Sterne had died so soon after the appearance of *A Sentimental Journey* that notices and reviews usually doubled as obituaries. There was a word of praise – a brief notice only – in the *Political Register* for May. The one French review, for the *Bibliothècque des Beaux Arts*, January–March 1768, translated

[7] *European Magazine*, XII (1787), 120. See *DNB*; A[lexander] Macalister, *History of the Study of Anatomy at Cambridge*, 1891, pp. 18–23; and D. A. Winstanley, *Unreformed Cambridge*, 1935, p. 154. The rumours about Sterne's bones remaining at Cambridge are nonsense. A guardbook at the University Archives entitled *Professors of Anatomy* (39.13, fol. 5) includes an inventory of the furniture and apparatus in the anatomy schools taken by Collignon in 1772: 'All that remains of the Bones, mentioned in former Catalogues, are some sections of them, to show their internal Structure. The rest were too dirty & bad for use.'

[8] Alan B. Howes, *Yorick and the Critics*, New Haven, Conn., 1958, p. 46 and n. 9, reports that the headstone was described as 'lately erected' in the *Literary Register*, I (1769), 285.

[9] Tom Sutcliff, 'Woodhall and Copley Hall', *Halifax Antiquarian Society*, 1904–5, pp. 251–62; R. Bretton, 'Wood Hall, Skircoat', *Halifax Antiquarian Society*, 1955, pp. 19–32.

in the *Annual Register*, 1769, was enthusiastic and complimented the late author as 'one of the first Beaux Esprits of the present age . . . a man full of sentiment'. But the animus against Sterne among English reviewers was not quieted by the news of his death. Ralph Griffiths in the *Monthly Review*, an essay begun in March and continued in April, and an anonymous reviewer in the *London Magazine*, March, had some complimentary things to say about the sentimentalism, but neither could resist saying that Sterne, when he appeared before his Maker, needed the help of a recording angel whose tears would blot out his sins. Whoever wrote the article for the *Critical Review*, which Smollett owned, was predictably incensed and implied that Sterne had stolen the idea of La Fleur from Smollett; as to Sterne's death, '*de mortuis nil nisi bonum*, said the traveller, when the landlord asked his opinion of his dead small-beer.'[10]

Though they spoke in private, some of Sterne's erstwhile friends and patrons were hardly more kind. 'Poor Sterne, whom the papers tell us is just dead,' wrote Bishop Warburton to Charles Yorke, 'was the idol of the higher mob, who have left the care of the public to Wilkes and the lower.' Wilkes had recently begun his canvas of the livery companies to represent the City of London,[11] and Warburton saw a parallel between Wilkes's adoring mob and Sterne's wealthy, doting clientele.

> He found a strong disposition in the many to laugh away life; and as now every one *makes himself*, he chose the office of common jester to the many. But what is hard, he never will obtain the frivolous end he aimed at, the reputation of a wit, though at the expense of his character, as a man, a scholar, and a clergyman. But I suppose he thought with Wilkes, (for mischief and folly are closely allied) who, in these last tumults, when he was upbraided with sedition and blasphemy, in one of his advertisements told the public, that the *essential part of his character was a love of liberty*: so poor Sterne's *essential part*, he would tell you, was to provoke a laugh. He chose Swift for his model: but Swift was either luckier or wiser, who so managed his wit,

[10] Exact dates of these and other comments given in HOWES, 197–204. The scribblers too were busy: OATES names *The Fig Leaf, or He's Gone! Who? Yorick!* and *Sentiments on the Death of the Sentimental Yorick. By One of Uncle Toby's Illegitimate Children.*

[11] See Wilkes's 'Address to the Livery of London, on Declaring Himself a Candidate for Member for the City', dated 10 March, *Gentleman's Magazine* for March 1768, p. 124.

> that he will never pass with posterity for a buffoon; while Sterne gave such a loose to his buffoonery, that he will never pass for a wit.[12]

Mrs Montagu was less harsh, but she still had not forgiven Sterne:

> Poor Tristram Shandy had an appearance of philanthropy that pleased one, & made one forgive in some degree his errors. However, as I think, there is but one way of a mans proving his philanthropy to be real & genuine, & that is by making every part of his conduct of good example to mankind in general, & of good effect towards those with whom he is connected. If Tristram gave an ill example to the Clergy, if he rendered his Wife and Daughter unhappy, we must mistake good humour for good nature. . . . Poor Tristrams last performance was the best, his Sentimental journey w[d] not have misbecome a young Ensign. I cannot say it was suitable to his serious profession.[13]

The *Court Miscellany* for April re-ran Dr John Hill's 1760 biographical sketch of Sterne, and a handful of sentimental elegies appeared:

> YORICK, farewell! peace dwell around thy stone;
> Accept this tribute from a friend unknown.
> In human breasts, while pity has a claim,
> Le Fevre's story shall enhance thy fame;
> Toby's benevolence each heart expand,
> And faithful Trim confess the master's hand.
> One generous tear unto the monk you gave;
> Oh let me weed this *Nettle* from thy grave.[14]

A more affecting comment came from Germany. When he heard of Sterne's death, Lessing said 'gladly would I have given him five years of my own life, if that could be done. . . . With the stipulation however, that he would have had to write. It would make no difference what.'[15]

Elizabeth and Lydia did not come to London, probably because Elizabeth did not feel strong enough. They had every confidence that the Rev. Mr John Botham would handle their affairs well. He did not. They asked him to

[12] *Letters from the Reverend Dr. Warburton . . . to the Hon. Charles Yorke*, 1812, p. 89.

[13] Addressed to Leonard Smelt; Huntington Library, MO 4999; extracted by CURTIS, 440–1. Parts of the letter have been quoted in previous chapters.

[14] One of two anonymous memorial verses published in the *Annual Register*, 1768, p. 227. HOWES, 204–7, gives two others.

[15] HOWES, 427.

sell Sterne's effects and to pay off the London debts with the proceeds. Botham did that, but ignored their instructions to sell Sterne's valuable gold snuffbox to Hall, who wanted it, or to offer other 'trinkets' to wealthy friends who would have been glad to pay prices above their market value.

They gave Botham specific instructions to send to York all the papers he found. Instead, he read every letter and manuscript he turned up and committed to the flames everything he thought unfit for his sister-in-law's eyes. Lydia, furious, wrote to Mrs Montagu:

> It was not mama's intention that any one shou'd read my Father's papers. well knowing that there was some amongst them which ought not to have been seen no not even by his Daughter nor sh[d] I have wish'd to see one of them! mama is very much chagrin'd at this for notwithstanding she can perhaps rely on M[r] Botham's secrecy yet it grieves that even he should be so well acquainted with certain anecdotes. but to burn any paper was very wrong.[16]

Biographers aside, few will regret the loss of the anecdotes, but the destruction of the 'comic romance' which Sterne had been writing on his deathbed was costly for Elizabeth and a loss to the world.

No will was found among his papers. Consequently, Elizabeth had to seek letters of administration for his possessions. On 4 June 1768, she appeared before Dr Francis Topham, Sterne's 'Didius', in the Exchequer and Prerogative Court of the Archbishops of York – the very court which had figured in the *Political Romance* as the great, warm watch-coat. She was granted the letters, but had to post bond for £500.[17]

The women were in a panic about money. The only regular income they could foresee was about £80 per annum from the estate Elizabeth had brought into her marriage, and the rent from Sterne's estate, the Tindal

[16] LETTERS, 434. CROFT tells of the burning of the papers, among them 'a large Parcel of Letters of Love and Gallantry from Ladies of the first Rank and Quality'. But Croft is incorrect in most of the details he gives about this event.

[17] The court handled all wills and administrations involving *bona notabilia* – the goods of the deceased who owned property outside his diocese, had died outside it, or, if a clergyman, had been possessed of more than one living: in effect, the goods of the wealthy dead. See Arthur H. Cash, 'Sterne as a Judge in the Spiritual Courts', in *English Writers of the Eighteenth Century*, ed. John H. Middendorf, New York, 1971, pp. 17–36. The original letters of administration granted Elizabeth Sterne are now housed at Borthwick Institute, dated 4 June 1768. Elizabeth was required to submit an inventory by 4 December 1768 and an account by 4 June 1769.

Farm and other lands, leased too cheap, said Lydia, at £50.[18] They had hoped in the autumn to sell Sterne's estate so that they could buy an annuity, but we do not know how much had been borrowed against it. Nor do we know how much money Sterne had on credit with Becket or his bankers; how much he had invested, as he once planned, in stocks (147); or how much the women could expect to receive for *A Sentimental Journey*. Sterne had lived well in both London and Yorkshire, and they kept getting bills for such items as shoes and wine – no less than £25 owed to a York wine merchant. Botham managed to pay off most of the London bills from the sale of Sterne's things at Bond Street, but Lydia said, with some exaggeration probably, that the Yorkshire bills amounted to £1100.[19] On top of this, they were threatened with a suit for dilapidations from Sterne's successor at Sutton, Andrew Cheap, who wanted to be reimbursed for the burned-out parsonage. 'The only thing for these people', wrote Mrs Montagu unkindly, 'would be to board in a cheap place, but my good cousin is si tracassiere, she puts every Town into a combustion in a month.'[20] No doubt Elizabeth and Lydia thought they had a right to live as gentlewomen, and the archbishop quite misconceived their situation at first when he pondered applying to the Corporation of Clergymen's Widows for a pension of £8. But they were not ridiculously proud. They were quite willing to move into the garret of their York house so that the landlord could let it during Race Week, thereby keeping their annual rent down to a reasonable £20.[21]

In the matter of the suit for dilapidations, the women appealed to Archbishop Drummond. Though he had 'properly nothing to do with it', he worked out a compromise with Mr Cheap, who agreed to accept £100. Elizabeth refused, Cheap filed suit, and the archbishop was furious: 'I . . . am not surprised at the absurdity of Mrs. Sterne wth regard to the dilapidations at Sutton; considering the different bubbles of Vanity and levity wch have upheld her for sometime.' But when the archdeacon's recorder presented her case to him, he was forced to change his mind. Mr Cheap had ambitions for a beautiful house, and eventually built one. But he

[18] LETTERS, 438. Lydia may have reduced the actual figure, or the lands may have been managed better after Sterne's death. But the York lawyer, John Graves, who acted as agent for Elizabeth and Lydia after they retired to France, forwarded to them £76 for the fiscal year 1771–2 and £94 for 1772–3: CURTIS, 455. I have not been able to locate this record.

[19] LETTERS, 437–8, 448.

[20] LETTERS, 434.

[21] LETTERS, 433, 438.

could claim of Elizabeth no more than the value of the ruinous old timber house which Sterne had found at Sutton when he first came there. Cheap took the £60.[22]

On 14 April, Sterne's personal effects were put up for auction at Coxwold, including his furniture, hand-painted china and a cow near calving. His gigantic chaise and long-tailed horses sold for £60, his books for £80. These books were bought by Todd and Sotheran, successors to Hinxman at the Sign of the Bible in Stonegate, who in turn put them up for sale during Race Week, but mixed in with the libraries of other recently deceased clergymen.[23] The returns from these sales and the settlement with Mr Cheap put it beyond doubt that the Sterne women would have enough to pay the debts. The question was: would they have enough left over with which to purchase an annuity? Would they be able to return to France?

The question was settled for them by Sterne's friends. In April it was known that Lord Rockingham would take the lead in raising a subscription for Elizabeth and Lydia during Race Week. The women were at first embarrassed by the thought of being objects of charity, but some 'judicious sensible gentleman' convinced them that a subscription raised by 'the principal gentlemen of the County & nothing less than 5 Guineas to be received is putting it upon such a footing that it is an *honour* to M[r] Sterne's memory & no small one to us & cannot lessen us in the eyes of the world.' Drummond had been informed of the value of Sterne's farms by one of Lord Fauconberg's stewards. 'The Inclosure was no merit of Sterne's,' he wrote to Mrs Montagu, 'but it was a profit to him.'[24] So he was suspicious of the Sterne women: 'There is generally falsehood mixed w[th] [a] little cunning' in what they were saying; 'as it is designed to have a subscription for them opened at York, they think it their interest to depreciate their estate.' He eventually changed his opinion, for he enlisted in the subscription for £10.[25]

[22] LETTERS, 436, 438; Andrew Cheap's angry note in the parish register, given in CURTIS, 437, was not altogether fair. On suits for dilapidations, see G. F. A. Best, *Temporal Pillars*, Cambridge, 1964, pp. 18–19. The house Cheap built at a cost of £577 lasted into the twentieth century.

[23] LETTERS, 438; advertisement for the auction: *York Courant*, 12 April 1768; for the book sale, *York Courant*, 16 August 1768. The catalogue for this sale has been discussed above, Chapter 2.

[24] LETTERS, 436. In the Sutton enclosure, Sterne had received two 30-acre fields, a small piece of 32 perches near the churchyard and a garden plot by the vicarage. One wonders whether Drummond thought that the larger Tindal Farm also came to Sterne in the enclosure. It did not, but was purchased by Sterne and Elizabeth in 1744: *EMY*, 261, 146–7.

[25] LETTERS, 435, 436, 438.

When Race Week came round, Rockingham led off with a generous £50. Sir George Saville gave the like amount, but not wanting to appear to give more than Lord Scarborough, his brother-in-law, he gave half of it in his own name and half anonymously. The subscribers' list has vanished, but many gentlemen must have taken part. The total raised came to about £800. 'How gracious, how merciful is God to us!' Lydia wrote to Mrs Montagu,

> what comfort has he sent us what friends has he rais'd us up! O may we ever retain a just sense of his mercy, and the most grateful remembrance of what we owe to our friends. indeed Madam I scarce can write for Tears when I think how peculiarly kind providence has been towards us. . . . my mother purposes to settle this Collection money upon me which is very kind considering the many debts she has to pay out of her estate.[26]

Then other Yorkshire friends of Sterne began to come forward. A maiden lady, Anne Eliza Morritt,[27] had taken the lead in another subscription among less wealthy citizens, and raised another £700. Mrs Montagu wrote to her sister on 4 September:

> I had a letter from Miss A. Moritt of York on Sunday telling me she had collected upwards of £700 for Miss Sterne, that she had promised the Subscribers it should be converted into an annuity for the girl for she added Mrs. Sterne was so little loved or esteemed there would not have been a single guinea given if that condition had not been made.[28]

In London, Lady Spencer mentioned the York subscriptions to John Craufurd, and that gentleman promptly raised another £108 among Sterne's London friends – Craufurd himself, Fox, Ossory, Shelburne, Hume, Commodore James, and others. Lydia was ecstatic: 'Judge, my dearest Cousin what pleasure this kind letter, & agreeable news gave us! how kind is providence to us!' And the collections continued into the autumn, Hall dunning Lord Irwin for a contribution, and Mrs Montagu her tightfisted father.[29] Even in far-off India, Eliza Draper, who had made the

[26] LETTERS, 437–8.

[27] Daughter of the prominent York Tory, Bacon Morritt. Her epitaph in Selby Abbey was composed by William Mason: CURTIS, 440.

[28] LETTERS, 439.

[29] LETTERS, 442, 444–5; Elizabeth Montagu to Sarah Scott, 1 December [1768]: Huntington Library, MO 5909.

awful mistake, when she heard of Sterne's death, of inviting Lydia to come to India without mentioning her mother, now tried to make amends by raising a subscription there, largely with the help of a romantic colonel, Donald Campbell of Barbreck.[30] The total of all these separate subscriptions must have come to something like £1800. One presumes that most of the money went to buy the annuity for Lydia. In any event, the generosity of Sterne's friends assured the Sterne women that they could take up the life in France they had planned before Sterne's death. Elizabeth Montagu, now convinced of their integrity, promised an annual allowance of £20, which before long she raised to £30.

The honour thus paid to Sterne's memory was so very great, one cannot but wonder that it had so little effect upon the traditions which grew up afterwards. Even so sound a scholar as Edmund Malone would write at the end of the century, 'The celebrated writer Sterne, after being long the idol of this town, died in a mean lodging without a single friend who felt interest in his fate, except Becket, his bookseller.'[31] Dr John Ferriar, the first serious student of Sterne, wrote in *Illustrations of Sterne*, 1798, 'It is known that Sterne died in hired lodgings, and I have been told, that his attendants robbed him even of his gold sleeve-buttons, while he was expiring.' This and similar stories persisted into the twentieth century.[32]

In the autumn of 1768, Lydia and her mother decided to offer the public another collection of Sterne's sermons. Sterne had left his sermons in a trunk in Hall's care, and in November Hall went through the manuscripts picking out those which had not been published. He found eighteen. He did some preliminary editing, he told Lydia, 'tho' not sufficiently to prevent your doing it yourself', and he found several passages which duplicated others in the published sermons. Sterne often plagiarized from himself. These, said Hall, had 'given me some trouble to patch and botch differently.' He advised Lydia to bring the sermons out in three volumes at a price of *2s. 6d.* per volume, the price of *A Sentimental Journey*, to gather subscriptions, and 'Then make a bargain to clear your subscriptions, and

[30] Eliza to Anne James, 15 April 1772, in *Works*, ed. Wilbur L. Cross, 12 vols, 1904, VIII, 173–268, reproduced in part in LETTERS, 458–64.

[31] 'Maloniana'.

[32] John Ferriar, *Illustrations of Sterne*, 1798, 175. In 1840 Isaac D'Israeli reported, 'Sterne died with neither friend nor relation by his side! A hired nurse was the sole companion of the man whose wit found admirers in every street, but whose heart, it would seem, could not draw one to his death-bed': *Miscellanies of Literature*, 1840, 1884 edn, 31; and Percy Fitzgerald, in the final edition of his *Life*, repeated Ferriar's story: see *Works*, ed. Cross, XII, 289–90.

sell the Copy.' In all these points she would follow his advice. Hall also thought she should deal with Becket if possible, 'because your father had a regard for him'. But the Rev. Mr John Botham was making trouble again: he had told Becket that not all the sermons were Sterne's, and Becket was uncertain whether to take them. To this Hall answered, in his letter to Lydia,

> I can aver upon my honour, and could I dare say, have the evidence of twenty people, who must have heard your Father, as well as myself, declare a hundred times, that all the Sermons which he had, were in a bag, and in order to make up the Volumes printed, he had no other method, than to put his hand into the bag, and take out what came first, therefore you have no reason to set a less value upon these, than your father did upon his other[s].[33]

Becket pointed to the preface to 'The Abuses of Conscience, Considered' in Volume IV of the *Sermons*, where Sterne had said that he had no more sermons except 'the sweepings of the Author's study after his death'. Lydia replied that it was no more than 'a Shandeism, like many others'. Since Botham had also spoken to Mrs Montagu, Lydia had also to write to her, assuring her that the sermons were genuine. Finally everyone was agreed. But Lydia was shy about soliciting subscriptions in York where so many people had already contributed to their welfare; so she asked Mrs Montagu to push them in London. Other friends soon joined in the effort.[34]

In the early spring of 1769, Lydia and Elizabeth came to London to publish the sermons. Commodore and Mrs James found rooms for them at the house of a paper merchant named Williams in Gerrard Street, close to their house. It was the first of many services which Anne James would perform for them. For the first time Lydia Sterne met her godmother,

[33] LETTERS, 443–4.

[34] LETTERS, 446–7; and two holograph letters of Lydia Sterne recently acquired by the Houghton Library. These lack complete dates and addressees, but clearly they were addressed to Thomas Becket in November and December 1768. One is a cover letter which Lydia wrote when she was sending to Becket the letter to her from Hall (i.e. Letter XXVI in LETTERS, 442–3). The other, dated only 'Monday', Lydia wrote subsequently, but before her next known letter to Becket (i.e. Letter XXVII in LETTERS, 443–4). Possibly the Sterne women anticipated having to put up some or all of the money for the venture, as Sterne would have done. Before departing for London, they borrowed £400 from Stephen Croft (see the receipt, dated 17 March 1769, at the Yorkshire Archaeological Society, Leeds, DD 58/BRA 487). In the end, they sold the book outright for that much or more (447).

Elizabeth Montagu. For the first time since they had been girls 'in hanging sleeves', Elizabeth Sterne met her cousin Elizabeth Montagu. Not in all of those years had Mrs Montagu said a kind word about Elizabeth Sterne, and her pointed failures to take her up had been a torment. Yet the meeting went off smoothly. For all her lack of popularity, Elizabeth Sterne still presented herself in 'finished Address supposed to be inferior to no Woman in Europe'.[35]

But the Sterne women were hard to get along with. Lydia's affected French manners offended many. Miss Morritt, the woman who had raised the second York subscription, wrote to Mrs Montagu begging her 'to advise Miss Sterne not to affect witt, a desire of being distinguished that way she says has ruined the whole family.' Mrs Montagu decided to do just that, and added, 'I shall now tell Miss Sterne I will allow her £20 per ann; and I hope that will give my advice more weight.' The result was a long letter of self-defence from Lydia in which she protested, 'as to inheriting my father's wit I have not the least grain in my composition we both thought it an unhappy turn in my father.' Moreover, Lydia had a hot temper, as her father had told her (417), and before long she was raging at Becket, calling him behind his back 'a *dirty fellow*'.[36]

Becket had offered the handsome price of £400 for the copyright to the three volumes of sermons, but he demanded a control of the project, which Lydia was not willing to give. She went secretly to a competitor, William Strahan, Johnson's publisher, the man who had been doing Sterne's printing.[37] In the end, Becket, Strahan and Strahan's partner Thomas Cadell published the volumes together.

[35] So Eliza Draper had been told: see her letter to Anne James, 15 April 1772, the source also of the information about Anne James's friendly services to the Sterne women. The address in Gerrard Street is to be found in LETTERS, 448; it is confirmed by John Wilkes's address book, BL, Add. MSS 30892. I have not identified Williams, the paper merchant.

[36] LETTERS, 417, 439–40, 446–7.

[37] LETTERS, 447. The MS of Lydia's letter to Strahan is now at the Beinecke Library, the gift of C. B. Tinker. It contains a few lines not given in LETTERS, which depended for text upon a Sotheby catalogue; but in these lines Lydia talks only about calling upon Strahan. Strahan's leadership in the project is evidenced by his papers at the BL. There is a ledger listing 50 proposals of subscriptions and 400 receipts for them: Add. MSS 48803, fol. 17. One of the receipts at Add. MSS 22261, fol. 48 – a receipt given to Lady Stafford for 7*s*. 6*d*., 'being the Subscription-Money for three Volumes of Sermons, by the late Reverend Mr. Sterne', dated 31 May 1769, and signed by Elizabeth Sterne. In later years Strahan and Becket sold off pieces of the copyrights in sermons and novels to various booksellers. See the 'Original Assignments

The sermons, numbered as Volumes V–VII but under a new title, *Sermons by the Late Rev. Mr. Sterne*, appeared on 3 June 1769.[38] A second edition was published before the year was out.

There were an astonishing number of subscriptions, over 700. As we know from a recently discovered letter that Lydia wrote to Garrick, many friends had helped, Garrick himself, Elizabeth Montagu, Anne James and the Dowager Countess of Carlisle. Lydia may have protested that she did not want to be the object of charity, but she did not hesitate to play upon the sympathies of Sterne's old friends. To Wilkes she painted her mother as 'nobly' paying off Sterne's debts from her own 'little estate of £40 per an which was all she had in the world' and said pathetically that they had sold the copyright to the sermons 'for a trifle'.[39] Perhaps Wilkes suspected this rhetoric: he did not subscribe, though his daughter did. The women were not always well treated. Sir Thomas Robinson, Bart, sent them 'a very great and noble list of subscribers', which they foolishly sent on to the printer, even though Robinson had not sent along any money. They dispatched a note: he was offended. They approached him at Ranelagh Gardens: he 'begg'd leave to tell us that it was our affair and not his that he was not a Collector of money &c. &c. & left us very abruptly.' So the women decided to deliver the books themselves to those whose names were published from Robinson's list. Lord and Lady Chesterfield, 'after having made us wait a quarter of an hour', sent word that they had not subscribed and the books must be taken away. Thereafter, they would not deliver them personally, but had the books sent out along with a printed notice asking politely for payment. Lord and Lady Beauchamp sent the volumes back with an indignant note, and Lydia feared 'we shall have a good many returned in this manner!'[40] As a consequence of Robinson's irresponsible

of Copy-rights of Books and other Literary Agreements . . . collected by William Upcott . . . 1925', BL, Add. MSS 83730.

[38] Advertised as appearing 'this day' in the *Public Advertiser*, 3 June.

[39] LETTERS, 448.

[40] Undated holograph at the Pusey Library, Harvard, bound in the William Upcott copy of the *Private Correspondence of David Garrick*, Vol. V of the *Life of David Garrick* by Arthur Murray, 1801–32. Thomas Robinson, Bart, of Rokeby, Yorkshire (?1702–77), often called 'Long Sir Thomas' to distinguish him from 'Short Sir Thomas' Robinson of Newby, Yorkshire (1695–1770, created Baron Grantham in 1761), was a cousin of Elizabeth Montagu and brother-in-law to Henry Howard, fourth Earl of Carlisle; MP for Morpeth, 1727–34; created baronet 1731; commissioner of excise, 1735–42; governor of Barbados, 1742–7. He was an amateur architect and one of the owners and builders of the Rotunda at Ranelagh,

behaviour, one ought to reduce the number of subscribers in the list from 770 to, say, 720 or 730. But, if this guess comes close to the truth, they still had more subscriptions than Sterne had been able to collect for the *Sermons* of 1760 or 1766. The list was yet another honour paid to the memory of Laurence Sterne.

Soon after the *Sermons* appeared, Elizabeth and Lydia departed for France, making enemies until the last. Hughes Minet, whose family owned the packet boat in which they crossed the Channel, wrote in the margin of his copy of *A Sentimental Journey*, 'Laurence Sterne, an unworthy churchman. . . . I knew him, and also Madam, his fool of a wife, and also Madam his daughter, as great a fool as her mother.'[41]

In 1772, Eliza Draper wrote a long letter to Anne James telling her about her present life and trying to make amends for slighting Anne in a matter which concerned the Sterne women.[42] She had not allowed Anne to negotiate with Elizabeth Sterne for the return of Eliza's letters; instead she had promised a reward to Becket if he would get them and turn them over to Anne for safekeeping. She was also at pains to explain how she could have invited Lydia to join her in India while ignoring her mother.

> How could I with any kind of Delicacy mention a Person, who was hateful to my departed Friend, when for the sake of that very friend—I wished to confer a kindness on his Daughter. . . . indeed I knew not, but Mrs Sterne, from the Description I had received of her, might be no more—or privately confined, if in Being, owing to a Malady, which I've been told the Violence of her temper subjects her to. . . . Miss Sterne, in her letter, tells me—*that her Father did sometimes misrepresent her mother, in order to justify his neglect of her*—I do not think highly of a Daughter, who would compliment a living Parent, however justly at the expence of a Deceased one.

where he was much in evidence. Called 'Ranelagh's maypole', he was said to have been 'a noted pest to persons of high rank and office': *DNB*; CLIMENSON, II, 275–7; Romney Sedgwick, *House of Commons 1715–1754*, 1970.

[41] William Minet, *Some Account of the Huguenot Family of Minet*, 1892, p. 169; see CURTIS, 465.

[42] The letter of 15 April 1772, cited above. My quotations are taken from pp. 210–13. Unless otherwise indicated, my account of Eliza is taken from WRIGHT AND SCLATER *as corrected* by Mr Sclater in his later article, 'Letters Addressed by Eliza Draper to the Strange Family, 1776–1778', *N&Q*, CLXXXVI (January–June 1944), 201–4, 220–4; CLXXXVII (July–December 1944), 7–13, 27–33, 48–54.

As to the things Sterne had told Eliza about his wife,

> I believed Sterne implicitly, I believed him! *I had no Motive to do otherwise than believe him just, generous & unhappy—till his Death gave me to know, that he was tainted with the Vices of Injustice, Meanness & Folly.* Nothing had ever offered to remove my prejudice against the Widows Character—till your assurances made me wish to be divested of it.

In 1773 Eliza left her husband for good. At first, Draper accused her of misconduct with Commodore Sir John Clarke, whose flagship lay in the harbour at Bombay, but he withdrew the charge. 'Suffer me to be unmolested,' Eliza wrote to Draper, 'and I will engage to steer through life with some degree of approbation, if not respect.' She was actually going to her maternal uncle, John Whitehill, the chief of the factory of Masulipatam, north of Madras, where she was to preside over his homosexual household. Her uncle's 'premier' was a twenty-four-year-old man, also in the service of the East India Company, named John Sulivan. Eliza wrote to her cousin, Thomas Limbrey Sclater,

> I am happy in having such a Companion for my constant associate.—He's Mild, yet Manly—a respectable understanding and a fine Disposition are his acknowledged Characteristics. So much goodness, without Parade, so much sensibility without a single foible. . . . My uncle doats on him with all the Extravagances of violent Passion—He cannot live without Him, He cannot even bear Him out of his Sight. He cannot like to have him Sleep in any apartment but his own.

In 1773 appeared in London a small volume, *Letters from Yorick to Eliza*, which contained the ten known letters which Sterne had written to Eliza in 1767 before she sailed for India. As the unidentified editor explained in the preface, 'Eliza's modesty was invincible to all the publisher's endeavours to obtain her answers.'[43] There is no doubt, from what the editor says, that Eliza was in possession of the letters which she had written to Sterne – letters she had finally got back from Elizabeth. It was scandalous of her to make public Sterne's letters, so flattering to her, without supplying her own to him, which would have revealed her part in this love game. It was especially reprehensible to release Sterne's letters while Elizabeth was alive.

[43] Wilbur Cross's edition of *Letters from Yorick to Eliza*, in *Works*, ed. Cross, VIII, 1–48.

The precise date of publication has not been established, but the book bears the date 1773. Elizabeth died in July of that year. Eliza was in India.[44] Since it took about a year to send a letter to India from England or France and to receive a reply, Eliza could not have known about Elizabeth's death when she released the letters. Her motives were probably not monetary, for the book was not advertised, so far as anyone has discovered, or pushed in any way. One is forced to conclude that Eliza took this step because she thought it would enhance her own image, and did so without regard for Sterne or his family.

In 1776, John Whitehill moved his Indian family, including Eliza and Sulivan, to Paris. It was there that the abbé Raynal fell in love with her. Guillaume-Thomas-François Raynal, a man in his early sixties, a longstanding member of the d'Holbach group, had recently shot to fame as the author of the *Histoire politique et philosophique de l'établissement des Européens dans les Deux Indes* (four volumes, 1770). Raynal gathered much of his information from interviews of people returning from the East or West Indies, and that is probably how he met Eliza. In the expanded edition of 1780, one finds a passage on the harems of the Moguls at Surat based on information Eliza had given him. The same edition contained, in the description of her birthplace, Anjengo, an *éloge* to Eliza, who by that time had died:

> Anjengo, it is to the influence of thy happy climate that she certainly was indebted for that almost incompatible harmony of voluptuousness and decency, which diffused itself over all her person, and accompanied all her motions. . . .
>
> Eliza intended to quit her country, her relations, her friends, to take up her residence along with me, and spend her days in the midst of mine. What happiness had I not promised myself? What joy did I not expect, from seeing her sought after by men of genius; and beloved by women of the nicest taste? I said to myself, Eliza is young, and thou art near thy latter end. It is she who will close thine eyes. Vain hope! Fatal reverse of all human probabilities![45]

[44] The tradition that Eliza had returned to England to publish the *Letters* was refuted by J. C. T. Oates, 'Notes on the Bibliography of Sterne', *Transactions of the Cambridge Bibliographical Society*, II (1955), 155–69. She did not leave India until 1776.

[45] I depend upon Cross's edition of a translation in the *European Magazine* for March 1784, in *Works*, VIII, 281–7. The *éloge* was attributed in a contemporary

Perhaps Eliza had made such a promise. When she found herself praising Raynal in a letter to the Strange family, 29 December 1777, she added, 'Not that I recant, what I have often said, and always thought, wch is that Men of this Stamp, are in general better known in their Works, than in a more familiar way—the Abbé, however, is an exception to this rule.' Obviously, at this stage, she regretted her intimacy with Sterne, but not that with Raynal.

Early in 1777, the entire household moved to London, where Whitehill purchased a handsome house in Queen Anne Street, Cavendish Square, and set Eliza up as its mistress. They were joined by her daughter, Elizabeth, now aged fifteen, her only surviving child. Then Whitehill was called back to India. There had been an uprising in Madras, and he went to restore order as interim governor. Eliza picked up her friendship with Anne James, who, she reported, was 'always with her'. She seems to have been accepted into the more intellectual polite circles. She had a friendship with John Wilkes, and with Charles Burney's second wife, and an acquaintance with Mrs Thrale.

In London, Eliza may have become something of a cult figure. Her letters are full of what she herself called 'homilies' upon self-love, benevolence, modesty, and the like. And she had become something of a feminist philosopher: on 25 August 1777, she wrote, 'I begin to think that the privilege of wearing petticoats is a very happy one as it excludes us the use of Offensive Weapons, and Sentencing People to Death, an advantage I think, very superior to that of fingering the Treasury, and disposing of Property.' But Mrs Thrale could not understand what people found so admirable: 'I saw no Rarety in Eliza—she was a Woman *all as another in my Eyes*.'[46]

She was in deplorable health and in her own opinion had long lost her beauty. Yet in December 1777 she was sitting for a painting by Bogle who 'is making a perfect Venus of me'. Bogle's painting is lost, but another by John Downman made about this same time has come to light. He painted her in a turban and oriental dress sitting in a romantic dell, gesturing toward a tree upon which her name is carved. Whether she actually sat for it we do not know, but Downman depicted her as a beautiful, fine-featured

review to Diderot, but Diderot denied authorship and said explicitly that Raynal had written it: Alice Green Fredman, *Diderot and Sterne*, New York, 1955, pp. 7–8.

[46] *Thraliana*, ed. Katharine C. Balderston, Oxford, 1942, p. 384, n. 3.

woman. The reality was that she was confined to her bed most of her last months. On 30 April 1778 she wrote that the doctors had pronounced 'a complication of Disorders—My Liver diseased, and dropsical too, is the Sentence pronounced against *Me*—this may be, for I am very yellow, & very much swelled.' At her own request, she was carried to Bath to see if the waters would help her. From there she was taken to Bristol for further treatment, and then to the nearby village of Clifton, then called Hot Springs. There she died on 3 August 1778. One account says that she died in the house of General Sir William Draper, a cousin to her husband. In any event, she was not alone. Someone, probably her daughter and John Sulivan, saw to it that she was interred in style beneath a diamond-shaped stone in the north aisle of the choir of Bristol Cathedral. At a later date Whitehill or someone else had a monument placed on the west wall, 'Sacred to the memory of Mrs. Eliza Draper, in whom Genius and Benevolence were united'. It has since been moved to the cloisters. Downman finished his painting the next year and exhibited it at the Royal Academy under the title *A Lady Surprised to Have Found Her Name Written on a Tree*.[47]

Commodore James died under a cloud in 1783. He had by that time served many years as a governor of the East India Company and since 1774 as Member of Parliament for East Looe. On 1 April 1783, a select committee of the Commons on Bengal affairs put before the House a report accusing James and his fellow governor, Laurence Sulivan, Sterne's correspondent, of altering the East India Company's accounts 'to deceive the committee about communications to India'. James vigorously denied the charge and strongly protested against the publication of the report when he and Sulivan had not been given an opportunity to answer it. He was ignored, for the accusation was largely a political move by supporters of Fox's East India Bill, which would have done away with the East India Company. James was forced to stay away when the Bill was voted in November.[48] He died three

[47] No. 73, 1779 exhibition. The identification of the subject was made by Malcolm Rogers, then Head of the Archives and Library of the National Portrait Gallery in a letter of 21 October 1982 to the then owner, Powsey and Payne art gallery. The painting, in oil, 18 × 14¼ inches, is signed and dated on the panel 1779. It was sold at Christie's on 13 July 1984 and was reproduced in colour in their catalogue for the sale, *Important English Painters*, No. 109. The title used at the Royal Academy exhibition is given in Algernon Graves, *The Royal Academy of Arts*, 1905, I, 363. John Downman (1750–1824) is noticed in the *DNB*.

[48] Sir Nathaniel William Wraxall, *Historical and Posthumous Memoirs*, 5 vols, 1884, III, 167–9; *Parliamentary Registers*, 1783, XXVI, 583–91; XXVII, 28–32; NAMIER AND BROOKE on James and Sulivan.

weeks later, on 16 December, during the celebration of his daughter's wedding. The very next day, the House of Lords roundly rejected the East India Bill. Anne James, grief-stricken, retired to their house in Eltham, Kent. In 1785 she erected a monument to the memory of her husband at the crown of Shooters Hill on the Kent Road close to London. It was a three-level tower of brown brick, built in a triangular configuration with smaller towers, replete with battlements, projecting upward from each of the three corners of the roof. A staircase connected at each level triangular rooms which were originally fitted out as a museum commemorating the battles in which Commodore James had distinguished himself. The tower, easily visible from London, soon became known as 'Lady James's Folly'. Today it is called Severndroog Tower and stands in a pleasant park where it serves to amuse children and picnickers.[49] Anne James died in 1798 and was buried beside her husband at Eltham.

In the early summer of 1769, Elizabeth and Lydia Sterne settled in the ancient city of Angoulême in southern France. From there Lydia wrote a long letter to John Wilkes, of whom she may have been slighty enamoured: 'thank my stars you promised me not to shew my letters to any one, not even to your Confessor.' Her practical purpose in writing was to ask Wilkes to keep his promise to collaborate with Hall on a life of Sterne. Wilkes and Hall had told her that she and her mother could publish the biography and keep the profits, or they could include it in the edition of Sterne's letters which Lydia had been contemplating. 'But entre nous', Lydia wrote, 'we neither of us wish to publish those letters but if we cannot do otherwise we will & prefix the life to them.' She and Becket had also been talking about an edition of *Tristram Shandy* which would reduce the nine volumes to six, and Wilkes had suggested she draw four more frontispieces to complement the two by Hogarth. 'What think you of Maria & the goat,' she asked him, 'with my father besides her?—the sick Bed of poor Le Fever for another with uncle Toby Trim by his bed side and Le Fever's son with the picture of his mother in his hand—the Cushion by the Bed side on which he had just pray'd[?]' Wilkes did not answer her letter. She wrote again. Then she wrote to Hall: 'let me urge press & entreat M[r] Hall to be as good as his word—if he will interest himself in our behalf. 'twill but be acting

[49] *Hasted's History of Kent*, ed. Henry H[olman] Drake, 1886, Pt I, 190. John Pavin Phillips, *N&Q*, second series, XII (28 September 1861), 244, as corrected by C. H. Cooper (2 November), 345, and augmented by Phillips (16 November), 402.

consistent with his character 'twill prove that Eugenius was the friend of Yorick.' Nothing came of either the life or the six-volume *Shandy*.[50]

The Sterne women moved further south, to Albi, in 1771. 'The situation of this Village is pretty,' Lydia wrote to Mrs Montagu, 'our little house is agreeable, but there is little society. and the little there is, is scarce worth the trouble of searching after.' Elizabeth had received a terrible fright from a man who had tried to break into the house by letting himself down the chimney on a rope. Soon after, she had 'an Epileptick fit and has continued ill ever since'. Lydia too was in bad health again and had grown thin. 'I partake too much of my Father's constitution.'[51]

In the spring of 1772, Lydia had an offer of marriage which she wished to accept from Jean-Baptiste-Alexandre-Anne Medalle, of Albi. She had reached the age of twenty-four. He was twenty. The young man's father 'insisted upon very hard terms': Elizabeth must give her entire estate as dowry. Lydia wrote to Mrs Montagu, pleading for her to continue their £30 allowance to her mother alone. 'My mother is willing almost to leave herself without bread for the advantage of her Lydia. . . . I here thrust my chair from me and write upon my knees, consider her, and her alone. and withdraw not your bounty from her whilst she lives!'[52] Mrs Montagu answered,

> I cannot hesitate a moment to transfer entirely to your Mamma during her life the little sum I used to send for your mutual service so that the article of your letter which relates to this point is most easily answered, and with as much pleasure on my side as it can be received on yours. The more momentous affair your marriage I cannot assent to with the same good will. . . . all you give your friends is that you are going to marry a man of a different Religion, and to reduce your Mother to almost beggary, both these things you confess. You seem at the same time to declare steadfastness in Religion and Filial piety to your parent. My dear cousin the actions not the words are what shall decide the judgment of God and man.[53]

What Mrs Montagu had not been told was that Lydia was pregnant.

On 25 April 1772 Elizabeth, Lydia, Jean-Baptiste and his father signed a

50 LETTERS, 449–53.
51 LETTERS, 455–6.
52 LETTERS, 456–7.
53 LETTERS, 458.

marriage contract.[54] Elizabeth settled upon the couple a dowry of 50,000 livres (about £2100), but reserved for herself the interest on half of it. The senior Medalle settled upon them half of his estate, but he was to have the use of it for his lifetime.[55] Elizabeth must have signed from her sickbed, for she did not attend the wedding, which was celebrated three days later, on 28 April 1772, in the chapel of the provost of the church of Saint Salvy. The registration states that Lydia had renounced the errors of the so-called reformed religion of England and become a Roman Catholic.[56] Four months later, on 6 August 1772, a son was born to Lydia. He was baptized the next day in the beautiful parish church of Saint Salvy and named Jean-François-Laurens.[57] In subsequent records he was called only Laurens or more often Laurent.

Elizabeth Sterne died on 11 July 1773, eleven months after the birth of her grandson. She had been confined nearly a year at No. 9, rue Saint-Antoine, the house of her physician and neighbour, Dr François Linières.[58]

Lydia and her husband lost no time in selling Sterne's estate. They did not come to England, but had the documents sent to them to be signed in France. They conveyed the Tindal Farm to the mortgagees, Dean John Fountayne and Stephen Croft, on 1 September 1773. What money the Medalles received is not recorded. Sterne's other lands, which had come to him in the Sutton enclosure, they sold on 5 November to Thomas Proud of Newborough for an unspecified sum.[59]

[54] Until recently, students of Sterne have depended for information about Sterne's family in France upon the work of the antiquarian, Emile Jolibois: *Inventaire-Sommaire des Archives Communales antérieures à 1790: Ville d'Albi*, Paris, 1869; and '1771–1783 – La Famille de Laurens Sterne à Albi', *Revue du Département du Tarn*, I (1877), 46. In 1941 appeared an article by Henri Duméril, 'La Descendance française de l'humoriste anglais Laurence Sterne', *L'Autra*, CXXVIII (1941), 122–4. The work of these men has now been superseded by that of Van R. Baker, 'Laurence Sterne's Family in France', *N&Q* (1975), 497–501, and 'What Happened to Lydia Sterne?', *Eighteenth-Century Life*, II (1975), 6–11. Professor Baker has kindly supplied me with copies of the original documents.

[55] Registre 107, Fonds Malaval: Archives Départementales du Tarn, III, E 8098.

[56] Parish registers, Saint Salvy, Albi, pp. 70–1: Archives Communales d'Albi, series GG 26.

[57] Parish registers, Saint Salvy, Albi, pp. 80–1.

[58] Death certificate: Archives Départementales du Tarn, series B 761; CURTIS, 458.

[59] North Riding Registry of Deeds, BD 864, pp. 478–9, dated 1 September 1773, recorded 30 May 1774; BC 839, pp. 508–9, dated 5 November 1773. There had been another mortgage besides that held by Croft and Fountayne, but Sterne must have paid it off. See AF 689, p. 491; AF 690, pp. 492–3, dated 2–3 June 1760, which reveals Sterne paying off the original mortgage but

On 21 December 1773, a second son was born to Lydia. He was baptized Jacques-François. This unfortunate little boy lived only into his fifth year, dying on 5 September 1778. He was buried in the cloister of Saint Salvy.[60]

Lydia made her last visit to England in the spring of 1775 to publish her father's letters. She found Becket ready to undertake the project, probably at a word from David Garrick, who acted as Lydia's chief adviser. Garrick had recently set Becket up in a shop at the corner of the newly finished Adelphi and the Strand, a move which made him the most fashionable publisher and bookseller in London. Lydia began to run advertisements asking her father's friends to send her any letters they had, and she with the help of Garrick and probably others wrote to known correspondents making the same request.[61] She managed to collect 114 letters.

Letters of the Late Rev. Mr. Laurence Sterne, to His Most Intimate Friends was published in three slight volumes on 26 October 1775.[62] There was a silly frontispiece, not of Sterne, but of Lydia, leaning on the bust of her father, engraved by James Caldwell from a painting by Benjamin West; a whimsical dedication to Garrick; Garrick's epitaph for Sterne; a couple of anonymous eulogies in verse; and a preface vouching for the genuineness of the letters. The miscellanies, however, were a valuable addition – Sterne's own 'Memoirs', which have provided so much critical information about his early years; 'An Impromptu'; and the 'Fragment in the Manner of Rabelais'.[63]

---

taking another to replace it; the second mortgage, held by Croft and Fountayne, he left intact. Until her death, Elizabeth Sterne had continued to pay rent on two pieces of land which Sterne had originally leased from Lord Fauconberg, presumably because they were being farmed by whoever had leased the other lands. See the *Fauconberg Rentual, 1755–1776*, MS at the Beinecke Library. CURTIS, 455, reported a sale price of the lands conveyed to Thomas Proud, £130, a record I have not been able to find.

[60] Parish registers, Saint Salvy, Albi, pp. 174, 444–5.

[61] See Garrick's note to Mrs Fenton: CURTIS, 121. In the scrapbook which L. P. Curtis gave to the Beinecke Library is a clipping of an advertisement in the form of a letter from Becket asking for Sterne letters for this edition: the date and periodical are not indicated. See also CROSS, 521.

[62] Monkman and Oates in WINGED SKULL, 306–7, indicate it was advertised in the *London Chronicle* of this date.

[63] The 'Memoirs' are included in LETTERS, 1–9. An edition by Kenneth Monkman of the holograph MS, recently come to light, is now in press. The other miscellanies may be found in *Works*, ed. Cross, VII, 255–67. The dedication to Garrick is also in *Works*, VI, 59–60. The MS of the 'Rabelasian Fragment' is now at the Morgan Library; see Melvyn New's edition, 'Sterne's Rabelaisian Fragment: A Text from the Holograph Manuscript', *PMLA*, LXXXVII (1972), 1083–92.

Lydia proved to be an incompetent, indeed an irresponsible, editor. The public was suspicious of her. Hannah More wrote to her sister in 1776.

> Mrs. Medalle (Sterne's daughter) sent to all the correspondents of her deceased father, begging the letters which he had written to them; among other wits, she sent to Wilkes with the same request. He sent for answer, That as there happened to be nothing extraordinary in those he had received, he had burnt or lost them. On which, the faithful editor of her father's works sent back to say, that if Mr. Wilkes would be so good as to write a few letters in imitation of her father's style, it would do just as well, and she would insert them.[64]

Lydia's willingness to forge letters was not demonstrated until the twentieth century, but we now know that the second letter of her edition, which appears to have been addressed to her mother, was adapted by Lydia from, possibly, passages in the *Journal to Eliza* or, more probably, a letter which Sterne himself had patched together from passages in the *Journal* to send to Eliza Draper.[65] Lydia bowdlerized letters and the 'Fragment in the Manner of Rabelais';[66] altered what she did not understand – changing 'the Bishop of Cork and Ross' to 'the bishops of C——, and R——';[67] indiscriminately replaced names with dashes, with or without initial letters, even her mother's name; changed dates for no apparent reason;[68] omitted postscripts and who knows what else;[69] and finally put the letters in a chronological order riddled with error. It was an edition carelessly thrown together for the purpose of making money and proved a great disservice to Sterne's memory. But Lydia by 1775 seems to have lost what affection she once had for her father and was embarrassed by the thought of him.

[64] *Memoirs . . . of Mrs. Hannah More*, ed. William Roberts, 4 vols, 1834, I, 67.

[65] *EMY*, 81, n. 3.

[66] CROSS, 523–5; New's edition of the 'Rabelaisian Fragment', cited above.

[67] LETTERS, 406; CURTIS, 407.

[68] Sterne's letter to Foley from Montpellier, No. 119 in LETTERS, 208–9, was dated by MEDALLE 20 January, which CURTIS presumed to be 1764. The MS, now at the National Library of Scotland, MS 2208, fol. 26, is clearly dated 'Nov 5, 1763'.

[69] The MS of Sterne's letter to Panchaud from London, No. 182 in LETTERS, 299–300, is now in the Robert H. Taylor Collection, Princeton Library. It had two postscripts which were omitted by MEDALLE. The first of these had been restored by CURTIS from a facsimile published in 1837, but curiously the facsimile had omitted the second. The heretofore unpublished second postscript reads, 'my best Comp^{s} to B. D'Holbach and all friends——.' The date too differs in the MS: it is 'Feb. 25', not 20 February.

In 1779 Lydia and her husband for unknown reasons moved to Toulouse. There she died at the age of thirty-two. She was buried in the burial ground of the church of Saint Sauveur on 10 January 1780.[70] Two years later her husband moved back to Albi. Little Laurent was put to school in an aristocratic military academy some thirty-five miles to the south, the Ecole de Sorèze, then run by Benedictine monks. There on 19 September 1783 Laurent Medalle, aged eleven, died. He was buried the next day at the church of Saint Martin.[71] Jean Medalle, who described himself as a 'man of letters', lost everything in the Revolution. For a time he supported the revolutionary leader of Toulouse, Jean-Joseph Janole, and tried to interest him in his political and social philosophy. Eventually he turned conservative and wrote a strong attack on Napoleon in support of the monarchy. Although he remarried, he proudly identified himself as the 'son-in-law of Sterne, the author of the famous Sentimental Journey'.[72]

In 1966 the Laurence Sterne Trust was established to preserve the memory of Sterne and his work and especially to restore Shandy Hall, which had fallen into ruin. Two years later, when repairs to the house were well under way, the Trust learned that St George's, Hanover Square, was selling the Paddington burial ground to a contractor who planned to build a block of flats there. Kenneth Monkman, honorary secretary and principal mover of the Trust, after many difficulties, obtained permission to search for and remove Sterne's remains. On 4 June 1969, Kenneth and Julia Monkman and a reporter from *The Times* watched as the workmen reached the site. The diggers, approaching from the south, had brought forth an assortment of bones and skulls. To be sure that those found in the marked grave were indeed Sterne's, the Monkmans called in a Harley Street surgeon and anatomist, Mr Harvey Ross, and Mr Monkman rushed home for his copy of the Nollekens bust of Sterne. Mr Ross laid the bones on a table and began piecing together individual skeletons and comparing the skulls with the

[70] Burial register of l'Eglise de Toulouse, commonly called l'Eglise Saint Etienne, for 1780, p. 1: Archives Municipales de Toulouse, series GG 357.

[71] Burial register of l'Eglise de Saint Martin de Sorèze, Item 137: Archives Départementales du Tarn, series E 5416, Vol. 41.

[72] Letter to Janole at the Archives Municipales de Toulouse, series 217, 'Germinal an II—Ventôse an III'; undated letter to the Duc d'Angoulême (*c.* 1815) and Medalle's pamphlet, *Un Bon Français à ses compatriotes*, 1815, both in the Archives Départementales de la Haute-Garonne (Toulouse), series 4 M 33; folder 'Première Restauration de janvier à avril 1815: correspondances diverses'. The story is told in greater detail by Baker.

bust. One matched perfectly. The crown had been sawn off. Evidence of autopsy is very rare in eighteenth-century graves; so the condition of the skull strongly corroborates the stories about Sterne's body having been stolen and anatomized.

On 8 June 1969 Sterne was given another funeral at Coxwold. His remains, in a small coffin, were interred on the south side of St Michael's, close against the church wall. The brother Masons' headstone, brought down from London, again marks the spot, and the stone which Captain Carrol added now lies flat upon the grave. In this traditional churchyard, all other headstones face east. Sterne's grave alone looks to the south, across lovely rolling fields and the stream that comes down from Byland to the pastures and woods of Newburgh Priory which rise on the other side. The sun strikes it squarely at noon.

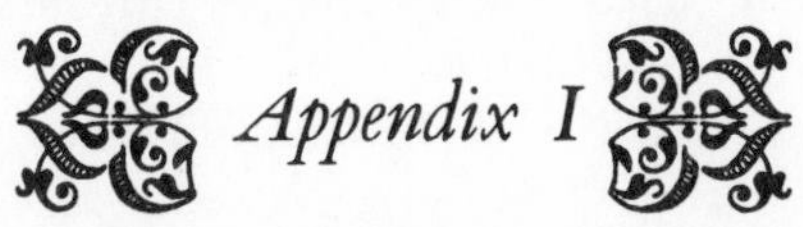

Appendix I

Unedited Sterne Letters

L. P. Curtis's edition, *Letters of Laurence Sterne*, 1935, contained 231 letters written by Sterne. By 1968 eleven others had come to light. Below are seven more, bringing to eighteen the total of Sterne letters discovered in half a century. L. P. Curtis had been thorough.[1]

First, I should like to remind students of where they can locate the eleven letters published between 1951 and 1968. I arrange this list, not in the order of publication dates, but in the chronological order in which the letters or groups of letters were written.

1. One letter to the Rev. John Dealtary, 20 November 1739, in which Sterne, yet a young man, talks about his love for Miss C——: L. P. Curtis, 'New Light on Sterne', *Modern Language Notes*, LXXVI (1961), 498–501.

2. One letter addressed to 'Dear Sir', 14 March 1758, in which Sterne defends himself against scandalous charges: Kenneth Monkman and James Diggle, 'Yorick and His Flock: A New Sterne Letter', *TLS*, 14 March 1968, p. 276.

3. Three letters to the Rev. Henry Egerton written during Sterne's 'flight from Death' into France, winter and spring 1762: Arthur H. Cash, 'Some New Sterne Letters', *TLS*, 8 April 1965, p. 284.

4. Five letters to Richard Oswald and his associate John Mill about the death of Oswald's son, dated from Toulouse, February and March 1763: Archibald Bolling Shepperson, 'Yorick as Ministering Angel', *Virginia Quarterly Review*, XXX (1954), 54–66.

5. One letter to Richard Davenport, 9 June 1767, thanking him for having procured subscribers to *A Sentimental Journey* and talking about his health, his wife and his writing: Earl R. Wasserman, 'Unedited Letters by Sterne, Hume, Rousseau', *Modern Language Notes*, LXVI (1951), 73–80.

In annotating the following letters I have felt free to omit from the notes biographical information about persons whose place in Sterne's life has already been discussed in either volume of this study. Pointed brackets enclose MS deletions made by Sterne.

[1]Since this was written, several Sterne letters have appeared in the *Shandean*, volumes I (1989) and II (1990), an annual periodical published by the Laurence Sterne Trust, Shandy Hall, Coxwold, York; General Editor: Peter J. de Voogd of Rijksuniversiteit te Utrecht.

I
To the Rev. John Blake

[September 1758]

. . . are better than what are prepared for you, & I would lose my Life, (wch You had better do than y^r^ Freedom) Before I would Stoop to them.—I Intreat You therefore, Sum[m]on up a good Stock of firmness & Resolution in the rema[in]ing Part of this Transaction—& let no Pênchent Incline You to any Thing or Concession, But what You believe, Y^r^ poor Father[1] had he been alive, would have deem'd hon^ble^ & Safe for You—

We join our Wishes for You & beg you'l think we are most

—Cordially Y^rs^

L S——

[Addressed in another hand:[2]]

To

The Revd Mr Blake

MS: The Laurence Sterne Trust

(Hitherto unpublished. This fragmentary letter and the two which follow belong to the series of letters from Sterne to the Rev. John Blake, advising him upon the marriage contract which Blake was negotiating with the family of Margaret Ash, whom he hoped to marry but, in the end, did not. See LETTERS, 52–5, 58–63.)

[1] Zachariah Blake (d. 8 August 1757) graduated BA from Christ Church, Oxford, 1712, MA, 1716; priest's orders, 1716; master of the Horse Fair Grammar School at York, 16 March 1726; Curate of Fulford, 1733, and later Rector of Goldsborough; resigned his mastership of the school in favour of his son on 13 May 1757: CURTIS, 51; S. L. Ollard and P. C. Walker (eds), *Archbishop Herring's Visitation Returns, 1743*, 5 vols, 1927–31, I, 196; *Chapter Acts*; Angelo Raine, *History of St. Peter's School: York*, 1926. On 1 August 1751, Sterne appointed him as one of his surrogate judges for the Peculiar Court of Pickering and Pocklington: *Deanery Court Book* at the Borthwick Institute, R. As. 87.

[2] The hand is childlike and may be that of Lydia Sterne, ten years old at this time.

II

To the Rev. John Blake

Sutton Thursday [? 5 October 1758]

Dear Sir.

I rec^{d} y^{rs} by Antony,[1] and am greatly astonished The Family should labour the point in question, at the rate you represent, wch I own gives just Cause to suppose something further arising from y^{r} Concession, Than we at first either of us saw clearly; wch is certainly a Consequence you have now hit upon in y^{r} Letter, That You thereby *virtually* settle your whole Fortune in Case you sh^{d} be left a Widdower with 2 or 3 Children. in such a Case it might be expedient, or perhaps y^{r} inclination to take a 2^{d} Wife— What then?—y^{r} hands are tied behind y^{r} back.—But suppose that should never happen, will not this Concession have an ill Effect in lessening the Dependence y^{r} Children ought to have on you, in wch Relation, There is no need to relax the Obligations between the Duties of Child & parent, but rather increase their Dependence.—I own, tho' I foresaw & mentioned this Objection wth some others, Yet I hastily, as you say, gave my Advice to give the Point up—But, my friend, it was only in a supposed Case, *to save* the breaking off of the Match, & That rather, Than suffer all to go to wreck in this Affair, to run the hazard of this Rock, wch I freely own, appears now more dangerous to you, than at that time, because Like Rocks but half discovered, we were ill Judges how near we were to venture. But now I am most absolutely for putting out to sea, rather than come into Port with this vile rock before you; For tho the Danger is distant, yet you will apprehend it & torment y^{r} mind ab^{t} it all the Days of y^{r} Life, & the longer You live, ye more new reasons will occur to You to prove the folly of it, as well as the vile Artifices of those who have led You into it.—But your Honor is engaged—Why so? I think they have fairly set you at Liberty by their own Conduct & the suspicions raised by it—And You may say with all plainess & Truth, that tho' You have underwritten so & so;—Yet as they seem resolved to consult wiser Heads, & thereby treat it as a Point of such Infinite Consequence to them, You have thought it prudent to follow the Example, they had set You, & that accordingly You had consulted some able & experienced friends, who forwarn you strongly against it, as a Conception of infinite ill Consequence to You—

—<Do> You are not to suppose you have treated with Miss Clark,[2] as with a tricking Attorney, or that y^{r} ill advised complyance *wrote*, could be taken any more advantage of, than If the same words had been unadvisedly *spoke*, & upon more mature consideration, retracted. In Conferring with a Sweetheart, a thousand changes of Scheems and Sentiments must happen & be allowed, as Things present themselves, & twould be ungenerous in 'em, to lay hold of it; nor would I be caught thereby—for more reasons than I can put into this Letter, being straitened in Time.

Pray consider, the Inconvenience wch w^{d} arise to y^{r} Children, if at y^{r} Death, there sh[d] happen, what is no uncomon Case, a Difference of 12 or 13 Years between the first born & the Youngest. perhaps the Estate could not be divided till 15 Years after it w[d] be absolutely of Service to the Elder Branches, which must pine away, till the Estate can safely be sold when the Youngest comes of Age—

Adieu. I am not very well so fear I shall not have the happiness of seeing You till the End of next Week—

All Services attend You—

Y[r] Goose was taken up in Owes[3] and I fear has been roasted—I think some one deserves roasting for not pulling her Wings—

dear Sir
y[rs].
L. Sterne

MS: Henry E. Huntington Library and Art Gallery
(First published by L. P. Curtis as the fragmentary Letter No. 29. On 30 September Sterne had mentioned his wife's intention of sending Blake two geese (LETTERS, 60) and, in another note written that same day, had indicated that one goose had been sent (61). The mention of the second goose in this letter – the goose which had escaped before it could be delivered – allows us to date the letter in early October. Blake has written to Sterne expressing his anxiety that he had agreed with Miss Ash's family to settle his entire estate, in case of his death, upon her and any children she might have. Sterne, who had originally thought it wise to concede this point, now thinks Blake should refuse. Should the wife die leaving a child, the child would be heir to the entire estate; any children Blake might have by a second wife could receive nothing.)

[1] John Hall-Stevenson, who was habitually addressed by Sterne as Antony. Sterne seems to have lied when he wrote to Bishop Warburton in June of 1760 that he had had 'nineteen years' total interruption of all correspondence' with Hall-Stevenson: LETTERS, 115.

[2] Possibly a connection of William Clark, whom Miss Ash would shortly marry.

[3] The River Ouse.

III

To the Rev. John Blake

[21–30 January 1759]

Dear Sir

I have been kept at home & to my Room ever since I gave You a Call, in y[r] absence——when I went home ill. My Romance wth a Serious Letter to D[r]

Topham[1] will come out to morrow night & I have ordered Mr Ward[2] to send 2 to Taylor's,[3]——one of wch is for You.[4]——That Criticism of ours upon the Passage—where the Stroke of Trim's Impudence is mentioned[5]——was not necessary——tis sense without ye intended Amendm^{t}.——This Impression upon the Parson's looks, exceeded all Description, & all power of resentm^{t},——that is, the Surprise disabled him from resenting it, as he sh^{d} have done. <as well as this Effect>. So I have let it stand——as it appeard to be sense, to one or two more[6] as it was. Let us know how You do &c——But pray tell me what is truely the gen^{l} Opinion of Topham's Reply.

All kind Resp^{ts} to You
Y^{rs} most truely
L. Sterne

[Postscript on the address-leaf:]
Say not a word of what [? is contained in it or when the] Romance is to come out——till You get it

[Addressed on the address-leaf:]
To
The Revd Mr Blake

MS: Robert H. Taylor Collection, Princeton University Library.
(Hitherto unpublished. Sterne and Blake have been looking at a proof copy of *A Political Romance*. Sterne writes to say he has decided against a possible change they had discussed. For Edward Simmen's discovery of a proof copy, see his article, 'Sterne's *A Political Romance*: New Light from a Printer's Copy', *Papers of the Bibliographical Society of America*, LXIV, 1970, pp. 419–29. The *Romance* was published in late January 1759.)

[1] Dr Francis Topham, the York ecclesiastical lawyer, as the character Trim the chief butt of the satire in *A Political Romance*. The *Romance* was written in two stages, the second part following the appearance of Topham's *Reply to the Answer to a Letter lately addressed to the Dean of York*, which appeared in mid-January 1759. Among the additions, Sterne included a letter to Dr Topham, dated 20 January 1759.

[2] Caesar Ward, the York printer.

[3] John Taylor, of Fulford, near York.

[4] These copies may be among the six known to have survived the burning of *A Political Romance*. They are listed by Simmen. The copy in the York Minster Library was reproduced in facsimile with an introduction by Kenneth Monkman by the Scolar Press, Menston, Yorkshire, in 1971.

[5] The passage describing the parson's facial expression when he sees that Trim has cut up the watch-coat – p. 8 in the Scolar Press facsimile.

[6] ? others.

IV

To the Marquis of Rockingham[1]

York. Dec. 14. 1759.

My Lord

You was so kind to me, as to bid me send You 8 Sets of Tristram Shandy, as soon as ever the 2 Vol^s^ came out, which, not having a better channel, I have taken the Liberty to do, by the Sheffield Carrier,[2] with my most humble Thanks to your Lords^p^ for the Honour You have done me in taking Notice of me & my Book.

There is an Anecdote[3] relating to this ludicrous Satyr, which I must tell your Lord^p^—& it is this, 'that it was every word of it wrote in affliction; & under a constant uneasiness of mind.[4] Cervantes wrote his humorous Satyr in a Prison——& Scarron his, in pain & Anguish[5]——Such Philosophers as will account for every thing, may explain this for me.

I am, my Lord

Y^r^ most faithful Servant Lau: Sterne

2 Sets directed to Wentworth house
The other 6 sets to Grosvenor Square

MS: The Robert H. Taylor Collection, Princeton University Library. (Hitherto unpublished.)

[1] Identified from Sterne's references to his seats at Wentworth, near Sheffield in the West Riding, and Grosvenor Square. He had a third seat at Malton in the North Riding.

[2] This statement constitutes the strongest evidence to date of the now generally accepted theory that the first edition of *Tristram Shandy*, I–II, appeared in York. See MONKMAN.

[3] Used in the first meaning given in the *OED*, 'secret, private, or hitherto unpublished narratives or details of history', but unusual in that the word is singular, whereas the idiomatic use is plural.

[4] Cf. the 'Anonymous Letter' in the *St. James's Chronicle* for 22–4 April 1788, published in the Wilbur Cross edition, *Works of Laurence Sterne*, 1904, VI, 24–32; see *EMY*, xix, 279 and n. 2.

[5] Cf. LETTERS, 416, and TRISTRAM SHANDY, 780.

V

To Thomas Becket

Montpellier. Sept: 26, 1763

Dear Sir

A week after I wrote my Letter of Complaint,[1] I rec^d^ y^rs^ at the Spaws in the South of France—& the Week after I arrived here, I rec^d^ your 2^d^ Letter. Your long

Silence however carried with it all the appearance of Neglect; for had I gone to Italy, I should most certainly have given you immediate Notice, as well as Mr Foley of my Rout—It always gives me pleasure to be convinced no wrong was intended me—& a man of common Justice and good nature will ever be satisfyed with it,—& take for granted That some Mistake was the Cause. If I should have Occasion for money before I set out for England, I will draw upon You for 20 Louis'd'ors, with the more willingness, as I trust so much will be in y^r^ hands, unless I am deceived by a gentleman just arrived here from London, who tells me, the Books have not wanted purchassers—they will go off I expect by next Spring——

Mr Hall[2] is decampd I suppose for Yorkshire, where I have wrote to him by this post—My Comp^s^ to Mr Edmunds and all friends. I am Y^rs^

sincerely
L. Sterne

PS

I Stay at Montpellier till I leave France for good & all————direct to me to Mr Ray Banquier[3]—

[Addressed:]
To
Mr Becket Bookseller
in the Strand
London
Angleterre——
[Postmark:] W[4]

MS: Boston Public Library.
(Hitherto unpublished.)

[1] Cf. LETTERS, 199.
[2] John Hall-Stevenson.
[3] Sterne's banker at Montpellier.
[4] MS endorsed: 'Mr Sterne / Montpellier / Sept 26, 1763 / requires no Ans.'

VI
To Thomas Astle[1]

[London, ? 23 March 1765]

My dear Sir

a perpetual round of engagements wherin, every moment of my time has been mortgaged—together with Some Days Illness, the natural fruits of so much dissipation—has put out of my power, what was so oft in my head—to wait upon You—I will do myself the pleasure of being an hour or two with You on Tuesday morning—being determined at noon to set out for Bath for a week to break this magic Circle—If I sh^{d} not be with You by half an hour after nine—will You suppose, I have been obliged to decamp sooner—& will You suffer me to see You upon my return?

Be assured of the Sense I have of y^{r} great civility to me, & that

I am dear Sir
most truly y^{r}
obliged
L. Sterne

Saturday
[Addressed:]
To
T. Astle[2]

MS: Houghton Library, Amy Lowell Collection.

(Hitherto unpublished. Since this letter was written on a Saturday before a Tuesday when Sterne planned to set out for Bath, it can be tentatively dated 23 March 1765. The exact date of Sterne's departure is not known, but he was planning to leave by the 23rd. On that date Elizabeth Montagu wrote to her sister in Bath, Sarah Scott, introducing Sterne, who would soon be arriving [Huntington Library MS, MO 5819]. By 11 April Mrs Montagu had heard from Mrs Scott about Sterne's visit [Huntington Library MS, MO 5820].)

[1] Thomas Astle (1735–1803), antiquarian and palaeographer, was the son of Daniel Astle of Yoxall, Staffordshire, Keeper of the Forest of Needwood. At a young age he gave up the study of law to become the cataloguer of the celebrated Harleian MSS. His catalogue was published in 1759. In subsequent years he was elected to the Royal Society of Antiquaries (1763), to the Royal Society (1766) and to the Board of Trustees of the British Museum. He served on royal commissions to regulate the public records at Westminster and to reorganize the records in the State Paper Office at Whitehall. He was one of the editors of the parliamentary papers published as *Rotuli Parliamentorum*, 6 vols, 1767–77. In 1775 he became chief clerk of the Record Office of the Tower of London and in 1783 Keeper of the Records. His chief work, *The Origin and Progress of Writing*, appeared in 1784. Astle built up an extensive collection of books and MSS, among them the major portion of the Stowe MSS, now at the British Library (*DNB*).

[2] MS marked at the top: 'Revd Mr Sterne (Tristram Shandy.) / No. 120', and endorsed in another hand, 'Tristram Shandy / to Mr Astle.'

VII

To Reverend Sir

Coxwould July 18. 1767

Revd Sir

I am directed by his Grace the Lord Arch Bishop of York to require you to send in a List of the papists or reputed papists within y^{r} parish wth all convenient Speed, & that you do it according to the manner pointed out by Order of the house of Lords

I am
Rev^{d} S^{r}
Y^{r} aff^{te} Brother
L. Sterne

The List to be sent in to
the Dean's Register Office
York

MS: Library of the Dean and Chapter of York.
(Hitherto unpublished. This is one of seven nearly identical notes now at the Minster Library. There were originally eight. Sterne intended them to be sent to the clergy of the various parishes which reported to the Peculiar Court of the Dean of York, of which Sterne had been the commissary, or judge, from 1751. On 22 May 1767 the House of Lords had ordered 'That an humble Address be presented to his Majesty, "That He will be Graciously pleased to give Directions to the Archbishops and Bishops, to procure from their Parochial Clergy, and . . . from all Persons invested with Peculiar Jurisdictions . . . as correct and complete Lists as can be obtained of the Papists or reputed Papists, within the same. . . ."' With each of Sterne's notes is a printed notice of the resolution and of the letter sent to Archbishop Robert Hay Drummond by the Secretary of State, Lord Shelburne. This investigation to determine the numbers of Catholics was quite routine, carried out in the manner of earlier investigations in 1706, 1735 and 1743.)

VIII

To John Clough[1]

Coxwould Aug. 7. 67

Dear Sir

——I have sent 8 Letters to the Clergy of the Dean's Jurisdiction—I know not whether I have wrote a sufficient Number—if not, let me know. & in the mean time direct the Inclosed, & get them sent.[2]

Y^{rs} L. Sterne

MS: Library of the Dean and Chapter of York.
(Hitherto unpublished. This is the cover letter for the eight notes described above. Although the notes were dated 18 July, Sterne did not get around to doing anything with them until 7 August, when it was too late. Cf. n. 2, below.)

[1] Registrar of the Deanery Court and to the Dean and Chapter. See CURTIS, 47.

[2] Clough's reply is self-explanatory:

> Rev[d] Sir
>
> I rec[ed] your favour this Morning with eight Let[s] Inclosed which I presume are intended for the Clergy within the Deanry in consequence of the Order of the House of Lords.
>
> The 9th of last Month the AB[p] Wrote to the D. & C. requiring them to procure Lists of the papists from their parochial Clergy and also to the Dean requiring the like lists from the parochial Clergy within his Jur[don] agreeable to the House of Lords. Upon the 20th of the same Month The D. & C. ordered me to get the Inclosed printed and the Dean directed me to get the Letter Signed by him printed, and one of each has been sent to the respective Clergy within the different Jur[dons] and by this I make no Doubt but his Grace has had returns made confirmable thereto from some of the Clergy—please to let me know what you would have me do with the Let[s] you sent me——I am
>
> Rev[d] Sir
>
> York 8th Aug[t] 1767
>
> Y[r] M[st] h[ble] Serv[t]
> John Clough
>
> P.S.
>
> You have above double the Number of places within the Deanry than you inclosed Let[s] for—M[r] Stables who has hitherto done such business as chanced to be in Court, for you, as the Dean's official lately hinted he wou'd do so no longer. The reason I know not. When you come to York I shall be glad of an opportunity of talking wth you upon the Subject.
>
> To the Rev[d] M[r] Sterne.

With this is a copy of the printed letter Clough had sent to the clergy.

The Mr Stables of whom Clough speaks in his postscript is William Stables, the York lawyer who held the post of commissary of the Peculiar Court of the Dean and Chapter. Sterne treated him kindly as William Doe in *A Political Romance*. Stables had been filling in for Sterne in the special trials which occasionally were carried over from the regular annual visitation: Arthur H. Cash, 'Sterne as a Judge in the Spiritual Courts: The Groundwork of *A Political Romance*', in *English Writers of the Eighteenth Century*, ed. John H. Middendorf, New York, 1971, pp. 17–36.

A copy of the final report sent to the House of Lords is at the Borthwick Institute: shelf mark R.Bp.H.2.9. Of the 956 parishes and chapelries, 389 reported the presence of papists – in all, 6583 Roman Catholics. The figures are conveniently compared to those for the earlier surveys – 3481 Catholics in 1706, 3526 in 1735, 5012 in 1743; but an anxious note explains that the actual increase is not as dramatic as it appears on paper because the earlier reports were imperfect. Sterne's specific report on Coxwold is discussed in Chapter 2, above.

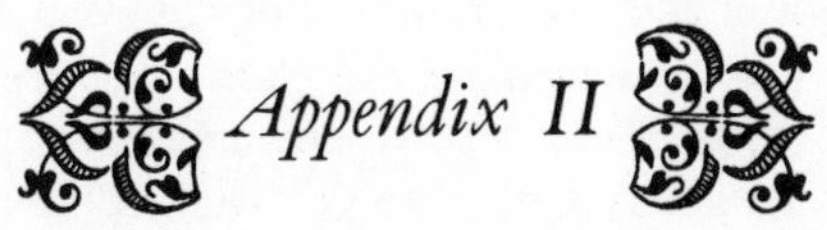

The John Hamilton Mortimer Caricature Group

In the late 1760s, John Hamilton Mortimer painted a caricature portrait of Sterne, one figure in a conversation piece. The painting, an oil on canvas in lively colours, 33 × 42 inches, depicts a group of friends enjoying a wine and oyster party. Mortimer himself is seen at the extreme left, happily surveying the scene (1), while his former master, Giovanni Battista Cipriani, whispers congratulations into his ear (2). Thirteen other tipsy men seem to be laughing at various witticisms or jests. John Ireland, in the foreground, dangles an oyster (3), perhaps preparing to throw it at a large-mouthed companion seated on the floor. Joseph Wilton, the sculptor (12), seems to be trying to open an oyster using a knife and fork like a hammer and chisel, but has only succeeded in knocking over his wineglass.

Sterne (9) has just risen from his chair and, pulling open his shirt, is calling attention to a large, heart-shaped locket on a chain resting against his bony chest. Three or four of the others are responding to Sterne's appeal for attention, and Dr Thomas Augustine Arne is raising his glass in a toast (4), no doubt to Eliza Draper. It must have been Mortimer's intention to make fun of Sterne's well-known foible of this period discussed above in Chapter 7, his passion for showing Eliza Draper's miniature portrait to every company in which he found himself. True, he was actually carrying Eliza's picture in a snuffbox, as was pointed out in a note. But a picture of Sterne displaying a snuffbox would have looked like a man offering snuff; so Mortimer probably invented the more dramatic heart-shaped locket. If this speculation is correct, the painting was made in 1767, a date which confirms that assigned independently by art historians, who had placed it in the middle to late 1760s.

Prior to his marriage in 1775, John Hamilton Mortimer lived in a studio he rented from the bookseller Jemmy Moran or Maronne in the Piazza of Covent Garden. He was known in the Covent Garden artist colony for the 'freedom and extravagence of his life', which, all accounts agree, ruined his health. Edward

Dayes described him as a '*bon vivant*' and told how once in a show of bravado he tossed off a glass of wine and then ate the glass.[1] The anonymous writer of a biographical sketch of 1796 disapproved of Mortimer's companions of this period, 'distinguished for the liveliness of their parts, rather than for any solid properties which they had to recommend them'.[2] But Henry Angelo, repeating what he recalled of conversations with his father and his father's friends, said that Mortimer's studio became the 'morning lounge' for numerous 'distinguished noblemen', the 'tip-top dramatic writers, players, sculptors, and painters', and 'all the professional men of talent of his day'.[3] Such a circle of friends offers a problem to the scholar who hopes to identify the revellers in Mortimers's painting: almost any outstanding person of the period might be represented.

It is possible that the painting depicts one of the several clubs Mortimer is known to have belonged to. He was president, said Thomas Jones, of the Howdalian Society, a club of artists that met at Munday's Coffee House in Maiden Lane.[4] According to Angelo, Mortimer belonged to a club of artists and actors which gathered at the Turk's Head in Gerrard Street. Dayes linked him with a group, largely artists, that met at the Feathers Tavern in Leicester Fields. John Thomas Smith chatted about this Feathers Tavern group, naming among its members Samuel Scott and John Ireland, both of whom appear in Mortimer's painting, but not Mortimer himself.[5] But there is some confusion in these accounts: there are two versions of a pleasant anecdote about how Mortimer sketched grotesque figures and caricatures on the margins of a newspaper and then auctioned the newspaper to raise money for a poor widow. Dayes placed the incident at the Feathers Tavern, Angelo at the Turk's Head. All in all, there does not seem to be enough evidence that the painting represents any of these clubs.

In strict logic, there is no need to postulate that the men here represented ever came together on a particular occasion, yet that possibility becomes more remote as one reflects upon the painting. More likely, it shows a circle of friends who often gathered in Mortimer's own studio. The room in the painting looks like an artist's studio because of the unframed canvases about, one on the wall behind and two propped up in the left foreground. On the other hand, the canvases are clearly a device; so one dare not make too much of them. Mortimer used them to represent absent members of the group, men who were away from London in the winter of 1767, perhaps, or friends who had moved away permanently, or possibly members who had died. Whatever the case, these portraits within the picture suggest that Mortimer was painting a distinct group that had met together for some time. As I

[1] *Works*, 1805, p. 340.

[2] 'Life of Mortimer, the Painter', by 'Libra', *Monthly Magazine*, I (1796), 4th edn [undated], 22–5.

[3] *Reminiscences*, 2 vols, 1828–30, I, 139.

[4] *Memoirs* (*Walpole Society*, XXXII, for 1946–8), 1951, p. 11.

[5] *Book for a Rainy Day*, ed. Wilfred Whitten, 1905, pp. 104–6.

identify the revellers here, the group was made up of artists from the Covent Garden artist colony, neighbours, or old friends of Mortimer.

How likely is it that Sterne would have been a member of such a coterie? He did not mention any of these men in his known letters. Yet several of them were friends of his friends. The artists knew or had professional connections with Sir William Chambers, who as a member of the Skelton Castle set was well known to Sterne. Samuel Scott (11) had been a close friend to Hogarth when he was alive, and John Ireland (3) would soon write the first scholarly studies of Hogarth. Dr John Armstrong (14) was a good friend of Reynolds. Sterne, there can be no doubt, would have enjoyed himself in this company. As an amateur painter, he would have had much to talk about with Mortimer and the other artists. As an amateur musician and the composer of at least one piece of theatrical music, the song for Catherine Fourmantel, he would have been happy to drink with Dr Arne (4), the foremost theatrical composer of his day. And, as a bawdy talker, he would have appreciated the talk of Dr Armstrong, the author of a well-known indecent poem. 'The Œconomy of Love'.

The strongest corroborative evidence that figure no. 9 represents Sterne comes from Henry Angelo, who named Sterne among the distinguished persons who frequented Mortimer's studio. To be sure, Angelo, not born until 1760, had his information at second hand. But he had grown up among the Covent Garden artists and as a boy was given drawing lessons by Cipriani and Bartolozzi, both of whom appear in the painting. And his father, a great favourite among artists, was in a position to know.

Moreover, Mortimer and his friends are known to have admired Sterne. In later years, when Ireland sat for a portrait by Mortimer, he had himself painted holding the first volume of *Tristram Shandy* open at Hogarth's illustration of Trim reading the sermon. The book and the illustration are visible in the engraving by W. Skelton used as the frontispiece for Ireland's *Hogarth Illustrated* (two volumes, 1791). (A copy by Thomas Tegg was engraved for later editions.)

Mortimer himself admired Sterne. He made a satirical etching complimentary to him, *The Reviewers Cave*, which appeared as the frontispiece to the second edition of Evan Lloyd's *Powers of the Pen* (1768). In a large cave, a fat figure in judicial robes presides over a hoard of critics, among them Dr Johnson. Scalps hang from the ceiling and a dead muse floats in a cloud. A slave staggers foreward under a basket of books, which the judge will pass to the reviewers to be devoured. Among the titles of the books in the slave's basket can be seen *A Sentimental Journey*. On the wall behind, trophies have been pasted up – title-pages of books already devoured; among them are *Tristram Shandy* and 'Sterne's Sermons'.

The earliest-known mention of Mortimer's caricature group appears in the article, 'The Life of Mortimer, the Painter', signed 'Libra', in the *Monthly Magazine*, I (1796). The author included a haphazard list of Mortimer's paintings, among them, 'A Group of Geniuses in Caricature, viz. Johnson, Churchill, Goldsmith, &c.' Yet we cannot find Johnson or Goldsmith in the painting, and Churchill was dead by 1767. To be sure, the writer may have been talking about another caricature group, now lost. But this does not seem probable, since Mortimer would not have been apt to include Dr Johnson in such a painting. He disliked Johnson and satirized him, not only in *The Reviewers Cave*, but in a comic pen-an-ink drawing of about 1776, *Literary Characters Assembled around a Medallion of Shakespeare*. More probably, the writer of the article was referring to the painting we have, but was wrongly informed about the identities of the sitters or simply made them up. Some time later, the painting came into the family of Sir Henry Roper. It was thought by that family to have been the work of Thomas Patch, and it had acquired a title suitable to Patch's career, *An Oyster Supper of Artists in Rome*. In 1966 it was put on sale by the Leger Galleries, bought by Mr and Mrs Paul Mellon, and soon thereafter identified as by Mortimer. It was exhibited in a show of Mortimer's work at the Towner Art Gallery, Eastbourne, and at Kenwood in 1968. In preparation for the exhibition, Basil Taylor and Benedict Nicolson published an article and query in 'Notes on British Art' (supplement to *Apollo Magazine*, new series, LXXXVII (1968), 3–4). They explained their reasons for attributing the work to Mortimer, made firm identifications of the figures of Mortimer and Ireland, and tentative identifications of some of the others, and asked for suggestions about the rest. One respondent, Dr Philip Traub, suggested Sterne. In 1977 the painting was shown in the exhibition 'The Pursuit of Happiness' at the Yale Center for British Art – No. 116 in the catalogue by Edward Nygren and Nancy Pressly. It was shown again in the exhibition organized by John Riely and Richard Godfrey, 'English Caricature 1620 to the Present', which opened at the Yale Center in 1984 and after other stops appeared at the Victoria and Albert Museum in 1985 – No. 79 in the catalogue, with notes by Richard Godfrey. Recently John Sunderland, Witt Librarian at the Courtauld Institute of Art and the leading authority on Mortimer, has worked on the painting in preparation for his study *John Hamilton Mortimer*, which with an accompanying *catalogue raisonné* will be published as Volume LI of the *Walpole Society* (for 1985). Mr Sunderland, while generously allowing me to use his notes, reserves his final opinion for his book. In 1981 the painting was given to the Yale Center for British Art, Paul Mellon Collection.

My own concern has been to identify the figures in the painting, in part to reinforce the identification of Sterne by showing connections between him and the other men in the picture, in part better to understand his world. Inheriting twenty-two suggestions about the identities of the sitters and adding another fifteen of my own, I proceeded to the Frick Art Reference Library, the Courtauld Institute of Art, and most importantly the National Portrait Gallery, where I could compare my photograph of the painting with photographs of portraits of the candidates. With due allowance for the age of the sitter in each portrait and his age in 1767 when Mortimer made his painting, I accepted or rejected the suggestions upon the basis of similarities in appearance. Ultimately, I reduced them to eleven. I list them below by the number assigned in the key, putting a question mark before the names of those I consider less certain.

Identifications (see key, facing p. 365)

1. JOHN HAMILTON MORTIMER (1740–79), known primarily as a pioneer in the genre of historical painting with such scenes as *King John Signing the Magna Carta* and *St Paul's Conversion of the Britons*. Mortimer also did portraits, theatrical paintings, scenes of terror and wild romance, and satirical drawings and etchings. He was active in the Incorporated Society of Artists, and during his bachelor years, which lasted until he was thirty-five, he lived in rooms rented from the bookseller Maronne under the Piazza of Covent Garden. Identified upon the basis of (1) *The Artist and Joseph Wilton, R. A., and a Student* at the Royal Academy; and (2) a self-portrait with his father and (?) grandfather after a shoot, *c.* 1760–2, in the Mellon Collection, Yale Center for British Art.

2. GIOVANNI BATTISTA CIPRIANI (1727–85), Florentine draughtsman and painter who made his home in England from 1755. Cipriani was Mortimer's teacher at the Duke of Richmond's gallery, where he served as drawing master, and later at the St Martin's Lane Academy. He became in 1768 a Royal Academician and a founding member of the Royal Academy. Identified upon the basis of (1) a sketch by Francesco Bartolozzi, *Cipriani at Work* (photograph at the Frick Art Reference Library); and (2) J. F. Rigaud's portrait of Carlini, Bartolozzi and Cipriani at the National Portrait Gallery.

3. JOHN IRELAND (d. 1808), watchmaker in Maiden Lane and author of the earliest major work on Hogarth, *Hogarth Illustrated*, in two volumes, 1791, augmented with a third volume, the earliest biographical study of Hogarth, 1798. Ireland frequented the Feathers Tavern in Leicester Fields and maintained with Mortimer 'an intimate, brotherly, and unbroken friendship'. Identified upon the basis of (1) Mortimer's painting, *Gentleman and Boy Looking at Prints*, in the Mellon Collection, Yale Center for British Art, thought by art historians to represent Ireland showing some Hogarth prints; and (2) Mortimer's portrait of Ireland holding *Tristram Shandy*, engraved for the frontispiece to *Hogarth Illustrated*, discussed above.

4. DR THOMAS AUGUSTINE ARNE (1710–78), prolific and highly successful composer of music for theatre and concert halls, brother of Susannah

Cibber, composer of 'Rule Britannia'. Arne broke with Garrick in 1760, began writing for the Covent Garden Theatre, and moved into rooms in the Piazza, Covent Garden, close to Mortimer's rooms. John Thomas Smith in *Book for a Rainy Day* (edition of 1905, p. 181) said that Sheridan once described Arne's eyes as 'like two oysters on an oval plate of stewed beet-root'. Wilfred Whitten, the editor of the book, in a footnote, attributed the remark to Mortimer. Identified upon the basis of (1) the caricature sketch by Bartolozzi, *c.* 1782, and Bartolozzi's hand-coloured engraving called *Harmony and Sentiment* at the National Portrait Gallery; (2) another print after a painting by R. Dunkarton, whereabouts unknown (photograph at the National Portrait Gallery).

5. CAPTAIN FRANCIS GROSE (1731–91), draughtsman, antiquary and soldier; said to have been 'a sort of antiquarian Falstaff'. Grose served as Richmond herald, 1755–63, paymaster of the Hampshire Militia from 1763, and captain in the Surrey Militia from 1778 or earlier. He was trained as an artist and active in the Society of Artists and the Society of Antiquaries. He wrote many antiquarian studies, for which he himself made many illustrations. His best-known works are *Antiquities of England and Wales*, four volumes, 1773–87, and *Antiquities of Scotland*, two volumes, 1789–91. Identified upon the basis of (1) Dance's drawing at the Scottish National Portrait Gallery, *c.* 1787; (2) Nathaniel Hone's painting, *Captain Grose and Theodosius Forrest Masquerading as Capuchin Friars*, 1770, whereabouts unknown (photograph at the National Portrait Gallery); and (3) the frontispiece to Grose's *Rules for Drawing Caricaturas: With an Essay on Comic Painting*, 1788 and later editions.

6. UNIDENTIFIED.

7. UNIDENTIFIED.

8. UNIDENTIFIED.

9. LAURENCE STERNE (1713–68). Said by Henry Angelo to have been a guest in Mortimer's studio (*Reminiscences*, two volumes, 1828–30, I, 139). Identified on the basis of (1) Reynolds's oil portrait, 1760; (2) Patch's oil caricature, 1766; and (3) Nollekens's sculpture bust, 1766, all of which are discussed and illustrated in the appendix on 'Portraits of Sterne' in the first volume of this work.

10. (?) FRANCESCO BARTOLOZZI (1727–1815), engraver and painter, friend of Cipriani since their childhood in Florence. Bartolozzi came to England in 1764 at the invitation of the royal librarian and soon thereafter was made engraver to the king. He shared rooms in London with Cipriani and became a well-known,

popular figure in the taverns and coffee houses habituated by artists. He would become, with Cipriani, a Royal Academician and founding member of the Royal Academy, but would leave England in 1802 to direct the Lisbon National Academy. Rigaud's painting of Carlini, Bartolozzi and Cipriani at the National Portrait Gallery serves to confirm this identification, as does a caricature portrait by Rowlandson in the Mellon Collection of the Yale Center for British Art. But the portraits by Opie, Reynolds and Henry Eldridge (photographs at the National Portrait Gallery) do not suggest the face painted by Mortimer. All, however, show a bump on the nose.

11. (?) SAMUEL SCOTT (?1702–72), marine painter and friend of Hogarth. Although Scott was said by John Thomas Smith to have been a member of the Feathers Tavern group, he made his home in Twickenham, where Horace Walpole, who bought many of his paintings, was a neighbour. Identified upon the basis of a pencil-and-wash sketch by James Deacon at the British Museum, reproduced as plate 713 in John Kerslake's *Early Georgian Portraits*, two volumes, 1977.

12. (?) JOSEPH WILTON (1722–1803), sculptor. Wilton studied in France and Italy, returning to England in 1755 in the company of Cipriani. He was appointed master for sculpture at the Duke of Richmond's gallery at the time Cipriani became master for drawing, and so knew Mortimer as a student. Wilton became in time sculptor to the king and Keeper of the Royal Academy. The identification is suggested by (1) Mortimer's painting *The Artist, Joseph Wilton, R.A., and a Student* at the Royal Academy; (2) Reynolds's portrait at the National Portrait Gallery; and (3) a Roubiliac bust at the Royal Academy. On the other hand, the identification is not supported by (1) Rigaud's painting of Wilton, Reynolds and Sir William Chambers at the National Portrait Gallery; or (2) the chalk-and-pencil sketch by Dance, 1793, at the Royal Academy.

13. (?) CAPTAIN WILLIAM BAILLIE (1723–1810), Irish-born soldier, connoisseur and amateur engraver. Baillie, a veteran of Culloden and Minden, retired from the cavalry in 1761 to devote himself to art. He made many engravings and etchings after the Dutch and Flemish masters, but was said by John Thomas Smith to have been a very bad engraver, though perfectly self-satisfied. He was an eccentric who always dressed in military garb and was well known in the Covent Garden artist colony. The National Portrait Gallery file contains a small print of a self-portrait, now lost, and a photograph of a self-portrait now in the possession of Baillie's descendants, but neither is helpful, since they both represent a very young man. So the identification of No. 13 as Baillie in Mortimer's painting rests entirely upon the military hat.

14. (?) DR JOHN ARMSTRONG (1709–79), Scottish-born physician and poet. Armstrong was made famous by the publication of his blank-verse poem, *The Art of Preserving Health*, 1744, but being an indolent man he wrote little thereafter. He had once moved in the rakish circle of John Wilkes but had broken with Wilkes. He wrote an indecent comic poem, 'The Œconomy of Love'. Armstrong was well known in artistic circles, being a friend of Reynolds and Fuseli, the latter of whom he accompanied on a tour of France in 1770. He lived in a house in Russell Street, Covent Garden, a man of learning who liked to associate with people of genius, but not very successful either as a poet or as a medical practitioner. Identified upon the basis of Reynolds's portrait, 1767, at the Adelaide Art Gallery; and (2) a silhouette at the National Portrait Gallery.

15. UNIDENTIFIED.

16. UNIDENTIFIED.

17. UNIDENTIFIED.

18. UNIDENTIFIED.

Rejected identifications

My reasons for rejecting an identification made by someone else or tentatively by me do not bear much discussion. Sometimes they have to do with chronology: e.g. Johnson was too old in 1767 for No. 2. Sometimes a lack of evidence forces me to discard a candidate: I can find no picture of Hall-Stevenson in his middle age. But usually I have rejected candidates upon the basis of the dissimilarity between the figure in Mortimer's painting and the figure in authenticated portraits.

I name first the candidates suggested by those who have previously worked on the painting, which I have been forced to reject. The numbers refer to the key. Samuel Johnson (2, 16); John Henderson (2); Henry Fuseli (4); Richard Wilson (6); Joseph Wright of Derby (7); Peter Perez Burdett (8); James Gandon (11, 17); James Boswell (15); Charles Churchill (15); Oliver Goldsmith (16); Samuel Foote (17); and Henry Woodward (18).

Finally, I list the men who seemed to me to be likely candidates, but whose faces I have not found in the painting: Sir William Chambers; Sir Francis Delaval; David Garrick; John Hall-Stevenson; Thomas Hearne; Edmund Malone; James Pine; Robert Edge Pine; Sir Joshua Reynolds; Luke Sullivan; James Stuart; Caleb Whitefoord; and Francesco Zucarelli.

Index

This is a selective index to people, places, and other details within the story of Sterne and his family, but not to source materials upon which the story is founded. It includes most persons whose lives touched upon Sterne's, but not Sterne's correspondents or those who told anecdotes of him, even when they are named in the text. It excludes scholars, critics, authorities, or owners of manuscripts and portraits, but includes book titles which come up in the discussion – indexed by author, if possible (except Sterne's own works, which are indexed by title). Information in footnotes is rarely included, and then only when the reader could not be expected to find it by looking up the material on the page to which the note is related. Under the entry, 'Sterne, Laurence', the reader will find only items which he could not locate readily by reviewing the major developments in the story of Sterne's life.